Code War

Code War

How Nations Hack, Spy, and
Shape the Digital Battlefield

Allie Mellen

WILEY

Published by John Wiley & Sons, Inc., Hoboken, New Jersey.

ISBNs: 9781394285570 (Hardback), 9781394285594 (ePDF), 9781394285587 (ePub)

For general information on our other products and services or for technical support, please contact our Customer Care Department within the United States at (800) 762-2974, outside the United States at (317) 572-3993 or fax (317) 572-4002. For product technical support, you can find answers to frequently asked questions or reach us via live chat at https://support.wiley.com.

If you believe you've found a mistake in this book, please bring it to our attention by emailing our reader support team at wileysupport@wiley.com with the subject line "Possible Book Errata Submission."

Wiley also publishes its books in a variety of electronic formats. Some content that appears in print may not be available in electronic formats. For more information about Wiley products, visit our web site at www.wiley.com.

Library of Congress Cataloging in Publication data available on request.

Cover Design: Jon Boylan
Cover Image: © C Design Studio/stock.adobe.com

Printed and bound by CPI Group (UK) Ltd, Croydon, CR0 4YY
C9781394285570_040226

For Jonathan

About the Author

Allie Mellen is a leading industry analyst who advises the Global 2000 on cybersecurity policy and practice, with a focus on detecting and responding to nation-state attacks.

She has held various engineering and research roles at MIT and multiple early-stage technology startups. Previously, she worked with government agencies on election and information security, conducted hardware security research, and partnered with product and infrastructure security teams as a hands-on security practitioner.

She is a featured speaker at many leading security conferences, including the RSA Conference, Black Hat, SANS events, and others. Her insights are frequently featured in top business and technology outlets such as NPR, *The Wall Street Journal*, and *The Washington Post*.

Read her newsletter, *The Latest Breach*, at `https://hackerxbella` `.substack.com`.

Acknowledgments

This book would not be possible without all of the interviewees who gave their time and insights. My sincerest thanks to Adam Meyers, Amy Robertson, Andrew Borene, Andrew Morris, Ankur Ahluwalia, Ari Schwartz, Brian Wrozek, Chase Cunningham, Chris Bisnett, Chris Hetner, Chris Kubecka, Cody Scott, Dmitri Alperovitch, Dragos Gavrilut, Elia Zaitsev, Enza Iannoppollo, Eva Galperin, Farijah St. Clair, Greg Linares, Iulian Timischi, Jamie Williams, Jeff Pollard, Jen Easterly, John Burger, John Clay, John Hammond, Katie Nickels, Keith McCammon, Mike Sikorski, Rick Holland, Robert McArdle, Ryan DuPre, Sam Curry, Sam Rubin, Sandra Joyce, Sean Nikkell, Sergio Calgitrone, Shawn Henry, Sherrod DeGrippo, Stefanie Metka, Steven McAndrews, Thaddeus Grugq, Visi Stark, Wasim Khaled, and Wendy Nather.

Thank you to everyone who helped coordinate these interviews. My sincere thanks to Andra Cazacu, Blair Campbell, Brendan Dodds, Daniel Lowden, Duquesa Pike, Erin Collier, Faith Wenger,

Ilina Cashiola, J.P. Szambelan, Josh DeButts, Kristina Moustakas, Lizzie Myers, Valerie Lattell, and Valerie Serino.

Thank you to the Wiley team, especially James Minatel, Annie Melnick, Kezia Endsley, Satish Gowrishankar, and Archana Pragash, for your incredible support and patience through this process.

Thank you to my researcher, Bogdan Nastasoiu, for your insights and time preparing countless background documents.

Thank you to Joseph Blankenship, Stephanie Balaouras, Jeff Pollard, and Jess Burn for your incredible support and guidance throughout this process.

Finally, to my family, friends, and loved ones—thank you for your patience and understanding through the long hours of research and writing. This book exists because of your support.

Contents

Introduction

For a successful technology, reality must take precedence over public relations, for Nature cannot be fooled.

—Richard P. Feynman[1]

This book is not about how the world ends. It will not tell you how a cyberattack will end society as we know it in the year 2030, or that a cyberattack alone will kick off the next world war.

Those ideas make for flashy headlines but fail to consider the nature of society and, as an extension, geopolitical conflict, which is inherently multidimensional. Every one of us, from the most technologically sophisticated 30-year-old engineer from MIT to the grandfather born during World War I, interacts with technology today—but never in isolation. For every social media message, there is a person to meet IRL; for every set of Maps directions, there

---

[1] Presidential Commission on the Space Shuttle Challenger Accident (1986) *Report of the Presidential Commission on the Space Shuttle Challenger Accident: Volume 2, Appendix F – Personal Observations on Reliability of Shuttle*, NASA. Available at: https://www.nasa.gov/history/rogersrep/v2appf.htm (Accessed: 7 January 2026).

is a location to go to; for every online search for a recipe, there is a kitchen and vegetables to cook.

The point of technology is to interact with the environment better. Even the most complicated, hidden kinds of technology are built for this ultimate goal. It may not seem like that, especially when you're looking at blockchain, middleware, or quantum computing. But much like physical technology, it is merely a means to a real-world end.

Take a simple axle—the axle alone may not have much effect on your life. You may look at an axle and think, that doesn't fit into my life at all. I've never seen that before, I don't know how it works, so it must not be important. But ultimately, rails connect to wheels, wheels connect to axles, axles connect to the chassis, the chassis connects to the floor, the floor connects to the seats, and all these parts make up a train that takes you to your parents' house for Sunday dinner.

When described separately, the components lose their meaning. But together, the meaning becomes clear: The train is technology you use to see your parents.

The same is true of software. A random number generator alone may not have much effect on your life. You may look at a random number generator and think, that doesn't fit into my life at all. I've never seen that before, I don't know how it works, so it must not be important. But ultimately, a random number generator is the basis for a strong key, which is required for strong encryption, which is used to encrypt your text messages so that only the people you want to read them, at the time you want them to read them, can.

The outcome always leads back to interactions with nature.

This is also the case in cybersecurity; for every ransomware attack, there is an organization trying to stay online—such as a hospital trying to keep equipment up and running so that patients get treatment. For every espionage operation, there is a piece of information that someone wants to keep secret, such as intellectual property of a new breakthrough electric vehicle, or the location and personal information of a spy. For every attack that defaces a public website, there are users trying to access it to get services.

If there is no real-world outcome to a cyberattack, nation-state attackers do not do it. Cyberattacks in a vacuum, without an environmental outcome, are meaningless. The motivation is always the interaction with nature. That is what this book is about—the real-world effects of nation-state cyberattacks and how, through understanding what motivates them, we can understand what will come next.

Chapter 1
The Currency of Control

Technology has infected every part of our lives; try to survive a day without your cell phone navigating an unfamiliar city, and you'll find that out immediately. But the key to technology is not the physical hardware itself. It is the data that is on it: The data that you as a user create, the data that you share with other people, the data that businesses generate. Manipulating that data is what changes things in the real world.

When interacting with technology, we all create data that serves as little breadcrumbs back to us and our lives. Every fitness tracker you use to track your jogging routes is a way for an attacker to see your name, your heart rate, exactly where you are, what time you exercise, and where you go. When Strava released a massive, supposedly anonymized global heat map of all user activities worldwide in 2017, people used it to figure out where military bases were and targeted it so they could see exactly who was exercising, where they were, and even what speed they were going.[1] They could track patrol schedules through it. Even years later, in 2024, researchers showed that they could figure out the exercise routes of world leaders like Joe Biden, Emmanuel Macron, and Vladimir Putin by

---

[1] www.wired.com/story/strava-heat-map-military-bases-fitness-trackers-privacy

tracking their bodyguards. The data was used to prove that Putin regularly runs near an almost billion-euro palace he has denied owning.[2] Stalkers use data like this to help them track the locations of their targets, creating opportune, seemingly accidental run-ins.

Modern cars you drive, like those from General Motors, can track the trips you take, the start and end times of your journey, the distance you traveled, your speed, and whether you had any sharp accelerations or braking. Not only do they have that data, but they've been known to sell it to insurers so that the insurers can reevaluate your premiums based on your driving history.[3]

If there's a video of you online, a scammer can use it to clone your voice with artificial intelligence. Once they've done that, scammers will use it to convince family members that their loved one is in danger and a ransom needs to be paid for their safe return. In 2025, a Florida woman received one such call from someone who sounded exactly like her daughter, claiming she had been in a car crash and that she needed to provide $15,000 in bail money at a specific location at a specific time. The mother paid it, and it wasn't until the scammer tried to get another $30,000 out of her that she realized it was a scam and her daughter wasn't in danger at all. She didn't get the $15,000 back.[4]

When an attacker gets access to your Social Security number, they use it to open new credit cards and personal loans, generating debt in your name. When they get your address, they use it to figure out when you won't be home and plan a burglary.

These types of scams are not rare. In 2024 alone, the FBI's Internet Crime Complaint Center (IC3) received over 800,000 complaints of illegal activity assisted by cyber-related means. Victims had an average reported loss of $19,372 from these crimes.[5]

---

[2] www.morningbrew.com/stories/track-heads-of-state-bodyguards-strava-accounts
[3] www.nytimes.com/2024/03/11/technology/carmakers-driver-tracking-insurance.html
[4] www.wfla.com/news/hillsborough-county/hillsborough-woman-duped-out-of-15k-after-ai-clones-daughters-voice
[5] www.ic3.gov/AnnualReport/Reports/2024_IC3Report.pdf

Data as National Power

For nations, data on citizens can be used to steal their economic well-being. It's a crime that is difficult to report, more difficult to attribute to a specific criminal, and even more difficult to effectively punish. When used for information operations, data on social media websites, like posts and comments, have the power to sway the political leanings of a nation, turning them for or against a particular idea; just look at the 2016 U.S. presidential election.

Nations have information they are invested in protecting: Data on their military apparatus, troop movements, strategic planning, and spy locations. Protecting that data is paramount to national security. It's also important to avoid the humiliation of appearing technologically behind or irrelevant—if you cannot protect your own nation's computer infrastructure, how could you possibly be equipped to protect your citizens?

Protecting information is now a core pillar of national stability. If a government cannot guarantee the safety of its data, it risks economic collapse, social unrest, and a complete erosion of the social contract that keeps it in power.

Cybersecurity is about this data: The confidentiality of it—who is authorized to access it and when, the availability of it—whether it can be accessed by those authorized to access it and how, and the integrity of it—whether it is accurate and complete.

It is about protecting that data by implementing security controls on computer infrastructure that stop attacks, whether it be more proactive measures, like keeping software up to date, enabling multifactor authentication, using strong passwords, or reactive measures, like finding and stopping attacks as they happen. For a single person alone, this is difficult, let alone for an organization or a nation.

For nations, it is a complex operation with many layers. There are core targets, which take on the brunt of cyber defense implementation and are the most critical to protect. These targets include organizations such as:

- Government entities, both agencies and people, civilian and military. This encompasses national entities and regional or local, which are often limited in staff and resources to support defense.
- Private-sector organizations, especially those designated as critical infrastructure that need to be protected for national security reasons. These are the companies that, if their services were disrupted, would severely limit the capabilities of a nation, like communications, the electric grid, hospitals, etc.
- Those within the private sector that are not critical infrastructure, but are still important, as they often collect citizens' personal data, which countries strive to protect.

Then there's the supportive apparatus built around all of this, which includes the organizations that are not necessarily the main targets for cyberattacks (though sometimes they are) but that are helping ensure the nation is innovating, pushing forward national and international policy, and bridging the gap between the public and private sectors. Some examples are:

- Intelligence agencies, which gather and disseminate threat intelligence within the government and with key partners that can help predict, identify, and stop attacks and national security threats.
- Policy organizations, which are focused on international diplomacy and alliances alongside economic security and sanctions in response to cyberattacks. These organizations build alliances and partnerships and establish mutual recognition of what defines a cyber norm.
- Organizations that execute legal deterrence measures, which focus on publicly attributing and punishing attackers to deter their behavior—for example, indictments or sanctions brought down on individuals.

- Community collaboration organizations that help to coordinate and bridge the gap between the public and private sectors. They are also the vehicles through which threat intelligence is disseminated.
- Research and innovation institutions that are responsible for advancing cybersecurity defense and offensive capabilities. They also develop standards, often in collaboration with the government and the private sector.

Depending on the style of the government, it may have limited or extreme control over one or all of these organizations. In most cases, it needs to provide a means by which to regulate its cybersecurity measures, ensure compliance, and detect and respond to cyberattacks.

Power Projection

Cyberattacks are the other side of this coin. A cyberattack is a deliberate, unauthorized attempt to access, disrupt, degrade, or destroy a computer system, network, or the data residing within it. Offensive organizations, including those within the government, are responsible for executing offensive cyber operations and for disrupting attacker infrastructure. They typically fall under one of a few categories:

- Nation-state threat actors, who are government or government-directed groups that execute offensive operations against other nation-state infrastructure and critical infrastructure. For example, when a nation-state targets an adversary's command-and-control systems to blind them before a kinetic strike, that is a military offensive cyber operation.
- Intelligence agencies, who can be offensive cyber operators, as they can be used for surveillance and espionage purposes. The goal here is most often theft over destruction. Intelligence agencies use these operations to steal state secrets, intellectual property, or sensitive data.

- Cybercriminals, who are often self-directed and execute offensive actions motivated by financial gain rather than geopolitical strategy. While they may use the same tools as nation-states (though often, not nearly as advanced), they lack the political authorization of nation-state activity. In some cases, nation-states will direct cybercriminal activity to avoid state attribution.
- Hacktivists, who are driven by nationalist sentiments and often operate independently or, in some cases, under the direction of the state. They are not formally part of the state apparatus, but they can be used by the state to gather intelligence or execute cyberattacks to avoid state attribution.

The attacks they perpetrate run the gamut, from distributed denial-of-service (DDoS) attacks that take down critical services to espionage operations that steal critical data. The attacks also have much crossover with information operations, especially attacks that spread online. Every major government uses a combination of cyber defenses and offensive cyber operations to protect its interests in the modern world. Just as the Cold War required a balance of nuclear deterrence and conventional military strength, cybersecurity requires a delicate balance between defenses and power projection.

A distributed denial of service (DDoS) attack is when an attacker uses many devices to flood a target system, service, or network with traffic or requests so that legitimate users can't access it. The flood of requests "deny service" to true users and can disrupt critical business operations.

Ultimately, a nation's cybersecurity capability is not just about technical controls like firewalls or encryption; it is a reflection of its national and geopolitical strategy. And the true potential of integrating it into combat operations became clearest during the Gulf War.

Chapter 2
The First Information War

Yours is a society that cannot accept 10,000 dead in one battle.[1]
—Saddam Hussein, July 25, 1990

S addam Hussein said these words in the last meeting with the U.S. Ambassador to Baghdad prior to the Iraqi invasion of Kuwait. The discussion centered on the rifts in U.S.–Iraq relations, Iraqi interests in the region, especially about oil and Kuwait, and U.S. interest in keeping a stable price for oil.

One message Saddam asserted during the meeting was that the United States didn't have the stamina or the mental fortitude to last through another bloody war, and that, because of this, it should stay out of future conflict in the region. To be quite frank, Saddam was likely right that the U.S. couldn't accept 10,000 dead in one battle; the Vietnam War was a recent and bloody memory, one that the United States had no interest in repeating. However, what Saddam and most of the world did not realize at the time was that by the 1990s, the military strategy the United States used in Vietnam was no longer its approach to conflict.

---

[1] https://www.nytimes.com/1991/03/01/opinion/this-aggression-will-not-stand.html

The Vietnam War was a brutal tipping point for the United States. It hung over the heads of the American military, especially those who served as officers there. But the lesson learned was not to *not* go to war. Instead, it served as a morbid reminder of the dangers of prioritizing body count as a metric of success, the failures and difficulties of poor coordination in joint operations, and the challenge of scope creep, where there was no clear end to a conflict, especially one that had fallen out of alignment with its original purpose.

During that time period, both the United States and the Soviet Union took lessons from another war as well: The Yom Kippur War. It began and ended in less than 3 weeks, and though the war started with a surprise attack by Egypt and Syria on Israel, the Soviet Union and the United States were heavily involved, supporting their respective allies with supplies. The 20 days taught the United States and the Soviet Union major lessons about the future of military conflict, though those lessons differed greatly.

For the Soviet Union, it was a resounding validation of its military technology and doctrine. It was proof that its Radio-Electronic Combat (REC) strategy, where the Soviets integrated electronic attack and physical destruction, was effective.[2] REC is grounded in the conviction that victory goes to the side that best controls the electromagnetic spectrum; the military must paralyze adversary's command, control, and communications while shielding its own from disruption.

For the United States, it showed that defeating a Soviet-style force required deeply integrated joint and combined-arms operations. It also demonstrated how timely changes in strategy on the battlefield could make a huge difference; Israel's early battlefield losses were turned around when they shifted to a more integrated air–ground approach. Effective coordination was paramount.

This led to significant changes within the U.S. military. *The Goldwater-Nichols Act of 1986* created unified command structures for military operations in different regions; to that end, it elevated the role of the chairman of the Joint Chiefs of Staff to military adviser to the President. Once the United States saw the Soviet approach to battle in Afghanistan, and because of its own oil interests in the

---

[2] https://www.airandspaceforces.com/article/0382radioelectronic

region, it established the U.S. Central Command (USCENTCOM) as a permanent unified command focused on the Middle East and Central and South Asia.[3]

This time was a catalyst for the United States to develop a counter strategy to REC, known as Command, Control, and Communications Countermeasures (C3CM). C3CM prioritizes protecting ones own C3 capabilities while degrading those of the enemy to deny them information.[4] It's the melding of electronic warfare, deception, operational security, and physical destruction to enable ground forces to more easily take control. C3CM uses information control to blind, paralyze, and destroy the enemy so they cannot strategically communicate and coordinate.

The United States also shifted toward a new doctrine, AirLand Battle, with intense coordination between air and land forces.[5] AirLand Battle underscores that joint forces exceed the sum of individual service capabilities—an idea that continues to shape U.S. military strategy to this day. Each branch relies on others' specialized capabilities to maximize mission success. Forces operate across diverse environments, from conventional battlefields to cyber and space warfare. By eliminating redundancy and improving coordination, joint operations allow commanders to tailor force composition to mission requirements, reinforcing the U.S. military's global responsiveness and strategic reach.

Thus, we return to the summer of 1990, which, to say the least, had been tense.

After its war with Iran in the 1980s, Iraq was stuck with at least $42 billion in debt, including some borrowed from Kuwait.[6] The best way for Iraq to solve that problem: Sell more oil for more money, as oil accounted for over 90 percent of Iraq's export revenue.[7] At a meeting with OPEC in July, Iraq insisted on a $25 price per barrel for oil, a major leap from the $18 at the time of the accords.[8]

---

[3] https://www.centcom.mil/ABOUT-US
[4] https://apps.dtic.mil/sti/citations/ADA242346
[5] https://www.armyupress.army.mil/Journals/Military-Review/English-Edition-Archives/MR-75th-Anniversary/75th-Doctrinal-AirLand
[6] www.merip.org/2003/09/a-clean-slate-in-iraq/#:~:text=By%201990%2C%20after%20the%20Iran,this%20task%2C%20he%20invaded%20Kuwait
[7] www.merip.org/1991/07/oil-and-the-gulf-war
[8] Ibid.

Saddam Hussein also sent a letter to the Arab League through Foreign Minister Tariq Aziz in which they accused Kuwait of stealing Iraqi oil, building military installations, and refusing to cancel the loans it made during the war. Compounding this was the ongoing Iraqi claim to Kuwaiti territory, which it had already tried to assert in 1938 and 1961. Pressures were high.[9] They attempted negotiations, with Iraq demanding concessions from Kuwait, particularly for what they viewed as its stealing what they claimed was $2.4 billion worth of oil from the Rumaila (الرميلة, Al-Rumaylah) oil field in southern Iraq.[10]

The negotiations failed, and by August, Saddam Hussein ordered the invasion of Kuwait. Iraqi forces took over Kuwait City with little difficulty and occupied the country in two days. Occupying Kuwait made it so that Iraq had more than 20 percent of OPEC's total oil output.[11]

But that didn't seem to be enough—Iraq appeared prepared to invade Saudi Arabia as well. Ostensibly, controlling Saudi Arabia would give Iraq control of more than 40 percent of the world's oil reserves.[12] This put the international community on edge; Iraq had already been attempting aggressive price hikes, and that much control in the hands of one nation over such a critical market could easily lead to price manipulation and disruption in the global economy.

Within days of the invasion, the United Nations Security Council passed a resolution to ban trade with Iraq and to compel UN member countries to protect the assets of the legitimate government in Kuwait. Twelve of the 21 Arab League countries also passed a resolution condemning the invasion and endorsing the UN resolution.

By August 7, the first phase of the war, Operation Desert Shield, had begun. The United States began sending troops to Saudi Arabia to

---

[9] www.tandfonline.com/doi/abs/10.1080/07075332.2002.9640981
[10] http://digitalcommons.law.umaryland.edu/cgi/viewcontent.cgi?article=1331&context=mjil
[11] https://jirfp.thebrpi.org/journals/jirfp/Vol_1_No_1_June_2013/1.pdf
[12] www.britannica.com/event/Persian-Gulf-War

help defend it in case of an attack. The deployment grew quickly; by mid-November, there were more than 240,000 U.S. troops deployed to the Gulf and another 200,000 coming. Countries including the UK, Egypt, France, Canada, Morocco, and over 20 others committed troops and weapons.

In the first UN authorization of use of force since the Korean War, the UN passed a resolution on November 29 that authorized the use of force if Iraq did not leave Kuwait by January 15, 1991—less than two months from then.

Enter: Operation Desert Storm, the second phase of the war. Iraqi forces refused to leave Kuwait by the deadline set by the UN, and so, two days later, the US-led coalition military campaign began. It started with an air campaign to wear down defenses before the ground offensive. The air campaign lasted from January 17 to February 24, with coalition forces achieving air superiority by January 28 before pounding vital targets, including and especially air defense systems, radar sites, command and control centers, and communication relays, taking from the ideas developed with the C3CM. The United States also coordinated a psyop campaign, which used radio communications, leaflets, loudspeakers, and other methods to encourage Iraqi soldiers to surrender.[13]

The ground offensive began February 24 with a strategy developed by CENTCOM, which used deception to convince the Iraqis of a seaborne assault. This pushed the Iraqis to concentrate forces in Kuwait. The most famous part of the strategy was the left hook, where forces from the left flank moved north from their position west of the border before making a left hook to the Euphrates River, intending to cut off Iraqi forces from the west. Meanwhile, the eastern flank met the main Iraqi line of defense.[14] Early forms of what would later be known as network-centric warfare were vital: GPS provided the coalition force with navigational accuracy in the

---

[13] www.armyupress.army.mil/Portals/7/combat-studies-institute/csi-books/perceptions-are-reality-lsco-volume-7.pdf
[14] www.nam.ac.uk/explore/gulf-war

largely featureless desert, and the Joint Surveillance Target Attack Radar Systems (JSTARS) gave near-real-time intelligence on enemy movements.

Within 100 hours, tens of thousands of Iraqi troops had surrendered due to the immense ground pressure immediately following the long air campaign. Saddam accepted a ceasefire on February 28. Nearly 87,000 Iraqi soldiers surrendered. During the campaign, 345 coalition troops were killed, and while official numbers are not known, Iraqi deaths are estimated between 30,000 to 100,000.[15]

There are a few reasons why coalition forces won so decisively. Iraqi forces were outmatched when it came to weaponry; they were operating with a majority of older Soviet equipment, much of which would have been new during the Yom Kippur War but was now several generations behind. Meanwhile, the allies had the latest, cutting-edge F-117A Nighthawk stealth fighter and new technology, like drones for surveillance and damage assessments. Iraqi soldiers were also majority conscripts, while the United States had an all-volunteer army by then (along with the British), with higher morale and support of the mission.

But by far the biggest reason the war was won so decisively was because of the massive change in strategy to integrate command, control, communications, computers, intelligence, and surveillance: C4ISR.[16] The Gulf War was the first major test of the power of U.S. Central Command. CENTCOM coordinated a coalition of over 30 nations, over 500,000 U.S. troops, and a combination of air, ground, and naval forces. They coordinated deception tactics, a psyops campaign, aerial maneuvers, a ground invasion, and naval forces in the Gulf. It was a massive validation and stress test of the value, strategic strength, and agility of an integrated combatant command. The United States didn't have to accept 10,000 dead in one battle; with coordination and information control, it could win anyway.

The Gulf War showcased the power of joint operations, electronic warfare, and an early form of multidomain warfare. It was

---

[15] www.nam.ac.uk/explore/gulf-war
[16] https://www.atlanticcouncil.org/in-depth-research-reports/issue-brief/in-brief-c4isr-a-five-step-guide-to-maintaining-natos-comparative-military-edge-over-the-coming-decade

a validation of the power of successful integration to create a new, overwhelmingly effective way of fighting. It showed the power of information dominance, coordination, and the importance of information control. It was a revelation—not in the power of a single technology, but in the creation of a system of systems that combined sensors, commanders, and weapons. It affirmed U.S. military doctrine and was the definitive proof of a sea change in warfare that became the blueprint for future operations. One early commentator said that "in Desert Storm, knowledge came to rival weapons and tactics in importance . . ."[17]

For the Soviets, it was validation of a strategy they had been accepting since the Yom Kippur War. It was proof that battles over perception and decision-making—what Moscow calls "information confrontation"—were now central.

It was also a wake-up call for one other major player: China. At the time, the PLA was technologically unsophisticated and more focused on territorial defense than projecting power abroad. The Great Leap Forward caused major challenges and chaos internally, which lingered. China's main adversary was the Soviet Union, especially following the Sino-Soviet split in the late 1960s.[18] They generally had a policy of non-intervention and were far more domestically focused at the time. However, the Gulf War was an unmistakable signal that the status quo could not last.

The Gulf War and the fall of the Soviet Union led to a profound shift in China's military strategy, where the PLA developed campaign concepts that combined traditional ground-centric approaches with modern joint warfare, where capabilities from all military services are coordinated.[19] It pivoted to *Winning Local Wars Under High Technology Conditions*, switching China from a primarily defensive posture to a much more offensive one. It was a major departure from the people's war ideology of the past 50 years; it focused on quick wars instead of attrition and on prioritizing the strength of China instead of assuming weakness. It also incorporated strategic

---

[17] https://www.army.mil/article/286292/army_cyber_corps_a_prehistory
[18] https://nsarchive2.gwu.edu/NSAEBB/NSAEBB49/index2.html
[19] https://media.setav.org/en/file/2020/02/chinas-evolving-military-doctrine-after-the-cold-war.pdf

deterrence, in line with the findings of the Cold War and other countries' nuclear weapons strategies. The switch laid the groundwork for China to focus on joint military campaigns.

Chinese analysts often reference U.S. operations like Desert Storm and Iraqi Freedom as examples where information dominance was key. In 1995, Major General Wang Pufeng published a paper in China Military Science that outlined his viewpoint on information warfare (信息战争), especially how its dominance and importance were demonstrated by the United States during the Gulf War.[20] His perspective was fundamentally different from how China had previously approached information warfare. He highlighted the importance of information dominance, often defined as the ability for a country to defend its information while exploiting the information of its enemy.[21] His work helped to dramatically change how China approaches information warfare. The PLA started to place great emphasis on information dominance, coordinating intelligence, surveillance, and reconnaissance to enable precise offensive actions and effectively assess the enemy's capabilities. Modern technology was central to this effort.

The Gulf War was the catalyst for joint military operations and an informatized future for Russia, China, and the United States. For Russia, it showcased the power of information for disruption and leverage; for China, the power of information for access and advantage; and for the United States, the power of information for control and deterrence.

---

[20] https://irp.fas.org/world/china/docs/iw_mg_wang.htm
[21] www.globalaffairs.ch/2022/06/08/chinese-definitions-of-information-warfare

Chapter 3

The Social Contracts of the Cyber Powers

There are three behemoth nations in cybersecurity that put more resources toward cyber defense and perpetrate more cyberattacks—and more effective cyberattacks—than any other nations in the world: The United States, China, and Russia. No geopolitical or cybersecurity conversation is complete without these three players. However, they do not approach cybersecurity in the same way. They each have unique defensive and offensive capabilities based on their histories, their military doctrine, and their social contracts.

The Difficult Balancing Act of the United States

The United States is pulled in three separate directions with three separate priorities: Ensuring national security, maintaining a strong economy, and keeping positive public opinion, especially on hot-button issues like freedom.

This is all driven by the social contract between the government and the people in the United States, which has been built from past traumas like the Revolutionary War, Civil War, and financial crises.

The government is expected to provide safety from tyranny, take minimal liberties with taxes, and provide the rule of law; if the state overreaches on any of these, the people are obligated to revoke the contract by either voting them out or revolting. The heart of the social contract is the promise that Americans can make a living and have opportunities for upward mobility and security through hard work.

In the view of American citizens, freedom is the promise of individual agency over collective security. Without maximum independence and individual agency, the government is considered repressive.

These competing and sometimes complementary interests make cybersecurity decisions in the United States a tough landscape to navigate.

On the defensive, the United States must strike a difficult balance. It has to protect its own systems at the federal and state levels across a highly distributed, heterogeneous environment of different agencies, confidentiality levels, equipment, and resources. At the same time, it needs to find a way to support and secure the private sector, which owns most of the critical infrastructure in the United States, without overstepping the social contract into perceived or actual tyranny. It also needs to find a balance between protecting Americans while also maintaining an open Internet, which helps project American values like democracy abroad. All of these face much debate and intermittent, chaotic changes from a changing regulatory environment as the nation becomes more divided.

On the offensive, the United States must avoid breaking the social contract by illegally surveilling Americans, yet it also still needs to gather the intelligence necessary for national security. It has to balance its own offensive cyber operations while operating within the bounds of international law to respect the ideological world it is trying to build. Many of its operations are clandestine, intentionally hiding the operation such that it remains completely undiscovered, while still accomplishing its goal in the name of operational agility and risk management . . . and to avoid bureaucratic hurdles.

All of this said, the United States has built and maintained the most powerful cybersecurity function in the world for decades. It is consistently ranked the most powerful cybersecurity country for its government strategies, offensive and defensive capabilities, private sector, workforce, and innovation.[1] It is the most sophisticated, yet also the most secretive, with many of the offensive cyberattacks perpetrated by the United States going unnoticed or unpublicized for decades, if they are ever revealed. Its partnerships with other nations—especially the *Five Eyes,* the intelligence-sharing alliance comprising the United States, the UK, Canada, Australia, and New Zealand—give it visibility into attacks happening in regions it otherwise would not. It also benefits from the wealth of cybersecurity researchers based in the West, who focus much of their efforts on finding and stopping attacks perpetrated by foreign adversaries.

The Total Control of China

China has three priorities: Maintaining the stability of its regime, protecting its national interests, and regaining its regional control and influence.

The social contract between the government and the people in China is that the people will comply with the state, so long as the government provides harmony and prosperity. This is driven by many points of trauma in Chinese history, from the Great Leap Forward when mass famine plagued the people, to World War II, when China was thrust into a brutal invasion by Japan while balancing a civil war, to all the way back in the Warring States Period, when seven distinct regional states fought for control. Harmony of the people and stability of the regime are the bedrock upon which modern Chinese society is built.

To accomplish this, the Chinese Communist Party (CCP) does not simply expect citizens to *accept* the party's messages; rather, it expects people to *believe* the propaganda given to them. In the view of Chinese citizens, freedom is ultimately the stability to live a life without starvation and chaos, even if you must wholeheartedly believe in and support the messages of the state. Without that stability, abstract civil liberties are meaningless.

On the defensive, China strives to reach total control: Privacy does not exist. For systems owned by the government, it prioritizes recognized, global cybersecurity standards. For the private sector

---

[1] www.belfercenter.org/publication/national-cyber-power-index-2020

and the public, however, it is a different story. It centralizes encryption standards such that it can decrypt any information from any company in the country. It requires data to be accessible by the government at any time, from any system. Every individual must be registered so that the government can track their Internet activity, no matter where they are. Propaganda and state media are the public narrative. Websites and online conversations are censored as they happen, and the Internet is under the complete control of the government—if they want to take down the Internet for a specific region in China, they can and will.

On the offensive, the CCP is targeted. It prioritizes espionage for diplomatic and military uses, but also for economic ones, and will feed back economic espionage to its top private sector partners. It prioritizes covert actions, those that create plausible deniability—and it denies almost every attack it is accused of perpetrating. This contrasts its strategy with regional states it wishes to bring under its control and influence, where; It is more overt, using threats and violence in person and online to intimidate. It has also expanded its capabilities in disinformation in recent years; in the past, its propaganda efforts were targeted at its own citizens, but more recently it has used information operations to manipulate the global narrative, both about China and about other countries.

China is consistently ranked the second strongest cyber power in the world after the United States. It had incredible foresight early on when building its defensive apparatus, understanding and addressing the power of the Internet and its regulation before most any other country. It had a strong base of hacktivists early on which, above all else, perpetrated cybercrime for love of country, a motivation that was unique to China at that scale and consistency at that time. According to then-FBI director Chris Wray in 2023, China has a bigger offensive cyber program than every other major nation combined. Chinese cyberattackers outnumber U.S. cybersecurity personnel by at least 50 to 1.[2]

---

[2] www.reuters.com/world/fbi-chief-says-china-has-bigger-hacking-program-than-competition-combined-2023-09-18

The Regime Power of Russia

Russia is driven to maintain economic stability, ensure loyalty to the regime, and prove itself a superpower capable of competing with the world's top countries, especially by regaining regional control and influence.

The social contract between the government and the people in Russia is that the people will be loyal to the state as long as the government provides economic stability and physical safety. It carries traumas borne out of the collapse of the Soviet Union, which was ultimately a collapse of the Soviet identity, with the deteriorating state of healthcare, a crushed economy, and skyrocketing poverty. It views World War II as a pinnacle of its power, both militarily and as a time that showcased its moral and geopolitical legitimacy. The path back to that legitimacy lies in loyalty to the regime.

The Russian government doesn't care if citizens believe the propaganda it is funneling to them; rather, it only expects them to accept and not challenge it. In the view of Russian citizens, freedom is the safety to live the life you want, even if you have to turn a blind eye to the acts of the regime. Private freedom—the ability to travel, buy what you want, and live without the state micromanaging—is most important.

Russia's defensive cybersecurity capabilities frame all of cybersecurity as a battle for information security (Информационная безопасность). It's all about the information, which is why much of its security measures revolve around national sovereignty and take place at the service provider level—it has specific requirements for Internet service providers such that the government can block traffic or throttle sites at will. It can surveil its citizens through lawful intercept, and makes use of it often. It also takes partial responsibility for the defense of private sector organizations through a collaboration between the private and public sectors. While it requires that all information companies, whether it be social media companies, email providers, or others, offer a way to decrypt communications and only use approved encryption services (those that the government can break into), it doesn't yet mandate encryption standards across the entire country for individual citizens, giving them a small pocket of privacy. All this said, it has consolidated media power such that it completely controls the media messages sent to citizens and continues to tighten those restrictions each year.

Its offensive capabilities parallel its defensive in how it prioritizes information warfare (информационная война). Deeply rooted in lessons on propaganda learned in the Soviet era, the Russian government spreads disinformation liberally through bot farms around the world. These efforts are widely known to have influenced activities in many countries, from Estonia during the Bronze Night to Ukraine during the Russo-Ukrainian War to the United States during presidential elections. It is a pioneer in information warfare, shaping how other countries use it today. Many of its operations are overt, done explicitly to draw attention and wreak havoc, promoting itself as an equivalent power to that of China and the United States. It also uses these attacks when trying to control former Soviet countries that refuse to submit to Russian interests.

The Battle for a Dominant Vision

These three nations are not just competing for dominance in cyberspace; they are fighting to impose their own vision on the very nature of the Internet. For the United States, the goal is a defensible and resilient digital ecosystem that aligns with its democratic values. For China, it is an instrument of state power, a carefully curated garden where harmony and prosperity are cultivated through absolute control. For Russia, it is a theater of information warfare, a battleground where stoking chaos is a weapon and undermining democracies is the prize.

Their cyber operations are a direct reflection of these irreconcilable worldviews. The attacks and defenses are not random acts, but calculated execution of doctrines forged by decades of unique historical traumas and political priorities.

The following chapters deconstruct the operational playbooks of these three powers and describe how they set out to fulfill the social contracts they have created with their people. We start with the world's most powerful and paradoxical: The United States.

Part I

The United States of America

Chapter 4
The Wars That Wrote the Code

World War I is known as a war fought in the trenches. The most iconic imagery of the war has always been of the death and destruction in the trench system. But soldiers didn't dig in because they wanted to, or because it, in and of itself, was a winning strategy. They dug in because to be caught in the open was to be annihilated.

The trenches were just a symptom of the true strategy; World War I was fundamentally a war of artillery. The machine gun could cut down charging infantry with terrifying efficiency, but it was artillery that could kill you from miles away, without warning, whether you were attacking or huddling for cover. The daily reality for most soldiers was the constant, soul-destroying stress of living under the ever-present threat of an artillery barrage. Of the 37 million battlefield casualties in World War I, 60 percent of them were caused by artillery.[1]

But artillery wasn't easy to aim. To figure out where to target, an officer needed detailed elevation maps with artillery tables—standard data used to calculate the expected path of a

[1] www.theworldwar.org/learn/about-wwi/artillery

shell. Artillery tables took hours to create by hand stateside before being sent to the front. Imagine being on a muddy, gray battlefield, doing paper calculations with artillery slide rules and trigonometry tables. That was the life of an artillery officer, calculating the elevation, azimuth, and time of flight for the shell so it could explode in the right place at the right time. In theory, the math was perfect. In practice, wind conditions could push artillery to a new angle; maps were often inaccurate and difficult to maintain; and equipment varied due to barrel wear and inconsistent ammunition. Calculations were done by hand under stressful conditions: Troops were being injured and dying, and the enemy was attempting to get a shot off first. The saving grace for the calculations was the minimal elevation across no-man's land and the machine gun fire, which kept troop movements to a minimum.

When the United States entered World War II in 1941, everything changed. The terrain varied, with urban, hilly, and mountainous areas that posed challenges for targeting. Hitting with one low-angle shot was a thing of the past, and they now needed to avoid obstacles like mountains and friendly forces. Artillery fire had also evolved thanks to advancements in metallurgy, propellant chemistry, and aerodynamics.

Compounding this was an arms race between nations for more advanced weapons. Each evolution of a new weapon was a double-edge sword: Yes, it meant better capabilities on a battlefield, but it also required new artillery tables. The speed of innovation in weaponry was being held back by the time it took to create these tables.

These factors led the U.S. government to realize that the way artillery tables were created was the ultimate bottleneck. In 1942, physicist John Mauchly proposed building an all-electronic counting machine to solve this problem, capable of performing artillery table calculations in seconds rather than minutes. The U.S. Army ate it up.[2]

They funded Mauchly's work at the University of Pennsylvania's Moore School of Electrical Engineering, and from 1943 to 1945, John and his partner, John Presper Eckert, developed the first large-scale computer to run without mechanical parts, known as the Electronic Numerical Integrator and Computer (ENIAC). This

---

[2] https://lemelson.mit.edu/resources/j-presper-eckert-and-john-mauchly

was a massive shift from previous counting devices, especially those championed by IBM, a juggernaut that dominated the market. Instead of electromechanical counting, which relied on movable parts prone to failure, ENIAC was completely electronic—no moving parts and much faster tabulations.

This was a remarkable breakthrough. ENIAC was a marvel for its time, but the machine was massive and had a lot of resource constraints. It took up 50×30 feet of floor space and needed almost 18,000 vacuum tubes to operate.[3] The tubes were roughly the size of a modern household lightbulb, and scientists had to replace one or two of them every single day. Despite its size, resource constraints, and its completion after the war ended, it didn't stop ENIAC from being useful. It performed calculations that helped construct the hydrogen bomb.[4]

Mauchly and Eckert wanted to commercialize ENIAC, but the University of Pennsylvania wanted them to accept tenure in exchange for releasing the patents. They declined, instead leaving the university and founding their own company, the Eckert–Mauchly Computer Corporation.

The Eckert-Mauchly Computer Corporation found immediate success and had two military contracts, but the contracts were closed when the FBI suspected the company had been infiltrated by communists. They suspected Mauchly of being a communist and conducted multiple investigations of him. This was all very poorly timed with the Korean War, which had just begun in 1950. Mauchly resigned as president in 1951 so the company could participate in military contracts. It took 8 years for Mauchly, who was innocent and not affiliated with communists, to be granted back his security clearance.[5]

Grace Hopper joined the Eckert–Mauchly Computer Corporation in 1949. By then, she was a lieutenant in the Naval Reserve and had already worked on the Mark I, the first large-scale automatic calculator, and had written the first computer manual that described how to operate it. She is also known for popularizing the term "debugging" while working on the Mark II computer in 1947.

---

[3] www.computerhistory.org/revolution/birth-of-the-computer/4/78
[4] https://www.ebsco.com/research-starters/history/univac-i-becomes-first-commercial-electronic-computer
[5] http://ds-wordpress.haverford.edu/bitbybit/bit-by-bit-contents/end-matter/appendix-the-fbi-dossier-of-john-william-mauchly

Though the term "bug" had been used previously to describe mechanical errors, her documentation helped propel the term.

Hopper designed the first compiler, A-0, which translated programmer instructions to machine code, in 1952. She served as head programmer for the Universal Automatic Computer (UNIVAC) I. The UNIVAC I was finished in 1951 and was used to tabulate parts of the 1950s population census and the entirety of the 1954 economic census.[6]

What helped popularize electronic computers was an election: Stevenson vs. Eisenhower in 1952. As a sideshow during vote counting, a CBS reporter showcased UNIVAC on election night. They wanted it to predict the outcome of the race. With only 3 million votes, UNIVAC correctly predicted that the odds of Eisenhower winning were 100 to 1. Even though the reporter asked repeatedly for UNIVAC's prediction, the company refused to provide it until much later, thinking the prediction was wrong, given how early in the race it was. Later, when it became clear that Eisenhower would win, the company had to sheepishly explain it was right from the start, and that next year they would believe it.[7]

UNIVAC became a cultural icon and signaled a transition for computers from military and academic use to commercial viability. For a time, the name "UNIVAC" became synonymous with the word "computer." From UNIVAC winning the Census Bureau business and correctly predicting the 1952 presidential election results, it pushed IBM over the edge to truly accept that the future was electronic. IBM developed the IBM 701 computer in just a single year to directly compete with UNIVAC, and despite it being late to market, it used its status as an electromechanical juggernaut to dominate the early electronic computer market.[8]

Cold War, Hot Tech

When the Second World War ended, the United States faced a new enemy: The Soviet Union. The Cold War led to major computing breakthroughs, in part because, in the void of direct military confrontation,

---

[6] www.census.gov/about/history/bureau-history/census-innovations/technol ogy/univac-i.html
[7] http://eisenhowermemorial.org/onepage/IKE%20%26%20Science.Oct08 .EN.FINAL%20%28v2%29.pdf
[8] https://www.ibm.com/history/700

research and development were seen as a proxy for national power and national success. It was a propaganda tool: The more innovation, the better the country must be doing over the other.

After the September 1957 launch of Sputnik 1 by the Soviet Union, U.S. President Dwight D. Eisenhower saw the public perception that the United States was falling behind the Soviets. With his Secretary of Defense, Eisenhower established the Advanced Research Projects Agency (ARPA) in February 1958. ARPA was created to innovate technology beyond imminent military requirements. It pursued high-risk, high-reward research to keep the United States ahead in science and technology.

In 1962, Joseph Carl Robnett Licklider joined ARPA to lead Command and Control Research.[9] Licklider changed things for ARPA—he pivoted it to prioritize interactive computing and creating a better world over military work, even renaming his department to the Information Processing Techniques Office (IPTO). This change was the foundation to push ARPA in a new direction, one that would come to define the modern age.

Command and control (C2) is the means by which a commander orchestrates the use of personnel, information, and materiel to achieve an objective. In cybersecurity terms, C2 is the infrastructure used to maintain communication with and control over compromised devices. It's HQ for their operations.

In 1966, a new IPTO director came aboard who was aligned with Licklider's ideas: Robert Taylor. Taylor and Licklider had a vision where computers could act as interactive devices that would communicate with one another, which would ultimately become the Internet.[10]

---

[9] https://users.cs.duke.edu/~chase/cps49s/licklider.html
[10] "The Computer as a Communications Device," https://archive.nytimes.com/www
.nytimes.com/library/tech/99/12/biztech/articles/122099outlook-bobb.html

In 1969, ARPA awarded a contract to develop the ARPANET to enable resource sharing between remote computers. It started with three time-shared systems, all at remote facilities; the team realized that, through these systems, interactive communities could develop. Many critical, related innovations emerged during that time, including packet switching to break data into smaller pieces and reassemble them on arrival at the destination, Telnet to remotely access and control another device, and the File Transfer Protocol (FTP) to share large files between machines, which paved the way for ARPANET to grow.[11]

Development of ARPANET continued in earnest thanks to collaboration between the Department of Defense, University of California, Los Angeles, Stanford Research Institute, University of California, Santa Barbara, and the University of Utah.[12] This collaboration was part of why requests for comments (RFCs) were created, which are a fundamental way that engineers and developers communicate and iterate on standards and policies, even today. The ARPA team used RFCs to communicate their ideas for changes and new developments, while giving the universities the opportunity to provide feedback.

Bolt, Beranek, and Newman (BBN), a company that would become RTX BBN (Raytheon BBN), was awarded the contract to build the Interface Message Processors, the packet-switching nodes that formed the backbone of the ARPANET.[13] A BBN employee sent the first-ever email. An engineer named Ray Tomlinson sent a message between two side-by-side computers using the @ symbol to link the username to the destination address. He created email just for fun; if you're tired of your email, you know who to blame. In a profile for *Forbes* magazine, he said that he showed a colleague what he had created and then said,

Don't tell anyone! This isn't what we're supposed to be working on.[14]

When he built it, he used three existing programs: SNDMSG and READMAIL, which let users leave messages for each other on the *same* machine. When combined with CPYNET, which copied messages *between* computers, he figured out that you could electronically mail someone a message.

---

[11] https://sites.cs.ucsb.edu/~almeroth/classes/F04.176A/handouts/history.html
[12] https://www.darpa.mil/news/features/arpanet
[13] https://www.walden-family.com/bbn/arpanet-rfq.pdf
[14] https://www.forbes.com/asap/1998/1005/126_print.html

Also in 1971, another BBN engineer and colleague of Tomlinson, Bob Thomas, created the first computer worm, Creeper. Creeper was designed to move between different computers on ARPANET. It didn't damage or disrupt systems, just displayed the message, "IM THE CREEPER: CATCH ME IF YOU CAN."[15] Even though it didn't cause damage, it was an early foreshadowing of what was to come: Computer worms for destructive purposes. After Creeper, Tomlinson created Reaper, which also moved across ARPANET, but instead deleted Creeper to clean up after itself. Paralleling Creeper's foreshadowing of future malware, Reaper foreshadowed future antivirus software to remove it.[16]

By 1974, ARPANET had grown significantly. It was connecting 46 different nodes that connected devices to the network.[17] Despite this, it still didn't even make the list of the most critical projects ARPA had on its plate. ARPA also lacked the legal authority to operate as a communications network—it was a research division, not equipped to maintain a functional utility. For these reasons, and because it was still important to the DOD to maintain it, they transferred ARPANET to the Defense Communications Agency (DCA) in 1975.[18]

The DCA made multiple changes; in 1983, it split off part of ARPANET into MILNET for military agencies, with ARPANET remaining as the civilian portion. The term "Internet" was originally used to refer to these two networks and how they interacted with one another. MILNET evolved into NIPRNET for unclassified military communications and is still used today.[19]

The DCA also mandated that the main communications protocol used by ARPANET, the NCP protocol, be replaced with TCP/IP, a new and more effective way for computers to exchange information on the Internet. This was one indication of ARPANET's future—it was a huge innovation for the time, but it was also the victim of aging infrastructure, and wasn't designed for the scale of its success.

---

[15] https://www.guinnessworldrecords.com/world-records/106836-first-computer-worm

[16] https://isc.sans.edu/diary/27208

[17] https://historyofcomputercommunications.info/section/8.1/Commercializing-Arpanet-1972-1975

[18] https://walden-family.com/bbn/arpanet-completion-report.pdf

[19] https://www.pcmag.com/encyclopedia/term/niprnet

In 1989, 15 percent of U.S. households reported that they had a computer, up from 8.2 percent in 1984.[20]

At the same time, the National Science Foundation (NSF) accounted for half of federal computer science research spending in the United States by 1980, at $20 million.[21] That funding was pushed toward NSFNET, a new national computing network with a stronger, more technologically advanced backbone. It supported the connection of numerous regional and local networks together in a network-of-networks approach, in sharp contrast to how ARPA targeted its partnerships to advanced universities. This new approach enabled more organizations to come online faster and quickly took the lead for core Internet infrastructure. NSFNET replaced ARPANET as the backbone of the Internet, and ARPANET was decommissioned in 1990.

Access and demand for the Internet grew steadily, especially commercially. However, NSFNET was at odds with commercial entities: Its acceptable use policy prohibited commercial activity.[22] The NSF believed the Internet should be focused on research and information sharing, not commercial gain. This wouldn't last; *The High Performance Computing Act of 1991*, championed by Al Gore, and *The National Information Infrastructure Act of 1993* encouraged the private sector to invest in the Internet.[23]

By 1997, 34.6 percent of U.S. households reported that they had a computer.[24]

---

[20] www2.census.gov/library/publications/1991/demographics/p23-171.pdf
[21] https://technicshistory.com/2020/09/01/internet-ascendant-part-1-exponential-growth
[22] http://www2.nmcc.edu/pages/information-technology/policies/nsfnet-aup.php
[23] https://www.congress.gov/bill/102nd-congress/senate-bill/272
[24] www.bls.gov/opub/btn/archive/computer-ownership-up-sharply-in-the-1990s.pdf

These changes, combined with Tim Berners-Lee's work inventing the World Wide Web at CERN in 1989 before it was released to the public in 1993, set up the Internet to flourish through a nonproprietary approach.[25] The World Wide Web was a defining moment for communication, as it gave users the ability to create and access webpages, which became the front face of the Internet. By 1995, NSFNET was decommissioned as a new industry of web browsers and Internet service providers flourished.

Also in 1995, members of the U.S. Naval Research Lab, David Goldschlag, Mike Reed, and Paul Syverson, started to experiment with how to make Internet connections more secure.[26] They built the first prototypes for onion routing, a way to route Internet traffic through multiple servers, encrypting it at each step to anonymize communication. Onion routing operates this way:

- The first relay in a circuit knows the IP address of the user but doesn't know where the traffic is going—all it does it pass the encrypted data to the middle node.
- The middle node doesn't know the user's IP or the final destination; it just passes it to the exit node.
- The exit node decrypts the data and sends it to its destination; this makes it so the destination node only sees the IP of the exit node, not the original user.

In this way, no single node in the process knows both the source and destination, just (potentially) one or the other. The first relay knows the source IP address but not the destination, the second knows neither, and the exit node knows only the destination, not the source. It's called onion routing because it is slowly peeling off layers of encryption to give different information to different nodes. Roger Dingledine out of MIT and Paul Syverson from the NRL started working on the onion routing (Tor) project in the early 2000s. In 2002, the Tor network was released under a free open source software license so that anyone could participate, which was important as this kind of routing relies on a decentralized system.[27]

The Tor project became an indelible part of the Internet landscape; it is incredibly powerful for anonymity. The Tor browser,

---

[25] https://home.cern/science/computing/birth-web/short-history-web
[26] https://www.torproject.org/about/history
[27] Ibid.

created in 2008, was used during the Arab Spring in late 2010 to protect online identities, access blocked websites, and organize protests anonymously, shielding protestors, citizens, and journalists from the government. Tor is used by legitimate users and criminals to access the dark and deep web. Cybercriminals use it to maintain anonymity online when selling breach data, weapons, or other illegal goods and services. For legitimate users, especially whistleblowers, Tor enables them to access services on the deep web, like dead-man switches. Dead-man switches are a service which, in the event the whistleblower is killed or jailed, will automatically publish and distribute their secrets. Access to the service and the files the whistleblower stores can only be done via Tor through a custom URL. If the user doesn't log in at a cadence they set (once a day, month, week), the documents will be published and sent to any and all individuals they specify.

From Niche Network to Daily Life

Internet use grew steadily as academics, then businesses, then consumers came online. By 1997, 18 percent of households had Internet at home. Just 3 years later, in 2000, that number more than doubled to 41.5 percent,[28] and it would only continue to increase over time. But as the Internet flourished, it presented new challenges for the U.S. government. It was especially challenging to balance growing and nurturing the Internet while maintaining data privacy for citizens, commercial success for American enterprises, and national security.

---

[28] www.census.gov/data/tables/time-series/demo/computer-internet/computer-use-1984-2009.html

Chapter 5
Splintering the Internet

One of the biggest challenges that the United States has is balancing maintaining an open Internet to further its international goals while still respecting data privacy, surveillance laws, and democratic values. The promotion of liberal democracy has been both an idealistic pursuit and a strategic tool for the United States, which uses support for democratic institutions to legitimize leadership, foster allies, and counter authoritarian influence. An open Internet is immensely valuable for this: It decentralizes the flow of knowledge and empowers citizens to share information widely. The open Internet is a tool of soft power, both for American national security interests and for international relations.

The Internet was initially heralded as an inherently democratizing force, promising to reshape politics by granting individuals unprecedented access to information. The ability for anyone with a connection to communicate instantaneously with a global audience was a monumental leap forward for free expression and the exchange of ideas. For social movements and previously marginalized groups, the Internet became an indispensable tool for organizing, raising awareness, and bringing new voices into the public discourse.

Look no further than the Arab Spring for an example of how freedom of communication in a secure and anonymous way can foster immense change and bring power back to the people. It allows individuals to connect and organize based on shared interests and ideas, enabling them to mobilize, advocate for their rights, and effect meaningful political change.

Before the Internet, traditional media was often controlled by a limited number of gatekeepers; in contrast, the open Internet provides a distributed, accessible public forum. It allows for widespread participation beyond the confines of local or regional constraints.

An open Internet has given the public direct access to official documents, legislative records, and real-time political developments. This level of transparency makes it more difficult for corruption to thrive and encourages elected officials to be more responsive to the public will.

All this said, the Internet has its own challenges. The optimistic view of the Internet as a purely democratizing tool has been challenged as it has matured. On its own, anonymity empowers individuals to bully, threaten, and lie without accountability. The power of scale provides groups with a platform to manipulate sentiment, sway public opinion, and create rifts in society. The same platforms that enable free expression have also become potent tools for spreading disinformation and propaganda, amplifying extremist views and conspiracy theories. The architecture of social media creates echo chambers where individuals are primarily exposed to opinions that align with their own, leading to increased political polarization and the erosion of constructive public dialogue.

An open Internet also makes it more difficult for nations to defend themselves and their citizens from cyberattacks, as its decentralized nature spreads out the points that need to be defended until they are difficult to manage.

How Democracies Lose the Internet

There is an alternative that threatens the advancements in democratic norms enabled by the open Internet: A controlled Internet. In a controlled Internet, nations command what their citizens see and share through digital sovereignty. The state can manipulate the populace through censorship and propaganda. It can more easily surveil, prevent individuals from sharing information anonymously, and hold citizens accountable for anything they say online—including things the state doesn't want them to be able to say. The government can shut down networks, preventing individuals from communicating with each other or the outside world. This model has led to a global decline in Internet freedom, turning a supposed tool of liberation into an instrument of repression. It is especially prevalent in countries like China, North Korea, and Iran, among others.

But Internet control has more than just an impact on the individuals of these countries. It also affects democracies around the world, including the United States. It is not in the best interest of any democracy for a controlled Internet that combines digital sovereignty with digital authoritarianism to thrive. Democracies prosper from the spread of ideas and freedom of expression. New ideas can flourish, revolutions can be planned, and differing perspectives can be debated. The more disjointed the Internet becomes, the more of a Splinternet it becomes, where there is a divide between regions of the Internet thanks to governments increasingly isolating their online services and data. In the Splinternet, it is more difficult to promote a different way of thinking through liberal democracy. New ideas can be repressed, dissidents can be subjugated, and propaganda can flood the zone.

The more fractured different sections of the Internet become, the more challenging it is for democratic values like freedom of speech and expression to spread and take hold. While maintain an open Internet (or freedom of speech in general) is complex, as it allows for dissent, it is important because it ensures a check on government tyranny.

This is not to say that over time the United States hasn't put restrictions on the open Internet; it has, and that is not just to be expected, it's realistic. There must be rules to protect citizens to some extent. But the choice of *which controls should be used where* is the real question.

Security or Repression

The United States bans some applications for use in different parts of the federal, state, and local government, such as DeepSeek, Kaspersky Labs, WeChat, and others.[1] This makes sense—there's no need to introduce potential risks to the U.S. government system given its sensitive information and activities.

The U.S. government also bans access to some sites for *all* U.S. citizens. They are typically websites that have been perpetrating illegal acts or information: Pirated or fraudulent sites, those made specifically for cyberattacks, or scam sites. However, there is another class of software and hardware that is restricted in the United States: Those that could be part of critical infrastructure. According to NIST, critical infrastructure is:

> System and assets, whether physical or virtual, so vital to the U.S. that the incapacity or destruction of such systems and assets would have a debilitating impact on security, national economic security, national public health or safety, or any combination of those matters.[2]

If critical infrastructure goes down, people get hurt and die. Activities grind to a halt. A great example of this is telecommunications infrastructure providers. Without them, people can't communicate. If they do not prioritize data privacy, user phone calls, chats, and data can be tracked, read, and shared with anyone.

A great example of this: Huawei. In 2017, the U.S. government began imposing restrictions on Huawei—first prohibiting its use in DOD networks, then, in 2018, prohibiting U.S. agencies from obtaining Huawei equipment with federal grants.[3]

By 2019, the United States Department of Justice (DOJ) indicted Huawei with bank fraud, wire fraud, and conspiracy to commit money laundering, among other charges. By 2020, it had filed a new, superseding indictment, which added charges including racketeering and stealing trade secrets from U.S. firms over two decades. The DOJ claims Huawei stole source code for Internet routers

---

[1] https://www.bis.gov/press-release/commerce-department-prohibits-russian-kaspersky-software-u.s.-customers

[2] https://csrc.nist.gov/glossary/term/critical_infrastructure

[3] https://www.congress.gov/crs-product/R47012

and stole proprietary information from cell antennas.[4] Huawei responded that these steps were attempting to damage its reputation. Regardless, in response to the criminal charges, in May 2019, the United States banned Huawei from doing business with U.S. companies by putting it on the *Entity list,* a trade restriction list in the United States.[5]

All Five Eyes countries have banned Huawei in some capacity. Eleven EU countries have restricted Huawei and other providers from deploying 5G and related equipment as well.[6]

Banning Huawei is a smart national security decision with little downside for U.S. citizens. The technology supports critical infrastructure, making it an important vulnerability in a wartime scenario. The tech is accessing extremely sensitive data, such as telephone conversations, chats, and other information, which could be a high-profile espionage target. There are direct competitors in the market that provide comparable goods and services, so it isn't a major loss in technological advancement. It is a fair trade-off between national defense and access to critical goods and services.

However, that's contrasted with other bans, which skirt a much more difficult line between national security and potential repression. The United States flirts with banning legitimate applications under the guise of national security. One recent example is attempts to ban TikTok. Unfortunately, banning a very popular app like TikTok for all U.S. citizens doesn't solve the real issue: That undesirable foreign companies create applications that gain widespread popularity among U.S. citizens, which pose a national security risk because of the attention they hold and the information they collect.

Banning these apps one at a time, playing whack-a-mole to knock them out, isn't timely or sustainable. In one such example, the U.S. government lost a case in 2020 due to free speech violations when the Trump administration was attempting to ban WeChat.[7]

---

[4] https://www.justice.gov/archives/opa/pr/chinese-telecommunications-conglomerate-huawei-and-huawei-cfo-wanzhou-meng-charged-financial
[5] www.congress.gov/crs-product/R47012#fn5
[6] www.euronews.com/next/2024/08/12/eleven-eu-countries-took-5g-security-measures-to-ban-huawei-zte
[7] www.npr.org/2020/09/20/914983610/federal-judge-blocks-trump-administrations-u-s-wechat-ban

These kinds of bans are also in direct opposition to U.S. national security interests to maintain an open Internet.

Freedom or Control

The battle for the Internet represents the same battle countries fight over freedom versus control. Every time a government walls off a section of its Internet from the broader world, we break into more of the Splinternet. As nations continue, it becomes more difficult to spread democratic values—American values—globally.

Chapter 6
Crimes and WarGames

I believe the real significance of the WarGames/hacker phenomenon is not that a group of amateurs could break into important databases, seemingly at will. The real significance of this phenomenon is the extent to which we as a society are accepting and using computers in all facets of our lives without full recognition of their vulnerability.

—*Joseph R. Wright, Jr.*[1]

I n 1983, the movie *WarGames* became a box-office hit, grossing $124.6 million.[2] In the film, Matthew Broderick is a young computer hacker who accidentally breaks into a U.S. military supercomputer and almost starts World War III.

While the movie had a major cultural impact, it played an even larger role that went beyond the culture. The day after the movie

---

[1] Deputy Director before the Subcommittee on Transportation, Aviation, and Materials of the Committee on Science and Technology of the House of Representatives on OMB's efforts to improve federal computer security.

[2] United States. Congress. House. Committee on Science and Technology. Subcommittee on Transportation, Aviation, and Materials, Computer and Communications Security and Privacy: Hearings Before the Subcommittee on Transportation, Aviation, and Materials of the Committee on Science and Technology, U.S. House of Representatives, Ninety-eighth Congress, First Session, September 26; October 17, 24, 1983 (Washington, DC: U.S. Government Printing Office, 1984).

came out, on June 4, then-President Ronald Reagan watched it at Camp David. After returning to the White House, he couldn't stop talking about it . . . with everyone. He even brought it up in a meeting with his national security advisers. He asked them whether what happened in *WarGames* could happen in the United States and directed General John William Vessey, Jr., the Chairman of the Joint Chiefs of Staff, to look into it. From the outside, this seemed like a fairly ridiculous request. However, Vessey did some digging, and a week later, he confirmed with the president that not only could it happen, but that "the problem is much worse than you think."[3]

That conversation led to a flurry of exchanges and memos that culminated in the *National Policy on Telecommunications and Automated Information Systems Security*, a new national security directive swiftly issued in 1984.[4] This directive was one of the first coordinated efforts to address vulnerabilities in federal civilian information systems for national security purposes. It charged the National Security Agency (NSA) with protecting the security of military and civilian information on *all* computers, not just U.S. government devices.

The directive had a fatal flaw: If you are going to protect civilian computer equipment, you have to be able to access it. This opened the door to the government spying on citizens through their own devices, which the NSA was explicitly forbidden from doing, especially after the Foreign Intelligence Surveillance Act (FISA) was passed in 1978.

Texas Democrat Jack Brooks, a civil liberties advocate, sponsored a law to override the directive: *The Computer Security Act of 1987.*[5] This law refocused the NSA on securing only government computer systems, not civilian ones. It also assigned the National Institute of Standards and Technology (NIST) the power to develop security standards with the NSA and to create security policies for

---

[3] www.nytimes.com/2016/02/21/movies/wargames-and-cybersecuritys-debt-to-a-hollywood-hack.html
[4] https://nsarchive.gwu.edu/sites/default/files/documents/2778589/Document-01-Ronald-Reagan-National-Security.pdf
[5] https://www.congress.gov/bill/100th-congress/house-bill/145

federal systems. This is one example of many skirmishes between privacy advocates and the NSA. There has been a constant push-and-pull between protecting citizens' privacy versus the NSA's desire to surveil for national security purposes. This instance set the precedent for civilians and the private sector to be responsible for protecting their own data and devices in the United States despite its growing importance to national power, creating a shared responsibility for national security.

In parallel with government efforts to improve the security of government systems, efforts were made to hold cybercriminals accountable. In the 1980s, early cybercriminal activities were difficult to prosecute; they fell under statutes governing mail and wire fraud, which made them prosecutable only in the context of an interstate scheme.[6]

The first effort to expand this was once again propelled by the movie *WarGames*. In 1983, a hearing on *Computer and Communications Security and Privacy* discussed the scope of the threat posed by cyberattacks. *WarGames* was mentioned at least four times during the hearing.[7] It was the catalyst for a specific section of *the Comprehensive Crime Control Act of 1984 (CCCA): The Counterfeit Access Device and Computer Fraud and Abuse Act of 1984.*[8] This was the first major federal legislation to specifically address computer crimes, and it expanded the rules against cybercrime, but only for specific scenarios. The act made it:

- A felony to use a computer without authorization when trying to obtain classified U.S. military or foreign policy information with the intent to harm the United States or benefit a foreign nation.
- A misdemeanor to access or use a computer without authorization for financial information protected by federal financial privacy laws.
- A misdemeanor to access a federal government computer without authorization and to use, modify, destroy, or disclose information from it, or prevent others from using it.

---

[6] https://groups.csail.mit.edu/mac/classes/6.805/articles/computer-crime/rasch-criminal-law.html

[7] https://www.ojp.gov/pdffiles1/Digitization/95323NCJRS.pdf

[8] https://www.congress.gov/bill/98th-congress/senate-bill/2864

The act steered clear of setting rules for stealing information or disrupting actions outside of the government or financial services. The law was a step forward, but was still limited, lacking broad authority over cybercriminal activity.

Even still, it's pretty funny that the movie *WarGames* is why the United States has cybersecurity policy.

Also within the CCCA is a critical law: *18 U.S.C. § 981*. This law defines the property that is subject to forfeiture in the United States; it enables the U.S. government to seize "Any property, real or personal, involved in a transaction or attempted transaction" in violation of certain laws.[9] As cybercrime evolved, prosecutors successfully argued that intangible assets like domain names and IP addresses, alongside tangible assets like servers, can be a form of personal property used in the commission of a crime and are therefore subject to forfeiture. This laid the groundwork for the U.S. government's efforts to combat cybercrime.

A more comprehensive act, *The Computer Fraud and Abuse Act (CFAA)*, was passed in 1986 as an amendment, which expanded coverage to "protected computers." Protected computers are considered any computer used in or affecting interstate or foreign commerce—so basically, almost any computer in use in modern day. The law also expanded the scope of federal crimes to those who knowingly cause computer damage, sell or traffic in passwords, or extort individuals using a computer. The CFAA became the cornerstone of U.S. cybercrime law and, importantly, resulted in felony charges in some cases. Computer extortion? Felony with up to five years in prison. Conspiracy to commit the offense? Felony with up to five years in prison as of 2008.[10] The USA PATRIOT Act of 2001 expanded the punishments and the definition of "protected computers" to include those outside U.S. borders if they affect U.S. commerce or communication.[11]

---

[9] https://home.treasury.gov/system/files/246/18usc981.pdf

[10] 18 U.S.C. § 1030 (2025).

[11] Uniting and Strengthening America by Providing Appropriate Tools Required to Intercept and Obstruct Terrorism (USA PATRIOT) Act of 2001, Pub. L. No. 107-56, 115 Stat. 272 (2001).

All of this sounds pretty reasonable when thinking about a cybercriminal trying to steal a civilian's life savings or breaking into national security systems and selling classified information to the highest bidder. However, some parts of the CFAA have been particularly vague, leaving room for interpretation (and misuse). One phrase in particular that has caused much strife is "exceeds authorized access":

> ... to access a computer with authorization and to use such access to obtain or alter information in the computer that the accessor is not entitled to obtain or alter ...

"Exceeding authorized access" is the intent of the individual to commit the act, not necessarily the act itself. This distinction is very important: Prosecutors argued that even if you had permission to access something, if you used it for a forbidden purpose (even something as benign as sending a personal email on a work computer or violating a website's terms of service), you were no longer "entitled" to that information and had broken the law. So, for example, if a website's terms of service state that users cannot download images from the website, but a user does, that could be considered a crime under the broad definition of "exceeds authorized access" in the CFAA. It would likely be a misdemeanor, unless you then used that image in a presentation at work, in which case it would likely become a felony. It's an issue of whether terms of service are enough (or should be enough) to hold someone legally liable for committing a crime, regardless of how extreme those terms are.

Take one tragic example: The case of Aaron Swartz. Swartz was a well-regarded computer programmer and entrepreneur. He was involved in some of the most high-profile and vital Internet projects in the 2000s. Swartz helped develop RSS, a web feed format built to automatically distribute content; the technical architecture for Creative Commons, a nonprofit dedicated to facilitating open access to creative works through free licenses; and the Python website framework web.py, which enables developers to write web apps in Python. He also helped define the syntax for Markdown, a common markup language to create formatted text in a plain-text editor, and was named co-founder of Reddit, an extremely popular social media platform.[12] He was also an Internet activist and believed strongly in the open access movement, especially the willful violation of copyright that restricts the distribution of knowledge.

In July 2011, Swartz was indicted by a federal grand jury.[13] The case involved JSTOR, a popular, subscription-based service that provides access to academic journals. JSTOR does not allow users to download articles en masse or to use the articles for anything other than personal use. Universities like MIT, Harvard, Yale, and many others use JSTOR to provide students and faculty with access to a digitized archive of primary sources.

According to the indictment, Swartz bought a laptop specifically to connect to the MIT network and download as many files as possible from JSTOR. He spent months downloading files and evading controls put in place by MIT and JSTOR to block his access.

All in all, Swartz downloaded 4.8 million articles from JSTOR.[14] He didn't actually do anything with the articles—he didn't make a profit from them, he just downloaded them. In 2011, a federal indictment was announced charging him with wire fraud, computer fraud, unlawfully obtaining information from a protected computer, and recklessly damaging a protected computer. He was charged based on the vagueness of the phrase "exceeds authorized access"—whereby authorized access, according to JSTOR terms of service, did not allow for downloading documents en masse.[15]

He would have faced a maximum of 35 years in prison and up to $1 million in fines had he been convicted. The indictment was divisive, and not everyone agreed that he should be prosecuted for stealing the files. Legal experts and digital rights advocates showed Swartz support, stating that the charges were disproportionate and far too aggressive for the crime.

Even JSTOR got its data back and considered the matter settled, declining to pursue civil litigation. However, the prosecution

---

[12] www.wired.com/2011/07/swartz-arrest
[13] United States v Swartz, No. 11-cr-10260 (D. Mass. indictment July 14, 2011).
[14] Ibid.
[15] Ibid.

continued. They unsealed a superseding indictment in September 2012, and Swartz was charged with 13 felony counts: Two counts of wire fraud and 11 counts of violating the CFAA. This increased the maximum to a potential 50 years in prison. *Fifty years in prison* for stealing documents online.[16]

Prosecutors attempted a plea deal—they offered a six-month prison sentence. The Swartz team rejected the offer and provided a counteroffer, but the prosecution rejected it. Two days later, on January 11, 2013, Aaron killed himself by hanging. He was 26 years old.[17]

His death sparked an online firestorm. Many called for the lead prosecutor on the case, Carmen Ortiz, to be investigated, with a petition gaining over 40,000 signatures. Anonymous targeted MIT websites, defacing them with tributes to Swartz.[18]

Did he commit a crime? Under the law, yes. Even still, his death was an undeniable tragedy. It's also undeniable that serving up to 50 years in prison for stealing academic articles is ludicrous. The CFAA's vague phrasing is ultimately what allowed this case to move forward. And it wasn't resolved with this case, in part because the case was dropped after Swartz's death. It would take eight more years for the CFAA to be challenged and changed.

The case that changed this vague language was *Van Buren v United States* in 2021.[19] Nathan Van Buren was a sergeant in the Cumming, Georgia, Police Department. From his work in the police department, he knew a man named Andrew Albo. Albo allegedly went to prostitutes for services, paid them, and then accused them of stealing money from him. Van Buren asked Albo for a loan, as he was struggling financially. Albo recorded the conversation and presented it to the Forsyth County Sheriff's Office, alleging that Van Buren was using his power as a police officer to get money from Albo. The FBI took the opportunity to conduct a sting operation against Van Buren. The FBI tasked Albo to ask Van Buren to look up a woman in the police database to see if she was an undercover

[16] United States v Swartz, No. 11-cr-10260 (D. Mass. indictment July 14, 2011).
[17] www.huffpost.com/entry/tom-dolan-aaron-swartz_n_2479980
[18] https://www.cnn.com/2013/01/17/tech/aaron-swartz-death
[19] https://www.supremecourt.gov/opinions/20pdf/19-783_k531.pdf

officer; Van Buren did, and the FBI arrested him the next day. According to the CFAA, he "exceeded authorized access" to police computers when he looked up the woman for reasons other than police business.

Van Buren admitted to the crime and was charged with one count of wire fraud and one count of felony computer fraud. He was convicted on both counts and appealed. When he appealed, he argued that the "exceeds authorized access" clause must apply only to those who obtain information they are not allowed to access, as opposed to accessing things they are allowed to, but for the wrong reasons. The Eleventh Circuit upheld the ruling, but Van Buren petitioned the Supreme Court.[20] The Supreme Court ruled that a person violates the "exceeds authorized access" language when they access data they are not allowed to access on a computer system they do not have permission to access. Thus, Van Buren was vindicated on that particular count. His case narrowed the focus of "exceeds authorized access" such that the clause only applies if you are not entitled to obtain the information in the first place, regardless of the intent.

This was a major win for more than just Van Buren; anyone who took action that violated the terms of service on a website could have been prosecuted with the broad scope of the CFAA. This was especially detrimental to security researchers, who often ethically violate terms of service to find vulnerabilities and aid companies in enhancing the security of their websites and products. For example, before the ruling, a simple port scan of computers open to the public could have been considered a crime by the CFAA if the computer owner had terms of service that specified it wasn't allowed.[21] This simple act is not a crime at all and may occur in the normal course of business, yet it could have resulted in a misdemeanor . . . or worse.

---

[20] www.law.cornell.edu/supremecourt/text/19-783
[21] http://www.networkworld.com/news/2007/080207-black-hat-storm-worms-viru lence.html

Criminalizing Botnets

The CFAA plays a critical role in shaping the U.S. government's response to cybercrime. It enables the DOJ to pursue cases involving foreign actors who break into American infrastructure or steal trade secrets, such as the indictments against Russian officers following cyber operations targeting the 2016 U.S. election. The CFAA also underpins civil lawsuits between private entities for breaches and data theft, making it one of the most litigated cybersecurity laws globally. However, its enforcement continues to evolve, as courts and policymakers grapple with how to protect national security without overcriminalizing digital behavior.

Charging under the CFAA became especially prevalent in the early 2000s, when botnets hit the scene hard.

> A *botnet*, a portmanteau of "robot network," is a collection of Internet-connected devices that have been infected with malware such that they can be remotely controlled by an attacker. These devices are often owned and operated by average citizens, but malware is running on their machines without their knowledge or control. The compromised devices, which can include computers, smartphones, and other Internet-of-things (IoT) devices, are controlled as a group to perform specific tasks, like perpetrating a DDoS attack. The individual devices in the botnet are called "zombies" because they carry out commands without the knowledge or consent of their owners.

At the time, two botnets were wreaking havoc worldwide: The Storm Botnet and the Zeus Botnet. The Storm Botnet infected anywhere from 250,000 to one million computers and was used for DDoS attacks.[22] The Zeus Botnet leveraged Zeus malware, a Trojan horse, to steal banking information by logging the keys that people

---

[22] https://www.eecs.umich.edu/techreports/cse/2009/CSE-TR-560-09.pdf

were typing as they typed them. Attackers used this to collect banking information and other data to sell online. By 2009, the Zeus Botnet had infected 3.6 million computers in the United States alone, more than any other botnet at the time.[23]

A Trojan horse, or simply *Trojan*, is a type of malware that deceives users by disguising itself as a legitimate program or file. It's named after the ancient Greek myth of the Trojan War, as the malware mimics the tactic of hiding in plain sight to gain access to a computer.

Because of these attacks and the national security implications, the FBI publicly announced Operation: Bot Roast in 2007.[24] It found and charged key individuals associated with a botnet that leveraged 1 million computers across the United States.

In one early instance of Operation: Bot Roast, the FBI arrested and charged Jeanson James Ancheta with attempting to cause damage to protected computers, causing damage to computers used by the federal government in national defense, accessing protected computers without authorization to commit fraud, and money laundering. This was the first ever prosecution of an individual for controlling a botnet. He was accused of using the botnet to install adware on people's computers, using the ads to make an alleged $60,000 in advertising affiliate proceeds.[25] Ancheta pleaded guilty. He was sentenced to 57 months in prison, had to pay the U.S. government $15,000, and had to forfeit the profits he made off the scheme.

---

[23] www.bloomberg.com/news/features/2015-06-18/the-hunt-for-the-financial-indus try-s-most-wanted-hacker
[24] https://archives.fbi.gov/archives/news/stories/2007/june/botnet_061307
[25] www.justice.gov/iso/opa/resources/5122014519132358461949.pdf

Charging China

The issue of attribution has always been a missing link in publicly understanding the landscape of APT cyber espionage. Without establishing a solid connection to China, there will always be room for observers to dismiss APT actions as uncoordinated, solely criminal in nature, or peripheral to larger national security and global economic concerns. We hope that this report will lead to increased understanding and coordinated action in countering APT network breaches.
                    —*APT1, Exposing One of China's Cyber Espionage Units*[26]

After years of lukewarm attribution to "individuals in China" or "China-based attackers," 2013 was a turning point. In February 2013, cybersecurity firm Mandiant released a report exposing a multiyear espionage campaign linked to one threat actor, which they refer to as Advanced Persistent Threat 1 (APT1).

The attacks, which Mandiant traced back as far as 2006, targeted at least 141 organizations across 20 major industries. APT1 stole data on a massive scale, including hundreds of terabytes of sensitive information like technology blueprints, manufacturing processes, business plans, and internal emails. The report was an incredible amount of information.

In Chinese hacker slang, *rouji*, 肉鸡, which, directly translated, means "meat chicken," represents a zombie computer used in a botnet.[27]

Yet, none of this was the mic drop moment. The true bombshell of the report was that Mandiant attributed APT1 to the 2nd

---

[26] https://services.google.com/fh/files/misc/mandiant-apt1-report.pdf
[27] https://blog.csdn.net/yeliuxiaozi/article/details/140516054

Bureau of the PLA, General Staff Department's 3rd Department, also known as Unit 61398.[28] Mandiant showed the building the unit works out of, its address in Shanghai, and the support units associated with the office, including an outpatient clinic, a kindergarten, and guesthouses.

It found that the unit received special fiber-optic communications infrastructure from China Telecom for national defense purposes. Its command-and-control infrastructure was concentrated in Shanghai, where they had registered hundreds of domain names. APT1 had also hijacked a series of hop points in other countries, which act as intermediaries between the unit and their target. Over just a two-year period, APT1 logged into the hop infrastructure in the United States from 832 different IP addresses in 1,905 instances. From 2011 to 2013, APT1 was running 937 confirmed command-and-control servers with 849 distinct IP addresses, though they are suspected of running hundreds to thousands more.

Mandiant was also able to identify some of the attackers, which had major consequences for the future of attribution and how governments handle these individuals. One of the ways Mandiant learned the identities of the attackers was because of the Great Firewall. Even the attackers did not appreciate being blocked from using services like Facebook and Twitter in China, so they would connect directly to the hop points in other countries, then use that attack infrastructure to log in to their personal Facebook, Twitter, and other accounts. This made it a lot easier for Mandiant to identify them.

This report was a watershed moment for cybersecurity; it was the first time a private entity publicly presented a comprehensive body of evidence attributing a major cyber espionage operation to a specific unit of the Chinese military in such great detail. Before this report, attribution of state-sponsored cyberattacks was speculative and confined to government intelligence circles. By naming

---

[28] https://services.google.com/fh/files/misc/mandiant-apt1-report.pdf

and shaming a specific PLA unit, Mandiant thrust the issue into the public domain and sparked an international conversation about state-sponsored economic espionage.

China's official response to the Mandiant report was swift condemnation and denial. Despite the denials, public exposure seemed to have an impact—APT1's activities appeared to decrease significantly following the report's publication.[29]

By issuing this report, Mandiant set a stake in the ground for when and how to attribute cyberattacks to specific nation-states. It also made it clear that private sector companies were not immune to or separate from the battles of nations; they have as much of a role to play as the government. The release of this report was a risk—not only did it face intense scrutiny and denouncement from China, but it also revealed Mandiant's methods and capabilities for tracking adversaries. This gives attackers information they can use to refine their operational security practices and prevent future detection.

In May 2014, the DOJ formally indicted five PLA officers from Unit 61398 for cybercrimes related to economic espionage against American companies. The Mandiant APT1 report laid the groundwork for the indictment, which spanned 31 counts, including conspiring to commit computer fraud and abuse, aggravated identity theft, economic espionage, and trade secret theft. This was a pivotal event that shaped the geopolitical consequences of cyberattacks, as it was the first time the U.S. government publicly filed criminal charges against known state actors for economic espionage.

The indictment is largely symbolic, as it's unlikely China would extradite its own military officers to face trial in the United States. Even still, China was furious. The Ministry of Foreign Affairs stated that:

> This US move, which is based on fabricated facts, grossly violates the basic norms governing international relations and jeopardizes China-US cooperation and mutual trust.[30]

---

[29] https://www.securityweek.com/lockheed-attackers-went-quiet-after-apt1-report-exposed-chinese-hackers

[30] https://spectrum.ieee.org/us-charges-chinese-military-hackers-with-cyber-espionage

China suspended its participation in the newly formed U.S.-China Cyber Working Group, a forum intended to de-escalate tensions over cybersecurity.[31] It also accused the United States of hypocrisy, citing global surveillance programs conducted by the National Security Agency that had been revealed by Edward Snowden.[32]

All this said, China did eventually come to the table. In late 2015, China and the United States signed *The 2015 United States–China Cyber Agreement,* a bilateral accord and mutual pledge that neither country's government would conduct or knowingly support cyber-enabled theft of intellectual property, including trade secrets or confidential business information, for commercial advantage. This was the first time China acknowledged a distinction between espionage for national security and economic espionage—previously, China had insisted that economic security was national security and there was no distinction between the two.

This led to a marked reduction in cyberattacks originating from China targeting U.S. commercial entities. Espionage for national security purposes continued, of course, but IP theft from commercial entities was on the decline.[33] That said, the results were temporary; by 2018, after indicting two more individuals for economic espionage, Deputy Attorney General Rod Rosenstein said in a press conference that:

> The activity alleged in this indictment violates the commitment that China made to members of the international community . . . The evidence suggests that China may not intend to abide by its promises.[34]

Dismantling Cybercrime Forums

In some instances, the CFAA is just one component of an operation, such as when taking down cybercrime forums. Cybercrime forums

[31] https://jsis.washington.edu/news/u-s-china-cybersecurity-cooperation
[32] https://www.nytimes.com/2013/06/28/world/asia/chinese-defense-ministry-accuses-us-of-hypocrisy-on-spying.html
[33] www.cfr.org/blog/us-china-cyber-espionage-deal-one-year-later
[34] https://www.justice.gov/archives/opa/speech/deputy-attorney-general-rod-j-rosenstein-announces-charges-against-chinese-hackers

are online discussion platforms that operate as a central hub for cybercriminal communications. They enable cybercriminals to collaborate, trade illicit goods and services, and share information. For example, it's relatively easy to access ransomware-as-a-service on one of these forums, so anyone, regardless of experience, can start attacking people with ransomware. These forums are a watering hole for cybercriminals. Taking the forums down makes it harder for cybercriminals to access services they need to engage in criminal activities online.

Ransomware-as-a-service (RaaS) is a cybercrime business model where cybercriminals build and operate ransomware, then rent it to affiliates who use it on their own targets. They don't have to build the ransomware themselves, lowering the skill barrier so anyone willing to pay can run a ransomware campaign.

The problem is, taking down cybercrime forums is no simple task. It takes years of work and international cooperation to identify and locate suspects, track down the infrastructure that keeps the forum up and running, and gather enough evidence to make a compelling legal case. It's also not just a digital operation—suspects are arrested, property is searched, and hardware and cash are seized.

For example, in 2025, German authorities led a Europol-supported operation with law enforcement from seven other countries (Australia, France, Greece, Italy, Romania, Spain, and the United States) to take down two huge cybercrime forums called Cracked and Nulled. Cracked and Nulled had over 10 million users who went to these sites to sell stolen data, buy malware, and pay for infrastructure to carry out attacks. Authorities seized the domains and servers used by the cybercriminals to support the forums. They also tracked down the administrator of Nulled and charged him with multiple counts from the CFAA.[35]

---

[35] www.justice.gov/opa/pr/cracked-and-nulled-marketplaces-disrupted-international-cyber-operation

Seizing the infrastructure and indicting the cybercriminals takes away the physical hardware and gives consequences to the criminals behind it. Takedowns like these are a reminder that behind every cyberattack are humans and real-world circumstances. Cybersecurity does not only exist online; it has concrete repercussions.

Follow the Money

Over time, the techniques the U.S. government uses to combat cybercrime have evolved into a whole-of-government approach. Sector-specific groups get involved, like the Department of the Treasury for financial crimes. Take, for instance, in 2025, when North Korea's Lazarus Group broke into an Ether wallet managed by cryptocurrency exchange Bybit and stole $1.5 billion USD in holdings.[36]

The holdings were in a cold wallet, which is supposedly more secure; it's isolated from the Internet most of the time, making it harder to reach. However, there is a process by which you can pull out funds when you need them. This process is exactly what the Lazarus Group exploited: The attackers targeted a vulnerability in the platform that Bybit uses for its transactions. The vulnerability allowed the attackers to make a transfer of Ethereum that seemed like a legitimate transaction. The attack was a shock to the crypto community, which had assumed cold wallets were the safest way to store their assets—Ethereum fell by over 20 percent.[37]

This was but the loudest of North Korea's plundering efforts. Since 2017, the Lazarus Group has stolen over $5 billion in cryptocurrency.[38] North Korea's campaigns to steal cryptocurrency have

---

[36] www.csis.org/analysis/bybit-heist-and-future-us-crypto-regulation#:~: text=On%20February%2021%2C%202025%2C%20a,48%20hours%20of%20the%20attack
[37] https://www.forbes.com/sites/siladityaray/2025/02/25/bitcoin-slips-below-90000-down-nearly-20-from-trumps-inauguration-day-all-time-high
[38] www.trmlabs.com/resources/blog/the-bybit-hack-following-north-koreas-lar gest-exploit#:~:text=A%20History%20of%20North%20Korean,or%20supply%20 chain%20compromise%E2%80%8B

become a defining feature of its foreign policy. As the country continues to grapple with crippling sanctions, it has few ways to fund its programs—including its nuclear program. Plundering is one of the most effective ways to do so with negligible risk . . . it's not like North Korea could be meaningfully sanctioned *more.*

The Department of the Treasury's Office of Foreign Assets Control (OFAC) sanctions individuals and entities for their role in these money laundering schemes. In November 2025, OFAC sanctioned two North Korean bankers who were responsible for managing stolen cryptocurrency on behalf of an already sanctioned and designated First Credit Bank.[39] These sanctions prohibit entities from performing transactions with any U.S. persons or any activities in the United States without being reported to OFAC.

In some cases, the DOJ has even been able to claw back cryptocurrency after it has been stolen. Investigators trace cryptocurrency through the addresses where it is stored. Attackers try to combat this by running cryptocurrency through mixers, which blend stolen funds with legitimate ones to make it difficult to trace their origin. To solve that problem, the DOJ just sanctions the mixers, too. If the funds are traced back to a regulated exchange or partner company, U.S. law enforcement issues seizure warrants and compels the exchange to freeze the assets. The DOJ also files civil forfeiture complaints against digital wallets holding stolen funds. Once a court approves the forfeiture, the government takes legal possession of the assets.

Between 2022 and 2025, the DOJ and partners have seized tens of millions of dollars' worth of cryptocurrency from North Korean state actors by tracking laundering trails and intercepting funds before they can be converted to fiat currency.[40] It's a drop in the bucket compared to what's stolen, but every bit helps and makes it more difficult for the attackers.

---

[39] https://sanctionssearch.ofac.treas.gov/Details.aspx?id=22985
[40] https://thehill.com/policy/cybersecurity/3635223-us-recovers-more-than-30m-in-cryptocurrency-from-north-korean-hackers

Chapter 7
Eligible Receiver

We had the Blue Team on the run by the third day of the exercise
... we only played about 30% of what we could have. So the message there is it could have been a lot worse.

*—The red team targeting officer in the Eligible
Receiver 97 exercise*[1]

In 1997, the U.S. government conducted war games called Eligible Receiver 97.[2] In a first-of-its-kind set of exercises meant to
simulate a real-life information operations attack, the NSA used off-
the-shelf equipment to demonstrate how easily it could break into civilian and DOD networks and disrupt command-and-control systems.

---

[1] https://nsarchive.gwu.edu/briefing-book/cyber-vault/2018-08-01/eligible-
receiver-97-seminal-dod-cyber-exercise-included-mock-terror-strikes-hostage-
simulations
[2] Ibid.

Red team and blue team exercises are where groups of security professionals simulate offensive and defensive roles to test an organization's defenses. These exercises help organizations identify and correct vulnerabilities before malicious actors can exploit them.

In the exercises, the NSA acted as the red team—the enemy—targeting and actually breaking into government systems. Meanwhile, the blue team—the defenders—was made up of individuals across U.S. agencies tasked with protecting against the attack. In one exercise, they simulated a cyberattack where North Korean and Iranian attackers target and take out the power grid and emergency communications for eight major U.S. cities to pressure American leaders to lift sanctions. In another, they simulated an attack where military communications networks at U.S. Pacific Command, the Pentagon, and other DOD facilities were disrupted to see how effective they could be without communications and visibility.

The result? The DOD was proven woefully unprepared for an incident. The red team prevented U.S. forces from communicating with and relaying commands to joint forces. It was a shock to DOD leadership, bringing to a marked change in how they approached cybersecurity.

However, they didn't act fast enough. Just a few months later, in February 1998, Iraq was flouting the UN's weapons inspections that had been agreed to after the first Gulf War. In the months prior, they had expelled American inspectors and, in January 1998, declared that three specific sites were off limits for inspection. By February, the United States had deployed around 2,000 Marines to the Gulf to enforce the weapons inspections in the region, along with a third U.S. aircraft carrier.

Just as the United States was preparing to deploy troops, DOD networks were breached. In tracing the attacker activity, investigators found the attackers had used one of the only Internet gateways into Iraq, Emirnet. The timing, scale, and technical details led the United States to believe Iraq had breached the DOD.[3]

---

[3] https://nsarchive.gwu.edu/briefing-book/cyber-vault/2023-02-28/solar-sunrise-after-25-years-are-we-25-years-wiser

The cyberattacks continued for three weeks. The attackers targeted domain name servers and gained root access to the machines by exploiting a vulnerability in Oracle Solaris 2.4, an operating system. The attack, named SOLAR SUNRISE, didn't breach any classified systems, but the attackers gained access to information critical to DOD operations in Iraq. At least 11 DOD systems were compromised, and the attack was described as incredibly sophisticated, likely a nation-state actor.

> *Root access* is the highest level of administrative privilege a user can have on a computer system. It is often referred to as "superuser" access because the root user has unrestricted control over the entire computer system.

After a feverish FBI investigation, they discovered the attack was not carried out by incredibly sophisticated Iraqi hackers or any other foreign nation-state, despite the bluster. It was actually carried out by two 16-year-olds in California, with the help of another Israeli teen.[4] A bit of an embarrassing moment for the DOD.

This incident and Eligible Receiver 97 led the DOD to create the first U.S. joint task force in 1998, built to address cyber warfare. The Joint Task Force – Computer Network Defense (JTF-CND) reported to the Deputy Secretary of Defense and was an early predecessor to United States Cyber Command. It also awakened a recognition that the U.S. government needed to secure its systems.[5]

> United States Cyber Command (*USCYBERCOM*) is the primary military body for cyber warfare in the United States, which operates under the DOD. It was created in 2010 and conducts offensive cyber operations, defends military networks, and coordinates cyber capabilities with conventional military strategy.

---

[4] https://nsarchive.gwu.edu/briefing-book/cyber-vault/2023-02-28/solar-sunrise-after-25-years-are-we-25-years-wiser
[5] https://www.cybercom.mil/About/History

One Size Fits None

The U.S. government has a handful of top-level departments and hundreds of agencies that differ in size, equipment, and resources. The agencies are not only numerous, but they are also disparate. The cybersecurity controls that work for the Department of Homeland Security (DHS) will not necessarily work for the U.S. Department of Agriculture. They face different types of attacks, vary in the sensitivity of the data they track, and employ people with wildly different backgrounds and strengths.

This makes it especially difficult to establish a uniform cyber defense policy for the entirety of the federal government. Much of this burden fell to the Office of Management and Budget (OMB), which oversees the implementation of government-wide policies.[6]

OMB gained its cyber-related power through *the Federal Information Security Management Act (FISMA)*, Title III of the E-Government Act of 2002.[7] FISMA was a win—it was the first implementation of a standardized information security framework across the entire federal government.

OMB became the oversight body for cybersecurity practices, requiring federal agencies to undergo annual reviews and get certifications for their security programs. Oddly enough, this was all done on paper. Agencies were required to catalog every system and its risks to determine where the most sensitive information is and prioritize its defense. When you have thousands of employees, computers, and other devices, it is very challenging to keep an up-to-date catalog like this. It can take months if not years.

The focus on cataloging and planning was intentional because of just how different each agency is: Mandating action is difficult when it's unclear what resources each agency even has. Unfortunately, spending so much time cataloging and planning didn't leave much time for action. As valuable as thorough planning is, without action—patching vulnerabilities, implementing security controls—you're still just as prone to a breach as you were before.

---

[6] https://www.congress.gov/crs-product/RS21665
[7] https://www.congress.gov/bill/107th-congress/house-bill/2458

FISMA fell short because of this. It wasn't until years later that this system was finally updated, with *the Federal Information Security Modernization Act of 2014*. This act changed the static annual review cycle to a continuous process with a lot less paper reporting. It also refocused reporting on actual attacks and security performance.[8]

All Vision, No Action

Meanwhile, the Bush administration was crafting a vision for the future of cybersecurity in the United States. In 2003, the administration released *the National Strategy to Secure Cyberspace*, a landmark for U.S. cybersecurity strategy. It was one part of the National Strategy for Homeland Security, a document that defined homeland security initiatives post-9/11.[9]

The strategy outlined voluntary suggestions to the public and private sectors on how to approach cybersecurity. The problem was, its recommendations were just that—recommendations. No mandatory action.

The document stressed that, in general, the private sector is best equipped to respond to "evolving cyberattack threats"—a statement that proved to be demonstrably false. Support from governments is a requirement for effective cybersecurity. However, it points to an early U.S. belief that rings true: The private sector has a huge responsibility in national cyber defense, yet the government has little control over it.

The strategy mandated that DHS be the go-between for cyber defense between the government and the private sector. In truth, the DHS has been an ideal landing spot for many of the cyber responsibilities outlined in the document: It has an aligned mission on

---

[8] www.insidegovernmentcontracts.com/2014/12/fisma-updated-and-modernized
[9] https://www.energy.gov/sites/prod/files/National%20Strategy%20to%20Secure%20Cyberspace.pdf

national protection, is civilian-led, and could be a primary interface with critical infrastructure providers, the majority of which are privately held. It tasked DHS with developing a national plan to secure critical infrastructure, support crisis management, and provide technical assistance to the private sector and government entities.

The DHS has played a major role in cybersecurity policy ever since. One of its most notable cyber agencies is the Cybersecurity and Infrastructure Security Agency (CISA), which was created in 2018. It is responsible for leading cybersecurity and critical infrastructure security programs, operations, and policy. It facilitates information exchange and supports remediation efforts for national incidents. CISA is now an established name in cybersecurity globally, most publicly supporting election security and providing threat advisories.

The heart of the Bush administration's strategy was five national priorities that quietly set the United States' cyber agenda for the next twenty years. These priorities were not implemented overnight but set a long-term direction: Create a national response system, address vulnerabilities, build a strong training program, improve federal security, and shape international cooperation.[10]

Good in Theory, Tough in Practice

Despite these efforts, these recommendations didn't always get put in place or work as expected. Without proper incentives, things don't change. One infamous case of this is the breach of the U.S. Office of Personnel Management (OPM).

OPM is the chief human resources agency and personnel policy manager for the federal government. It manages the federal civil service, from benefits to hiring to a secure employment process, for millions of current and former federal employees. It tracks and

---

[10] www.energy.gov/sites/prod/files/National%20Strategy%20to%20Secure%20 Cyberspace.pdf?utm_source=perplexity

maintains background checks for security clearances, housing some of the most sensitive personal information held by the U.S. government. As of the early 2010s, it was under significant scrutiny for deficiencies in its security practices.

The inspector general warned OPM repeatedly that it had material weaknesses in its information security program. Every year, from 2009 to 2014, the inspector general would report on just how poor OPM's security practices were. Yet, year after year, FISMA audit after FISMA audit, nothing changed.

By 2015, OPM would have to face the consequences of its inaction: It announced it had been breached. Attackers had stolen personnel files of 4.2 million former and current government employees and security clearance details for 21.5 million individuals.[11]

The attackers targeted Social Security numbers and other personal identifying information, but it was unclear whether the attack was for commercial gain or espionage.[12] The Committee on Oversight and Government Reform released a scathing report that criticized OPM leadership for failing to implement security controls and for misleading the public about the extent of the attack.[13] But what incentives had OPM been given over the years to implement security controls? None.

A class action lawsuit on the breach was settled for $63 million, and the OPM director resigned.[14] Finally, some consequences! Just like private sector organizations that only invest in security after a breach, OPM put new security controls in place to modernize systems and ensure government contractors were secure.

---

[11] https://oversight.house.gov/wp-content/uploads/2016/09/The-OPM-Data-Breach-How-the-Government-Jeopardized-Our-National-Security-for-More-than-a-Generation.pdf

[12] https://www.nytimes.com/2015/06/05/us/breach-in-a-federal-computer-system-exposes-personnel-data.html

[13] Ibid.

[14] www.govexec.com/pay-benefits/2022/10/judge-finalized-63m-opm-hack-settlement-feds-two-months-damages/378950

This illustrates the fundamental problem with FISMA at that time: Recommendations do not result in action. OPM struggled with being under-resourced and with failing to prioritize resources for cybersecurity . . . because it didn't have to.

The Prescriptive Pivot

Things started to change in 2018, when the Trump administration released the most comprehensive strategic approach to cybersecurity since the Bush administration: *The National Cyber Strategy of the United States*.[15] It prioritized a far more aggressive, offensive stance than the previous, mostly defensive strategy. This was a marked change at the right moment: Offensive cyber operations toward the United States were at an all-time high.[16]

The strategy prioritizes securing federal networks but recommends doing so in tandem with combating cybercrime through law enforcement partnerships and stronger apprehension efforts of criminals abroad. It advocates for developing the cybersecurity workforce, together with prioritizing innovation. It pushes for the establishment of cyber norms to impose consequences, while also performing counter-influence operations. And it promotes an open, reliable, and secure Internet by building an international cyber capacity, especially across partners.

The strategy is heavy on deterrence and imposing high costs on those who target the United States. This approach has helped frame and support a wave of law enforcement actions to take down and indict cybercriminal gangs and forums.

The other major adjustment from catalogs and plans to prescriptive action came from the Biden administration in *Executive Order 14028 in 2021, Improving the Nation's Cybersecurity*.[17] Instead of recommendations, it made mandates. It required federal agencies to adopt Zero Trust and migrate to secure cloud services wherever

---

[15] https://nsarchive.gwu.edu/media/16821/ocr
[16] https://www.iwp.edu/active-measures/2020/10/22/a-review-of-the-trump-administrations-national-cyber-strategy-need-for-renewal-and-rethinking-of-the-public-private-partnership-in-u-s-national-security-policy
[17] https://www.nist.gov/itl/executive-order-14028-improving-nations-cybersecurity

possible. It underscored the importance of security controls such as multifactor authentication (MFA) and encryption.

Zero Trust is a security model that follows the core principle, "never trust, always verify." It prioritizes least privilege access such that individuals, devices, and other entities have as few permissions as possible, preventing them from accessing things they shouldn't.

The executive order standardized the playbook for responding to cyber incidents across federal agencies. It established a Cybersecurity Safety Review Board, composed of leaders from the public and private sectors. This board convened after significant incidents to analyze events and give concrete recommendations for improving cybersecurity practices moving forward. They supported response efforts for many notable incidents like Log4Shell. However, it was disbanded in January 2025 by the Trump administration as part of an effort to eliminate the misuse of resources, per Acting Secretary of the DHS Ben Huffman.[18]

The executive order hasn't been all sunshine and rainbows, though. Agencies were expected to make this pivot without receiving the funding to actually make it happen. They were also expected to put these security controls in place on systems, some of which haven't been updated for decades—it just wasn't realistic. The original problem—agencies being disparate and having very different systems, yet needing uniform mandates and leadership—remains unsolved.

---

[18] https://www.cybersecuritydive.com/news/dhs-disbands-advisory-board-csrb/737976

Chapter 8
Private Power, Public Risk

At DHS, we believe cyberspace is fundamentally a civilian space.
—Homeland Security Secretary Janet Napolitano[1]

The United States has long prided itself and anchored its global power on its economic might. Its technological innovation over the past century and the preeminence of the U.S. dollar has allowed the American economy to adapt and lead in successive waves of industrial change.

The American economic system is built on a foundation of free-market capitalism and a fear of government overreach. There have always been strong cultural and political headwinds against government actions that could infringe on the autonomy of private enterprises.

Part of the reason the United States has been able to dominate is its approach to regulation: Fairly hands-off. The American regulatory system is complex but focuses on mitigating liability, enforcing anti-corruption measures, and ensuring a level playing field among companies. U.S. labor laws are much more flexible

---

[1] http://www.dhs.gov/ynews/speeches/sp_1303766068994.shtm

than those in other Western countries, such as the EU, thanks to policies like at-will employment. The regulatory culture prioritizes business efficiency and economic growth, seeking to minimize interventionist practices. This is one of the things that keeps the United States so competitive; flexibility in the labor market and a focus on productivity encourage innovation and advancement. This environment is especially attractive for startups and high-growth companies that thrive on agility. American companies pride themselves on innovation and see regulations as a path to stifling it.

Compounding this, industry groups and lobbyists fight tooth and nail against new regulations, especially those they deem too burdensome. Lobbying groups are constantly advocating for self-regulation over government regulation.

In the majority of instances, new laws do not come about in the United States unless something is negatively affecting free and fair enterprise, children, or national security. These limitations are a significant barrier to data privacy when user data is fundamental for mass profit, which corporations crave. Incentives for strong, comprehensive, and consistent data privacy laws aren't just misaligned; they are nonexistent.

This is exactly why laws for protecting data privacy in the United States are fragmented and sector-specific. Laws that mandate data protection obligations focus on specific industries, and many were not even originally intended to protect consumer privacy.

The Telecommunications Act of 1996 requires that telecommunications providers protect customer proprietary network information—but even that was not originally for consumer privacy. It was to prevent telecommunications providers from having an unfair advantage over competitors.[2]

The Health Insurance Portability and Accountability Act (HIPAA) is the preeminent law that protects personal health information. It was originally created to make it easier to share health information between insurance providers when citizens moved between jobs (and thus insurance providers), not to protect data privacy. The P in HIPAA stands for portability, not privacy.[3]

---

[2] https://www.congress.gov/bill/104th-congress/senate-bill/652
[3] https://www.congress.gov/bill/104th-congress/house-bill/3103/text

The Gramm–Leach–Bliley Act (GLBA) protects financial information.[4] *The Children's Online Privacy Protection Act (COPPA)* was passed in 1998 to protect children's privacy under the age of 13.[5]

But is there anything like the EUs General Data Protection Regulation (GDPR), which provides a centralized, rights-based framework for all personal data at the federal level within the United States? Nope. There is simply no appetite for it.

Prepare for Penalties

A fragmented system leads to fragmented enforcement. Rather than imposing consistent data privacy obligations on businesses prior to a breach, the U.S. government imposes penalties *after* a breach through regulatory bodies such as the Federal Trade Commission (FTC), Consumer Financial Protection Bureau (CFPB), Securities and Exchange Commission (SEC), Federal Communications Commission (FCC), and Department of Health & Human Services (HHS), as well as through state laws. It is a complex web that makes compliance challenging, and every regulator wants their pound of flesh.

The FTC is the primary federal agency responsible for consumer protection and is among the most active regulators of data breaches. Under *Section 5 of the FTC Act*, the agency may bring actions against companies for "unfair or deceptive" practices, including failing to implement reasonable data security measures or misrepresenting their privacy policies.[6] The FTC can and has imposed significant fines and mandated corrective actions on companies. The FTC is also responsible for enforcing the GLBA's Safeguards Rule and Privacy Rule for non-bank financial institutions, while federal banking regulators handle bank financial institutions.

The CFPB also plays a role in regulating data privacy in the financial sector. It can take action against Unfair, Deceptive, or Abusive Acts or Practices, which it has successfully argued includes

---

[4] https://www.congress.gov/bill/106th-congress/senate-bill/900
[5] https://uscode.house.gov/view.xhtml?path=%2Fprelim%40title15%2Fchapter91&edition=prelim
[6] https://www.ftc.gov/news-events/topics/protecting-consumer-privacy-security/privacy-security-enforcement

failing to implement adequate data security measures, as it can lead to significant harm to consumers through identity theft and fraud.[7]

The SEC is focused on protecting investors and ensuring the integrity of the financial markets, which means it can fine publicly traded companies for failing to disclose cybersecurity risks and data breaches in a timely and accurate manner. SEC rules adopted in 2023 require companies to report material cybersecurity incidents within four business days, increasing the likelihood of enforcement actions for noncompliance.[8]

The FCC has the authority to enforce data privacy rules for telecommunications carriers and has acted against companies for failing to protect customer data.[9] If the U.S. government can't have your telecommunications data without a warrant, neither can anyone else.

The HHS Office for Civil Rights enforces HIPAA and can impose civil monetary penalties on healthcare providers, insurers, and their business associates for violations, including data breaches. Fines can range from a few thousand to over a million dollars per violation, depending on the culpability.[10]

Take Anthem's data breach in 2015.[11] Anthem, the largest U.S. national health benefits company by membership, disclosed it had been breached in 2014, when attackers accessed up to 80 million health records, including social security numbers, birthdays, addresses, email information, financial information, etc. At the time, it was the largest breach in U.S. healthcare history.

An employee at Anthem's Amerigroup subsidiary was targeted by a phishing email that they opened, enabling the attacker to access their computer. The attacker spread across Anthem's environment, compromising at least 50 accounts and 90 systems. Anthem brought in Mandiant for incident response and was able to remove the attacker within three days of discovering the breach.

In a subsequent regulatory settlement agreement between Anthem and the insurance departments of multiple states,

---

[7] https://www.consumerfinance.gov/about-us/newsroom/cfpb-finalizes-perso nal-financial-data-rights-rule-to-boost-competition-protect-privacy-and- give-families-more-choice-in-financial-services

[8] https://www.sec.gov/newsroom/press-releases/2023-139

[9] https://www.law.cornell.edu/cfr/text/47/64.2011

[10] https://www.hhs.gov/hipaa/for-professionals/compliance-enforcement/data/ enforcement-highlights/index.html

[11] https://www.insurance.ca.gov/0400-news/0100-press-releases/anthem cyberattack.cfm

CrowdStrike confirmed the attacker's identity and, with moderate confidence, that the attacker was acting on behalf of a foreign government. At the time, they did not publicly identify which government or individuals.[12]

The fallout was a brutal barrage: Anthem paid $115 million in a class action lawsuit; $16 million to the HHS Office for Civil Rights for the HIPAA violation; another $39.5 million to the attorneys general of 43 states; and another $8.7 million to settle with the California attorney general.[13]

The findings from the regulatory settlement indicated that Anthem had done the right things. It had a security program in place that was appropriate for its size and business. It took reasonable steps to secure its data, including using security technologies. Yet still, it was breached and required to pay a large settlement to both HHS and multiple states.

The breach was a clear indicator that, unlike what the U.S. government had previously stated, the private sector *was* at a disadvantage, especially against nation-state attackers. Four years later, the DOJ indicted two Chinese nationals for their role in the Anthem attack and attacks on three other U.S. companies.[14]

Follow the Money

None of this even scratches the surface of state laws or sector-specific state laws, which adds another layer of complexity. Take, for example, the Cambridge Analytica scandal. In 2018, a massive scandal rocked the United States and the tech world as a whole when Christopher Wylie came out as a whistleblower and revealed that Cambridge Analytica, a British political consulting company that specialized in data analysis, had been tracking the personal data of millions of Facebook users and monetizing it to support political purposes without consent.[15]

---

[12] www.commerce.alaska.gov/web/Portals/11/Pub/Companies/Exams/MCE16-09.pdf?ver=2016-12-12-083253-927
[13] https://cyberscoop.com/anthem-data-breach-settlement
[14] https://www.justice.gov/archives/opa/pr/member-sophisticated-china-based-hacking-group-indicted-series-computer-intrusions-including
[15] www.theguardian.com/news/2018/mar/17/cambridge-analytica-facebook-influence-us-election

Cambridge Analytica originally collected data through legitimate means in a personality quiz app called "This Is Your Digital Life," which was released in 2014 by an academic at the University of Cambridge. Some 270,000 people downloaded the app and consented to the collection of their data for academic purposes. Hundreds of thousands were paid to fill out the personality test. However, at the time, Facebook had weak data collection policies, which enabled the app to also pull personal data from the users' friend networks, who had not consented to data collection—think things like status updates, likes, and even private messages of up to 87 million Facebook users.

Using this data, Cambridge Analytica built psychographic profiles of American voters, which contained up to 5,000 data points per voter. They fed this data to their clients, who would use it to create targeted and manipulative advertisements that played on people's likes, dislikes, and perspectives.

It turns out, Facebook found out this was happening in 2015. However, they didn't tell their users; instead, they sent a letter to Cambridge Analytica requesting that they delete the data. They never verified that Cambridge Analytica had deleted it, aside from receiving a certificate stating that it had.

Once Wylie came out as a whistleblower, the Cambridge Analytica CEO was suspended, and two months later, the company filed for bankruptcy. Mark Zuckerberg was called to testify before Congress, and Facebook paid the FTC $5 billion, a record-breaking amount, for using deceptive privacy practices.[16] However, shareholders allege that the FTC was only estimated to fine Facebook around $100 million, far below the $5 billion paid. They claim the $4 billion and change difference was to protect Zuckerberg from being held personally liable.[17] The payout doesn't show the priority of user privacy in the United States; it just shows the lengths a company might go to protect a CEO.

The FTC required Cambridge Analytica to delete the data it had collected. The SEC fined Facebook $100 million for misleading

---

[16] https://www.ftc.gov/news-events/news/press-releases/2019/07/ftc-imposes-5-billion-penalty-sweeping-new-privacy-restrictions-facebook
[17] https://arstechnica.com/tech-policy/2021/09/facebook-paid-ftc-4-9b-more-than-required-to-shield-zuckerberg-lawsuit-alleges

investors regarding the risks the company faced from the misuse of customer data.[18]

While this was a major political scandal, especially given its prominence in the 2016 presidential campaigns of Donald Trump and Ted Cruz, as well as in Leave.EU on Brexit, it also had significant cybersecurity implications.[19]

This got to the heart of why data privacy matters: Because otherwise, it can be used and abused to manipulate individuals. In this instance, it was to try to sway votes. In others, it could have been to get them to buy the latest fad. But most importantly, it's able to do this at a massive scale.

One of the ramifications of this incident was that it prompted state lawmakers to consider and enact privacy laws to protect constituents. In 2020, California enacted the California Consumer Privacy Act. The act ensures that Californians know what personal data is being collected and have rights to it: To have it deleted, to opt out of data collection or sharing, and to correct inaccurate information.[20]

However, the incident wasn't enough to get a federal privacy law passed. Instead, it highlighted what comparative juggernauts the FTC and the SEC had become in providing some form of recompense for misuse of user data. The best defense the American public has is laws that protect shareholders and free and fair markets.

Eat the Carrot or Get the Stick

The U.S. government is not just there to impose policies and fines. CISA has done significant work to prioritize information sharing between the public and private sector, and to provide the private sector with helpful and timely guidance on threats and vulnerabilities.

> Threat intelligence is analyzed information about threats and threat actors that can directly inform security decisions and defensive actions. Organizations use threat intelligence

---

[18] https://www.ftc.gov/business-guidance/blog/2019/07/ftc-sues-cambridge-analytica-deceptive-claims-about-consumers-personal-information
[19] www.theguardian.com/uk-news/2019/jul/30/cambridge-analytica-did-work-for-leave-eu-emails-confirm
[20] https://oag.ca.gov/privacy/ccpa

to understand attacker activity, prioritize vulnerabilities, and improve defenses.

In 2015, *the Cybersecurity Information Sharing Act* was enacted to promote the exchange of cyber threat information between private companies and the government. It provided companies with legal protections from liability for sharing threat intelligence, thereby protecting sensitive business data from public release and allowing companies to share information without fear of violating antitrust laws.[21] At the time, the security community was wary; they were concerned about the potential for government surveillance when sharing sensitive information. There's a strong fear among Americans of being ruled by a surveillance state, which makes information sharing an especially difficult endeavor. Few companies want to share information with government bodies that could use the information against them.

Even still, information sharing is a critical part of cyber defense because no single organization, no matter how large or well-resourced, can see the entire threat landscape on its own.

CISA managed the information sharing system created by the *Cybersecurity Information Sharing Act* and built it up to where there were almost 10 million shared indicators of threats in 2021. When the main group responsible for sharing data from the federal side shifted from the Defense Cybercrime Center to what most deduce is the NSA, that well of indicators dried up. They pretty much entirely stopped sharing data, as the NSA has a different, tightly constrained information-sharing group with which they share information. That dropped the shared threat intel indicators down to under 500,000 in 2022.[22]

CISA had begun to build back the program, and with private sector partners, increased the number of shared indicators back up to over 10 million in 2024.[23] However, the law expired on October 1, 2025, effectively ending the program, as companies no longer have liability protection for information sharing.

---

[21] https://corpgov.law.harvard.edu/2016/03/03/federal-guidance-on-the-cybersecurity-information-sharing-act-of-2015
[22] www.sans.org/blog/reflections-on-the-us-governments-oig-report-on-cisas-automated-indicator-sharing-program
[23] www.oig.dhs.gov/sites/default/files/assets/2025-09/OIG-25-46-Sep25.pdf

Even when these partnerships work, they go both ways. If you're given fair warning by the government of an impending attack or vulnerability, it's not just a warning—it's a directive. Equifax found this out the hard way.

On March 7, 2017, a critical vulnerability in Apache Struts, an open source framework for building modern Java applications, was publicly disclosed. A day later, DHS notified Equifax about the vulnerability. Equifax used Apache Struts across a series of applications, which made this vulnerability—and addressing it—a critical priority. Though Equifax staff were instructed to patch their systems to address the vulnerability, not everyone did. Critical systems remained vulnerable, and two months later, attackers had used the vulnerability to breach Equifax's systems. In the 76 days the attackers had in the network, they accessed 48 databases and sent 9,000 queries to them. Equifax didn't notice until months later.[24]

On September 7, 2017, Equifax announced the breach—it had exposed the credit information of 148 million consumers, nearly half of all Americans, along with around 700,000 UK consumers and 19,000 Canadians. This included the sensitive personal information you would expect a credit reporting agency to have: Names, Social Security numbers, birth dates, addresses, and driver's license numbers.[25]

Eight days after they announced the breach, Equifax's CIO and Chief Security Officer retired early. The CEO left the company, and Equifax paid a massive amount of money in response to the breach, including $425 million in a settlement with the FTC, CFPB, and multiple U.S. states.[26]

Regulating Elections

From protecting against foreign cybercrime, to enhancing federal and state cybersecurity measures, to ensuring the private sector prioritizes data security, all of these defensive measures culminate in and are personified by the work of securing elections.

---

[24] https://oversight.house.gov/wp-content/uploads/2018/12/Equifax-Report.pdf

[25] https://www.hbs.edu/faculty/Pages/item.aspx?num=53509

[26] https://www.nbcnews.com/business/consumer/equifax-executives-step-down-scrutiny-intensifies-credit-bureaus-n801706

Chapter 9
The Coop of Amontillado

O n a rainy October 3rd in 1849, a man found Edgar Allen Poe lying in a gutter outside of a polling location called Gunner's Hall in Baltimore, Maryland. He was entirely incoherent and not his usual well-dressed self; instead, he was reeking of alcohol and dressed in secondhand, poorly fitting, and dirty clothes. After he was found, he never regained consciousness—he was in and out of hallucinations, calling out for an unknown "Reynolds," and died four days later.[1]

Poe had left Richmond, Virginia, a week earlier to go to Philadelphia—yet he never arrived and instead turned up in the gutter in Baltimore on election day. It's all very mysterious and remains so to this day. However, Poe biographers have one particular enduring theory: Poe died after being a victim of *cooping*.

During this time, Baltimore (and much of the United States) faced rampant voter fraud. One of the most common methods of voter fraud was called cooping, where people were kidnapped and forced to vote for one candidate multiple times. The kidnappers would beat them into submission and dress them up in different outfits each time they went to vote so they wouldn't be noticed as

---

[1] www.smithsonianmag.com/history/still-mysterious-death-edgar-allan-poe-180952936

repeat voters. This was a different time in America, one where voters were given a little treat of alcohol after voting as a reward, so anyone voting multiple times in one evening would undoubtedly get a little drunk. The polling location was well-known for being used for cooping, and some speculate that Poe was a victim of it left to die after the work was done.

By the late 1800s, many reforms were introduced to prevent cooping and other methods of voter intimidation. Instead of party-distributed ballots, secret ballots administered by the government were adopted, ensuring voter anonymity. Voter registration requirements were adopted to ensure that voters would register in advance to be eligible to vote, and to prevent repeat voting.[2]

Reforms like these, implemented through the late 19th and early 20th centuries, fundamentally changed voting in the United States, making it nearly impossible to execute voter fraud on a large scale. Yet, fears of voter fraud persist.

A major turning point in voter confidence occurred during the 2000 U.S. presidential election, when, at around 8 p.m. on November 7, 2000, broadcast networks projected that Al Gore had won the state of Florida over George W. Bush. This would have been a huge victory; the election was decided by Florida's 25 electoral votes. However, the reality was more nuanced—the results became too close to call in the state of Florida, and the networks retracted their statement. Later, they would report Bush had actually won Florida and thus the presidency. Gore conceded the election to Bush, but the vote margin continued to shrink, and the race became far closer than expected. Gore retracted his concession, and Florida became too close to call once again. Over the next 36 days, anxieties ran high in the United States—the margin in Florida was less than 0.5 percent, just 537 votes. One automated recount and a court case appealed to the Supreme Court later, and the state ran out of time to complete the manual recount, making Bush the certified winner of the election. Hanging chads and butterfly ballots led to thousands of votes not being counted properly, causing frustration and raising doubts about the results of the election.[3]

[2] https://www.smithsonianmag.com/history/the-vote-that-failed-159427766
[3] https://www.npr.org/2018/11/12/666812854/the-florida-recount-of-2000-a-nightmare-that-goes-on-haunting

Ever since this moment, the United States has been tumbling toward a broader divide in confidence, split by party. Voter concerns have become especially prevalent with the introduction of electronic voting machines. In 2003, Walden O'Dell said the following to invite Bush supporters to a fundraiser, "I am committed to helping Ohio deliver its electoral votes to the president next year."[4]

There's one major problem with this: Walden was the chief executive of Diebold, Inc., one of the most prolific creators of voting machines in the United States at the time.[5] It raised immediate concerns about his potential bias as a public advocate for the Bush campaign while also being the owner of a company that makes voting software. In addition, Diebold wasn't exactly known to be open with its technology—the software was not available to the public until a voting activist, Bev Harris, found the source code on an unprotected server.[6] Researchers at Johns Hopkins and Rice University found multiple vulnerabilities: The system failed to log important events that needed to be recorded; there was an option that would delete all audit logs (and thus any record of what happened); and in Humboldt County, California, the tabulation software deleted 200 votes for no reason. Internal emails show that Diebold employees knew about the vulnerabilities but avoided tests that would show them.[7]

Not only that, but in 2006, HBO released a documentary, *Hacking Democracy,* which brought election security and the security of voting machines to the public. The documentary showed one particularly eye-opening attack against Diebold machines, the *Hursti Hack,* which could change election results in a completely undetectable way. It manipulated the contents of the memory card in the machine by modifying scripts and vote counts on the card in a way that wouldn't be identified by the administrator.[8]

By 2009, Diebold sold its voting machine division to Election Systems and Software (ES&S), which had accounted for about half the votes in the last four major elections at the time.[9]

---

[4] www.nytimes.com/2003/12/02/opinion/hack-the-vote.html
[5] https://www.wired.com/2005/12/ceo-quits-embattled-diebold
[6] https://blackboxvoting.org/bbv_chapter-1.pdf
[7] https://blog.citp.princeton.edu/2006/09/20/refuting-diebolds-response
[8] https://www.hackingdemocracy.com
[9] www.wired.com/2009/09/diebold-sells

Voting Machines Aren't the Problem

The hacker community has tried to work more closely with the election equipment industry, especially through events like the DEF CON (a popular hacker conference) Voting Village. The Voting Village started in 2017 and gives hackers the opportunity to try to break into voting machines and find new vulnerabilities. Ethical hackers like these operate in many industries, breaking into systems to help make them stronger. The hackers access the system, then show the company how to repeat the hack so they can fix it.[10]

Unfortunately, the conference has been used to spread lies about election integrity. In 2020, after being defeated in the presidential election, Donald Trump tweeted a video from the conference, which he claimed was evidence that the election was rigged, even though that is not the case.[11] Identifying technical flaws does not mean an attack has happened, just how one *could* happen. Even the attacks that DEF CON hackers were able to perpetrate could not necessarily be done at scale. The main reason for this is that the United States electoral system is remarkably decentralized. It was structured this way from the beginning—the framers of the Constitution were concerned about the power to control through centralized authority, as they had experienced it under British rule. To ensure states retained their own independence, they distributed control over the electoral process at the state level, instead of centralizing it federally.[12]

States are responsible for holding their elections as they see fit, and the Electoral College system enabled the states to decide how their electors were chosen. Over time, the states further delegated operational activities to local governments at the county, city, and town levels.

As a result, almost 13,000 local authorities now manage nearly every facet of the electoral process, from voter registration and ballot design to the procurement of voting equipment and vote counting.

---

[10] https://harris.uchicago.edu/files/cpi_-_def_con_25_report_-_final_3.pdf
[11] https://arstechnica.com/tech-policy/2020/11/voting-security-experts-refute-trump-claims-of-voting-machine-hacking
[12] https://effectivegov.uchicago.edu/primers/the-electoral-college

Election administration is overseen by a mix of appointed partisan officials, civil servants, and elected officials, resulting in wide variation in procedures across the country. Nothing is standardized, not even the equipment they use.[13]

Even the structure of voting is different in different regions. Some use winner-take-all systems, others use majority-vote systems, while still others use ranked-choice voting or proportional representation. Some use hand-marked paper ballots and optical scanners, like Alabama, New York, and Virginia; others use ballot marking devices that get scanned in, like Georgia, South Carolina, and Arkansas; others still use direct recording electronic machines, where voters tap a screen to vote, like Louisiana; others have a mix of technologies, like Nevada, Ohio, and Utah; lastly, some states mostly vote by mail, like California, Colorado, and Oregon. Many use a combination of these options.[14]

Instead of a single, uniform national election process, the United States is a complex patchwork: More than 8,000 distinct election jurisdictions each have their own rules, procedures, technical equipment, and computer infrastructure, including networks.[15] For attackers, that means different personnel to phish, different operating systems to build malware for, different networks to access, different vulnerabilities to target, and different counting methods to change. There is simply no centralized way to attack every single jurisdiction in a coordinated fashion, or even to attack them all in the same way at the same time. Even if it were possible to tip the scales in a single one with a cyberattack, it wouldn't be enough—there are 8,000 others to be targeted separately, too.

Because of this complexity, instead of targeting the voting equipment, it's easier to target where that data *is* centralized: In the reporting infrastructure.[16] If you can't easily target and change the vote count, because the systems are not connected to the Internet or are not easily accessible, instead, change what information is presented to the public. At the very least, it will cause confusion and potential chaos.

---

[13] https://effectivegov.uchicago.edu/primers/nonpartisan-election-administration
[14] https://ballotpedia.org/Voting_equipment_by_state
[15] https://www.eac.gov/election-officials/election-security-preparedness
[16] https://www.ic3.gov/PSA/2022/PSA221004.pdf

The Iranians tried to do this during the 2020 U.S. presidential election. Iranian contractors broke into the election reporting infrastructure for one city. They were planning on using the access to change the reported vote count being shared with the public to create doubt in the results. U.S. Cyber Command identified and stopped the attackers before the attack was able to achieve its goal.[17]

Even in this instance, the attackers would have only been able to change the *reported* vote count, not the *actual* vote count, for one city of thousands. Even if that city was the deciding factor in the election, the integrity of the vote count remained: There is a record of the actual vote count that can be reviewed and compared to the reported totals. This is why auditing the results is so important—secondary testing and validation would have caught this even if U.S. Cyber Command did not. A layered defense involves layers of validation checks, too.

---

[17] www.nbcnews.com/tech/security/iran-linked-hackers-broke-election-results
-website-2020-general-says-rcna81304

Chapter 10
Fractured Truths

In 1782, the American Revolutionary War was waning. The Siege of Yorktown was a major defeat for Great Britain that broke its will to continue major fighting.[1] Even still, Benjamin Franklin was concerned about potential reconciliation. He had refused peace offers that would keep the 13 states as part of the British Empire, insisting on American independence. To ensure that independence, he undertook many diplomatic actions, alongside some less morally sound ones, including disseminating disinformation in American newspapers.

He crafted a supplemental sheet to be included with the newspaper that held a letter, purportedly from Capt. Gerrish of the New England militia.[2] Only, Gerrish didn't exist—he was a fiction created by Franklin. In the sheet, "Gerrish" reported that American forces had found packages with the scalps of women and children taken by the Seneca Nation. The letter went into gruesome detail—yet it was all lies from the mind of Benjamin Franklin.[3]

He filled the sheet with more falsehoods, including a fake letter from a famous and well-regarded naval commander, John Paul

---

[1] www.battlefields.org/learn/revolutionary-war/battles/yorktown
[2] https://founders.archives.gov/documents/Franklin/01-37-02-0132
[3] https://slate.com/human-interest/2015/07/history-of-benjamin-franklin-diplomacy-propaganda-newspaper-with-stories-of-native-american-atrocities.html

Jones, saying that independence was paramount, because the king "engages savages to murder their defenseless farmers, women and children."[4]

These lies were published multiple times in different American papers and in newspapers in the UK. It helped Franklin sabotage reconciliation and put diplomatic pressure on the British on their home turf.

It goes to show that the very first information operations against the United States did not happen on the Internet, or even with radio during World War II—it helped shape the very founding of the United States. Disinformation and information operations have always been part of the U.S. experience, they are just more easily scalable with the Internet.

Priming the Pump

The United States became primed to be manipulated by online information operations and disinformation in the early 2000s.

By this point, the existing fault lines among Americans had naturally grown deeper. Ideologically, in 1994, 16 percent of Democrats viewed the Republican Party very unfavorably. In 2014, that number had more than doubled to 38 percent. In 1994, 17 percent of Republicans viewed Democrats very unfavorably. In 2014, that number had more than doubled to 43 percent.[5] Ideological differences divided Americans more than they had in a long time, and this was compounded by differences in racial, religious, geographic, and class issues.

Exacerbating this, the media environment was freshly and incredibly fractured. In the early 2000s, the traditional media landscape was still fairly dominant, but that was all about to change. In 2007, Twitter gained massive popularity, shooting up from 5,000

[4] https://founders.archives.gov/documents/Franklin/01-37-02-0132
[5] www.pewresearch.org/politics/2014/06/12/political-polarization-in-the-american-public

tweets per day to 300,000 just a year later.[6] Social media numbers would only continue to skyrocket. In 2008, Facebook had 100 million users; by 2009, it had 300 million.[7] By 2008, more Americans were getting their news from online sources than from newspapers for the first time.[8]

The media landscape shifted; instead of being dominated by a few established news outlets, Americans now found themselves in a digital environment with infinite sources. Social media platforms driven by algorithms that prioritize engagement over accuracy are inherently vulnerable to sensationalist and emotionally charged content. False stories, particularly about politics, have been shown to spread significantly faster and more broadly because they are often more novel and evocative.[9] The same data-driven tools that allow advertisers to target consumers with precision can be used to target specific demographics with tailored disinformation. Adversaries can target groups based on their interests, fears, and political leanings, delivering customized messages designed to be as persuasive and inflammatory as possible.

Lastly, the state of the Internet in the United States made it ripe for manipulation. The United States has very little appetite for anything that could be considered a violation of free speech, including on the Internet. *Section 230 of the Communications Decency Act of 1996* makes managing this a problem for companies, instead of a mandate from governments.

Much of what enables the best and worst parts of the Internet today comes down to Section 230. Some call it the "26 words that created the Internet" for how influential it has been over the past few decades.[10] Section 230 shields interactive computer services, including social media companies, from liability for content that is posted by their users. It states that they cannot be held accountable for or treated as publishers of content produced by others, even on their own sites,

---

[6] www.internetlivestats.com/twitter-statistics
[7] https://faculty.lsu.edu/fakenews/elections/sixteen.php
[8] www.ebsco.com/research-starters/information-technology/old-media-traditional-media
[9] https://news.mit.edu/2018/study-twitter-false-news-travels-faster-true-stories-0308
[10] www.cfr.org/in-brief/trump-and-section-230-what-know

but that they do have the power to censor. It has led to many debates. On the opposing side, critics argue that this law fails to hold companies accountable for the damage their users could inflict by posting hate speech online, and that the platform gives them the vehicle to do so. Proponents state that Section 230 is what makes the Internet what it is today, and without it, many of the best parts of the Internet, especially the freedom of expression without accountability, would be lost.

This leads independent companies, especially social media companies, to get sucked into the political vortex for censoring content as they choose on their own websites. Efforts to combat disinformation by removing content or blocking sources inevitably face backlash over alleged censorship and violation of free speech. On an open Internet, there is no single arbiter of truth. Measures that are too aggressive risk stifling legitimate dissent, creating a censored information reality, and empowering corporations to decide what information is considered acceptable.

The anonymity enabled by the Internet compounds this issue. You can claim to be from the United States, but that doesn't mean it's actually where you are. In the past, publishing information to a mass audience required significant resources and approvals from traditional gatekeepers like editors and publishers. The Internet removed these barriers. Anyone with an Internet connection can create content and distribute it globally at virtually no cost, all while claiming to be whoever they want. This makes it incredibly difficult to verify sources and the credibility of information.

The Perfect Storm

This leads us to the perfect-storm moment: The 2016 U.S. presidential election. During the election, Russia went full force, pumping disinformation towards U.S. citizens specifically designed to divide. In the three months before the election, fake news stories favoring Trump were shared 30 million times, and those favoring Clinton were shared 8 million times. And the real kicker: Over half of

American adults who recall seeing fake news say they believed the stories.[11]

The goal of the Russians' disinformation campaigns was to undermine the democratic process and deepen existing divisions in the United States. According to an intelligence assessment from the Office of the Director of National Intelligence, the Russians wanted to boost Trump's candidacy and harm Clinton's campaign. The report states that

> . . . Putin and the Russian Government aspired to help President-elect Trump's election chances when possible by discrediting Secretary Clinton and publicly contrasting her unfavorably to him.[12]

All three agencies agreed with this assessment: The CIA and FBI with high confidence, the NSA with moderate confidence.

One of the more horrific examples of the direct impact of these disinformation efforts is Pizzagate.[13] After John Podesta's emails were posted by WikiLeaks in 2016, Reddit and 4chan users began scouring them for any nefarious activities. What did they find? Emails between Podesta and his brother about going to a pizza place for dinner. Benign, right? Apparently not.

Users made the gigantic leap that "cheese pizza" must have been in reference to pedophiles, since some use the phrase "c.p." as online shorthand for "child pornography." They also found that John Podesta had emailed the owner of the popular pizza joint Comet Ping Pong about political fundraisers. The assumption became, based on a series of innocuous words, that Democrats were operating a secret child sex-trafficking ring out of the pizza joint.

This gained a lot of steam online and became its own hashtag, #PizzaGate. In November 2016 alone, nearly a million tweets were sent using the term "pizzagate."[14] Protestors congregated outside of Comet, and the owner even let some of them in to try to convince

---

[11] https://faculty.lsu.edu/fakenews/elections/sixteen.php
[12] https://www.intelligence.senate.gov/wp-content/uploads/2024/08/sites-default-filesations-ica-2017-01.pdf
[13] https://www.nytimes.com/interactive/2016/12/05/us/document-Edgar-Welch-Criminal-Complaint-Comet-Ping-Pong.html
[14] www.bbc.com/news/blogs-trending-38156985

them it wasn't true. The theory was that the conspiracy was run out of the basement of the store, but there was one big problem with that: The store didn't have a basement.[15]

Individuals in Macedonia, the purported "fake news capital of the world," were paid to spread more information on social media related to Pizzagate. At least 14 Russia-linked accounts masquerading as Americans tweeted about Pizzagate.[16]

Compounding the problem, American leaders and influencers promoted these fake ideas. One of the Russian accounts, @Pamela_Moore13, had been retweeted by those close to Trump, including Trump supporters like Donald Trump Jr. and Roger Stone. Alex Jones was also a big promoter of the Pizzagate conspiracy theory until he had to publicly apologize to the owner to avoid damages in a libel suit.[17] The fake news flourished on Reddit r/The_Donald, 4chan, and Twitter.

This all culminated in one Sunday afternoon around 3 p.m., when a man walked into Comet with a rifle.[18] He pointed the gun at an employee before firing three rounds at a locked closet inside the building, scaring employees and customers, including children. After finding no evidence of any hidden rooms or sex trafficking in the pizza place, he surrendered and was arrested outside the restaurant. No one was injured.[19]

This case is just one among many instances in which disinformation translated to violent kinetic action and accelerated American divisions.

After the election was over, the reality was undeniable; the Russian government had worked to influence the 2016 U.S. presidential election. However, the extent to which Russian influence affected the outcome remains heavily debated. The outcome was decided by

[15] https://www.justice.gov/usao-dc/pr/north-carolina-man-sentenced-four-year-prison-term-armed-assault-northwest-washington
[16] https://misinforeview.hks.harvard.edu/article/russian-disinformation-campaigns-on-twitter
[17] www.npr.org/sections/thetwo-way/2017/03/26/521545788/conspiracy-theorist-alex-jones-apologizes-for-promoting-pizzagate
[18] www.starnewsonline.com/story/news/crime/2016/12/05/dc-pizza-place-shooter-former-cfcc-student-local-actor/24400830007
[19] www.washingtonpost.com/local/public-safety/comet-pizza-gunman-to-appear-at-plea-deal-hearing-friday-morning/2017/03/23/e12c91ba-0986-11e7-b77c-0047d15a24e0_story.html

a mere 80,000 votes across three states, and with a razor-thin margin like that, it is highly likely it had some effect.[20]

What is less debatable is Russia's success in achieving its broader strategic objective. By injecting conspiracy theories and inflammatory content into American political discourse, Russia successfully eroded public trust, exacerbated social tensions, and damaged faith in the democratic process itself—a victory for any adversary looking to weaken the United States from within. These tactics have since become a model for other hostile actors, including China and Iran, and continue to pose a threat to democratic societies.

The Iranian Shotgun

The Iranians copied the Russians' work in later elections by attempting to erode trust in the electoral system. However, their approach was more of a shotgun: Numerous small activities at once that are hard to track, forcing authorities to play whack-a-mole.

Ahead of the 2020 U.S. presidential election, contractors working for the Iranian government sent phishing emails to senior officials and individuals associated with the political campaigns to try to gain access to their data. They targeted vulnerabilities in 11 different U.S. state election websites, and successfully broke into one; they did not manipulate or alter any vote counting, but they were able to steal voter information for 100,000 voters because of it.[21]

In some cases, Iranian attackers used this information to harass voters. They sent emails masquerading as the Proud Boys to tens of thousands of registered voters, especially democratic ones, in Florida. These emails called them out by name and demanded that the voters switch parties and vote for Trump, or they would be physically attacked.[22]

---

[20] www.washingtonpost.com/news/the-fix/wp/2016/12/01/donald-trump-will-be-president-thanks-to-80000-people-in-three-states
[21] https://s3.documentcloud.org/documents/25176482/us_v_seyyed_mohammad_hosein_et_al_signed_indictment_redacted-1.pdf
[22] https://www.osi.af.mil/News/Article-Display/Article/2395806/bulletin-iranian-spoofed-emails-portraying-the-proud-boys

They also targeted and breached a U.S. media company, Lee Enterprises, which owns numerous newspapers across America and maintains their content management systems.[23] The attackers were testing their ability to add disinformation to the systems to spread it through trusted sources. The day after the election, the attackers tried to log in using the stolen credentials they had harvested previously, but failed because the FBI and the media company had identified the breach and revoked access prior to election day.

Iranian attackers masqueraded as Proud Boys volunteers and sent Facebook messages and emails to members of Congress, White House advisers, the media, and Trump campaign officials that claimed the Democratic Party was going to exploit "serious security vulnerabilities" in state voter registration websites. It claimed they would "edit mail-in ballots or even register non-existent voters." Attackers created a video that supposedly showed someone breaking into state voter websites to create false ballots, but the methods they used were fake and not possible with the systems that exist today.[24]

The goal of their disinformation efforts was not to prop up any particular candidate, but instead to denigrate Donald Trump. The attackers wanted their disinformation to cause chaos and uncertainty.

Immediately following the 2020 election, but before Biden was sworn in, Iranians once again began to try to stoke tensions. They created a website called Enemies of the People (enemiesofthe people.org). The website was a veritable hit list of American political figures responsible for carrying out and securing the election, as well as those who spoke out against Trump's claims of rigging, like Michigan Governor Gretchen Whitmer and Director of CISA Chris Krebs.[25] It included images of the targets, along with any personal information they had, such as home addresses and email addresses.

---

[23] www.wsj.com/politics/national-security/iranian-hackers-broke-into-news-paper-publisher-lee-enterprises-ahead-of-2020-election-11637359741
[24] https://home.treasury.gov/news/press-releases/jy0494
[25] www.nbcnews.com/tech/security/irans-history-elaborate-election-interference-efforts-trump-campaign-h-rcna171312

These types of attacks haven't stopped: Russia, China, and Iran all targeted the 2024 U.S. presidential election in different ways.

Iranian disinformation has also focused on targeting and widening gaps in divisive issues in the United States, like COVID-19 pandemic response, the economy, civil unrest, and the electoral process.

These attacks become even easier to perpetrate when leadership promotes the messages for you. During the COVID-19 pandemic, there was a significant rise in online disinformation. Part of it was caused by actors like the Iranians, but it didn't help that political figures were lying and suppressing stories; then-Governor of New York Andrew Cuomo covered up deaths in nursing homes, while then-President Trump promoted a factually false "cure" in the anti-malarial drug hydroxychloroquine and bleach.[26,27] The more confusion from the top, the easier it is for the attackers to divide Americans.

The Censorship Tightrope

The United States and social media companies did learn lessons from this. Leading up to the 2020 election, especially in the days and weeks prior, social media organizations tightened their policies.

From October 27 to November 11, 2020, Twitter labeled 300,000 Tweets as disputed or potentially misleading, and 456 of those were restricted so they could not be retweeted, replied to, or liked. Tweets were also marked with a warning before someone quote-tweeted, which reduced the number of quote-tweets by 29 percent.[28] They introduced prebunk prompts, which told people that election results were likely to be delayed and that voting by mail is safe and legitimate; these prebunking measures were seen 389 million times. Twitter created an election hub page for the 2020 U.S. presidential

[26] https://trumpwhitehouse.archives.gov/briefings-statements/remarks-president-trump-vice-president-pence-members-coronavirus-task-force-press-briefing-31
[27] https://oversight.house.gov/release/covid-select-refers-former-new-york-governor-andrew-cuomo-for-criminal-prosecution
[28] https://blog.x.com/en_us/topics/company/2020/2020-election-update

election to give citizens more information from trusted media outlets and election officials. On YouTube, credible and official sources were prioritized in search results.[29]

Debunking is correcting misinformation or disinformation after exposure. *Prebunking* is anticipating disinformation and warning about it prior to exposure. Social media companies do this with fact checks from media outlets, notices from government agencies, or videos and other media from political parties.[30]

Facebook introduced a voting information center to give information to the public. It also created prebunking banners for election day that highlighted that votes were still being counted. Prior to the election in 2020, between March and September, they denied 2.2 million ad submissions that targeted the United States without completing the authorization process. They removed more than 120,000 pieces of content on Instagram and Facebook that violated voter interference policies and put warnings on more than 150 million pieces of content that were debunked by fact checkers.[31]

The policies worked. Removing reshares greatly reduced the political news, including disinformation, that users interacted with.[32] Later studies found that adding warning labels to questionable content reduced people's belief in false headlines by 27 percent and the sharing of false headlines by 25 percent.[33]

Some of these policies started to relax after the election—only to pick back up again significantly after the January 6 attack on the Capitol in 2021. After January 6, media outlets and social media

[29] https://www.congress.gov/118/meeting/house/115561/documents/HHRG-118-IF16-20230328-SD022.pdf

[30] https://democratic-erosion.org/wp-content/uploads/2024/10/Correcting-U.S.-Election-Misinformation-What-Works.pdf

[31] https://abcnews.go.com/Technology/social-media-giants-counter-misinformation-election/story?id=73563997

[32] www.princeton.edu/news/2023/07/28/social-media-polarization-and-2020-election-insights-spias-andrew-guess-and

[33] https://mitsloan.mit.edu/ideas-made-to-matter/online-content-moderation-what-works-and-what-people-want

platforms recognized that far more had to be done. The violence was a catalyst for action. Post-January 6, they focused on fire-fighting measures for content moderation, ad policies, and rapid response bans.

For content moderation, Facebook has experimented with using third-party fact checkers to identify and remove, prevent sharing, deprioritize, or label misleading content. The labels often refute the claim, mark it as misleading, or link to more information.[34]

When it comes to ad policies, the platforms created searchable databases for political ads. For example, Meta created an ad library so journalists and researchers can see who paid for what advertisement, what creative content was used, how much money was spent on the ad, and who the ad targeted. All ads now have a "paid for by" disclaimer. They also built stricter ad policies, so advertisers have to prove their identity and location to be authorized to run political ads.[35]

Rapid response bans are used in cases where there is potential for real-time escalation of violence during a crisis. In those instances, the social media platform demotes or throttles harmful content, disables engagement features, or suspends and removes accounts. Take, for example, Donald Trump's social media after January 6. His accounts were suspended on Twitter, Facebook, Instagram, and YouTube, though they were all reinstated in the years following. Snapchat locked his account permanently and has not reinstated it as of 2025.[36]

The tides shift considerably depending on the party in power. Take one example: Trump is a big opponent of what he considers censorship by social media platforms. After he came back to power in 2025, Meta moved away from the third-party fact check model, instead promoting community notes as fact checks.[37] Effectively, what the community says the loudest now becomes reality.

---

[34] https://transparency.meta.com/features/how-fact-checking-works
[35] https://transparency.meta.com/researchtools/ad-library-tools
[36] https://www.pbs.org/newshour/politics/trump-returns-to-facebook-youtube-after-reinstatement
[37] https://www.pbs.org/newshour/nation/meta-says-it-will-follow-x-replace-fact-checking-with-community-notes

Global Consequences

Amnesty International called out that changes in social media policy, especially pulling back on fact-checking, pose a grave threat to communities globally. Their research shows that Meta's algorithms prioritize and amplify harmful content, such as in Myanmar in 2014.[38]

In one instance in July, a lie spread online that two Muslim tea shop owners raped a Buddhist employee.[39] U Wirathu, a well-known Buddhist monk and militant leader of the 969 movement in Myanmar, shared the falsehood on his Facebook page, and it took off like wildfire. He is known as the "face of Buddhist terror" and had hundreds of thousands of followers at the time.

This led to four days of violence and resulted in two people dead and 14 injured. Myanmar authorities attempted to contact Meta, but were unable to reach them, and decided to block access to Facebook in Mandalay until the incident subsided.

U Wirathu's page was finally banned by Facebook, but not until 2018.[40]

The Rise and Fall of CISA

One of the most important defensive measures against disinformation is the work that governments and leaders undertake to protect the electoral system and to communicate election integrity to the public. CISA has been central to this effort; it has been at the forefront of election security in the United States, aiding local election officials in preparing for cyberattacks during the 2020 and 2024 elections. It became the primary federal agency responsible for protecting election infrastructure from cyberattacks.[41]

---

[38] www.amnesty.org/en/latest/news/2025/02/meta-new-policy-changes
[39] www.amnesty.org.au/wp-content/uploads/2022/09/The-Social-Atrocity-Meta-and-the-right-to-remedy-for-the-Rohingya.pdf
[40] https://www.bbc.com/news/world-asia-58471535
[41] https://www.intelligence.senate.gov/wp-content/uploads/2024/08/sites-default-files-os-jeasterly-051524.pdf

The first head of CISA, Chris Krebs, was nominated in 2018 by then-President Trump. Krebs had worked in the DHS and at Microsoft before leading CISA, and is a self-described lifelong member of the GOP.[42] During his tenure as CISA director, Krebs quickly elevated CISA through clear and direct communication with the general public, effective defense of U.S. critical infrastructure, and protection of U.S. elections.

He led CISA in defending the 2020 U.S. presidential election by prioritizing efforts to clearly communicate the state of election security to the American public. CISA stated publicly that the election was "the most secure in American history."[43] While Trump and some of his supporters pushed claims of election fraud, Krebs and CISA stood fast that the election results were accurate. Trump and his supporters lost more than 60 court cases that challenged the outcome of the election, and many republicans came out to publicly state the election was not rigged.[44]

Krebs continued to state publicly that the election was not fraudulent, and shortly after the election, Trump fired Krebs from his role leading CISA via a tweet for doing so.[45] Trump continued to spread disinformation about the 2020 election results, despite there being no meaningful evidence of voter fraud or inaccurate results.

The most recent setback to strong election security is the Trump administration's 2025 decision to curtail CISA's election-security responsibilities. They downsized the agency and paused all election security activities pending a review of funding, activities, and personnel.[46] That means activities like threat intelligence sharing, internal resources and security support, incident response services, and physical security assessments are no longer being provided to state and local election organizations. No other federal agency has been established to support this effort, meaning no other federal agency is taking the lead to protect U.S. elections.

---

[42] https://www.cbsnews.com/news/election-results-security-chris-krebs-60-minutes-2020-11-29
[43] https://www.hsgac.senate.gov/wp-content/uploads/imo/media/doc/Testimony-Krebs-2020-12-16.pdf
[44] www.pbs.org/newshour/politics/fact-check-trumps-2024-win-doesnt-prove-claims-that-the-2020-election-was-stolen
[45] www.nytimes.com/live/2020/11/17/us/joe-biden-trump
[46] https://apnews.com/article/trump-election-security-fbi-cisa-foreign-interference-98f1e17c8a6d5923db945a27f06458e7

Reality Is Believability; Believability Is Reality

Once disinformation gets started, it's difficult to stop and easy to continue. It develops its own momentum. If there's one thing Benjamin Franklin shows us, it's that disinformation continues and will always continue. Our response to it is what matters.

At this point, we have entered into a post-truth world, where instead of reality, we are in a battle for believability. Winning the battle over believability is not easy. It requires a combination of fact-based messages on repeat, prioritized education, and controls that limit and manage the spread of disinformation. But what it requires more than anything else is civilian trust in government institutions. There's one thing that makes trust in government more difficult: Deceit.

Chapter 11
No Holds Barred

There are days that go by, but not many, that you're not balancing national security against civil liberties when you're addressing terrorism . . . So they are not easy decisions.

—*Robert Mueller, then Director of the FBI, 2011*[1]

Throughout history, the United States has surveilled individuals that it considers to be "other." One infamous example is its surveillance of Martin Luther King, Jr., an unwavering supporter of nonviolence. Through a domestic counterintelligence program, COINTELPRO, the FBI did everything they could to discredit him; to quote the man in charge of the operation, "No holds were barred."[2]

After King's 'I Have a Dream' speech, the FBI deemed him a threat as an effective leader; they suspected he could "unify and electrify" the "black nationalist movement." They surveilled him and sent him threatening messages and packages.[3]

---

[1] https://time.com/archive/6595643/cover-story-is-the-fbi-up-to-the-job-10-years-after-9-11

[2] https://www.intelligence.senate.gov/wp-content/uploads/2024/08/sites-default-files-94755-ii.pdf

[3] https://www.intelligence.senate.gov/wp-content/uploads/2024/08/sites-default-files-94intelligence-activities-vi.pdf

The FBI mailed King a tape recording made using microphones they had hidden in his hotel rooms, which one agent testified was an attempt to destroy King's marriage. The tape recording was accompanied by a note, which King and his advisers interpreted as threatening to release the tape recording unless King killed himself.[4]

According to findings by the U.S. Senate select committee known as the Church Committee, the FBI conducted numerous outright violations of the law, including warrantless break-ins, opening citizens' mail, and wiretapping without warrants.[5]

This operation is now widely condemned as one of the most unethical and abusive acts in the history of American intelligence operations, revealing the extreme lengths the U.S. government was willing to go in an attempt to "neutralize" a nonviolent leader advocating for justice and equality.

The Reckoning

In the 1970s, Washington was scrambling to clean up decades of intelligence abuses uncovered by the Church Committee, including COINTELPRO and the FBI's actions against King. Congressional investigations shone a light on secret surveillance programs and wiretaps run without judicial oversight, revealing how national security could be used as a convenient excuse to violate constitutional rights, especially against political adversaries and journalists.

Many changes came out of this time, though they were eroded rather quickly. *The Privacy Act of 1974* governed how federal agencies handle personally identifiable information (PII) in their systems of record. It established privacy practices that (a) restrict the disclosure of records about an individual without their consent, and (b) give individuals the right to access their records.[6] Keep in mind, this act only governed federal agencies—it did not create rules about PII for the private sector.

---

[4] www.intelligence.senate.gov/wp-content/uploads/2024/08/sites-default-files-94755-ii.pdf
[5] Ibid.
[6] https://www.justice.gov/opcl/privacy-act-1974

The Foreign Intelligence Surveillance Act (FISA) of 1978 established the legal framework for gathering foreign intelligence through electronic surveillance and other means on U.S. soil. The act requires law enforcement to obtain a warrant to conduct such surveillance.

Congress initially limited FISA to regulating government use of electronic surveillance. It established two foreign intelligence courts to approve FISA investigative authorities: The Foreign Intelligence Surveillance Court (FISC) and the Foreign Intelligence Surveillance Court of Review (FISCR). FISC hears government requests and third-party challenges to FISA orders, whereas FISCR hears appeals from the FISC. FISC scrutinizes government applications for wiretaps and searches targeting "agents of foreign powers." The catch: These proceedings are done *ex parte*—targets have no clue and no representation—so the opportunity for abuse remains high. Compounding this, while the existence of FISC was technically public knowledge, its operations, proceedings, and decisions were secret for decades.[7]

Instead of obligating the government to show probable cause of a crime, which is the requirement for the vast majority of criminal warrants, FISC judges looked for probable cause that the target was tied to a foreign government or terrorist group. This distinction gave U.S. intelligence room to maneuver when surveilling—all they had to do was present evidence that an individual could be tied to a foreign government, and they were good to go.[8]

Many of the practical limits imposed after the Church Committee began to erode in 1981, when President Ronald Reagan signed *Executive Order 12333*. Although it didn't make a large splash at the time, it gave the NSA, CIA, and FBI a legal document to protect themselves from some of the restrictions that emerged from the Church Committee findings, while still providing oversight and limitations. Government agencies invoked *EO 12333* to justify conducting warrantless bulk data collection abroad. This surveillance often included the communications of Americans by accident—if an agency was collecting data on foreign agents, it

---

[7] https://www.congress.gov/110/plaws/publ261/PLAW-110publ261.pdf
[8] https://www.congress.gov/crs-product/IF11451

was likely that at some point those foreign agents would inter-act with an American citizen. FISA remained the gatekeeper for foreign surveillance domestically, but *EO 12333* allowed the intelligence community to bypass traditional oversight overseas, running operations with less friction and very little court involve-ment. *EO 12333* is the authority behind U.S. Internet surveillance and monitoring today.[9]

"Fatally Flawed"

This leads us to the day that many things changed in the American psyche. On the morning of September 11, 2001, nineteen ter-rorists from the Islamist extremist group al-Qaeda hijacked four commercial airplanes in a coordinated terrorist attack against the United States.

What came to be known as 9/11 was a moment that redefined American politics, culture, and foreign policy. In the immediate aftermath, President George W. Bush declared a global War on Terror, and U.S. forces invaded Afghanistan to dismantle Al-Qaeda and overthrow the Taliban regime that harbored them. This marked the beginning of a new era of counterterrorism strategy character-ized by preemptive military action and expanded intelligence oper-ations worldwide.[10]

It also led to significant changes in the homeland. After the attacks, Bush authorized a series of secret intelligence activities known as the *President's Surveillance Program (PSP)*. Under this pro-gram, the NSA began secretly surveilling Americans' and foreign-ers' communications metadata—things like call records, emails, and Internet browsing histories. The NSA surveilled individuals affiliated with known terrorist groups as well as anyone associ-ated with those people. To do so, the NSA had to find "reasonable grounds to believe" that at least one person in the communication chain was a member of an "affiliated terrorist organization," which gave them the power to target U.S. persons or other individuals

---

[9]https://www.archives.gov/federal-register/codification/executive-order/12333.html
[10]https://9-11commission.gov/report

who weren't terrorists. This warrantless surveillance program was directly at odds with FISA because of its inevitable surveillance of U.S. citizens.[11]

The legal justification at the time was grounded in a broad interpretation of the president's inherent constitutional authority as commander-in-chief, an argument advanced by the Justice Department's Office of Legal Counsel. This legal theory claimed that in a time of national emergency, the president could bypass statutory restrictions like FISA to protect the country. The practice continued for years, until 2003, when Jack Goldsmith took over as the head of the Office of Legal Counsel. He concluded that collecting Internet metadata in bulk from American citizens was legally unsound, given the focus on domestic surveillance.[12]

This caused a stir in the Bush administration. James Comey, then Deputy Attorney General, agreed it was unsound, whereas the White House counsel, David Addington, disagreed. When debating, Comey said that the legal justification was "flawed—in fact, fatally flawed. No lawyer reading that could reasonably rely on it."

Addington responded, "Well, I'm a lawyer and I did."

In reply, Comey said, "No *good* lawyer."[13]

The debate continued until days before a new authorization was required in 2004, when Attorney General John Ashcroft's Justice Department decided that parts of the PSP were illegal and should not be authorized. Unfortunately, Ashcroft fell ill the next day with acute pancreatitis. In an absolutely absurd decision, Bush sent two aides to the hospital to try to convince Ashcroft, who was in critical condition, to sign a document that would authorize it. They failed.[14] Robert Mueller, then Director of the FBI, visited the hospital shortly after the aides left; his notes said that Ashcroft was feeble and barely articulate.[15]

---

[11] https://oig.justice.gov/reports/report-presidents-surveillance-program-unclassified-prepared-offices-inspectors-general
[12] Ibid.
[13] www.politico.com/magazine/story/2017/05/18/james-comey-trump-special-prosecutor-robert-mueller-fbi-215154
[14] https://www.cato.org/blog/what-ashcroft-hospital-showdown-was-about
[15] https://www.nytimes.com/2007/08/17/washington/17inquire.html

The next day, Bush signed a new authorization for the PSP despite the Justice Department's decision. In protest, Mueller shut down the FBI's part in it and wrote a letter to the president stating that he would resign if the FBI were forced to continue to participate in the program. Comey was also prepared to resign.[16] In capitulation, Bush modified parts of the PSP to remove provisions that the DOJ stated were not legally supported, although the program did not officially end until 2007. It wasn't until 2005, in an exposé by *The New York Times*, that the world learned about the *President's Surveillance Program* and the surveillance measures that were part of it.[17]

Just 45 days after 9/11, Congress fast-tracked and passed the *Uniting and Strengthening America by Providing Appropriate Tools Required to Intercept and Obstruct Terrorism Act*, or USA PATRIOT Act. Only one U.S. Senator, Russ Feingold, voted against the legislation in defense of civil liberties.[18] The House votes were more split. The USA PATRIOT Act granted legislative authorization for broad surveillance capabilities, rather than leaving it to executive authority, like the PSP.[19]

The act was a smorgasbord of new surveillance measures. It updated wiretap laws, introducing roving wiretaps. Instead of having to name a specific phone or computer to be tapped in the warrant, law enforcement could monitor people across different communications devices without having to specify precisely which device. The act made it easier to legally monitor electronic communications, including voicemail and emails. It enabled law enforcement, like the FBI and the CIA, to more easily share information about criminal investigations and national security concerns, which previously had a clearer separation. That information sharing allowed authorities to turn over evidence from terrorist cases to a different authority for a criminal case, or vice versa.[20]

---

[16] https://www.brookings.edu/articles/james-comeys-damning-testimony
[17] https://www.nytimes.com/2005/12/16/politics/bush-lets-us-spy-on-callers-without-courts.html
[18] https://ballotpedia.org/Fact_check/Was_Russ_Feingold_the_lone_U.S._Senate_opponent_of_the_US._Patriot_Act
[19] https://www.congress.gov/107/plaws/publ56/PLAW-107publ56.pdf
[20] Ibid.

The act introduced "Sneak and Peek" warrants, which allowed law enforcement to delay notification of a search warrant so they could search a property *before* notifying the owners. They could now collect records and physical items that they deemed relevant to national security investigations without immediately notifying the owner; the act also allowed these requests to be delivered with gag orders, so record holders couldn't disclose that it had happened. The NSA used it for bulk collection of telephony metadata, like phone numbers, call durations, dates and times, and sometimes location information.[21]

For a while, many of these changes flew under the public radar. But when the extent to which the U.S. government was surveilling individuals did come to light, it rocked the country and the world.

No Place to Hide

In June 2013, Glenn Greenwald published an explosive article in *The Guardian* titled "NSA collecting phone records of millions of Verizon customers daily."[22] This was a *shocking* headline on its own, but it was just the tip of the iceberg.

This article kicked off the Snowden disclosures, when Edward Snowden—a then-29-year-old NSA contractor working for Booz Allen Hamilton—went public with details of U.S. government surveillance of American citizens. All in all, Snowden took more than 1.5 million classified documents from the NSA.[23]

The day after Greenwald's article, new disclosures came; the NSA had access to systems at Google, Facebook, Apple, and other large tech companies through a program called PRISM. The documents alleged that the NSA collected data directly from these providers' servers with their support. Many senior technology executives insisted that they neither supported nor were aware of a program like this.[24]

---

[21] https://www.congress.gov/107/plaws/publ56/PLAW-107publ56.pdf
[22] https://www.theguardian.com/world/2013/jun/06/nsa-phone-records-verizon-court-order
[23] https://intelligence.house.gov/uploadedfiles/hpsci_snowden_review_declassified.pdf
[24] www.theguardian.com/world/2013/jun/06/us-tech-giants-nsa-data

PRISM used FISA Section 702 as a legal framework to conduct surveillance of non-U.S. persons abroad without individualized warrants for each target. The law allowed authorities to collect electronic communications from service providers—that includes emails, chats, videos, photos, file transfers, anything service providers were storing, really. This meant that when a foreign target communicates with someone in the United States, both parts of the conversation are collected. While the NSA was not legally allowed to target U.S. citizens or people inside the United States without a warrant, given the global nature of communication on the Internet, they collected information on U.S. citizens anyway. While they may not have intended to, in practice, they collected information from many U.S. citizens through this process, given the law's broad scope.[25]

Just days later, Snowden revealed himself as the whistleblower.[26] Snowden worked at the CIA with top secret clearance from 2006 to 2009, and claims that during that time, he grew disillusioned with the U.S. government. His supervisor wrote a derogatory report in his file, which noted that his work patterns had changed and that they suspected he was trying to access classified files he wasn't authorized to access. After his time at the CIA, he started working as an NSA contractor through Dell.[27] He got a new role at Booz Allen Hamilton in March 2013, which he said he got solely so he could steal additional evidence.[28]

Additional disclosures included XKeyscore, a search to give NSA staff access to databases with emails, chats, browsing histories, and other information of millions of individuals, and MUSCULAR, a program that harvested data from companies like Yahoo! and Google overseas.[29] MUSCULAR directly targeted fiber-optic cables

---

[25] https://www.nytimes.com/2013/06/07/us/nsa-verizon-calls.html
[26] www.theguardian.com/world/2013/jun/09/edward-snowden-nsa-whistleblower-surveillance
[27] www.nbcnews.com/feature/edward-snowden-interview/edward-snowden-timeline-n114871
[28] www.scmp.com/news/hong-kong/article/1268209/snowden-sought-booz-allen-job-gather-evidence-nsa-surveillance
[29] www.washingtonpost.com/world/national-security/nsa-infiltrates-links-to-yahoo-google-data-centers-worldwide-snowden-documents-say/2013/10/30/e51d661e-4166-11e3-8b74-d89d714ca4dd_story.html

used to transmit data to and from data centers. It stole the metadata and contents of communications, including text, video, and audio, transferring it all to NSA servers en masse.

NSA employees spied on many people. They stole data, such as chat and financial information, from gamers in World of Warcraft and Second Life in case criminals were using the games to communicate their plans.[30] They spied on Tor users. In a more salacious example of government tool misuse, employees would spy on their romantic interests, a phenomenon so common that they nicknamed it LOVEINT.[31]

The U.S. military and intelligence services use a standard pattern of abbreviations. For example, signals intelligence becomes SIGINT, human intelligence becomes HUMINT, etc. LOVEINT is internal NSA slang for spying on romantic partners.

The leaks also revealed more details than had been disclosed previously about a program developed in the late 1970s, the Special Collection Service, codenamed F6. F6 was established as a joint operation between the NSA and CIA headquartered in Maryland, though it places operatives around the world, often near U.S. embassies. It is the intersection of CIA covert action capabilities and NSA intelligence capabilities, whereby agents are tasked with deploying covert listening devices that the NSA can then use for intelligence purposes. To date, it hires mostly foreign agents who are physically on location in these regions to enhance espionage efforts with physical hardware. They spied on UN programs like UNICEF and Médecins du Monde, along with allies like then German Chancellor Angela Merkel and then-Israeli Prime Minister Ehud Olmert.[32]

---

[30] www.propublica.org/article/world-of-spycraft-intelligence-agencies-spied-in-online-games

[31] www.washingtonpost.com/news/the-switch/wp/2013/12/31/heres-what-we-learned-about-the-nsas-spying-programs-in-2013

[32] www.theguardian.com/uk-news/2013/dec/20/gchq-targeted-aid-agencies-german-government-eu-commissioner

These are just some of the details found in the Snowden leaks. But here's the kicker: Section 702 of FISA, the section that gave the NSA some of the powers to do this, is still in force. American citizens' data can still be collected "incidentally" when collecting data on foreign targets. The data that's collected can still be used against Americans in criminal cases for serious crimes.[33]

The FBI can still compel companies to turn over communications or data on specific individuals and impose secrecy orders. The gag orders following the notice must be periodically reviewed at around 3 years, but can be extended if the FBI wants it to.[34]

On the plus side, the NSA now has annual improved oversight: Annual reviews, yearly reporting to Congress, and rigorous audits.[35]

Sovereignty Strikes Back

The most significant change coming out of the leaks was the *USA Freedom Act*. The law, passed in 2015, re-upped a modified version of the USA PATRIOT Act. It prohibited bulk telephone metadata collection. The NSA can still collect metadata on specific targets, just not a broad swath of data in bulk. Instead of collecting and storing the data itself, the NSA has to access the data stored by telephone companies. To get that data, the NSA has to get a search warrant from the FISA court. Personal data of U.S. and non-U.S. citizens can only be kept for five years, unless it is considered a national security concern.[36]

The law introduced some oversight: The government must disclose to Congress details on the number of orders it sought and how many people were targeted and affected annually. Tech companies are able to report on how many times and what types of orders they receive from the government on an annual or semi-annual basis. This is not just a handful of requests. The requests have picked up precipitously: In 2011, Google reported over 12,000 requests

[33] https://www.intel.gov/assets/documents/702-documents/FISA_Section_702_Booklet.pdf
[34] https://www.eff.org/wp/the-failed-fix-to-NSL-gag-orders
[35] https://www.dni.gov/files/documents/0421/702%20Unclassified%20Document.pdf
[36] www.pbs.org/wgbh/frontline/article/how-the-nsa-spying-programs-have-changed-since-snowden

for disclosure of user information across over 23,000 accounts by the U.S. government. In 2024, the U.S. government submitted over 118,000 requests for disclosure of user information across over 224,000 accounts.[37]

In what's called the "Snowden Effect," the U.S. global brand was tarnished by the leaks. U.S. cloud providers were estimated to lose up to $35 billion over 3 years due to lost business from other countries.[38] Companies like Google immediately accelerated their adoption of stronger, end-to-end encryption.[39]

Countries introduced or sped up requirements for data localization and sovereign cloud offerings from cloud providers and software-as-a-service (SaaS) vendors, aiming to shield their data from foreign intelligence services.[40] The introduction of data localization and sovereign cloud offerings directly hampers U.S. efforts to maintain an open Internet, as it disjoints the Internet along regional borders. *The European Union's General Data Protection Regulation (GDPR)* was also shaped and accelerated by the leaks as the EU grappled with how to protect citizens' data.[41]

The situation is tricky—on the one hand, espionage is fundamental to preparedness and diplomacy in a geopolitical context. On the other hand, protecting American citizens' data should be paramount. This is one of the challenging balancing acts American intelligence agencies have faced: How to protect Americans' data while still protecting national security.

---

[37] https://transparencyreport.google.com/user-data/overview?hl=en
[38] https://archive-yaleglobal.yale.edu/content/snowden-effect-threatens-us-tech-industrys-global-ambitions
[39] https://jolt.law.harvard.edu/digest/google-encrypts-its-network-to-counteract-nsa-surveillance
[40] https://academic.oup.com/ijlit/article-abstract/25/3/213/3960261?redirectedFrom=fulltext
[41] https://cyberdefensereview.army.mil/Portals/6/Documents/CDR%20Journal%20Articles/Fall%202019/CDR%20V4N2-Fall%202019_COYNE.pdf?ver=2019-11-15-104104-157

Chapter 12
The Hacker Ethic

My hacking activity actually was a quest for knowledge, the intellectual challenge, the thrill and the escape from reality.
— *Kevin Mitnick, March 2000*[1]

T he culture of hacking started in 1943 at MIT, when they constructed an unassuming, temporary plywood building known as Building 20. Building 20 was meant to serve as a temporary Radiation Laboratory during World War II to support war efforts, specifically to develop radar. It was intended to last no more than 6 months after the war.[2]

In spite of that, it evolved from its original purpose, and the building stood for many years as an icon at MIT. It lasted until 1998 as MIT's Magical Incubator and housed many groups that created ground-breaking developments. One of those groups was the Tech Model Railroad Club (TMRC), which found its home in Building 20 in 1946. One group within TMRC, the Signals and Power (S&P) Subcommittee, was responsible for designing train circuits. It was here that the term "hacking" was created, as S&P members would tinker with electronic

---

[1] Mitnick, K. (2000, March). Testimony of Kevin Mitnick Congressional hearing. U.S. Senate Committee hearing on computer crime and cybersecurity.
[2] https://www.blackhistory.mit.edu/archive/building-20-time-capsule-1999

and mechanical devices. At the time, hacking was very different than what we associate it with today—it was not a criminal activity, but a curious one. "Hacking" was to tinker with technology, explore what it could do, and push systems beyond their intended design.[3]

This group expanded its activities to programming as computers became more mainstream, but not without challenges. There was one IBM 704 on campus, and access was heavily restricted—so S&P broke in to use it and understand how it worked.[4]

The computing culture that emerged at MIT during the 1960s crystallized into a distinct philosophy, as documented by journalist Steven Levy in 1984 in his book *Hackers: Heroes of the Computer Revolution*. Levy articulated what became known as the "hacker ethic"—a set of principles that guided the early computing pioneers and that continues to influence technology culture today. The core tenets of the Hacker Ethic are unlimited access to computers, freedom of information, and the promotion of decentralization.[5]

One early embodiment of the hacker ethic was the Incompatible Timesharing System (ITS), an early time-sharing operating system developed by the MIT Artificial Intelligence Laboratory in the late 1960s. It was designed for openness, interactivity, and sharing of ideas. Timesharing systems enable multiple users to access a single computer simultaneously. Previous batch-based systems relied on users submitting "jobs" to be run, with the results returned to them at a later date. Unlike most other operating systems of the time, ITS initially had no passwords and no login requirement, enabling remote guest access via the early ARPANET. The ITS was developed to be collaborative, allowing for maximum access to user files—not the best from a security standpoint. The first versions of Emacs, MACLISP, and CLU were created on an ITS system.[6]

While hacker culture has a very different message and goal than cybercriminals, its foundations align with those of many early American hackers. Early American hackers, in the cyber sense of the term, were curious and wanted to take that curiosity and explore what it meant for computers.

---

[3]https://tmrc.mit.edu/old/history/index.html
[4]www.wired.com/2014/11/the-tech-model-railroad-club
[5] Steven Levy, Hackers: Heroes of the Computer Revolution (Anchor Press/Doubleday, 1984).
[6]https://gunkies.org/wiki/Incompatible_Timesharing_System

The Rise of the 414s

In the 1980s, IBM sponsored computer and technology programs for high school students to get them interested in computing.[7] One of the students who participated in these programs was Tim Winslow, a teen in Milwaukee. During the program, he bonded with five other teens to form a group that called themselves the 414s, after the Milwaukee telephone area code.[8]

They used their home computers to find and play computer games. After reading computer manuals, they would explore ways to break into other machines by using the default usernames and passwords they found in those manuals. However, things escalated quickly. In 1983, they broke into computers at Security Pacific National Bank. Then, they broke into computers at Los Alamos National Laboratory. Despite targeting a large financial institution and a government facility working on nuclear weapons development, they didn't get caught . . . until they broke into Memorial Sloan Kettering Cancer Center and caused $1,500 worth of damage, as they deleted billing records to hide their activity. The center alerted the FBI to a potential breach of its systems, and the FBI immediately began investigating the incident.[9]

The FBI tracked the teens down and arrested them after installing data capture devices on their telephone lines to track their communications and collect evidence. At the time, the ages of the group members ranged from 17 to 21 years old. Two of the adults were charged with a misdemeanor for making harassing telephone calls, while the minor, Neal Patrick, was not prosecuted (though he did go on the media circuit to talk about what the group did).[10]

The World's Most Wanted Hacker

The World's Most Wanted Hacker also came up out of this time: Kevin Mitnick. Although first charged in 1981 as a 17-year-old for

---

[7]https://www.ibm.com/history/importance-of-education
[8]https://edition.cnn.com/2015/03/11/tech/computer-hacker-essay-414s
[9]www.taylorfrancis.com/chapters/mono/10.1201/9781315155852-3/414s-bruce-middleton
[10]www.discovermagazine.com/the-story-of-the-414s-the-milwaukee-teenagers-who-became-hacking-pioneers-41882

stealing computer manuals from Pacific Bell, his activities over the next two decades became much more prolific.[11]

In 1988, he was sentenced to a year in prison and 3 years of supervised release for breaking into the computers of the Digital Equipment Corporation and copying their software. He continued throughout the 1990s, breaking into machines from companies like Sun Microsystems and Motorola. He was especially effective at social engineering, pretending to be an employee at a company so he could get legitimate usernames and passwords to log in.

In 1995, he was charged again following a two-year manhunt. The government accused him of breaking into and damaging systems, causing millions in damages to Novell, Nokia, Sun Microsystems, and Motorola, estimated at $300 million.[12] The losses were not reported to the IRS or shareholders, and the prosecutors presented limited evidence, raising doubts about its legitimacy. However, after his arrest, investigators found 20,000 credit card numbers copied from Netcom on his computer, which gave them the evidence they needed.[13]

His incarceration started a massive underground movement, with protestors outside of the prison holding banners that read, "Free Kevin." Other supporters defaced websites with the same message.[14] Many of the stories of what he was capable of were vastly exaggerated, with prison officials concerned that he could start a nuclear war simply by whistling into a pay phone to emulate a modem, hack NORAD, and trigger a ballistic missile—impossible and ridiculous.[15]

He pleaded guilty to the charges after 4 years in custody and spent a total of 5 years in prison, 4 already served by the time the plea deal was agreed to, before being released. He was also banned from using any communications technology other than a landline for 2 years.[16] Mitnick became a well-respected cybersecurity

---

[11] Shimomura, Tsutomu, with John Markoff. *Takedown: The Pursuit and Capture of Kevin Mitnick, America's Most Wanted Computer Outlaw—by the Man Who Did It.* New York: Hyperion, 1996.
[12] www.ulm.edu/news/2016/104-worlds-most-famous-hacker-kevin-mitnick-to-speak-ulm-business-symposium.html
[13] www.wired.com/1999/05/how-much-damage-did-mitnick-do
[14] https://cybernews.com/editorial/the-passing-of-kevin-mitnick
[15] www.nbcnews.com/tech/tech-news/pioneering-hacker-kevin-mitnick-felon-turned-security-guru-dead-59-rcna95401
[16] www.wired.com/2012/02/feb-15-1995-mitnick-arrested

consultant, renowned for his ability to understand how to attack systems and use that information to help businesses defend themselves more effectively. He passed away in 2023.

The Day the Internet Stalled

In 1988, a tenth of the computers connected to the Internet worldwide stopped working for over 24 hours. That's 6,000 computers out of the 60,000 on the Internet at the time. A worm had spread from computer to computer, affecting organizations like Harvard, Princeton, and NASA. Military and university functions were slowed, and emails were delayed for days. Some companies opted to wipe their systems entirely to remove the worm and start fresh.[17]

It turns out that the entire incident was caused by one man, a PhD student at Cornell named Robert Tappan Morris. Morris created the worm just to see if it was possible. He released it from an MIT computer to avoid it being traced back to him at Cornell. The worm wasn't intended to slow down computers—it was designed to spread from computer to computer and showcase the weaknesses in networks at the time. The reason it slowed down machines to such an extent was because he programmed the worm to copy itself 14 percent of the time regardless of whether it was already running on the target machine. As an unintended side effect, a target machine could be infected multiple times, which caused the machines that were reinfected to slow down to the point where they were unusable. It served as a form of denial-of-service attack, albeit unintentionally.[18]

He originally programmed the worm to check if it had already infected the computer before installing itself, but ended up removing the feature, as it slowed the system down and he didn't want to be detected by an administrator.[19]

Morris was reportedly distraught by the damage the worm caused, and told two of his friends about it, asking them to issue a message across the Internet on how to stop the worm and remove it. One of his friends called the *New York Times* anonymously to

---

[17] https://www.doncio.navy.mil/CHIPS/ArticleDetails.aspx?ID=10969
[18] https://ntrs.nasa.gov/api/citations/19900014594/downloads/19900014594.pdf
[19] https://st.llnl.gov/news/look-back/1988-morris-worm-internets-first-cyberattack

report on it, leading to the first-ever explicit mention of the term "The Internet" in *The New York Times*.[20]

After the incident, the FBI launched an investigation into Morris. He was the first individual to be charged under *the Computer Fraud and Abuse Act in 1989*, just 3 years after it was enacted. While Morris avoided jail time, he did receive a fine, probation, and was required to do 400 hours of community service.[21]

In the aftermath of the attack, DARPA directed the creation of the nation's first computer emergency response team at Carnegie Mellon University in Pittsburgh. Carnegie Mellon's Software Engineering Institute operates CERT/CC, which was established to be staffed around the clock to respond to computer incidents, to provide a forum for discussing and communicating prevention measures, and to manage coordination and awareness. Over the years, its goals shifted toward awareness and research when the DHS took over national CERT efforts.[22]

The Western Bias

It's very difficult to know exactly when the U.S government started leveraging offensive cyber operations. Unlike many nation-state actors, such as Iran, Russia, or China, malware is rarely attributed to the United States, and the U.S. is even more rarely classified as a threat actor. There are a few reasons for this.

First, there's an extremely Western-centric view of the world when it comes to threat research. The majority of security researchers are from Western nations, especially the US, Israel, and the United Kingdom. Nations like China and Russia have researchers, but it is difficult to determine if these groups are independent or under the direction of the state, and whether they are disseminating accurate information or disinformation, often discrediting their analyses.

---

[20] www.nytimes.com/times-insider/2014/08/06/1988-the-internet-comes-down-with-a-virus
[21] https://www.nytimes.com/1990/01/23/us/computer-intruder-is-found-guilty.html
[22] https://cacm.acm.org/news/computer-security-who-you-gonna-call

Take, for example, in 2017, when WikiLeaks released Vault 7, the code name for a series of classified documents dating from 2013 to 2016 that detail the extensive cyber warfare and electronic surveillance capabilities of the CIA. This was a massive leak. It exposed critical CIA tools like the Marble framework, which was designed to make sure malware could not be attributed back to the CIA. It allowed malware authors to make it appear as though they had set their spoken language to Chinese, Russian, Korean, or other languages to avoid attribution to a Western nation. Another tool, Weeping Angel (which was named after an alien in *Doctor Who*), directed smart TVs to record video and audio, even when they appeared off. These are just two of many tools uncovered in the leak.[23]

It was a major look into an otherwise highly secretive and tight-knit operation, and one that Beijing-based cybersecurity firm Qihoo 360 used to attempt to attribute a cyberespionage campaign in China to the CIA in 2020. They codenamed the group APT-C-39, stating it had attacked targets in China since 2011, especially critical information systems, scientific research, and government agencies. They compared the CIA tools leaked in Vault 7 to attacks observed in the wild in China. The report speculated that the CIA may have acquired highly classified business and government data, including real-time flight tracking and passenger information.[24]

This was a major departure for the Chinese—though they had spent years accusing the United States of being hypocritical and targeting them with cyberattacks, this particular instance was notable because of just how much detail it went into about the techniques and capabilities it suspected the CIA had, largely based on Vault 7.

Following the publication of the report, the Chinese Foreign Ministry demanded a clear explanation. The China Institute of International Studies wrote an article titled "Qihoo 360's report exposes U.S. hypocrisy in cybersecurity." China's Foreign Ministry denounced the United States as a "hacker empire"—the Chinese translation for "The Matrix."[25]

[23] https://wikileaks.org/ciav7p1
[24] https://blog.360totalsecurity.com/en/the-cia-hacking-group-apt-c-39-conducts-cyber-espionage-operation-on-chinas-critical-industries-for-11-years
[25] www.ciis.org.cn/english/ESEARCHPROJECTS/Commentaries1/202007/t20 200715_3245.html

The wider cybersecurity community, including independent researchers, did not have enough evidence to validate Qihoo's claims. This is part of what makes identifying Western threat actor groups so challenging; much of the proof required to do attribution is not shared by Chinese companies with Western companies. Western companies are also reticent to attribute cyber activity to their home countries, like the United States. And, of course, information coming out of China is notoriously manipulated and crafted to fit the party line. When information becomes unreliable, it's difficult to trust that attribution is done in good faith.

Masters of Shadows

One of the other factors that makes it difficult to find attacks perpetrated by the United States is that it is known to have extremely high levels of operational security. *Operational security* is the process of analyzing critical information to determine how adversaries could find or exploit it, and applying countermeasures to prevent its disclosure. It's about controlling indicators of sensitive activities so your enemies won't know it's you. Cyberattackers will avoid using the same servers, IP addresses, or domain names, or they will work at unusual hours and on holidays or weekends, as only running cyber operations 9–5 on weekdays can help researchers pinpoint your location based on your time zone. Some malware writers will write malware differently each time so that researchers cannot identify a signature technique.

Much of the tradecraft of the U.S. government, especially the NSA and a specialized team within the NSA known as the Office of Tailored Access Operations (TAO) is extremely sophisticated. TAO relies heavily on creating its own zero-day exploits, which are new ways to break into systems. They continually develop new malware and techniques to breach systems more effectively while maintaining anonymity and evading detection.

Take, for example, one of the more recent times China accused the United States of breaking into its systems. In 2022, China accused the United States—specifically the NSA—of breaking into China's Northwestern Polytechnical University (NWPU), a very prominent university for military and aerospace research. Qihoo 360 and China's National Computer Virus Emergency Response Center (CVERC) claimed that TAO targeted the university with phishing emails to staff and students. Once they got access, the attackers leveraged 40 different strains of malware and zero-day vulnerabilities—including NOPEN and SECONDDATE, two forms of malware linked to the NSA from 10 years prior. With that access, they stole critical research data.[26]

Qihoo 360 tied four things to the attackers: First, nearly all attacks occurred during business hours in the United States, with no activity on holidays or weekends; second, the attackers were using an American English keyboard setting; third, there was a misconfigured script with directory paths linked to TAO's tools. Fourth, IP addresses involved in the incident were associated with companies like "Jackson Smith Consultants" and "Mueller Diversified Systems."[27]

There are a few problems with these being used to tie the attack to the NSA. The IP address naming, the times when the attacks were conducted, and the misconfigured script are all sloppy and signal poor operational security practices. This would be highly unusual for the NSA, which is meticulous. But the bigger problem is the TAO tools—while these tools were used by the NSA, they were made publicly available a decade prior to the attack. TAO would not use burned tools again, but other attackers could use them to hide their own attribution.

While the attack could very well have been perpetrated by the NSA, the evidence provided isn't substantial enough to make that claim. All that said, China's response and attribution served a specific purpose. Both nations have long accused each other of engaging in state-sponsored cyber espionage to gain a technological and military edge, and China's response was a calculated move to counter the U.S. narrative that portrays China as the primary aggressor. By presenting what it claimed was a clear and

---

[26] https://jm.china-embassy.gov.cn/eng/zgxw/202209/t20220906_10762573.htm
[27] https://www.securityweek.com/how-china-pinned-university-cyberattacks-on-nsa-hackers

complete chain of evidence, the CCP sought to expose alleged U.S. cyber operations on a global stage. Foreign ministry spokesperson Mao Ning stated that the actions "seriously endanger China's national security."[28]

For all the effort U.S. intelligence agencies poured into keeping its attacks hidden, the United States has not always stayed in the dark. In a handful of operations, the cloak slipped—and the world got a rare look at how U.S. cyber power actually works.

---

[28] https://www.cbsnews.com/news/china-accuses-us-nsa-cyberattack-spying-northwestern-polytechnical-university-military-research

Chapter 13
Crypto War

There is a trade-off between individual privacy and society's safety from crime . . . Our society needs to decide where to draw the line.
—*A U.S. government official, in reference to the Clipper chip*[1]

Since the 1970s, more than 120 countries have trusted a single company to create devices for encryption: The Swiss firm Crypto AG. Countries like Iran, India, Pakistan, and the Vatican were among the many that depended on its encryption technology. Governments entrusted their secrets to Crypto AG—yet little did they know, the company was run by American and West German intelligence: The CIA and the BND (*Bundesnachrichtendienst*).[2] The intelligence agencies used Crypto AG to spy during some of the most critical geopolitical incidents of the time. In Iran, the intelligence agencies listened in on communiques during the 1979 hostage crisis. In Egypt, they gathered intel from the communications of the Egyptian president during the 1978 peace negotiations with Israel. Forty percent of diplomatic cables and other

---

[1] https://www.nytimes.com/1993/04/16/us/electronics-plan-aims-to-balance-government-access-with-privacy.html
[2] https://www.washingtonpost.com/graphics/2020/world/national-security/cia-crypto-encryption-machines-espionage

transmissions by foreign governments went through Crypto AG devices in the 1980s. Yet no one would learn the truth until 2020.[3]

It all started with Boris Hagelin, a Russian inventor who fled to Sweden during the Russian Revolution. He created encryption that was difficult to break, even for the U.S. government. The U.S. government called it the "Hagelin problem"—they worried that, if Hagelin could create more secure technology, they wouldn't be able to crack it. The CIA made a deal with Hagelin. If he restricted sales of his most advanced encryption equipment to those approved by the United States and provided other countries with the less advanced models, the United States would compensate Hagelin for the lost sales. By 1960, Hagelin and the CIA had a licensing agreement under which the CIA would pay him $855,000, including $70,000 per year as a retainer, and $10,000 for marketing expenses to ensure that Crypto AG was the primary supplier to as many governments as possible.[4]

In the mid-1960s, the NSA saw an opportunity to take things a step further. Hagelin had to innovate to convert from mechanical manufacturing to electronic circuits, but lacked the knowledge to do so. The NSA took advantage of the moment, and by 1970, Crypto AG was releasing an all-electronic model designed by the NSA. It used a base system that, instead of a true random number generator, repeatedly generated the same output, allowing the NSA to crack it.[5]

By the late 1960s, Hagelin was 80 years old and preparing for the company's next phase. The CIA and the BND made a bid to surreptitiously buy his company. They succeeded, and for the next 20 years, they collaborated to maintain the business and plant easily breakable encryption in as many governments as possible. But there were points of friction; the CIA wanted to sell the easily crackable equipment to more than just their enemies, including NATO members like Spain and Greece. The BND didn't want to. They did anyway.[6] Thanks to bribes, smear campaigns, and the support of

---

[3] www.washingtonpost.com/graphics/2020/world/national-security/cia-crypto-encryption-machines-espionage

[4] https://www.cryptomuseum.com/people/hagelin/boris.htm

[5] https://www.nsa.gov/portals/75/documents/news-features/declassified-documents/friedman-documents/reports-research/FOLDER_110/41743639078284.pdf

[6] https://www.cryptomuseum.com/intel/cia/rubicon.htm

private industry, especially Siemens and Motorola, the intelligence agencies built an empire out of Crypto AG; sales increased from 15 million Swiss francs in 1970 to more than 51 million by 1975.[7]

At the same time, intelligence officials were concerned that those hired to work at Crypto AG—who were kept in the dark about their ties to intelligence officials—would begin to recognize something was amiss: The encryption standards weren't working as expected. One man was fired after flying to Syria to address complaints with the technology, as once he got there, he patched vulnerabilities, which caused U.S. intelligence to lose access to Syrian communications. In another case, the CEO was warned by U.S. officials not to hire Mengia Caflisch, an electrical engineer and radio-astronomy researcher. The officials cautioned that she was "too bright to remain unwitting." She was hired anyway and did in fact begin investigating vulnerabilities, just as the NSA feared.[8]

Many countries suspected that Crypto AG was selling them sub-par encryption equipment and that it might be associated with an intelligence organization. In one of the most notable instances, the Hydra crisis, Iranian authorities arrested a Crypto AG employee, Hans Buehler. Unfortunately for Buehler, he knew nothing about the intelligence agencies that owned Crypto AG. He wasn't released until 9 months later for $1 million, secretly provided by the BND. Buehler never trusted Crypto AG again after the incident, even appearing on Swiss television at one point in a report against the company. This signaled the beginning of the end for the program.[9]

In the 1990s, the BND was concerned about its exposure in Operation Rubicon, and because of this, reached an agreement where the CIA would buy out Germany. After that, the company's customer base dwindled over time, though Crypto AG continued until 2018, when the company's assets were split and sold. This served as the cover for the CIA to exit the business, though they were revealed in 2020 by a joint publication between *The Washington Post* and German public broadcaster *ZDF*.[10]

---

[7] www.washingtonpost.com/graphics/2020/world/national-security/cia-crypto-encryption-machines-espionage
[8] Ibid.
[9] https://www.bbc.com/news/world-europe-51487856
[10] www.washingtonpost.com/graphics/2020/world/national-security/cia-cryptoencryption-machines-espionage

The U.S. government's attempts to break encryption extend beyond external and foreign interests. They've also made efforts to reduce the encryption capabilities of U.S. enterprises.

Encryption as Arms Trafficking

The United States has had a difficult relationship with encryption for a long time. In 1954, the U.S. government restricted encryption technology as a "munition" under the United States Munitions List, a classification that now seems absurd. However, at the time, cryptography was almost exclusively used by the military. The United States wanted to protect its own cryptographic technologies from being leveraged or reverse-engineered by other governments during the Cold War.[11] This classification served as the basis for a legal battle that would target Philip Zimmermann.

In 1991, Zimmermann wrote a very popular program that encrypted Internet communications using public key cryptography. Known as Pretty Good Privacy (PGP), it provided privacy controls, particularly for securing email communications. However, despite the proliferation of the Internet, encryption technologies were subject to export controls because they were classified as munitions in the U.S.. When PGP was distributed outside the United States after foreigners downloaded it from the Internet, Zimmermann was investigated for violating federal arms export laws.[12] To combat this, in 1995, Phillip released a book published by the MIT Press that contained all the source code for PGP. Exporting the software was a felony comparable to arms trafficking; exporting a book with the same information is protected speech under the First Amendment. The investigation lasted three years before the U.S. government dropped the case in 1996, as a separate case held that computer code constitutes an expression of free speech protected by the First Amendment.[13]

---

[11] https://dspace.mit.edu/bitstream/handle/1721.1/28754/59822564-MIT.pdf?sequence=2&isAllowed=y
[12] http://www.usnews.com/usnews/news/articles/950403/archive_010975.htm
[13] https://jipel.law.nyu.edu/wp-content/uploads/2017/04/NYU_JIPEL_Vol-6-No_2_1_Baranetsky_PressClause.pdf

In another related instance in 1993, the NSA introduced the Clipper chip, an encryption device using the then-classified Skipjack algorithm, which the Clinton administration intended to use to replace the existing federal standard. The catch? It used key escrow, also known as key surrender, which required that the government be given a copy of the cryptographic key so that government agencies could decrypt communications on the device. The algorithm itself was developed by the NSA and was classified SECRET, so independent cryptographers couldn't review it. Once it was eventually released, multiple researchers found vulnerabilities that made it easier for attackers to break the encryption.[14]

The initial rollout of the Clipper chip focused on government devices but was expected to expand to commercial telephones and computers later. The Clinton White House, congressional committees, and the Department of Commerce debated whether or not it should be a government *and* private sector standard. An immense firestorm of public debate followed: Was installing the Clipper chip worth the loss of privacy, especially for private companies?[15]

This launched what is widely considered the first Crypto War, a fight against government-mandated backdoors. Many considered it a tool to violate free speech and to justify unreasonable searches and seizures. Privacy advocates and technologists, in particular, expressed concerns about the system. Groups such as the Electronic Frontier Foundation and the American Civil Liberties Union (ACLU) were among the strongest opponents of the Clipper chip, along with individuals such as Rush Limbaugh.[16]

Meanwhile, companies such as Apple and Microsoft raised concerns that adopting the chip would hinder innovation and put U.S. companies at a disadvantage in international markets. So-called cypherpunks—activists advocating for privacy and strong encryption—pushed hard against the Clipper chip. They gathered at the first annual Hackers on Planet Earth conference in 1994 and held a two-hour panel to debate the Clipper chip's technical capabilities and political ramifications.[17]

---

[14] www.wired.com/1994/06/nsa-clipper
[15] https://cs.stanford.edu/people/eroberts/courses/cs181/projects/1995-96/clipper-chip/history.html
[16] www.nytimes.com/1994/06/12/magazine/battle-of-the-clipper-chip.html
[17] https://hope.net/about.html

In 1996, the Clinton administration formally withdrew support for the Clipper chip. Legal challenges, fears that competing encryption standards would outperform American ones, and pressure from the tech sector prompted Clinton to sign an executive order transferring commercial encryption from the Munitions List to the Commerce Control List. The government still retained control over exports, but it simplified the rules and permitted higher-quality encryption software to be exported from the United States.[18]

The Second Battle of Bullrun

This brings us to the mid-2000s, when instead of personal computers, smartphones were taking the world by storm. The iPhone was officially released in June 2007. By January 2008, it accounted for 20 percent of the U.S. smartphone market, having sold 4 million units in six months.[19] It didn't take long for smartphones to have a ton of data on them that law enforcement agencies wanted. For example, in 2008, Apple assisted the Secret Service in investigating a child-exploitation case by bypassing the iPhone's login screen after a court order. Apple and Google were repeatedly asked to help access locked devices, typically during drug investigations. According to the ACLU, from 2008 to 2016, there were 63 confirmed cases in which the government asked Apple or Google to help it access a locked device, predominantly in drug cases.[20]

The tide began to turn against this practice in 2013, when the Snowden leaks revealed the NSA's efforts to weaken encryption both within and outside the United States. By September, it was made clear how far the NSA was willing to go to weaken encryption through Bullrun.[21]

Bullrun (stylized BULLRUN) is a classified operation built to evade, weaken, and control encryption so that the NSA can more easily access data.

---

[18] https://cs.stanford.edu/people/eroberts/cs181/projects/export-controls/references.html
[19] https://www.macworld.com/article/194150/iphone_2008.html
[20] www.npr.org/sections/alltechconsidered/2016/03/30/472391092/apple-google-ordered-to-unlock-smartphones-since-at-least-2008
[21] www.nytimes.com/2013/09/06/us/nsa-foils-much-internet-encryption.html?pagewanted=2&_r=1

The NSA helped build the standards issued by NIST and the International Organization for Standardization (ISO) that intentionally weakened encryption and made it easier for the NSA to break in. Given its status as a recognized expert in cryptography and its mandated role in securing federal communications, the NSA was able to influence these standards easily. Because of the *Federal Information Security Modernization Act (FISMA)*, the NSA is also obligated to coordinate with NIST when NIST develops federal cryptographic and information security standards.[22]

In its 2006 cryptography standards, NIST recommended the known insecure algorithm Dual Elliptic Curve Deterministic Random Bit Generator (Dual_EC_DRBG) in part because the NSA advocated for it. The algorithm makes session keys predictable, so the NSA could easily reverse-engineer it and break the encryption.[23]

The U.S. government coerced manufacturers to use the algorithm to introduce backdoors into their products for the NSA. In one instance, the NSA paid $10 million to security company RSA to use Dual_EC_DRBG as the default for one of its widely used products, BSAFE.[24]

In another instance, the U.S. government worked closely with Microsoft to get pre-encryption access to products like Outlook, Skype, and SkyDrive (Microsoft's cloud storage service at the time).[25]

Dual_EC_DRBG remained a standard until 2014, after the Snowden leak confirmed it was a deliberate strategy by the NSA to weaken encryption. Because of this, Apple and Google announced that they would introduce new privacy features to protect users. NIST also had to repair its reputation, overhauling its standards process to be more transparent and independent of NSA influence.[26]

---

[22] https://csrc.nist.gov/topics/laws-and-regulations/laws/FISMA

[23] https://www.wired.com/2013/09/nsa-backdoor

[24] https://www.eff.org/deeplinks/2014/01/after-nsa-backdoors-security-experts-leave-rsa-conference-they-can-trust

[25] https://www.theguardian.com/world/2013/jul/11/microsoft-nsa-collaboration-user-data

[26] https://www.nist.gov/news-events/news/2014/04/nist-removes-cryptography-algorithm-random-number-generator-recommendations

Blame the Technology, Not Us

Before 2014, Apple was known to assist law enforcement under court order in breaking into older devices and extracting data from them. However, they drew the line at building a backdoor into their systems. The boundaries were clear: If data wasn't protected by device-level encryption, law enforcement could access it. Apple was following the rules.

But after the Snowden leaks, Apple and Google decided to add encryption set by the user so that they couldn't unlock the phones and give access to others, including, and especially, governments. The law enforcement community in the United States was distraught.[27] Some, like the chief of detectives for Chicago's Police Department, said that Apple would become the phone of choice for pedophiles.[28]

That is a popular refrain from those in power to justify surveillance—it always comes back to "protecting the children." Law enforcement also argued that user-controlled encryption was unnecessary; the Supreme Court had recently held that police must obtain a search warrant before collecting data from a cell phone in most circumstances. However, Apple and Google continued to make clear that, once these encryption capabilities were in place, they would be unable to comply with subpoenas seeking information from customer devices, not because of their own refusal, but because of the technology itself.

All this came to a head in 2015, after the San Bernardino, California, terrorist attack. On December 2, 2015, a married couple, Syed Rizwan Farook and Tashfeen Malik, carried out a terrorist attack at Farook's work, the Inland Regional Center. They targeted a training event and a Christmas party, killing 14 people and injuring 22 others in a shooting. They also attempted a bombing, but the pipe bombs failed to go off. The couple fled the scene and were killed in a shootout after a police chase.[29]

---

[27] www.washingtonpost.com/opinions/compromise-needed-on-smartphone-encryption/2014/10/03/96680bf8-4a77-11e4-891d-713f052086a0_story.html
[28] www.theguardian.com/world/2014/feb/27/gchq-nsa-webcam-images-internet-yahoo
[29] https://portal.cops.usdoj.gov/resourcecenter/ric/Publications/cops-w0808-pub.pdf

After the incident, the FBI collected mobile phones from the scene of the crime and the shootout, including one iPhone 5C. The iPhone was owned by the county but issued to Farook for work purposes.

The FBI executed a search warrant, which authorized them to access the iPhone; however, its encryption capabilities and security features prevented them from accessing it. When the FBI requested Apple's assistance, Apple cooperated to the best of its ability but declined to create custom software to bypass encryption and security features. The DOJ filed a motion to compel assistance, pursuant to *the All Writs Act*. In the end, the FBI found a third-party solution and dropped the case, and Apple walked away without sanctions.[30]

Since this point, other tech companies that have built phones have implemented similar device-level security features, making it virtually impossible for them to support government intervention or break into a device without creating custom software. Device encryption is the barrier that enables them to deny the government. The companies intentionally set technical barriers to prevent forced compliance and breach of user trust.

No major U.S. tech company has built a universal unlocking tool for the government. Once full device encryption (FDE) became standard for both Apple and Google, the official policy everywhere became clear: If it's technically feasible under the law, basic account-level data can be provided, but device-level backdoors are out of bounds. Cases where law enforcement requests access almost always end with investigators finding other ways to access data—either through remote account access, device vulnerabilities, or specialized forensic hardware—rather than compelling the manufacturer to weaken its own security.

The government has continued to try to find ways around this. However, rather than the government attempting to compel Apple to yield, legislation was proposed in 2020. This legislation, *the Eliminating Abusive and Rampant Neglect of Interactive Technologies Act (EARN IT)* would amend Section 230 of Title 47, thereby making Internet platforms liable for user-generated content posted on their

---

[30] https://jolt.law.harvard.edu/digest/federal-court-orders-apple-to-unlock-iphone-apple-refuses

platforms. This would force platforms to monitor user behavior and content so that they could ensure it wasn't malicious or in violation of U.S. regulations.[31]

The big problem here is that the EARN IT Act would require tech companies to break their end-to-end encryption and monitor all messages from all users, destroying user privacy on the Internet. Companies would have to choose: Comply with EARN IT and make their products less secure, or leave the U.S. market.

The proposed legislation would have a massively detrimental effect on the privacy and the security of the Internet. If it became law, it would have ramifications for national security, as backdoors would be built into every piece of technology. Information would be easier to find, people would be easier to surveil, and privacy would be next to impossible to ensure.

Our Eyes Only

By the end of World War II, the United States had revealed itself to be a powerful ally to Great Britain, especially in its intelligence capabilities. The two worked closely after 1943 on decrypting communications between Axis powers, most notably the German Enigma cipher.

In 1946, Britain and the United States agreed to be transparent with each other and to share intelligence gathered from intercepted communications. Much of this was fueled by the Venona project, a counterintelligence program run by the United States that revealed the extent of the Soviet Union's intelligence gathering.[32]

Over the next decade, Canada, Australia, and New Zealand were added to the mix, forming a strategic global network of intelligence sharing across the most geopolitically important continents of the time, with a special focus on intelligence gathering on the Soviet Union.[33]

---

[31] https://www.congress.gov/bill/118th-congress/senate-bill/1207/text
[32] https://www.nsa.gov/Helpful-Links/NSA-FOIA/Declassification-Transparency-Initiatives/Historical-Releases/UKUSA
[33] https://natoassociation.ca/if-knowledge-is-power-then-shared-knowledge-is-lethal-the-story-of-the-five-eyes

This became a multilateral intelligence-sharing arrangement between Australia, Canada, New Zealand, the United Kingdom, and the United States. Its name, Five Eyes, comes from the security classification of shared intelligence documents: "SECRET – AUS/CAN/NZ/UK/US EYES ONLY," shortened to Five Eyes.

Over time, other nations became part of an extended intelligence network, which shares some intelligence, though not to the same level of confidentiality as the Five Eyes. France, the Netherlands, Denmark, and Norway are members of the Nine Eyes. The addition of Belgium, Germany, Italy, Sweden, and Spain makes up the Fourteen Eyes.[34]

No Place to Hide

Some of the documents leaked by Snowden revealed how the Five Eyes collaboration really works. There is deep cooperation among the Five Eyes in the collection and sharing of intelligence globally. In 1971, the Five Eyes created a global espionage apparatus called ECHELON to intercept electronic communications worldwide. STATEROOM is another program that collects international radio, telecommunications, and Internet traffic.[35]

The Five Eyes also treats one another as subcontracting partners. In cases where one country cannot collect data for legal reasons, another Five Eyes member can do so on its behalf. Take, for example, this comment from then-NSA Director Lt. General (now four-star General Ret.) Keith Alexander, where he suggests the UK's Government Communications Headquarters (GCHQ) Menwith Hill spying site surveil for the NSA: "Why can't we collect all the signals all the time? . . . Sounds like a good summer project for Menwith."[36]

---

[34] https://law.yale.edu/mfia/case-disclosed/newly-disclosed-documents-five-eyes-alliance-and-what-they-tell-us-about-intelligence-sharing
[35] https://www.ebsco.com/research-starters/law/echelon-uk-usa-agreement
[36] https://arstechnica.com/tech-policy/2016/09/snowden-leaks-collect-all-signals-surveillance-born-in-uk

In February 2014, Optic Nerve came to light. Optic Nerve is a program developed by GCHQ with assistance from the NSA, which can capture still images of Yahoo! webcam chats. They collected these images of anyone, not specific targets, in bulk and stored them on agency databases. In just six months, they collected images from 1.8 million Yahoo! users.[37]

Eyes Wide Shut

The Five Eyes gives its members a distinct global intelligence advantage through broad surveillance coverage, code-breaking expertise, and the deployment of listening posts worldwide. It also helps coordinate activities to disrupt cybercriminal networks or other nation-state infrastructure.

However, the partnership can be precarious, as the joint operations between West Germany and the United States with Crypto AG showed. Priorities must be aligned across countries for information to be shared in good faith. Enemies have to be aligned. If that starts to fall apart, so too does the alliance.

One recent example of this came in March 2025, when Defense Secretary Pete Hegseth ordered USCYBERCOM to cease offensive cyber and information operations against Russia. Intelligence allies immediately began considering scaling back intelligence sharing with the United States, as they were concerned about protecting foreign assets whose identities might be inadvertently disclosed.[38] Foreign intelligence assets are highly valuable; they must be cultivated over years, and their identities are kept as strict secrets to ensure their safety in enemy territory.

This isn't the only method the United States has to break into equipment, both foreign and domestic—sabotage also plays a central role.

---

[37] www.theguardian.com/world/2014/feb/27/gchq-nsa-webcam-images-internet-yahoo

[38] https://www.nbcnews.com/politics/national-security/trump-pivots-russia-allies-weigh-sharing-less-intel-us-rcna194420

Chapter 14
Sabotage by Design

Covert sabotage efforts are a favorite pastime of the U.S. government. It's a quiet, effective way to degrade enemies' capabilities.

In the 1970s and '80s, the Soviet Union was far behind Western innovation in computers. To catch up, it treated computer innovation as an exercise in KGB industrial espionage, stealing schematics, then building copies of the technology for itself.[1] In one instance, the Soviets cloned Digital Equipment Corp.'s DEC PDP-11/40 minicomputer, the computer that popularized Unix, the operating system that forms the basis for many operating system variants used in the modern era. The United States caught on to this copycat program, and the FBI launched Operation Intering to sabotage efforts to steal and copy American computing. Through a complex network of intermediaries in various countries, the FBI orchestrated the sabotage of microchips and computer processors so that they would only fail once deployed.[2] The FBI sold these parts through partners from Austria, London, and Zurich, among other places, and was able to stagnate Russian technology development through this strategy.

---

[1] Intersect, Vol. 8, No. 3 (2015) Chan, Fallen Behind.
[2] www.politico.com/news/magazine/2024/08/04/us-spies-soviet-technology-00164126

In the modern era, one of the most effective U.S. sabotage operations took place in Iran.

Operation Olympic Games

1987 marked the start of Iran's nuclear weapons ambitions when it acquired design plans for a P-1 centrifuge, used to enrich uranium.[3] Yet, its nuclear weapons plans weren't put under a global microscope until 2002, when an exiled Iranian opposition party revealed the location of two nuclear sites: Arak and Natanz.[4] In 2003, Britain, Germany, and France had begun negotiating with Iran over its nuclear policy; just a few months later, Iran suspended its nuclear enrichment program. By 2005, a pro-nuclear president was elected in Iran, who told the UN that Iran had the right to develop peaceful nuclear technology, and by 2006, Iran revealed it was once again enriching uranium. China, Russia, the United States, Britain, Germany, and France came together as the P5+1 group, with a "framework for an agreement" to stop Iran's uranium enrichment; Iran rejected the proposal. For the next four years, the UN, EU, and U.S. imposed sanctions against Iran.[5]

Diplomatic pressures and attempts to negotiate weren't working . . . Iran was building nuclear capabilities anyway. It's right around this time in 2006 that the United States and Israel started developing malware to sabotage Iran's nuclear capabilities through Operation Olympic Games. If diplomacy wasn't going to work, sabotage would.

Operation Olympic Games started with the NSA and CIA gathering as much intelligence as possible on the Natanz center and its infrastructure. The NSA collected reconnaissance on the infrastructure in the center, especially information like the centrifuges in use, which are fundamental to uranium enrichment. This reconnaissance would prove critical: The centrifuges became the ultimate target.[6]

U.S. intelligence officials and Israeli Unit 8200 worked together to develop malware to slowly sabotage and destroy the centrifuges.

---

[3]https://theworld.org/stories/2016/07/30/timeline-explains-long-bumpy-road-iran-nuclear-deal
[4]https://carnegieendowment.org/posts/2012/12/the-international-atomic-energy-agencys-decision-to-find-iran-in-non-compliance-2002-2006?lang=en
[5]https://2001-2009.state.gov/r/pa/prs/ps/2008/jun/105992.htm
[6]https://www.congress.gov/crs_external_products/R/PDF/R41524/R41524.3.pdf

Throughout their work, they performed extensive testing, going so far as to build a replica of the Natanz facility in the Israeli desert with P-1 centrifuges from Libya's discontinued nuclear program.

By 2009, the malware, known as Stuxnet, was so effective that they pushed forward to the next stage: Deploying it. This was the tough part. It wasn't like the NSA or Israeli Mossad could just stroll into Natanz and deploy it. The Iranians also didn't enable many Internet connections from within Natanz. Instead, the US and Israel used a Dutch engineer recruited by the Dutch intelligence service to deploy the malware. Though the Dutch were not aware of the full operation, Erik van Sabben was tasked with getting the malware deployed.[7] He went to Iran often and was married to an Iranian, which made for the perfect cover. To get the malware in place, he got a job installing a water pump in the Natanz facility. The water pump had Stuxnet on it, which spread to other machines once it was connected to the network infrastructure in the facility. Van Sabben left Iran immediately after installing the pump but was killed in a motorcycle accident two weeks later.[8]

Multiple variants of the malware were deployed over time—at least one was deployed through a USB drive. It's unknown exactly how the USB drive got into the facility, but it's likely it was introduced through a spy or an unsuspecting victim. Once the USB drive was plugged into a machine on site, it operated as a worm, replicating from one target machine to another, looking for Siemens Step 7 software on computers managing a programmable logic controller. It was designed to hide its files and processes so that it could not be easily detected.[9]

Once Stuxnet found the right targets, it constantly repeated a sequence: Change the frequency of rotation of the centrifuge to slightly above safe speed for 15 minutes, then restore it to normal speed for 10 to 20 days, then slow below the safe speed for 50 minutes, then again return to the normal state for another 27 days.[10]

---

[7] www.securityweek.com/dutch-engineer-used-water-pump-to-get-billio-dollar-stuxnet-malware-into-iranian-nuclear-facility-report

[8] https://www.securityweek.com/dutch-engineer-used-water-pump-to-get-billion-dollar-stuxnet-malware-into-iranian-nuclear-facility-report

[9] Zetter, Kim. Countdown to Zero Day: Stuxnet and the Launch of the World's First Digital Weapon. New York: Crown, 2014.

[10] https://securityanddeence.pl/Operation-Olympic-Games-nCyber-sabotage-as-a-tool-of-American-nintelligence-aimed,121974,0,2.html

Constantly repeating this cycle degraded the centrifuges. It was initially reported to have destroyed around 1,000 centrifuges at Natanz, however, later reports stated it wiped out a fifth of Iran's centrifuge supply.[11,12]

The attack was never meant to be discovered, especially not outside of Natanz, but it was. The worm escaped the facility and started to spread to unintended victims around the world. In 2010, Belarusian security company VirusBlokAda identified it when a customer outside of Iran began experiencing random system reboots. Symantec found 14,000 unique IP addresses infected with the malware. Siemens and Microsoft confirmed that it was a worm targeting industrial control systems.

The United States chose to ramp up its attacks with Stuxnet, even after it was discovered.[13] Although the United States and Israel never directly confirmed that they perpetrated the attack, the geopolitical motivations, sophistication of the malware, reporting from *The New York Times* and others, and some tongue-in-cheek comments from U.S. officials all but confirmed it.[14]

[11] www.washingtonpost.com/wp-dyn/content/article/2011/02/15/AR20110
21505395.html
[12] www.nytimes.com/2011/01/16/world/middleeast/16stuxnet.html?pagewanted=all
[13] https://www.nytimes.com/2012/06/01/world/middleeast/obama-ordered-
waveof-cyberattacks-against-iran.html
[14] Ibid.

Chapter 15
Defend Forward

In November 2008, a flash drive was inserted into a laptop at a U.S. military base in the Middle East. Many tales have been shared about how this may have happened; one story claims someone found it in the parking lot and plugged it into a laptop out of curiosity. That remains in question, as there's no confirmation that it's the true origin story. Another theory is that an American soldier or contractor in Afghanistan used a thumb drive in an Internet cafe on an infected computer, picking up the malware by accident. Regardless of how the malware got access, it did, and once it did, it spread across U.S. computers globally through the U.S. Central Command network, which included devices in combat zones and at the Pentagon. The NSA was the first to detect the attack after spotting some of the infected machines attempting to communicate back to the attacker.

The attack was a worm that had spread incredibly quickly across the U.S. Central Command network, affecting both classified and unclassified systems.[1] It also infected the Joint Worldwide Intelligence Communications System, which is used to share top-secret information with U.S. officials globally.

---

[1] www.latimes.com/archives/la-xpm-2008-nov-28-na-cyberattack28-story.html

The worm became known as Agent BTZ.[2] It gave attackers access to incredibly important information about battlefield operations. It was never confirmed what data the worm collected from U.S. military devices; nevertheless, it represents a massive failure in U.S. military cyber defense and is one of the most significant breaches of U.S. military computer networks to date.

Because of the attack, the Pentagon took the unusual step of banning external flash drives on all DOD networks and government computers worldwide. This ban made information sharing during war especially challenging, as sharing combat plans and after-action reports, especially in theaters like the Middle East, is difficult to do securely without physical hardware.[3]

The worm remained in U.S. military networks for a long time—it took the DOD 14 months to remove it. The removal operation was called Operation Buckshot Yankee.[4]

Though initial speculation pointed to China as the perpetrator, intelligence experts strongly suspected Russia. It wasn't confirmed by the U.S. government publicly until 2016, when the FBI included the malware in a report on Russian intelligence services' capabilities.[5]

This attack led to the creation of the world's most consequential military command for cybersecurity: U.S. Cyber Command. In 2009, Defense Secretary Robert Gates consolidated Joint Task Force-Global Network Operations (responsible for DOD cyber defense) and the Network Warfare Unit (responsible for offensive cyber operations) into a single four-star command known as the U.S. Cyber Command (USCYBERCOM). It is responsible for defending the DOD from cyberattacks, supporting counterterrorism and military efforts, and working with partners in and out of the U.S. government, including private industry, to share threat intelligence and help coordinate defense.[6]

USCYBERCOM sits in a unique position. Not only does its commander also lead the NSA in a dual-hat capacity, but what's more, it oversees commands in each military branch (Army Forces Cyber

[2] https://docs.broadcom.com/doc/waterbug-attack-group
[3] https://www.brookings.edu/articles/insiders-doubt-2008-pentagon-hack-was-foreign-spy-attack
[4] www.wired.com/dangerroom/2010/08/insiders-doubt-2008-pentagon-hack-was-foreign-spy-attack
[5] Department of Homeland Security and Federal Bureau of Investigation, JAR-16-20296: GRIZZLY STEPPE – Russian Malicious Cyber Activity, December 29, 2016.
[6] https://www.cybercom.mil/About/History

Command, the U.S. Navy's Tenth Fleet, 16th Air Force, and Marine Corps Forces Cyberspace Command), providing a central operational authority for military cyber activities.[7] This coordination is critical – without it, joint operations can easily fall apart.

USCYBERCOM is also both an offensive and defensive organization, as offensive and defensive cyberattacks are uniquely intertwined. It may actively disrupt adversaries before an attack occurs, which is considered an offensive cyber capability but is done for defensive reasons. On the other hand, USCYBERCOM may be performing intelligence gathering, which is critical to a strong defense but often occurs during offensive operations.

For example, from an offensive standpoint, since at least 2012, the United States has performed reconnaissance on control systems in the Russian electric grid. USCYBERCOM has taken this even further, using that access to actually deploy malware. They deployed malware implants, which establish persistence, then can be used to surveil or attack at a later date. Such implants can be particularly useful in unexpected military incursions, as the attackers can activate an implant and gather reconnaissance information or, say, take the electric grid offline. However, it's risky business—the act of prepositioning can be considered its own form of escalation.[8]

> The original USCYBERCOM mission statement is cryptographically encoded into its insignia as an MD5 hash.[9]

There have been growing pains for USCYBERCOM, however. It initially reported to the U.S. Strategic Command (USSTRATCOM), a more strategic, slow-moving organization responsible for managing the nuclear force. USSTRATCOM was not built for the agile, rapid, and persistent engagements for which USCYBERCOM was created. USSTRATCOM prioritizes deterrence, which is reasonable

---

[7] www.foreignaffairs.com/articles/united-states/2010-09-01/defending-new-domain

[8] https://www.nytimes.com/2019/06/15/us/politics/trump-cyber-russia-grid.html

[9] https://www.wired.com/2010/07/code-cracked-cyber-command-logos-mystery-solved

in the nuclear context, but much different and more difficult in the cyber context. In kinetic attacks, weapons, equipment, and blast patterns often bear manufacturing marks, serial numbers, and technical characteristics that link them to specific states. Cyberattacks are much more difficult to attribute.

The Problem with Proof

Attribution—the act of ascribing a cyberattack to a particular threat actor or nation-state—is the cornerstone of establishing accountability for cyberattacks. Without accurate attribution, we don't know whether a cyberattack is perpetrated by a government, a cybercriminal organization, a hacktivist group, or someone else entirely. Without accurate attribution, we cannot definitively accuse, let alone prosecute or sanction, a group or country.

To do attribution well requires the right resources—skilled security researchers and time—and the right data. That means (a) having sufficient evidence, (b) having enough global data to identify and understand common attack patterns of the perpetrator, and (c) having confidence in the results of the analysis.

Security researchers need to be accurate and timely with their attribution. It can be easy to misattribute attacker activity without a thorough view of the attack landscape on all domains—not just the devices we use every day, but also the cloud resources, networks, identities, and the data itself.

Attribution also has consequences. Both attribution and misattribution can heighten geopolitical tensions and escalate a conflict.

At the same time, attackers are looking for ways to prevent attribution. They may use a strategy as simple as using a proxy like a cybercriminal group, or as complicated as using virtual private networks (VPNs) to hide their true location or spoof a user's IP address or other information to appear to be someone else. Attackers know just as well as cybersecurity professionals that their activity can be tracked, and they will attempt to hide their breadcrumbs to ensure attacks can't be traced back to them or their nation.

It gets even more complicated when nation-states share their malware with cybercriminals. Once cybercriminals start using it, it becomes difficult to tell if and when the malware is being used by a cybercriminal or a nation-state, further obfuscating nation-state activities.

Some nation-states may even manufacture a false flag operation. Just as some criminals will try to plant evidence at a crime scene, nation-state attackers will also plant evidence—documents, malware written in certain languages, different types of malware that are known to be associated with another nation-state—to mislead researchers into suspecting another group.

Attributing an attack with confidence can take weeks, months, or even years, and the nation-state typically denies responsibility.

Unleashing Disruption

Two big changes affected how USCYBERCOM approached deterrence and cyberattacks overall. First, in 2017, President Trump announced USCYBERCOM would be elevated to a Unified Combatant Command, taking it out from under USSTRATCOM and increasing its autonomy and reach within the DOD. This was a much-needed change and validation of the importance of cyber to the military. USCYBERCOM's new status as an equal combatant command enabled it to integrate with joint operations more effectively and gave it more responsibility for planning and conducting global operations.[10]

The second factor was a military authorization bill passed in 2018, which authorizes USCYBERCOM to conduct clandestine military activities without special presidential approval. Titled the *John S. McCain National Defense Authorization Act for Fiscal Year 2019*, it has enabled USCYBERCOM to take action faster and with less oversight.[11]

---

[10] https://trumpwhitehouse.archives.gov/presidential-actions/presidential-memorandum-secretary-defense
[11] www.nytimes.com/2018/10/23/us/politics/russian-hacking-usa-cyber-command.html

This is when USCYBERCOM started experimenting with more complex and innovative deterrence efforts like Defend Forward. Defend Forward was introduced in 2018, when USCYBERCOM recognized that traditional methods of deterrence are not nearly as effective against cyberattacks because of how difficult attribution is.[12]

To avoid the attribution problem, USCYBERCOM started to embrace deterrence by disruption through its Defend Forward initiative. Defend Forward disrupts attackers at the source in adversary networks *before* they reach U.S. systems. It is a form of proactive disruption that consists of targeting and attacking adversarial infrastructure, such as infiltrating enemy networks to take them down. USCYBERCOM continuously engages with foreign cyber actors to ensure the adversary is under constant pressure.

For example, in 2018, USCYBERCOM was targeting Russian operatives who were leveraging disinformation to interfere with elections. In an effort to deter them through intimidation, USCYBERCOM was reportedly reaching out to Russian operatives to tell them that Americans knew what they were doing and were tracking their activity.[13]

Operation Glowing Symphony

In another instance in 2016, ISIS had turned the Internet into one of its weapons and its main source for recruiting. They produced extensive propaganda, including numerous foreign-language websites; published a popular magazine, *Dabiq*; and even created a mobile app for official news.[14]

Task Force ARES, a special task force that is part of USCYBERCOM, was responsible for taking out ISIS propaganda operations through Operation Glowing Symphony. ARES had been playing a cat-and-mouse game with ISIS computer network operators: ARES would disable a communication hub, and yet another would appear.

---

[12] https://dodcio.defense.gov/Portals/0/Documents/Library/CyberStrategy 2018.pdf

[13] www.nytimes.com/2018/10/23/us/politics/russian-hacking-usa-cyber-command .html

[14] www.npr.org/2019/09/26/763545811/how-the-u-s-hacked-isis

However, everything changed when the team realized that ISIS was using only 10 primary accounts and servers for its global media distribution. Everything—finances, file sharing, online posts—was managed through one of those accounts. It made sense for efficiency, but left them vulnerable to concentration risk; a coordinated attack could potentially disrupt the entire system.

Unfortunately, ARES couldn't just shut down the servers ISIS was using because ISIS had hijacked legitimate systems. The servers were shared for both attacker and civilian activity, which the United States didn't want to disrupt. They had to somehow stop the ISIS activity without also taking out civilian activity, all on the same computers. ARES spent years monitoring and tracking the attackers so they could gather enough information about ISIS operatives and about the infrastructure ISIS was using to take out their systems entirely.

Once they were ready to attack, ARES started by locking ISIS out. In the first phase of the operation, ARES took control of all systems and began resetting credentials and deleting data. They exfiltrated copies of intel, locked ISIS out of accounts, and deleted files. The second phase was all about making ISIS operations more difficult. ARES slowed down ISIS's ability to download files, denied them access to programs, caused programs to crash unexpectedly, and locked them out of their accounts. It was a slow-burn denial-of-service attack, except instead of blocking access entirely, ARES just made the computers intolerable to work with, like trying to use an iPhone with hardware more than 5 years old. The attacks looked like normal IT issues, but in reality, it was the U.S. government slowing them down. Six months later, ISIS media operations were a shadow of their former selves.[15]

Dabiq magazine missed its deadlines until it had to shut down. The foreign language websites and mobile apps shut down, too. Because of the challenges with obtaining new servers and forms of payment in war-torn Syria, ISIS simply didn't have the resources to start over again.[16]

---

[15] https://www.stratcom.mil/Portals/8/Documents/FOIA/FOIA%2017-023,%2017-033,%2017-064%20-%20USCYBERCOM%20Joint%20Task%20Force%20Areas.pdf?ver=2017-04-19-111941-797
[16] https://nsarchive.gwu.edu/briefing-book/cyber-vault/2018-08-13/joint-task-force-ares-operation-glowing-symphony-cyber-commands-internet-war-against-isil

What made the biggest difference in this attack was that it was not whack-a-mole. It was a continuous effort to wear ISIS down over months. It degraded their resources and will to continue—a true mission of deterrence by disruption.

The Best Defense Is a Good Offense

USCYBERCOM has also prioritized certain Defend Forward measures ahead of upcoming high-profile events. Before the 2020 U.S. presidential election, there were fears that a botnet could be used to launch attacks against infrastructure before election day, such as against voter registration systems.

USCYBERCOM was particularly concerned about attackers using malware like TrickBot, which is known to deliver ransomware and infect computers on a massive scale. In the 2010s, it was highly prolific in scale and impact—from late 2016 to 2020, more than a million devices were infected with TrickBot.[17]

To defend against it, USCYBERCOM distributed new configuration files to infected Windows computers. This update redirected TrickBot to look for new updates and commands from localhost instead of its command-and-control (C2) server. In other words, the malware was looking for updates on the computer it infected rather than the C2 that actually had updates. It's like if your PC tried to get a software update, but only checked its own hard drive instead of reaching out to Microsoft's servers. It's not going to update properly. Since the malware could no longer receive updates or commands from its controller, it was effectively disabled, even though the computer remained usable for the end user.[18]

Interestingly enough, Microsoft also took action to disrupt the TrickBot botnet. In conjunction with the Financial Services Information Sharing and Analysis Center (FS-ISAC), Broadcom's Symantec, ESET, and other partners, it cut off key infrastructure

---

[17] https://blogs.microsoft.com/on-the-issues/2020/10/12/trickbot-ransom ware-cyberthreat-us-elections
[18] https://krebsonsecurity.com/2020/10/attacks-aimed-at-disrupting-the-trickbot-botnet

that TrickBot relied on. To do so, Microsoft's team investigated where and how TrickBot infrastructure operated, specifically where its C2 servers resided. The U.S. District Court for the Eastern District of Virginia granted Microsoft and its partners authorization to disable the IP addresses associated with the C2 infrastructure and also block the operator's ability to purchase additional servers.[19]

It was critical that Microsoft obtain a court order to reduce its liability—Microsoft isn't a nation-state and, as a private entity, can't just attack providers at will. But the way they approached the court order was interesting. It was based on, of all things, a trademark violation. Microsoft argued that the attackers were misusing its software, thereby providing a legitimate basis for revoking access. This operation set a major precedent for how private companies can engage and stop malicious cyberactivity even overseas: Engage the courts to get permission and a legal shield, even in a roundabout way.

Both Microsoft's and USCYBERCOM's approaches were temporary by design, yet Microsoft demonstrated that a private company could act as effectively as the U.S. military in disrupting cyberattacks. Large companies have true power in the geopolitical and cyber landscape, even as they face hurdles in navigating local and international law.

---

[19] https://www.microsoft.com/en-us/security/blog/2020/10/12/trickbot-disrupted

Part II

The People's Republic of China

Chapter 16
From Nationalism to Informatization

中国好古而忽今,西人努力于今以胜古。

I think the greatest difference between China and the West, which can never be made up, is that the Chinese are fond of antiquity but neglect the present.

—*Learning From the West, Yan Fu*[1]

To set up a conversation about modern warfare in the People's Republic of China (CCP) and its use of cyber operations, we must look very far into the past, to when *The Art of War* was written. Historians argue whether one person or multiple people wrote it, but most reference Sun Tzu. It is even less clear when the text was written, though it is assumed to be during the late Spring and Autumn period of ancient China, roughly in the fifth century BCE, during the Warring States Period.[2]

---

[1] https://afe.easia.columbia.edu/ps/china/yanfu_learning_west.pdf
[2] www.britannica.com/biography/Sunzi

For the Communist Party of China (CCP) and PLA, informatization (xìnxīhuà, 信息化) is the process of integrating
information technology into every aspect of warfare, governance, and the economy. It is the Information Age analog
to industrialization.

The Art of War is fundamental to Chinese military strategy; since
2006, it has been required reading for officers, soldiers, and sailors in the People's Liberation Army National Defense University.[3]
Chinese generals can cite entire passages from the book. It permeates the culture. But it also permeates the culture of another group:
Cybersecurity professionals. They are notorious for religiously
quoting Sun Tzu and *The Art of War*. Quotes like "If you know the
enemy and know yourself, you need not fear the result of a hundred
battles" are commonly referenced when talking about the importance of threat intelligence and understanding an organization's
infrastructure.[4] Other quotes, such as "In the midst of chaos, there
is also opportunity," call on security teams to leverage moments of
high stress, such as during a cyberattack, to their advantage.[5]

Despite keeping its roots, aspects of Chinese military strategy
have also evolved over time. Shortly after the CCP was founded, the
Central Military Commission began developing and implementing
the doctrine of active defense.[6] China's active defense is a strategic
approach to warfare that emphasizes asymmetric advantage, peacetime vigilance, balanced use of force, guerrilla warfare, and prioritizing defense alongside counterattacks.[7] It emphasizes the role of
non-military personnel for a whole-of-nation approach to warfare.

Mao's view was that China was at a disadvantage but could
succeed through a combination of mobile guerrilla and positional

---

[3] https://ndupress.ndu.edu/Media/News/Article/577507/sun-tzu-in-contemporary-chinese-strategy
[4] Sun Tzu, The Art of War, trans. Lionel Giles, in The Internet Classics Archive.
[5] Ibid.
[6] http://eng.mod.gov.cn/xb/Publications/WhitePapers/4887928.html
[7] https://media.defense.gov/2024/Dec/18/2003615520/-1/-1/0/MILITARY-AND-SECURITY-DEVELOPMENTS-INVOLVING-THE-PEOPLES-REPUBLIC-OF-CHINA-2024.PDF

warfare. *Be on the defensive constantly, never fire the first shot, always take defensive actions offensively.*[8]

To this day, China demonstrates just how much its geopolitical strategy has been inspired by this approach. China is consistently playing the long game, developing methods and means to wear down the adversary while avoiding direct, high-profile conflict. This is especially true of its cyber strategy, which does not rely on flashy, explosive attacks that take down electric grids or ransom hospitals, but instead on gathering strategic intelligence and prepositioning in the event of a conflict.

The Great Leap Backward

The mid-1950s were a time of opportunity and development. China established a formal computing development program and created its first vacuum-tube computer based on Soviet designs. Over the years, it copied many technology designs from the Soviet Union through technology transfer programs until the relationship began to deteriorate.[9]

Unfortunately, this effort stalled out once the Great Leap Forward began in 1958. Mao Zedong, Chairman of the Communist Party of China and party leader, sought to thrust China into industrialization, a necessity for any growing nation at the time, especially those on the wrong end of colonial rule and the world wars. But Mao's approach was devastating: It led to the most deadly famine in history.[10] Private farming was abolished. Farm labor was reorganized into industrial labor, and farming communes were established, led by individuals loyal to and known by the Communist Party. The communal kitchens had unrealistic quotas, and Goodhart's Law reared its ugly head. Metrics were falsified to appear to meet quotas, which only exacerbated the problem.[11] As the Chinese people faced a devastating famine, scientific and technological progress, including in computer development, stalled.

---

[8] www.marxists.org/reference/archive/mao/selected-works/volume-2/mswv2_09.htm
[9] Mullaney, Thomas, S. (2024). *The Chinese Computer: A Global History of the Information Age.* MIT Press.
[10] https://ourworldindata.org/famines
[11] www.asianstudies.org/publications/eaa/archives/chinas-great-leap-forward

Importing the Information Age

It wasn't until Deng Xiaoping championed the *Four Modernizations in 1978* that the Chinese technology market would start to catch up. Originally proposed in the '60s, the *Four Modernizations* refers to the drive to develop agriculture, industry, science and technology, and defense. They helped China boost productivity, embrace new technologies, modernize its industrial base, and reform education. The modernization was buoyed by the opening up of international engagement, with formal participation in global trade.[12]

The Four Modernizations led to a substantial increase in China's computer imports. China jumped from 600 foreign-built microcomputers in 1980 to 130,000 by 1985.[13] The biggest challenge for Chinese users at the time was that computers lacked sufficient memory to render Chinese characters, as computers were designed for Latin character sets.

Work by Louis and Bruce Rosenblum, a father-son team, helped to address this. Rosenblum set out to create a low-cost microcomputer at a fraction of the cost of the Sinotype II. They succeeded, developing the Sinotype III. To make it compatible with the Chinese character set, they expanded the on-board memory to support more Chinese characters and used external hard drives to store additional characters. Even still, this came with trade-offs in recall speed. It also still could not address the entire Chinese character set—far from it, given that there are thousands of Chinese characters.[14]

To resolve these constraints, Ni Guangnan invented the Han card at the Chinese Academy of Engineering. Han cards, or Hanka, were hardware expansion cards that could store thousands of Chinese characters on chips installed in the motherboard expansion slots. Engineers at Tsinghua University were some of the earliest to focus on the development of Hanka. The cards were originally developed for custom systems but were translated over to personal computers, which enabled the Chinese market to adopt computers on a larger scale.[15]

---

[12]https://www.britannica.com/topic/Four-Modernizations
[13]https://techcrunch.com/2021/06/29/the-engineering-daring-that-led-to-the-first-chinese-personal-computer
[14]https://www.technologyreview.com/2021/05/31/1025599/history-first-chinese-digital-computer-fonts
[15] Ibid.

Computer adoption continued to grow slowly, and by 1987, after years of work, the first email was sent in China with the subject line, "First Electronic Mail from China to Germany." It began,

"Across the Great Wall we can reach every corner in the world."[16]

It was sent by the team at the Institute of Computer Applications in Beijing and addressed to CSNET computer scientists, a group of scientists responsible for a network established in the 1980s, and members of Karlsruhe University, both of which collaborated on the effort with the Chinese.

Back to Disconnect and Isolation

The Four Modernizations led to rapid growth and technological progress. Unfortunately, it also led to widespread corruption and inflation. By 1988, inflation was at 18.5 percent.[17] The economic challenges began to grate on the population, and in 1989, weeks of student protests across China were held to promote political and economic reform, especially to protect individual rights and freedoms. It's difficult to know exactly how many gathered to protest, as the CCP refuses to disclose the number, but estimates range from tens of thousands to up to a million. The protests culminated in the Tiananmen Square massacre, where martial law was declared, and protesters were forcibly subdued.[18] Hundreds to potentially thousands of peaceful protesters were murdered, with thousands more arrested.[19] Some were shot to death; others were crushed by military vehicles. In China, even discussing the incident is banned to this day, and those who do speak on it are arrested and jailed. As China's influence has spread, so has its crackdown on mentions of Tiananmen Square—in Hong Kong in 2024, several individuals

---

[16]https://www.thechinastory.org/lexicon/the-internet
[17]http://news.bbc.co.uk/2/hi/asia-pacific/5237748.stm
[18]www.britannica.com/event/Tiananmen-Square-incident
[19]www.amnesty.org.uk/china-1989-tiananmen-square-protests-demonstration-massacre

were arrested just for posting on social media in remembrance of the incident.[20]

After Tiananmen Square, the international community was outraged and hit China with sanctions that caused its economic growth to plummet, with GDP dropping from 11.7 percent in 1987 to 3.9 percent in 1990.[21]

Between its economic challenges and the massacre, China reverted to its more modest economic approach, limiting foreign joint ventures and tightening monetary controls. This continued until 1992, when Deng Xiaoping, then 87 years old and no longer technically in power, took a tour of southern China. He used the 35-day trip to advocate for economic reforms to liberalize the market. The tour ultimately compelled CCP leadership to embrace foreign investment, and just in time. The Internet was about to reach China, and the economic boom would transform the country.[22]

By 1994, the first permanent Internet connection had been established in China.[23] China's first website was launched for the Institute of High Energy Physics, www.ihep.ac.cn. Internet access in China shot up, and by 1996, the first Internet cafés opened in Shanghai.[24] However, computer adoption was far from realistic for the average citizen. The most popular personal computer among consumers in 1995, the Compaq Presario, was $2,100, while the average after-tax yearly income for urban residents in China was 4,283 yuan, the equivalent of about $515.[25,26] The PC was far out of reach at just shy of four times the average yearly take-home pay of an urban Chinese citizen.

[20] www.amnesty.org/en/latest/news/2024/05/hong-kong-arrests-under-new-national-security-law-a-shameful-attempt-at-suppressing-peaceful-commemoration-of-tiananmen-crackdown

[21] www.reuters.com/article/world/timeline-chinas-post-tiananmen-re-emergence-onto-the-world-idUSKCN1SX0IE

[22] https://www.jstor.org/stable/45316396

[23] www.osti.gov/servlets/purl/1834055

[24] https://edition.cnn.com/2014/04/23/world/asia/china-internet-20th-anniversary

[25] www.wsj.com/articles/SB834350462479023000

[26] pubmed.ncbi.nlm.nih.gov/12347914

Unleashing ChinaNET

It wasn't until 1995 that the Ministry of Posts and Communications set up ChinaNET, the first commercial network in China, which enabled the public to access the Internet. It created massive opportunities for foreign investment, given the nearly one billion people living in China at the time.[27]

Instead of buying their own computers, many early computer users were students, as much of China's computing efforts were concentrated in universities. Technical information sharing took place between two primary networks for many years: the China Education and Research Network (CERNET), a joint initiative among multiple Chinese universities to facilitate information sharing, and its sister network, CSTNET. These networks were foundational to the development of technology and cybersecurity in early China, as they provided students who could not otherwise afford to own a computer or access the Internet with a means to experiment and learn.[28]

By 1997, 1.6 percent of Chinese families owned a computer.[29]

In 1996, the CCP established a 5-year development plan focused on computer literacy and education. The release of this plan marked an inflection point in the development and education of computer literacy among the Chinese; it stipulated that teachers must be adept at using computers, that research on computer science teaching must be strengthened, and that experiments must be conducted in computer instruction.

[27] https://scholarship.law.vanderbilt.edu/cgi/viewcontent.cgi?article=1716&context=vjtl
[28] http://en.internet.cn/history/niandu/1994.html
[29] www.wired.com/1997/06/china-3

The Internet mainly afforded well-educated, predominantly male computer users in China the opportunity to access information they never had before and to become more entrepreneurial as a result. There was a sharp divide between those who had access and those who did not, but that divide got smaller quickly. In less than a decade, China became the country with the largest number of Internet users in the world. As of 2025, it still holds that record, now at over 1.1 billion people.[30]

---

[30] https://english.www.gov.cn/archive/statistics/202507/21/content_WS687d d259c6d0868f4e8f4501.html

Chapter 17
New Bricks in the Great Wall

天網恢恢, 疏而不失。

Heaven's net is vast, so vast. It is wide-meshed, but it loses nothing.

—*Lao Tzu*[1]

Though individual fortifications were built during the War-ring States Period, the first unified Great Wall of China was started in 214 BCE. It was one of the largest construction projects ever undertaken, spanning over 2,000 years and at least nine dynasties.[2] As many as 400,000 people died during its creation, some of whom were buried in the wall itself during the building process.[3] It was designed to protect against attacks and to communicate quickly over long distances with early warnings. The wall is an

---

[1] Tao Te Ching, ch. 73, in D. T. Suzuki & Paul Carus (trans.), various reprints.
[2] www.britannica.com/topic/Great-Wall-of-China
[3] www.history.com/articles/great-wall-of-china

156 THE PEOPLE'S REPUBLIC OF CHINA

iconic part of Chinese history that also speaks to China's approach to its own information system: Keep in what China wants kept in, and keep out what China wants kept out.

To that end, information control in China began early. In 213 BCE, Qin, the first emperor of China, ordered that books on poetry, philosophy, and history be burned to control information among the populace and consolidate power. Over his fears of others talking or writing about him, Qin had 400 scholars arrested and buried alive.[4] Control of information was paramount.

The Hundred Flowers Ruse

Mao took a similar approach to Qin. In the mid-1950s, Mao initiated a cultural movement that loosened the state's control over history and information. The movement, called "Let a Hundred Flowers Bloom," purported to promote intellectual freedom and to encourage criticism. To quote Mao, "Carrying out the policy of letting a hundred flowers blossom and a hundred schools of thought contend will not weaken, but strengthen, the leading position of Marxism in the ideological field."[5]

Whether the campaign was a plot to identify dissenters (as some speculate) or just one man who couldn't take criticism, the result was the same. Turnabout was swift, and retribution was brutal as critics lost their jobs or were imprisoned. Criticism of the state was not tolerated.[6]

Akin to Qin and the scholars, in the mid-1960s, the Red Guard, Mao's student-led paramilitary force during the Cultural Revolution, destroyed Chinese symbols of the past and cleansed China of the Four Olds: Old ideas, culture, customs, and habits.[7] From 1966

[4] https://www.smithsonianmag.com/history/brief-history-book-burning-printing-press-internet-archives-180964697
[5] www.marxists.org/reference/archive/mao/selected-works/volume-5/mswv5_58.htm
[6] https://www.ebsco.com/research-starters/history/maos-hundred-flowers-campaign-begins
[7] www.nationalarchives.gov.uk/education/resources/the-cultural-revolution

to 1967, they beat, imprisoned, and sent individuals for reeducation in the millions. Up to 2 million people died.[8,9]

Laying the Groundwork

Censorship of a similar kind continued decades later as the Internet became popular. By 1995, the Internet had hit the mainstream and was starting to explode globally. With the events of Tiananmen Square ringing in the ears of state leaders and the fall of the Soviet Union laid bare before them, the CCP saw just how critical dominance of the ideological beliefs of the populace was. Controlling the burgeoning Internet was a natural next step to those efforts, but it had to be handled carefully; the state needed to reap the economic benefits of the Internet while still maintaining control.

As early as 1996, the State Council started issuing Internet regulations. The first step: Establish choke points. *Decree 195 of the State Council of the People's Republic of China* mandated that computer networks looking to connect to the Internet must connect through channels approved by the state, specifically by the Ministry of Post and Telecommunications.[10] The Internet backbone and local Internet Service Providers (ISPs) had to be approved by the state. Any new networks attempting to connect to ISPs would be classified as "work units" and required to register as network operators. Individual users had to register with their "work unit" to gain access to the Internet.

A "work unit" is effectively an Internet choke point. They are registered groups responsible for providing Internet access. By mandating that all international communications pass through state-controlled infrastructure and connect exclusively to approved

---

[8] www.nationalarchives.gov.uk/education/resources/the-cultural-revolution/#:~:text=The%20Cultural%20Revolution%20took%20place,impacted%20China%20and%20its%20people

[9] https://spice.fsi.stanford.edu/docs/introduction_to_the_cultural_revolution

[10] https://www.cac.gov.cn/1996-02/02/c_126468621.htm

ISPs, the government created registered funnels at the national, regional, and local levels, thereby giving authorities visibility into every Internet connection.

The second step: Control the data. The regulation held network operators responsible for maintaining the security and secrecy of their networks and for providing the state with access to the data passing through those networks. With these two requirements, the state now had the legal authority to know the locations of all Internet access points and to build a system to monitor, control, or block citizens' Internet access at will.

Building the Golden Infrastructure

To transform regulation into technical reality, the CCP began *The Golden Projects* (三金工程), a series of special programs to enhance China's information infrastructure. For example, *the Golden Card Project* is the infrastructure for online finance, and *the Golden Customs Project* is the infrastructure for trade and related licensing. *The Golden Bridge Project* is a massive project launched in 1993 to create a nationwide, state-owned, commercial Internet backbone using fiber-optic cables and satellites. It not only supports Internet expansion in China but also enables the state to maintain direct control over the Internet.[11]

The Golden Shield Project (金盾工程), run by the Ministry of Public Security, began in the late 1990s as the basis for China's national public security system, a broad surveillance network covering the majority of the Internet in China. It is the largest, most coordinated, and most sophisticated national surveillance network in the world.[12] *The Golden Shield Project* was launched to enhance police control through advanced technology, but it has evolved significantly over time. It became the software and hardware that enables the authorities to identify, catalog, track, surveil, and persecute anyone the state wants within China. Initial deployments in the early 2000s focused on speech-recognition software to surveil phone calls, video surveillance, a nationwide database on Chinese

[11] https://www.cac.gov.cn/2019-12/02/c_1576821721222367.htm
[12] https://www.hrw.org/legacy/backgrounder/asia/china-bck-0701.htm

citizens, closed-circuit television to monitor public spaces, finger-printing technologies, firewalls to control external Internet access outside of China, and pilots of facial recognition technologies. It also helped establish rules for Internet service providers (ISPs) to track and store detailed records of individual Chinese citizens, which feed the database.

A core component of the Golden Shield is its massive, intercon-nected web of surveillance infrastructure and databases. Its Inter-net surveillance system is designed to monitor all online activity of individuals, from search history to email accounts to other personal data. Once an individual is identified as relevant, especially if they are a dissident, they are tracked more closely than others.

One prominent component, PoliceNet, is a database of the national population. By just scanning a citizen's identification card, police can retrieve their photo, employment history, family infor-mation, political affiliations, Internet browsing history, and 60 days of emails.[13] One database tracks all records of encounters with Chinese security forces, including their physical and online loca-tions, characteristics, and ability to evade capture, as well as any information relevant to justify arrest.[14]

Depending on the location and use case, information about the target individual is customized—for example, if the Golden Shield is accessed at re-education through labor camps, it gives the author-ities personal information about the individual to help them carry out psychological or physical torture.[15] It tracks information like whether the target continued to follow religious practices and their susceptibility to forced conversion.

The Golden Shield takes a multilayered approach to censorship – catch as much as possible while balancing computational costs and potential network latency issues. It maintains blocklists of websites it doesn't want its citizens to access, like CNN and the BBC. It uses intrusion detection systems, which are designed to detect cyberat-tacks, to filter specific websites that the state doesn't want citizens

---

[13] www.irb-cisr.gc.ca/en/country-information/rir/Pages/index.aspx?doc=455174&pls=1
[14] https://www.hrw.org/news/2017/11/19/china-police-big-data-systems-violate-privacy-target-dissent
[15] https://cyberlaw.stanford.edu/content/files/sites/default/files/ciscos_customization_of_chinas_golden_shield_to_suppress_falun_gong.pdf

to see. Email providers and instant messaging services are required to install keyword filtering to censor data as it reaches a user's device. Chats are recorded so that the police can later inspect them at will. Websites go through content filtering to screen for specific keywords. Discussion forums are required to self-censor and filter out messages that use state-deemed banned words about politics, religion, and pornography.[16]

> A *firewall* monitors and controls incoming and outgoing network traffic, permitting or blocking data transmission based on security rules. It is a barrier between a trusted internal network and untrusted external networks, including the Internet.

By 1997, the Public Security Bureau had begun implementing a national Internet filtering and censorship system via a firewall, a core component of the Golden Shield. It was first referenced by its more popular name, the Great Firewall (防火长城), in a *Wired* article in 1997.[17] The firewall provides "preventative interference"—it filters out certain words and phrases as the data passes over the Golden Bridge. For example, the system filters out commentary on China's unity and sovereignty before the information can even enter the country. The implementation of the Golden Bridge and *Decree 195* was paramount to implementing the Great Firewall. If all foreign Internet connections did not pass through the Golden Bridge by law, the state would not be able to easily control the information flow.[18]

The Great Firewall started as a part of the Golden Shield, but by the end of the first phase of the project in 2006, it grew into its own distinct undertaking. The core difference: *The Golden Shield Project* is primarily responsible for surveillance within national

---

[16] https://www.opensocietyfoundations.org/uploads/e7d8b223-df0a-4975-b40b-c9914a58b626/china-internet-censorship-20041101.pdf
[17] www.wired.com/1997/06/china-3
[18] https://cs.stanford.edu/people/eroberts/cs181/projects/2010-11/FreedomOfInformationChina/the-great-firewall-of-china-background/index.html

borders, while the Great Firewall is responsible for surveillance and for blocking data leaving or entering the country.[19]

The Golden Shield and Great Firewall are ultimately tools to subjugate, as in the case of the Falun Gong, a movement founded in 1992.[20] The Falun Gong gained traction in China in the late 1990s as a spiritual movement with Buddhist, Taoist, and Confucian roots, promoting physical and mental health through meditation.[21] Thanks in large part to the Internet, the Falun Gong quickly gained popularity worldwide. Its acclaim and thus potential influence were concerning to the CCP, whose main priority is to ensure regime stability at all costs. The state quickly labeled the Falun Gong an evil cult.[22]

In 1999, some 10,000 Falun Gong followers organized a peaceful protest in Beijing. They used the Internet to communicate and spread information about the protests. The state cracked down on the protestors, prosecuting followers and making it a crime to practice. They confiscated books and blocked access to websites related to the Falun Gong. Followers were taken to re-education camps, beaten, and tortured into compliance and disavowal of the cause.[23]

The attacks against the Falun Gong that China perpetrated even spread overseas. Two Canadian Internet service providers, Bestnet Internet and Nebula Internet Services, experienced sustained denial-of-service attacks that took down website access for days.[24] They traced the attacks back to Beijing state offices, providing some evidence that the state would go so far as to target even the movement's websites to suppress dissident voices abroad.

Though *the Golden Shield Project* was not specifically meant to target the Falun Gong, but instead all dissidents, over time, many components of the project were built to track them. Its real-time monitoring capability and signature library identify specific

---

[19] https://www.andrew.cmu.edu/user/nicolasc/publications/Phong-USENIXSec24.pdf
[20] www.britannica.com/topic/Falun-Gong
[21] www.ebsco.com/research-starters/religion-and-philosophy/falun-gong-spirtual-movement
[22] https://digitalcommons.wcl.american.edu/cgi/viewcontent.cgi?article=1435&context=hrbrief
[23] https://amnesty.ca/features/legacy-tiananmen-square
[24] www.wired.com/1999/07/isps-accuse-china-of-infowar

indicators of individuals likely to be affiliated with Falun Gong. For example, one capability inspects images online for anything related to the Falun Gong, like flyers.[25] By the end of April 2004, a reported 108 Falun Gong followers had been sent to forced labor camps because of their Internet-related activities.[26]

Safe From Whom?

In 2003, China began implementing its Safe City project (平安城市), launched by the Ministry of Public Security (MPS) and the Ministry of Science and Technology. Safe City is responsible for giving disaster warnings, managing traffic, and providing public security and urban management. It leverages the infrastructure from *the Golden Shield Project*, particularly the data on Chinese citizens and its surveillance via CCTV networks, which it also expanded independently. The underlying infrastructure for the Safe City project is the same as that used for other surveillance initiatives in China. As of 2005, it was active in 22 provinces and 21 cities.[27]

Safe City is closely linked to another project, Skynet. No, it's not named after Skynet from the *Terminator* movies (even though it is disturbingly similar). It's actually named after the idiom from Lao Tzu at the start of this chapter. Tianwang (天网) translates to "heavenly net" or "Skynet." Skynet was created in 2005, when the MPS and the Ministry of Industry and Information Technology (MIIT), which is responsible for industrial standards and telecommunications infrastructure, initiated a real-time urban surveillance system using CCTV. It's built to give 24/7 coverage of specific districts, schools, and business areas. As of 2018, more than 200 million surveillance cameras were deployed across China.[28]

---

[25] https://cdn.ca9.uscourts.gov/datastore/opinions/2023/07/07/15-16909.pdf
[26] www.opensocietyfoundations.org/uploads/e7d8b223-df0a-4975-b40b-c9914a58b626/china-internet-censorship-20041101.pdf
[27] https://cset.georgetown.edu/wp-content/uploads/CSET-Designing-Alternatives-to-Chinas-Surveillance-State.pdf
[28] Ibid.

While dual use as public safety infrastructure, the Safe City project and Skynet are fundamentally sophisticated surveillance systems. They integrate hundreds of millions of surveillance cameras with facial and license plate recognition, crowd- and situational-awareness detectors, and geolocation platforms across cities. Data from utilities, commercial establishments, banks, and public cameras is funneled into centralized "city brain" systems operated by public security bureaus, allowing authorities to build detailed, searchable profiles of individuals and groups. These systems monitor urban populations, enabling law enforcement to respond to crimes and predict and preempt activities deemed threats to social stability, including protests and dissent—often targeting minorities, migrant workers, and those on watch lists. In practice, China's Safe City is designed less for community safety and more for total, real-time social control at an unprecedented scale.

Cracking the Golden Shield

While the Golden Shield has been effective for surveillance and blocking, ways around the controls exist, particularly via VPNs, proxy servers, and Tor. Practically, if users can directly connect to the Internet outside China, the controls within China don't matter.

To that end, in 2017, MIIT announced a 14-month nationwide campaign to "clean up and regulate" the Internet.[29] At the time, the Great Firewall was blocking traffic well enough, but some users were dodging the censorship controls with VPNs. This directive functionally outlawed any VPN provider that did not agree to state oversight. It explicitly stated that all VPN services must obtain state approval to operate legally. The mandate targeted ISPs' Internet data centers and content delivery networks, requiring them to verify their clients' use of network resources. Authorities also directed China Unicom, China Telecom, and China Mobile—the three largest state-owned telecommunications companies—to block access

---

[29] https://chinadigitaltimes.net/2017/01/china-reinforces-great-firewall-new-vpn-rules

to any unauthorized VPNs. This ensured that the state would not only police what its citizens saw online, but also who was allowed to provide the tools that might let them see more.[30]

The Green Dam Has Broken

In one instance of China's failed efforts at control, MIIT mandated the installation of Green Dam software on all new computers. It issued a notice on May 19, 2009, stating that the mandate would take effect in July.[31]

MIIT stressed that the technology was developed to protect children online, especially from pornography. However, the reality was far from what they stated. The software reportedly had blocked keywords, only 15 percent of which were related to pornography, while the other 85 percent were related to topics the CCP wanted to restrict discourse on, like the Falun Gong and Tiananmen Square.[32] It was a lot like parental controls on software—it limited what users could see directly on the device they were using, and it couldn't be uninstalled. The software also recorded the user's screen. It was riddled with vulnerabilities that made it a target for attackers, and users quickly broke into the software. Users found ways to disable and bypass the software, and surveys showed that 80 percent of Chinese Internet users refused to install it.[33] By June, the Publicity Department issued a notice to the media instructing them not to question the mandatory installation of the Green Dam software and instead to promote positive commentary about it.[34] It didn't help, and by June 30, the mandatory installation was postponed. By August, computer manufacturers were no longer required to include it on new PCs. Public outcry was too strong, even for the CCP. It is a salient example of how large and public changes draw criticism and ire, whereas small, incremental, and hidden changes persist.

---

[30] https://www.xinhuanet.com//politics/2017-01/25/c_1120378818.htm
[31] https://cpj.org/2009/08/chinas-green-dam-finally-cracks
[32] http://hk.news.yahoo.com/article/090623/4/cujx.html
[33] http://tech.163.com/09/0611/03/5BGEP73T000915BD.html
[34] www.rfi.fr/chinois/actu/articles/114/article_14265.asp

Importing Control

In 2015, China implemented the Police Cloud (警务云), a predictive policing tool that operates as a data-driven surveillance system to support its public security bureaus. An upgrade over PoliceNet, Police Cloud gives authorities a centralized, cloud-based platform that aggregates data and enables police to track individuals and predict criminal activity and social unrest. It tracks personal data on individuals, including home addresses, family members, religious affiliations, travel records, biometrics (e.g., facial recognition scans), online activity, and other data, such as healthcare or mail delivery records.[35]

It continuously evaluates surveillance data and looks for anomalies to determine whether a person deviates from their normal routines. Most of the tracking done in this system is targeted at political activists, dissidents, or ethnic minorities like the Uyghurs. The Police Cloud is a national project, but it is organized by province. Shandong and Jiangsu Provinces claim to have some of the most established capabilities in the country.[36]

American companies facilitated the creation of much of the surveillance software and hardware used by Chinese authorities to persecute their citizens. In just the most recent reporting on this in 2025, the Associated Press found that many American companies, including Microsoft, Thermo Fisher Scientific, Oracle, Motorola, Amazon Web Services, Cisco, and others, supported China's digital police state.[37] IBM helped design *the Golden Shield Project*, assisted China in building its national intelligence and counterterrorism systems, and sold its i2 police surveillance analysis software to Xinjiang. Intel and NVIDIA have added AI capabilities to camera systems for video surveillance in China, including in regions such as Xinjiang and Tibet. IBM, Oracle, and HP sold geographic and mapping software to the Chinese police, which was deployed in the Police Cloud to identify when Uyghurs left their provinces or

---

[35] https://www.hrw.org/news/2017/11/19/china-police-big-data-systems-violate-privacy-target-dissent
[36] Ibid.
[37] https://apnews.com/article/chinese-surveillance-silicon-valley-uyghurs-tech-xinjiang-a80904158b771a14d5a734947f28d71b

altered their typical routines. Dell and VMware provided cloud software to the police in Tibet and Xinjiang.

China's reliance on Western technology highlights a critical paradox in modern tech diplomacy. While the US actively pursues decoupling strategies to limit China's technological rise, American firms have spent decades effectively architecting the very surveillance state the United States condemns.

Chapter 18
The New Danwei

群众的眼睛是雪亮的。

The people have sharp eyes.
                              —*Mao Zedong during the Cultural Revolution*[1]

China has a long history of social surveillance and informer culture. The state *expects* citizens to report on one another.

In the state of Qin, communities were organized into units of up to 10 households, which were required to supervise the other households in the unit and report activities deemed harmful by the state. Collective liability (连坐) was the structure by which the government ensured compliance—if you didn't report a crime, you were also considered guilty.[2]

Much of the social surveillance in China has been wrapped in other, more mundane tasks, like taxes. The Han dynasty used social surveillance as the first real basis for registering the population, collecting taxes, and recruiting troops. Citizens reported tax evaders

---

[1]https://cset.georgetown.edu/article/sharp-eyes-surveillance-program-expands-dramatically
[2]https://www.ebsco.com/research-starters/history/qin-dynasty-founded-china

and were rewarded with half of the tax evader's wealth.[3] Officials like Zhao Guanghan created boxes known as *xiangtong* (缿筒), akin to a suggestion box for citizens to report corrupt officials or issues with local clans.[4]

During the Ming dynasty, community compacts were common; agreements made by citizens in the countryside established rules for local community members to follow.[5] The baojia (保甲) also spread during the Ming dynasty and functioned as a local militia while also facilitating surveillance.[6] Today, social surveillance helps the state neutralize threats to regime stability at the source.

Mao's Panopticon

In the 1950s, China attempted to transform its economy into the Soviet model. It regarded the Soviet approach as strong, given that it enabled the Soviet Union to withstand Germany during World War II and expand its influence in Europe. In urban areas, they implemented the *danwei*, based on the Soviet *kombinat*, as the core work unit. However, the danwei extended far beyond work: Individuals in a danwei shared almost every aspect of life, from work to living to bathing to cooking.[7] People were stuck with their danwei; they had no autonomy to move, which led to political and social control. Conformity was essential, especially politically, and was always under scrutiny. Citizens were under mutual surveillance, whereby any individual with "incorrect" thoughts or anyone who didn't enthusiastically participate in political campaigns was considered suspicious and was subjected to criticism.[8]

---

[3] www.theworldofchinese.com/2023/11/how-chinas-emperors-encouraged-informers
[4] Ibid.
[5] https://open.library.ubc.ca/media/stream/pdf/24/1.0391821/4
[6] https://chinesehistoryforteachers.omeka.net/exhibits/show/first-five-year-plan/first-five-year-plan-overview
[7] Ibid.
[8] Saich, Tony. From Rebel to Ruler: One Hundred Years of the Chinese Communist Party. Cambridge, MA: Harvard University Press, 2021.

The CCP continued to rely on local citizens to report even the slightest suspicious behavior by their peers or family members, and also enlisted many agents, especially in urban areas and within the danwei, to spy.[9] Agents reported back on domestic dissent, foreign actors, and suspicious behavior.

During the Cultural Revolution, Mao encouraged citizens to spy on their own family members and neighbors who might be disloyal to communism, urging them to "sweep away all monsters."[10]

This laid the groundwork for the future, when the Internet would introduce an entirely new way of finding and tracking the populace. Instead of relying on individual groups, China could compel service providers to report on their users, compel users to report on their service providers, and compel citizens to report on one another, all while monitoring them through a vast, interconnected web of surveillance equipment. The Internet offered a new type of danwei, one that could scale infinitely and give the government more information and control than ever.

The state made clear its intention to repeat history and treat Internet service providers and tech companies as the new danwei early on, with *Decree 195*, which established a new hierarchy of control between ISPs, network operators, and users.[11]

Issued in 1997, *Decree 33* expanded on this, requiring ISPs to register users and retain user records.[12] Critically, this decree also standardized what online content network operators were prohibited from disseminating. Anything that could be considered inciting resistance, subversion, separatism, distorting facts, or harming the prestige of state organs was prohibited.[13]

In 2000, the state expanded the purview of the decree so that content providers and websites were also forbidden from disseminating prohibited information. If a user posted illegal content on their website, websites were now legally required to report it to the appropriate security bureau.

---

[9] https://assets.cambridge.org/97811070/17870/excerpt/9781107017870_excerpt.pdf
[10] www.marxists.org/subject/china/peking-review/1966/PR1966-23c.htm
[11] https://www.cac.gov.cn/1996-02/02/c_126468621.htm
[12] https://www.mps.gov.cn:9080/n6557558/c7684568/content.html
[13] https://digichina.stanford.edu/work/computer-information-network-international-interconnection-security-protection-management-rules

The decree sets up a system of self-censorship. The terminology they used was intentionally vague, the ambiguity giving the state room to adjust what's "prohibited" whenever it decides. Providers need to predict what the state might consider as "destroying national unity" or "harming national interests," which inevitably leads to excess censorship.

In practice, the requirements make the primary method of accessing the Internet—using an Internet café—more challenging than one might expect. The state requires the café to track each user's identification, residence, and workplace. Individuals are prohibited from accessing or downloading information from banned sites, and the café is required to maintain a record of all Internet activities. Just like many of the news outlets in China self-censor, so must the Internet café owners. Before requests even reach the Great Firewall, the Internet café has its own filtering system in place to avoid the risk of a fine.

Comply or Get Out

In 2002, the Internet Society of China, a state-affiliated group, put forth an agreement called *the Public Pledge on Self-Discipline for the Chinese Internet Industry*.[14] The agreement is a pledge by companies operating in China to censor information deemed objectionable by the CCP, including content that the state deems capable of threatening national security or disrupting social stability. This pledge was presented as optional, but in practice, refusal to comply risked a company's eligibility for an Internet content provider license. No license, no Chinese market. At the time, Yahoo! was the only major Western company to sign the pledge, much to the chagrin of human rights advocates.[15]

In 2005, Microsoft entered the Chinese market with its blogging platform, Windows Live Spaces, and signed the 2002 pledge. Google also did so in 2006.[16] At the time, it argued that it would

---

[14]https://www.amnesty.org/es/wp-content/uploads/2021/06/asa170072002en.pdf
[15]www.cnet.com/tech/services-and-software/yahoo-yields-to-chinese-web-laws
[16]https://www.hrw.org/news/2006/02/01/us-put-pressure-internet-companies-uphold-freedom-expression

better facilitate Chinese citizens' access to information if it were present in the Chinese market, even if it were required to censor certain websites.

China continued to tighten its controls on Internet companies. In 2009 and early 2010, the China Internet Network Information Center enacted a domain name registration policy. This policy required new and existing .cn domain name holders to provide a photo ID to acquire a new domain name—something that is not typically required, so users can maintain anonymity online. Following this change, the world's largest domain name registrar, GoDaddy, announced it would stop issuing domains in China. It did not want to participate in the Chinese authorities' increased control over the Chinese Internet.[17]

In 2010, Google published a blog titled "A new approach to China."[18] In it, they outlined a massive attack against them and over 20 other organizations, codenamed Operation Aurora by McAfee. Google's team had evidence that the attackers were trying to break into Google to access the Gmail accounts of Chinese human rights activists. They also had evidence that some Gmail accounts of human rights advocates in the United States, China, and Europe were compromised in separate attacks.

The attack on Google also attempted to steal intellectual property from Adobe, Rackspace, Akamai, and many other companies. Symantec attributed the attack to the Elderwood Gang, and Secure-Works released similar findings. MIIT denied it.[19]

The most interesting part of this attack was not the attack itself; it was the rest of the blog post from Google. In it, they stated that, because of the attacks and the additional measures China had taken in the past several years to curb freedom of speech on the Internet, Google had decided to stop censoring results in China, and it exited the Chinese market shortly after.

---

[17] www.wired.com/2010/03/godaddy-stops-selling-cn-domains-over-china-censorship-concerns
[18] https://googleblog.blogspot.com/2010/01/new-approach-to-china.html
[19] www.secureworks.com/blog/research-20913

This reversal showed that, despite their best intentions, even the largest companies in the world are not on equal footing with nation-states. Private companies are under the thumb of these governments because they have what the companies want: Access to an incredibly large market. Instead of providing more rights to citizens, these companies aid the erosion of freedoms—until they choose to leave the market.

By 2010, 30 journalists and 72 Internet users had been jailed for their online speech in China. They were charged with subversion and dissemination of state secrets.[20]

In late 2010, WikiLeaks published cables from the U.S. embassy that outlined potential reasons for the attack on Google. In an embarrassing moment of insecurity and vanity, a member of China's Politburo Standing Committee Googled himself on the uncensored version of Google and, when he found critical and unflattering information, he demanded that any links to Google.com be removed from Google.cn, the censored version.[21] Another cable stated that the attack was directed by the Politburo Standing Committee and was politically motivated.[22]

Privacy, Unless It's From the State

In 2016, China enacted the *Cybersecurity Law of the People's Republic of China*, a groundbreaking national law on cybersecurity that was more comprehensive than the laws concerning cybersecurity in the vast majority of countries at the time.[23]

---

[20] www.refworld.org/reference/annualreport/rsf/2010/en/73333
[21] www.theguardian.com/world/us-embassy-cables-documents/207610
[22] www.theguardian.com/world/us-embassy-cables-documents/245489
[23] https://digichina.stanford.edu/work/translation-cybersecurity-law-of-the-peoples-republic-of-china-effective-june-1-2017

However, the law is also very broad. It was the first time the CCP had introduced cyberspace sovereignty (though it didn't define it). It did define cybersecurity and critical information infrastructure at a national level, but the definition was intentionally vague. Vague definitions are open for interpretation, which gives the state space to define, and therefore control, any organization it wants under this banner.

The law focuses on three main things. First, it prioritizes China's education and research, mandating cybersecurity education through mass media. Second, it explicitly bans targeting anyone with cyberattacks or participating in illegal activity online. It requires citizens to "respect social morality"—an intentionally vague statement that can be used to later persecute those who speak out against the regime. Third, it establishes the state as responsible for monitoring the cybersecurity of the nation. That includes implementing a multi-level protection system (MLPS), a combination of technical measures to prevent cyberattacks and to control response to attacks if they occur. The catch here: This gave the state more access to network equipment and operators. The law requires network equipment to meet the requirements of a state security inspection before it is sold, and the state maintains a database of approved network equipment and specialized security products, which are typically products the state knows it can break into or surveil as needed. Network operators are also required to support national security and public security organs upon request in cases of national security. The law is broadly worded such that the state can ask for virtually any information, and the network operator must comply.[24]

There's some good in this document, particularly when it comes to user privacy from companies (though that privacy does not extend to protection against the state). It requires providers to indicate where user data is collected and obtain consent from the user. While later than other privacy laws, like in Canada and the EU, China was part of a second wave of privacy-forward regulation. It also requires providers to report when they observe attacks and vulnerabilities, thereby increasing public awareness and coordination against attacks.

The stuff that starts to infringe on personal rights is more buried. For example, network operators, which includes services like instant messaging (QQQ, Weibo, WeChat), social media,

---

[24]https://www.cac.gov.cn/2016-11/07/c_1119867116.htm

e-commerce, news services, or information publication (like message boards and forums) must require users to provide real identity information upon registration. This expands a 2012 law, which mandated that providers ensure that users link their true identities to their online personas. While this may seem innocuous, it helps authorities tie online actions (even seemingly benign ones) to real-life consequences, including jail time.[25]

In keeping with tradition, every person has the right (and is mandated to) report conduct that endangers cybersecurity or public security. If anyone fails to comply, they will be fined significantly.

The Apps Have Sharp Eyes

China is a geographically large country (one of the five largest in the world) with a mix of urban and rural areas.[26] Urban zones are far easier for the state to surveil—Skynet is able to use facial recognition effectively because of the concentration of people and surveillance equipment in urban areas, which rural areas lack. It's simply too expensive and technically difficult to deploy surveillance equipment and staff in all rural areas. To address this, the state launched the Sharp Eyes surveillance program (雪亮工程) in 2015 under the guise of addressing rural crime.[27]

Sharp Eyes extends surveillance beyond the more populous urban regions into rural areas and integrates urban and rural monitoring. Its primary goal is to integrate public and private camera networks to expand surveillance into rural communities. China wanted to reach 100 percent coverage of public spaces by 2020, and it seems like the project has been a relative success in surveillance, though data siloes between regions remain.[28]

To conduct surveillance at scale, the state relies on citizens for assistance. Geographic areas are divided into grids, and citizens within these grids are encouraged to spy on their peers. In some areas, the state installed television boxes in local residents' homes so they could watch live security footage and report on their

---

[25] https://www.cac.gov.cn/2012-12/29/c_133353262.htm
[26] https://www.britannica.com/place/China/Government-and-administration
[27] https://cset.georgetown.edu/article/sharp-eyes-surveillance-program-expands-dramatically
[28] https://www.gov.cn/zhengce/2015-04/13/content_2846013.htm

neighbors.[29] In another instance, the state launched an initiative called "Everyone Is a Safety Officer" that encourages citizens to report potential crimes via a mobile app.[30]

Ultimately, Sharp Eyes represents the final mile of the surveillance state. It relies on not just technology, but its own citizens to solve the last-mile problem.

Rules for Thee, Not for Me

Ironically, keeping information private has been an obsession of the Chinese for millennia. For a country that does everything in its power to surveil its populace and access almost all aspects of their lives, including the ability to read and modify their messages, the security and privacy of government documents remain a major priority.

This obsession goes back to the Shang Dynasty and grew throughout subsequent dynasties. After the Zhou Dynasty, information transmission capabilities were so vital to the country's day-to-day operations that they were known as the "vein of the nation."[31]

While early transmission methods in battle included drums, signal fires, and verbal messages delivered by couriers, each faced logistical challenges. There were many concerns about potentially leaking critical information to the enemy or being tricked into accepting bad information. To prevent this, during the Warring States Period, they adopted a physical tally system known as the Tiger Tally, Hufu (符), in which messages were passed on paper while a courier traveled with one half of a bronze, jade, or wooden artifact. The commander had the other half of the artifact; if the two halves did not match when the courier arrived, it was likely a

---

[29]https://cset.georgetown.edu/article/chinas-sharp-eyes-program-aims-to-surveil-100-of-public-space
[30]https://cset.georgetown.edu/wp-content/uploads/CSET-Designing-Alternatives-to-Chinas-Surveillance-State.pdf
[31]https://journals.plos.org/plosone/article?id=10.1371%2Fjournal.pone.0250622

fake message.[32] There is a direct parallel here to a common cybersecurity defense known as token authentication, in which a specific token is used to verify the legitimacy of incoming data.

Many dynasties continued this legacy. Ming Dynasty military treatises, such as the Bingfa Baiyan (兵 法 百 言), described the importance of transmission (傳), the ability to communicate information, especially in military scenarios.[33]

In modern times, the CCP uses a highly structured information-sharing process called the Neibu system, introduced in the 1950s. The system gives a clear distinction between public-facing propaganda and internal documents, known as *neibu wenjian* (内部文件). Documents are split into a few categories: Neibu (内部), meant for internal circulation to the party; *mimi* (秘密), confidential; *jimi* (机密), secret; and *juemi* (绝密), top-secret.[34]

Special sensitive documents, known as Neibu Cankao, are exclusive news reports containing sensitive information that are not meant to be shared with the broader public. They often contain threats to the stability of the state, geopolitical challenges, or information on public sentiment. The biggest difference between internal and publicly available media is that internal media must be accurate and factual. This is how the CCP manages to stay up to date with the realities on the ground while still spreading propaganda to the public.[35]

All of this comes back to one thing: Control. Control of what the public sees, control of what the media sees, control of what the party sees.

---

[32] https://english.cctv.com/2022/06/07/VIDEZuI141RNnvd4WJAjLrto220607.shtml

[33] https://www.cia.gov/resources/csi/static/Traditional-Chinese-Conceptions.pdf

[34] www.thechinastory.org/eyes-only-how-chinas-party-leaders-get-their-information

[35] Dimitrov, Martin K. Dictatorship and Information: Authoritarian Regime Resilience in Communist Europe and China. New York: Oxford University Press, 2022.

Chapter 19
The Red Guests

就狭义而言,信息战是指交战双方通过控制信息与情报的流动,
来争夺战场主动权的战争。

In a military sense alone, information warfare refers to both side's
attempt to gain the initiative of the battle through their control over
information and flow of intelligence.
> —*Dr. Shen Weiguang, considered China's father of*
> *information warfare*[1]

Dr. Weiguang's book, *Information Warfare*, served as an early example and the foundation for future theories on information warfare. His belief that wars could be fought and won without bloodshed, solely through the information domain, was in keeping with tradition in China. It harkens back to Sun Tzu in *The Art of War*: One of its most famous quotes exemplifies this, "All warfare is based on deception."[2]

The Red Guests

Hacktivists played an important role in China's threat actor ecosystem; they were the first major cyberattackers to emerge from China.

---

[1] www.globalaffairs.ch/2022/06/08/chinese-definitions-of-information-warfare
[2] Sun Tzu. The Art of War. Translated by Ralph D. Sawyer. Boulder, CO: Westview Press, 1994.

The word for hacker in Chinese is *heike* ((黑客), which literally translates to "dark guest." Hacktivists were labeled red hackers, or *hong-ke* (红客), "red guest," since China's identity and culture are so strongly tied to the color red. Because of this, red hackers were also known as Honkers (the pronunciation of *hong-ke*).

Red hackers served as the foundation of China's cybersecurity community, which is critically important in understanding how China's cybersecurity apparatus grew. What unites them is their love of country, which has enabled China to build a strong, mission-aligned cybersecurity force.

Many early red hackers went on to become executives at some of the largest Chinese companies, while others led hacking groups or worked in the state apparatus. In *Before Vegas: The "Red Hackers" Who Shaped China's Cyber Ecosystem,* Eugenio Benincasa outlines the Red 40—the top 40 Chinese citizens who, after starting in a hacktivist group, had a significant impact on the cybersecurity landscape in China.[3] These individuals founded or played a major role in prominent patriotic hacking groups, then went on to build or hold high-level leadership positions at companies such as Huawei, Alibaba, Tencent, NSFOCUS. Others ended up in PLA positions or as state contractors. For example:

- The founder of the China Eagle Union, Tao Wan (eagle), later took on a leadership position at Huawei.
- The founder of Xfocus, Zhang Xundi (xundi), worked for Alibaba, and the founder of Ph4nt0m Security, Wu Hanqing (ci), took a leadership position at Alibaba.
- The founder of NCPH, Tan Dailin (wicked rose), became a state contractor affiliated with the PLA before joining a Ministry of State Security–affiliated offensive cyber threat actor.

In the 1990s, the cyber community operated independently of the state but shared nationalist interests. Chinese hacktivist groups had thousands of members, with discussion boards and training programs to uplevel new ones. Much of it thrived because of early university networks like CERNET. It provided the perfect

---

[3] https://css.ethz.ch/en/center/CSS-news/2025/07/before-vegas-the-red-hackers-who-shaped-chinas-cyber-ecosystem.html

infrastructure for students to experiment with technology, the Internet, and hacking.[4]

Red hackers carried out their first major cyberattack against Indonesia in 1998, kicking off a series of patriotic cyber wars. For many years prior, ethnic Chinese had experienced discrimination and violence in Indonesia. Tensions were high, as it was suffering from the Asian financial crisis, and had seen divisive vote rigging during the 1997 legislative election. Many demonstrations by students were taking place across Indonesia, some of which turned deadly between protestors and security forces. Over the ensuing period, rioters raped and killed native Chinese Indonesians and looted and burned their homes, churches, and properties.[5]

China's response was . . . tepid, for many reasons. It had spent years working to not be perceived as a threat, as it had a tumultuous history with Indonesia and had only recently (as of 1990) reestablished strong relations between the two nations; it prioritized state sovereignty and saw its own potential response as marring that; and it had, in the 1950s, established Chinese citizenship through birthplace instead of blood, limiting the ties of Indonesian Chinese back to China.[6]

Red hackers in China felt differently. In response to the attacks on ethnic Chinese in Indonesia and as a show of just how independent they could be from the state, hacktivists defaced Indonesian websites and targeted them with distributed denial-of-service (DDoS) attacks to take them down.[7]

The Honker Crusades

Over the next few years, red hackers broadened their attacks beyond Indonesia. After Taiwan's president advocated for Taiwan's sovereignty, attackers responded by defacing websites with messages like, "There is only one China in the world, and the world only needs one China."[8]

---

[4]https://www.wired.com/story/china-honkers-elite-cyber-spies
[5]https://journals.sagepub.com/doi/10.1177/18681034221084320
[6]https://s3.us-west-1.wasabisys.com/p-library/books/ddc263a6633cc5d8af9e146624497e3a.pdf
[7]https://www.wired.com/1998/08/cyber-vandals-target-indonesia
[8]https://yris.yira.org/essays/freedom-for-authoritarianism-patriotic-hackers-and-chinese-nationalism

In 2000, a conference was organized in Osaka, where the leading topic was the organizer's belief that the 1937 Nanjing Massacre was the "biggest myth of the twentieth century."[9] The Japanese government allowed the event to continue, causing widespread outrage, especially from the likes of the CCP and state media. The event and the response to it led red hackers to target Japanese government sites en masse, flooding Japanese government email inboxes and trying to break into banks and government agencies. They defaced websites with messages like:

> Japanese, as all people know, it's a folk which has no concern to face the truth of history. They are the disgrace of Asia.[10]

Red hackers were initially applauded as defenders of China and viewed positively by the public. A report claimed that 84 percent of Internet users supported red hackers.[11]

Several large red hacking groups were founded during these years. The first known hacktivist organization in China was the Green Army, founded in 1997 by a hacker from Shanghai.[12] Other hacking groups were founded as well, like China Eagle Union (1997), Xfocus (1999), Honker Union (2000), Ph4nt0m Security (2001), EvilOctal Security (2002), 0x557 (2003), and Network Crack Program Hacker (2004).[13] These groups had thousands of registered users, but the core users that took an active role in ongoing engagements were far fewer. The disparate groups also led to the creation of the Red Hacker Alliance (红客), a loose coalition of hacker groups that ultimately disbanded in 2004.[14]

Over time, and especially as the CCP recognized they could not control them and wield them as they saw fit, red hackers fell out of

---

[9] www.nytimes.com/2000/01/23/world/japanese-call-37-massacre-a-war-myth-stirring-storm.html
[10] https://css.ethz.ch/content/dam/ethz/special-interest/gess/cis/center-for-securities-studies/pdfs/Cyber-Reports-2020-01-A-one-sided-Affair.pdf
[11] https://chinascope.org/archives/6519
[12] https://books.google.fr/books/about/The_Dark_Visitor.html?id=NYIiAQA AMAAJ&redir_esc=y
[13] https://css.ethz.ch/content/dam/ethz/special-interest/gess/cis/center-for-securities-studies/pdfs/before-vegas-cyberdefense-report.pdf#page39
[14] https://css.ethz.ch/en/center/CSS-news/2025/07/before-vegas-the-red-hackers-who-shaped-chinas-cyber-ecosystem.html

favor. The tipping point came in 2001 when a U.S. spy plane on an intelligence-gathering mission collided with a Chinese air force jet in the South China Sea.[15] The collision killed the Chinese pilot and downed the U.S. plane, forcing an emergency landing on a nearby island. On the way down and prior to being detained, the U.S. crew feverishly destroyed as much data on board as possible. The crew was detained, interrogated, and was not released until 10 days later, when the United States provided a letter known as the "letter of two sorries." The letter stopped short of issuing a formal apology but stated regret for the death of the Chinese pilot and for entering Chinese airspace and landing without clearance. It was the difference between a form apology, a *zhengshi daoqian* (抱歉), and a casual apology, a *baoqian* (道歉).[16]

This kicked off a series of cyberattacks on both sides in a show of patriotic attacks. Red hackers held a "week-long May Day war" on U.S. sites starting on April 30.[17] They targeted many U.S. websites, including the U.S. Department of Labor and Department of Health and Human Services, gaining access to and illicitly posting eulogies and pictures of the fallen pilot on their websites. Red hackers shut down the website of the White House for hours, and Eastern Ohio's Bellaire School District website was defaced. The red hackers made the school district's website play the Chinese national anthem with an image of China's flag on it.[18] U.S. hackers fought back, defacing Chinese state websites with pornographic images.[19]

Attempting Order from Chaos

These unchecked attacks made the CCP aware of just how out of their control the red hackers were. In the *People's Daily*, they referred to it as "web terrorism" and stated that "While we do not

---

[15] www.nytimes.com/2001/04/02/world/us-plane-in-china-after-it-collides-with-chinese-jet.html
[16] https://www.history.navy.mil/research/archives/Collections/ncdu-det-206/2001/ep-3-collision-crew-detainment-and-homecoming.html
[17] https://www.cnn.com/2001/WORLD/asiapcf/east/05/03/china.hack
[18] www.nytimes.com/2001/05/13/weekinreview/may-6-12-the-first-world-hacker-war.html
[19] https://www.nytimes.com/2001/05/13/weekinreview/may-6-12-the-first-world-hacker-war.html

wish to offend patriotic web surfers, it is important to alert the public to the risks of such acts and prevent further disasters."[20]

Between the change in sentiment, increased regulation resulting from the implementation of the Great Firewall, and economic conditions in China, the red hackers reached an inflection point. From here on, many of the groups slowly declined in membership or disbanded.

Economics were a major factor—China was one of the fastest-growing economies of the early 2000s, yet even those in urban areas struggled with financial uncertainty. This statement from the Ph4nt0m Group shortly before it shut down its blog in 2008 says it all:

> In China, it is hard to have an easy life until you've earned a lot of money. So, we don't have enough spare time to do the things we enjoyed before finding a stable place to live.[21]

Chinese hacktivists persist to this day, but in a very different form. One example is the Little Pink (小粉红) group, young Chinese hacktivists named after the pink background of the discussion forum where they got their start, Jinjiang Literature City.[22] In 2016, when Taiwan elected a pro-independence president, Little Pinks hammered the president's Facebook pages and Taiwanese media outlets with memes that were pro-China and pro-unification.[23]

The CCP rarely denounces these groups, instead trying to cultivate their nationalist tendencies as a tool of state power. That said, hacktivists like these can pose challenges for diplomacy and are often derided by academics. In one instance, Yu Liang, a journalist and academic at Fudan University in Shanghai, criticized the efforts of Little Pinks as "video-clip Marxism."[24]

[20] https://ethz.ch/content/dam/ethz/special-interest/gess/cis/center-for-securities-studies/pdfs/before-vegas-cyberdefense-report.pdf
[21] Segal, Adam. The Hacked World Order: How Nations Fight, Trade, Maneuver, and Manipulate in the Digital Age. New York: PublicAffairs, 2016.
[22] https://www.economist.com/china/2016/08/13/the-east-is-pink
[23] https://dominotheory.com/chinese-nationalist-groups-are-launching-cyberattacks-often-against-the-wishes-of-the-government
[24] https://insidestory.org.au/little-pinks-and-their-achy-breaky-hearts

Chapter 20

Borrow a Corpse to Raise the Spirit

借尸还魂。

Revive something from the past by giving it a new purpose or bring to life old ideas, customs, or traditions and reinterpret them to fit your purposes.

—*Stratagem 14 of the* Thirty-Six Stratagems[1]

One book became popularized in 1961 when it was reviewed in a CCP newspaper: *The Thirty-Six Stratagems* (三十六计). Compiled at the beginning of the Qing dynasty, it is a military treatise that focuses on psychological strategies in warfare, particularly deception and manipulation.[2] It focuses on six sets

---

[1] https://ia601605.us.archive.org/30/items/the-direction-of-war-contem porary-strategy-in-historical-perspective-pdfdrive/The%20Thirty-Six%20 Stratagems%20-%20A%20Modern%20Interpretation%20Of%20A%20Strategy%20 Classic%20(%20PDFDrive%20).pdf
[2] Ibid.

of stratagems: Advantageous, opportunistic, attacking, confusion, deception, and desperate. These stratagems have been fundamental building blocks to China's cyber strategy.

Failure to Join

In the mid-1980s, Deng Xiaoping deviated from Mao's era of protracted warfare to focus on *Local War Under Modern Conditions*, a military strategy wherein speed, mobility, and precision were prioritized on smaller battlefields.[3] This transition took the PLA from a force awaiting World War III to a peacetime military focused on development. The PLA reduced troop numbers and focused on military modernization to build a more targeted, mobile, and responsive army.

Later on in the 1990s, in direct response to the Gulf War, Jiang Zemin introduced *Local Wars Under Modern High-Tech Conditions*. In theory, this strategy prioritized technology and joint operations.[4] In practice, despite this and many attempts over the next 3 decades, the PLA would struggle to integrate its units equally. The army continued to dominate, with other units treated as subordinate. China hadn't been in a true war since 1979, and because of that, PLA officials often described its force as struggling with "peace disease"—troops were complacent.[5]

Once again in 2003, this time under Hu Jintao, China pivoted its force, this time as it tried to develop strategies to soften a potential battlefield. In the 2003 version of China's Three Warfares doctrine, the PLA broadened wartime capabilities to include psychological warfare, public opinion warfare, and legal warfare as official, coordinated tools for advancing Chinese interests in peacetime and conflict.[6]

Other doctrines, like *Local Wars Under Informatized Conditions* in 2004, pushed for more joint warfare, but the structure of the PLA

---

[3] www.uscc.gov/sites/default/files/Cheng_USCC%20Testimony_FINAL.pdf
[4] www.congress.gov/crs-product/IF11719
[5] https://jamestown.org/military-operations-other-than-war-antidote-to-the-plas-peace-disease
[6] https://www.esd.whs.mil/Portals/54/Documents/FOID/Reading%20Room/Litigation_Release/Litigation%20Release%20-%20China-%20The%20Three%20Warfares%20%20201305.pdf

continued to prevent it from taking hold. That said, this doctrine did recognize the increasing impact of advanced information technologies on combat operations. It helped build acceptance for *informatization*, the process of integrating information technology into every aspect of warfare.[7] The PLA saw how control over information could ensure superiority during crucial phases of a campaign. It led the PLA to prioritize a systems-to-systems approach to warfare that the PLA developed into a strategy known as "system destruction warfare" in 2005.[8] This strategy shifts the approach from taking out individual assets, like tanks or armies, to taking out the operational systems of the enemy. Once the enemy's operational systems cannot function, they lose the will and ability to resist. The goal is not necessarily to annihilate the enemy's forces but to incapacitate their systems, rendering them unable to function as an integrated whole.

Too Little to Too Much

Integrated Network-Electronic Warfare (INEW) is a military strategy that directly resulted from China's shift in focus to information warfare. INEW marked the convergence of cyber and electronic warfare into a unified strategy focused on disrupting an adversary's operations by gaining information superiority.[9] However, initial efforts to implement INEW were fragmented and lacked full integration across military branches because of the disjointed structure of the PLA.

It wasn't until after Xi Jinping was elected in 2012 that the PLA would fundamentally change.[10] He pushed a vision of a military force capable of conducting joint informatized operations through system destruction warfare.[11]

To get there, *Winning Informatized Local Wars* was introduced in 2015. This led to a major reorganization of the PLA to transform it from a ground force–centric operation to one that prioritized integration of joint forces.

---

[7] M. Taylor Fravel, "Shifts in Warfare and Party Unity: Explaining China's Changes in Military Strategy," International Security 42, no. 3 (Winter 2017/18): 45.
[8] https://www.rand.org/pubs/research_reports/RR1708.html
[9] https://jamestown.org/chinas-new-military-strategy-winning-informationized-local-wars
[10] https://www.britannica.com/biography/Xi-Jinping
[11] https://keystone.ndu.edu/Portals/86/PLA%20Systems%20Attack%20-%20Key stone%2025-1%20Jan%2025.pdf

The new PLA was structured around three organs: The Army Leading Organ, the Rocket Force, and the Strategic Support Force (SSF). This made a profound difference in how consolidated the cybersecurity capabilities were—instead of being spread across multiple divisions, the PLA Strategic Support Force consolidated intelligence, space, cyber, electronic, and psychological warfare.[12] A 2015 China's Military Strategy document explicitly identified cyberspace as a "new commanding height" in modern military competition, and under Xi Jinping's leadership, China's investment in cyber capabilities accelerated.[13] However, the consolidation didn't help the way Xi hoped it would. Instead of serving as an effective one-stop shop for cyber in the PLA, it became a bottleneck. It was responsible for building and defending the military network along with fighting in specific domains, and it was simply too much.

Breaking the Bottleneck

In 2024, China once again restructured the PLA to try to fix joint operations. It dissolved the Strategic Support Force and replaced it with the Information Support Force, Aerospace Force, and Cyberspace Force. These three, plus the Joint Logistics Force, make up the key support arms for the major service branches. It separated out defensive and offensive cyber capabilities.[14] The Information Support Force coordinates the PLA's network information systems, ensuring the PLA has communications and network defense support. Meanwhile, the Cyberspace Force is responsible for cyber warfare, electronic warfare, and psychological warfare, including offensive and defensive cyber operations. It's too early to say if these changes will fix the problems of before, but they have helped reduce the bottleneck formerly established by the SSF.

---

[12] www.cfr.org/blog/chinas-strategic-support-force-new-home-plas-cyber-operations

[13] https://english.www.gov.cn/archive/white_paper/2015/05/27/content_281475115610833.htm

[14] https://www.cna.org/our-media/indepth/2024/08/chinese-information-support-force

Chapter 21
Beijing's Trojan Dragon

韬光养晦。
Hide your strength and your bide time.

—Deng Xiaoping[1]

China was first to create many inventions that fundamentally changed warfare, with some of its most well-known being the Four Great Inventions of China (中国古代四大发明). These are prominent symbols of Chinese pride and innovation, especially when it comes to the compass, papermaking, printing, and gunpowder. These technologies enabled incredibly consequential changes to military and global history, and, like many ideas, goods, and cultures, they spread to the rest of the world via the Silk Road.[2]

Lay the Foundation

China underwent a period of economic inward focus, especially through the 1970s. That changed with Deng Xiaoping's economic reforms in 1978, which marked a turning point in China's global

---

[1] https://www.hoover.org/research/defending-taiwan-0
[2] https://ag.china-embassy.gov.cn/eng/zgyabjw/202302/t20230210_11023529.htm

strategy. Rather than exporting revolution, China focused on economic development and integration into the global economy.[3]

While there were some hiccups along the way, by the early 2000s, China was encouraging Chinese companies to invest overseas. It formalized this approach in its "going out" strategy, which marked China's transition to an outward-facing economy that encouraged overseas investment and laid the groundwork for broader economic initiatives to come.[4]

Since 1991, China has been building out its "national team"— a group of corporate champions for Chinese interests that receive state benefits and that are directly empowered by the state.[5] These companies are responsible for advancing China's national interests and generating business profits. Among other benefits, they receive subsidies and grants, preferential credit, procurement preferences, diplomatic facilitation, and policy guidance by the state.[6]

Many members of the national team have a party member in a leadership position, such as a CEO or a board seat. For example, Jack Ma, founder of Alibaba, is a member of the CCP.[7] Ren Zhengfei, founder and CEO of Huawei, is a party member and has said that, in a dispute between the interests of Huawei and the CCP, he would "choose the CCP, whose interest is to serve the people and all human beings."[8]

If they do not have a party member as a leader, they often still have party influence. Private enterprises in China are required to have a party branch if they have three or more CCP members as employees. The branch spreads party propaganda and ensures party oversight of the business.[9]

Here's the problem with this: Being part of the CCP is not a mere political affiliation, it is a lifestyle. Membership is relatively exclusive; as of 2025, the CCP has 100.27 million party members, about 7 percent of the population.[10] Party members pay dues, are

[3] https://www.cctv.com/english/special/60anni/20090907/107082.shtml
[4] https://ecfr.eu/archive/page/-/China_Analysis_Facing_the_Risks_of_the_Going_Out_Strategy_January2012.pdf
[5] www.tcd.ie/Economics/TEP/2006_papers/TEP8.pdf
[6] www.nber.org/system/files/working_papers/w20930/w20930.pdf
[7] https://time.com/5926062/jack-ma
[8] Marquis, Christopher, and Kunyuan Qiao. Mao and Markets: The Communist Roots of Chinese Enterprise. Yale University Press, 2022.
[9] https://www.csis.org/analysis/new-challenge-communist-corporate-governance
[10] http://english.scio.gov.cn/pressroom/2025-06/30/content_117954482.html

well-versed in party theory, and are expected to give the party complete and total loyalty above all other organizations. Their lives are monitored, and if they are accused of a crime, they will be tortured into giving confessions. It is a totalistic ideological movement. The CCP also has very different incentives from a business. A business is out for profit; the CCP is out to pursue "happiness for the Chinese people and rejuvenation for the Chinese nation."[11]

Spread the Message

China's accession to the World Trade Organization (WTO) in 2001 was a critical milestone in its integration into the global economy.[12] It had leveraged its manufacturing capacity and was emerging as an economic powerhouse. Over the next ten years, it focused on securing the raw materials and markets necessary for sustained economic growth, which enabled it to leapfrog to a new strategy in the 2010s.

In 2013, a modern Silk Road, leveraging new innovations, was being built: The Belt and Road Initiative (BRI).[13] BRI is a global infrastructure development strategy launched by Xi Jinping. This was a fundamental shift in China's primary focus from its own economic transformation to global integration and influence.

In the initiative, the "belt" refers to a vast network of railways, highways, energy pipelines, and other infrastructure projects that extend across Central Asia to Europe. The "road" consists of the developing ports and maritime routes from Southeast Asia to East Africa and Europe.

With total investments already exceeding $1 trillion, the BRI is one of the largest infrastructure and investment projects in history. As of 2025, about 150 countries have signed cooperation agreements, including 17 member states of the EU and 8 G20 nations.[14]

---

[11] www.idcpc.org.cn/english2023/tjzl/cpcjj/20thPartyCongrssReport
[12] https://www.brookings.edu/articles/issues-in-chinas-wto-accession
[13] www.cfr.org/backgrounder/chinas-massive-belt-and-road-initiative
[14] www.griffith.edu.au/__data/assets/pdf_file/0028/2184418/Nedopil-2025-China-Belt-and-Road-Initiative-BRI-Investment-Report-2025-H1.pdf

Much like the Silk Road was during the Han Dynasty, the BRI is the connective tissue between East Asia, Europe, and now Africa, Oceania, and Latin America.

It's been a partial success for China, expanding its influence while also exposing it to financial risks and political backlash. Geopolitically, the BRI expands China's global political and economic influence by making participating nations more economically interdependent with China. However, the initiative has drawn significant criticism over concerns of debt-trap diplomacy, where countries become financially beholden to China. For example, the China-Pakistan Economic Corridor is a massive $62 billion infrastructure project that has put Pakistan in debt—in 2022, 30 percent of its foreign debt was owed to China.[15]

Wire the World

There's another part of the BRI that has faced considerable skepticism: Its counterpart launched in 2015, the Digital Silk Road (DSR).[16] The DSR is the technology and digital infrastructure component of China's BRI. It finances and develops infrastructure, including 5G networks, fiber-optic cables, data centers, surveillance technologies, and e-commerce platforms for participating nations. It provides support to recipient states and to Chinese exporters such as Huawei.

On the buyer side, at least 16 countries are formally part of the DSR, though estimates suggest over 80 have DSR-related technology.[17] On the seller side, many prominent companies associated with the Digital Silk Road are also part of the national team, including Huawei, ZTE, Inspur, Alibaba, Tencent, Baidu, and JD.com.[18]

This seems like a win; companies like Huawei are making major advancements in areas like 5G, which can be brought more easily

[15] www.bloomberg.com/news/articles/2022-09-02/china-s-funding-to-pakistan-stands-at-30-of-foreign-debt
[16] https://www.cfr.org/china-digital-silk-road
[17] www.cfr.org/china-digital-silk-road
[18] https://www.eurasiagroup.net/files/upload/Digital-Silk-Road-Expanding-China-Digital-Footprint.pdf

to countries that otherwise wouldn't have access. Pakistan, Saudi Arabia, and the UAE have projects to integrate Huawei into their national digital transformation agendas, including the deployment of 5G networks.[19]

But it's not all sunshine and rainbows. As much as the DSR supports countries' digital transformation efforts, it also puts them under the CCP's thumb. There's no saying that China won't pressure these Chinese companies to do the same things they have already done in China: Provide the CCP direct access, censor, or surveil. In fact, evidence exists that China is set up to do just that.

In 2017, *China's National Intelligence Law* formalized the powers of China's state intelligence agencies, which were previously fairly vague.[20] The most far-reaching and consequential part of the law comes with Article 7, which outlines that "all organizations and citizens shall support, assist, and cooperate with national intelligence efforts in accordance with law."[21]

The law creates a legal, affirmative duty for any Chinese citizen or company, regardless of their location, to collaborate with the state's intelligence services upon request, whether that company is Huawei, TikTok, or any other in China. The law codifies powers that would make Chinese companies and citizens use their global presence and resources to aid the state. Under these laws, a Chinese citizen working for a U.S. company in the United States would be legally required by the Chinese state to spy on that company or pass information from that company back to the state if the CCP wanted. It opens up China's intelligence-gathering apparatus to a degree far broader than it has ever been, at a unique time when the Belt and Road Initiative and the Digital Silk Road have embedded China, Chinese companies, and Chinese citizens in the core infrastructure of many nations.

---

[19] https://www.pta.gov.pk/category/pta-and-huawei-pakistan-sign-mou-to-strengthen-collaboration-in-it-and-telecom-sector-1577608552-2025-01-01

[20] www.cfr.org/backgrounder/chinas-huawei-threat-us-national-security

[21] www.chinalawtranslate.com/en/national-intelligence-law-of-the-p-r-c-2017

As of 2020, the Chinese had built at least 186 government buildings in Africa. Huawei built more than 70 percent of the continent's 4G networks.[22,23]

Surveil the World

To complicate matters further, China is also exporting its surveillance technologies, especially Safe City, to other countries as part of the DSR. Countries around the world that want to strengthen state control are increasingly adopting Chinese surveillance platforms. Sixty-three different countries, 36 of which are part of the Belt and Road Initiative, have bought AI surveillance technology from Chinese companies.[24]

These Safe City initiatives are marketed as comprehensive solutions for public safety, incorporating technologies like facial and license-plate recognition, social media monitoring, and intelligent surveillance systems. Much of Huawei's marketing makes bombastic claims about dramatically reducing violent crime and improving emergency response. In one instance in Kenya, Huawei claimed that crime rates in Nairobi and Mombasa declined by 46 percent compared to the previous year[24]—yet Kenya's National Police Service reported that, for those same cities, there was only a slight decrease in crime in Nairobi and an increase in Mombasa.[25,26]

Geopolitically, Huawei's Safe Cities are a key component of China's strategy to expand its global influence. By embedding its technology in the urban infrastructure of other nations, China can set technological standards, create long-term economic dependencies due to high replacement costs, and gain a commercial foothold in next-generation markets.

[22] https://www.heritage.org/africa/commentary/chinas-palace-diplomacy-africa
[23] https://www.uscc.gov/sites/default/files/Hruby_Testimony.pdf
[24] https://carnegieendowment.org/research/2019/09/the-global-expansion-of-ai-surveillance?lang=en
[25] www.huawei.com/en/news/2016/10/safe-city-summit-africa
[26] www.csis.org/analysis/watching-huaweis-safe-cities

Critics describe it as exporting authoritarianism, an apt phrase. But given Huawei's status in China, these surveillance systems don't just export authoritarianism—they also give China access to vast amounts of foreign data. China could very well use the surveillance infrastructure Huawei has sold to these nations to spy on them.[27] In 2018, in Ethiopia, Huawei-provided servers inside the African Union headquarters had been exporting data daily to Shanghai over a period of 5 years.[28] The headquarters, which had been built by the Chinese, was also filled with listening devices. African Union members had already known for a year about the surveillance but had chosen to keep it a secret. Much like the self-censorship of the people in China, African Union members' hesitation showcases just how much influence China has over Africa—and how much Africa stands to lose if it picks a fight with the Chinese that it can't win. China and Huawei were accused of stealing the data and planting the listening devices, but they vehemently denied it.

---

[27] www.csis.org/analysis/watching-huaweis-safe-cities
[28] www.cfr.org/blog/african-union-bugged-china-cyber-espionage-evidence-strategic-shifts

Chapter 22
Stealing Fresh Air

打开窗户，新鲜空气进来了，苍蝇也会飞进来。

There are those who say we should not open our windows, because open windows let in flies and other insects . . . They want the windows to stay closed, so we all expire from lack of air. But we say, "Open the windows, breathe the fresh air and at the same time fight the flies and insects."

—*Deng Xiaoping*

Following Deng Xiaoping's initiation of *the Four Modernizations* in 1978, Deng instituted China's Open Door economic policy, which opened it to foreign investment. Though the state reaffirmed that the Chinese economy is fundamental to China's national security, it also recognized that, at the time, China's semiconductor market was nonexistent, its computer industry was just beginning to be viable, and multiple industries—including telecommunications, automotive and aviation, and manufacturing—all relied heavily on imported tools from foreign nations.[1]

China recognized how far behind other major powers it was. It had a major problem: How does China catch up? The answer:

---

[1] https://www.cato.org/publications/chinas-post-1978-economic-development-entry-global-trading-system

Industrial espionage. While industrial espionage was not new to the Chinese, before the 1980s, it was ad hoc and relied on replicating Soviet designs. The state needed to create more strategic support to do this at scale effectively.

The main organization that would have supported it, the Central Investigations Department, had been decimated during the Cultural Revolution. It was reconstituted in 1983 and merged with parts of the Ministry of Public Security, responsible for counterintelligence, to form the Ministry of State Security (MSS). The MSS became the centralized civilian national security and intelligence function responsible for foreign intelligence and counterintelligence.[2] One of its first major actions was to facilitate industrial espionage to support China's development.

Around this same time, European companies sought to tap into the large Chinese market and made efforts to establish a presence there. There were many things that made this difficult—cultural differences, anti-Western sentiment within China, long selling cycles, and an uneven balance on the cost of goods, to name just a few. China used these roadblocks to its advantage. The long selling cycles and cultural differences in particular gave the Chinese time and access to European intellectual property so they could copy these companies' designs.[3]

For example, in 1980, the China New-Type Building Materials Company was considering inviting Bally to China to negotiate a potential collaboration. They demanded "as many documents as possible" from Bally about their technology so they could supposedly determine whether a collaboration would be feasible.[4] In reality, this was one of many examples of China attempting to negotiate its way to accessing intellectual property. It was to the point where some Western companies had to train their employees on the signs of IP theft during the buying process.[5]

In another instance, Swiss watchmakers opened watch centers in Chinese cities like Beijing and Shanghai. Chinese authorities

[2] www.uscc.gov/sites/default/files/John%20Costello_Written%20Testimony 060916.pdf
[3] https://journals.sagepub.com/doi/10.1177/00220094251323798
[4] http://pmc.ncbi.nlm.nih.gov/articles/PMC12240485
[5] Ibid.

used these facilities to train Chinese watchmakers. The watchmakers would get trained by the Swiss, then immediately leave and work for a Chinese manufacturer. One Swiss company claimed it was forced to close due to high turnover and staff poaching.[6]

Once the Internet became ubiquitous, China could scale these efforts.

Drilling for Data

Since the late 1990s, Chinese oil and gas companies have been shifting toward a more global energy strategy, driven by their substantial energy needs and economic growth. *The 11th Five-Year Plan* in China for 2006–2010 prioritized state-owned energy companies, particularly those on the national team.[7] It recommended they pursue an aggressive global strategy, particularly through overseas asset acquisitions. In 2009 alone, Chinese companies accounted for 13 percent of total global oil and gas acquisitions and 61 percent of all acquisitions by national oil companies.[8] The market was hot, and China recognized it as a strategic priority for national growth.

Enter 2011, when cybersecurity company McAfee announced it had found a new cyber espionage campaign targeting the global energy sector. The attacks, known as Night Dragon, began in 2006 and targeted at least 71 organizations, primarily oil, gas, and petrochemical companies. The attackers stole high-value confidential data, like proprietary operational data and bidding information for oil and gas field exploration and production contracts. That information could be worth millions and give a competitive advantage to any energy companies that got their hands on it. Companies could undercut competitors, better understand their corporate strategies, and leverage or weaponize any geological assessments, technical development plans, or risk calculations they could get.[9]

---

[6] https://pmc.ncbi.nlm.nih.gov/articles/PMC12240485
[7] https://www.cnsa.gov.cn/english/n6465652/n6465653/c6478484/content.html
[8] www.oecd.org/content/dam/oecd/en.publications/reports/2011/02/overseas-investments-by-chinese-national-oil-companies_g17a1f69/5kgglrwdrvvd-en.pdf
[9] www.mcafee.com/blogs/wp-content/uploads/2011/02/McAfee_NightDragon_wp_draft_to_customersv1-1.pdf

In the report, McAfee stopped short of stating the attack was perpetrated by the CCP, instead saying they had strong evidence to suggest the attackers were *based* in China.[10] The attacks used hacking tools developed in China, were launched in several locations in China, and used Beijing-based IP addresses. In addition, the attackers operated only from 9 to 5 p.m. Beijing time, which is typically indicative of attackers who do this for a living, rather than part-time or freelance.

The attack also aligned with China's national plans and would help it establish a competitive advantage in the energy space. It's likely that the attack was perpetrated by, at the very least, a group associated with the CCP, and that the information was spread to the national team energy companies to help them differentiate in global markets.

The Price of Entry

In 2008, Coca-Cola issued a formal, public, cash offer to acquire China Huiyuan Juice Group Limited. Coca-Cola had been operating in China for years; China was its fourth-largest market. It had worked closely with Beijing during the Olympics, and it had pledged an additional $2 billion in investment in China.[11] It saw China Huiyuan Juice Group as a big opportunity—if the deal went through, it would have been the largest foreign takeover of a Chinese company, at $2.4 billion.[12]

In the heat of its 6-month-long negotiations in 2009, the deputy president of Coca-Cola's Pacific Group received an email seemingly from the Coca-Cola Pacific Group general counsel, which contained a link to a file supposedly from the CEO—only it wasn't from the CEO at all. It was actually from attackers in China's PLA Unit 61398. Unaware, the deputy president clicked the link in the email, and the malware installed code to track every single thing he did with his keyboard. It started stealing essential documents and emails to send back to China. The attackers spread their access across multiple machines, stole passwords from other employees,

---

[10] www.mcafee.com/blogs/wp-content/uploads/2011/02/McAfee_NightDragon_wp_draft_to_customersv1-1.pdf

[11] www.reuters.com/article/business/china-scuttles-cokes-bid-for-juice-maker-idUSTRE52H0QH

[12] www.npr.org/2009/03/18/102064714/china-scraps-cokes-bid-for-juice-company

and accessed Coca-Cola systems daily.[13] The deal collapsed shortly thereafter, when China's Ministry of Commerce disapproved the deal under its new *Anti-Monopoly Law*.[14] Although there were legitimate concerns over the control Coca-Cola would gain over the Chinese market, many speculated that this was a form of economic protectionism, that China was avoiding foreign control in a significant industry. There's good reason to suspect this, as it was the first instance of the state invoking the *Anti-Monopoly Law* since its enactment in 2008.[15]

Coca-Cola kept the attack hidden for years until it became public in 2012.[16] When it came to light, it was highlighted as a clear example of economic espionage. It's likely, though unconfirmed, that the attackers sought to access sensitive internal documents that could provide the Ministry with a better understanding of Coca-Cola's position and be used in the negotiations.

Sick Money

The COVID-19 pandemic created opportunities for many threat actors to attack businesses struggling to transition to fully remote work, both for financial gain and espionage. Especially at the start of the pandemic, IT staff were inundated with requests to enable secure work-from-home access. It left a major opportunity for APT41, a Chinese state-sponsored threat group, to complete two objectives: Espionage and financially motivated cybercrime.

Between January and March 2020, APT41 targeted entities in multiple countries across various industries. They leveraged a vulnerability in Citrix systems, one in Zoho ManageEngine, and a Cisco router exploit to gain access to over 75 different entities.[17] Their goal: Steal as much information as possible.

---

[13] https://www.wired.com/2013/02/chinese-army-linked-to-hacks
[14] https://www.npc.gov.cn/zgrdw/englishnpc/Law/2009-02/20/content_1471587.htm
[15] https://www.wilmerhale.com/en/insights/publications/coca-cola-huiyuan-china-prohibits-its-first-merger-under-the-aml-march-20-2009
[16] https://www.securityweek.com/coca-cola-hid-hack-2009-report
[17] https://cloud.google.com/blog/topics/threat-intelligence/apt41-initiates-global-intrusion-campaign-using-multiple-exploits

APT41 also executed a brazen series of financially motivated attacks, stealing at least $20 million in U.S. COVID-19 relief funds, including Small Business Administration loans and unemployment insurance funds from multiple states.[18] This type of cyber activity from China was unusual. The vast majority of Chinese state-aligned actors rarely target victims for financial gain. APT41 is the exception and has attacked targets for financial gain before, but most were in the video game industry.[19] Some U.S. officials speculate that while the espionage was state-directed, the CCP may have simply tolerated the hackers profiting from their access due to its frustrations with the United States.[20]

By May, an arms race for the COVID-19 vaccine was underway; APT41 directed its espionage against health care, pharmaceutical, and research organizations in the United States and other nations to steal data on COVID-19 vaccines and treatments.[21]

In September 2020, the U.S. Department of Justice indicted five alleged members of APT41 on racketeering, money laundering, fraud, identity theft, and access device fraud.[22]

---

[18]www.nbcnews.com/tech/security/chinese-hackers-covid-fraud-millions-rcna59636
[19]https://cloud.google.com/blog/topics/threat-intelligence/apt41-dual-espionage-and-cyber-crime-operation
[20]https://www.nbcnews.com/tech/security/chinese-hackers-covid-fraud-millions-rcna59636
[21]www.nytimes.com/2020/05/10/us/politics/coronavirus-china-cyber-hacking.html
[22]https://www.justice.gov/archives/opa/pr/seven-international-cyber-defendants-including-apt41-actors-charged-connection-computer

Chapter 23
Learn from the Barbarians to Control the Barbarians

師夷長技以製夷
Learn from the barbarians the superior techniques to control the barbarians.

—The Illustrated Treatise on the Maritime
Kingdoms, *Wei Yuan*[1]

In 1861, after a series of defeats during the Opium Wars, the Qing dynasty recognized that the military needed major reforms. They wanted to maintain Chinese culture and Confucian values while adopting Western technology and knowledge. This is like putting on new clothes and claiming you are a different person—if you don't change the underlying structure, you can reap the benefits for only a short time.

China began appropriating Western approaches—building out Western-style arsenals, shipyards, and military schools. The Jiangnan Arsenal (江南機器製造總局) was built in Shanghai to manufacture firearms and other military technologies and build ships.[2] The

---

[1] Wei Yuan, Haiguo tuzhi 海國圖志 (Illustrated Treatise on the Maritime Kingdoms), 1st ed., 1843.
[2] https://www.britannica.com/topic/Jiangnan-Arsenal

arsenal translated Western books on technology and science into Chinese in collaboration with Western missionaries.[3] This was a massive shift for a country that for centuries had required neighboring states to speak in Chinese when meeting with its emperor. Students were sent to study in the United States under the Chinese Educational Mission, a program in which 120 Chinese children studied science and technology in New England.[4] Upon returning to China, the students supported engineering efforts for the military and the state.

In 1895, General Zhang Zhidong revolutionized the Qing army into the New Army, structured around Western-style techniques. He brought German instructors to teach and recruited individuals to the army based on their strength, not familial ties. He believed Western drills and German artillery would meet the modern era. In a very consequential decision, he nixed the long tradition of using swords, replacing swords with modern rifles.[5]

Many of the reforms China built out in science and technology were not as effective as they could have been due to inherent corruption. The reforms were focused on changing science and technology, instead of changing the underlying system. Even if China wasn't willing to change the cracked foundation to make its own advancements, it still had to find innovation somewhere. This moment established that, in order to keep up with the technological advancements in the rest of the world, China had to use industrial espionage in its favor.

Clash of the Titans

In 2003, Shawn Carpenter, a cybersecurity analyst at Sandia National Laboratories, helped investigate a cyberattack on Lockheed Martin.[6] A few months later, he investigated another cyberattack on his own employer with a strikingly similar methodology. The attackers

[3] www.erudit.org/en/journals/meta/2016-v61-meta02902/1038684ar
[4] https://earlychinesemit.mit.edu/chinese-educational-mission
[5] https://cedar.wwu.edu/cgi/viewcontent.cgi?article=1485&context=wwuet
[6] https://time.com/archive/6674509/the-invasion-of-the-chinese-cyberspies

quietly broke in, grabbed as much data as they could, then left without a trace—sometimes in under 30 minutes. The similarities between this incident and the one at Lockheed Martin were so stark that Carpenter decided to bring it to the government's attention, and got in touch with his contacts in the U.S. Army cyber counterintelligence division, who eventually referred him to the FBI. Outside of his day job, he hunted the attackers, attempting to find where they were operating out of, then passed that information back to the FBI. U.S. officials codenamed the attacks Titan Rain.[7] Carpenter discovered that, despite the attackers trying to evade attribution (in part by treating machines in South Korea, Hong Kong, and Taiwan as waypoints before phoning home back to China), he could prove that the attacks were perpetrated by individuals in China. Over the next several years, the attackers stole data from many other defense-related firms, including NASA, the UK Ministry of Defense, the House of Commons, and contractors, stealing information on sensitive documents, including data related to advanced military systems.

While his findings alone are typically not enough for solid attribution to a nation state, as it could be any individual in China responsible, many analysts at the time suspected this attack was carried out with state resources. It was far too fast, effective, and targeted to be much else.[8] It wasn't acknowledged until 2007 that China was responsible, and even then, it was just as a comment in congressional testimony.[9] Even still, Titan Rain marked a turning point; China was no longer experimenting—it saw just how valuable cyber espionage could be.

Catching the RAT

In 2011, then-VP of Threat Research for McAfee, Dmitri Alperovitch, and his team went public with a 5-year-long attack they dubbed Operation Shady RAT.[10] RAT is a little play on words: It

---

[7] www.homelandsecuritynewswire.com/lesson-titan-rain-articulate-dangers-cyber-attack-upper-management
[8] https://time.com/archive/6674509/the-invasion-of-the-chinese-cyberspies
[9] www.govinfo.gov/content/pkg/CHRG-110hhrg48926.html/CHRG-110hhrg48926.htm
[10] https://graphics8.nytimes.com/packages/pdf/technology/mcafee_shadyrat_report.pdf

stands for Remote Access Tool, a piece of software that lets an individual remotely access and control a computer. The attack started in mid-2006 and was a massive cyber espionage campaign that targeted over 70 different organizations. It targeted these entities for inconsistent amounts of time: They accessed the U.S. Department of Energy Research Laboratory for 3 months and a South Korean construction company for 17 months. They siphoned sensitive documents, from defense secrets to business contracts to Olympic strategy files. Several U.S. state and federal government agencies were targeted, alongside defense contractors, news organizations, and other companies. A government agency in Taiwan and one in Canada, the United Nations, a technology company in Canada, and an Indian government agency were all breached.

In 2008, leading up to and following the 2008 Summer Olympics in Beijing, the World Anti-Doping Agency, the Olympic committee of a Western country, and the International Olympic Committee were all targeted.

Many analysts didn't definitively attribute these attacks, but suspect the attackers were affiliated with the CCP. The attack was likely a state actor, as there is little commercial or financial value in stealing documents from these specific government-affiliated organizations, governments, and Olympic-affiliated groups.

Shady RAT was a demonstration of China's growing confidence in prolonged, low-visibility cyber campaigns. The broad range of targets, from defense contractors to the International Olympic Committee, revealed Beijing's interest in using cyberattacks not just for military advantage, but also for soft power, industrial knowledge, and international influence. The operation helped shape the modern concept of advanced persistent threats (APTs) as long-term, targeted cyberattacks that are typically perpetrated by a nation-state.

Seeds of Doubt

Cybersecurity company RSA is named after the RSA public key cryptography algorithm, one of the oldest and most widely used public key cryptosystems for secure data transfer. The company created and sold SecurID, a very popular two-factor authentication product. The tool enabled a user to log in to a device using a token, a key fob, or software that creates a new authentication code every 60 seconds based on a "seed"—basically, a key. Both the token and the server know this seed, and so when you enter it to access the server, the key recognizes that you are the legitimate user and allows you to access the system. Since the code constantly changes based on the seed, it's very difficult for an attacker to guess it, as long as they don't know the seed. As was found out later, that's a problem: The seed is a concentrated point of vulnerability. Because of its ability to provide what most considered more secure authentication, the software was very popular with companies like Lockheed Martin as well as the U.S. Department of Defense. This made it an ideal target for attackers—if you can't break into Lockheed Martin directly, break its security software and get in that way.[11]

And in 2011, that's exactly what attackers did. They sent phishing emails to a small group of RSA employees, with one message containing a malicious Excel file titled "2011 Recruitment plan." An employee in Australia opened the attachment, which installed a backdoor so attackers could easily access the system time and time again. The attackers stole usernames and passwords from the machine, then quickly spread to other RSA computers. Eventually, the attackers reached a treasure trove: A server with hundreds of user credentials. RSA's security team was seeing and stopping the attacks as they were happening, but, they were consistently just behind the attackers. Then came the moment the attackers attempted to access the devices containing the most important information of all: Copies of the seeds on which the entire SecurID system relied.

At the time, executives believed these seeds were secure because they were in an air-gapped environment—an environment completely separate from any machine that accesses the

---

[11]http://wired.com/story/the-full-story-of-the-stunning-rsa-hack-can-finally-be-told

Internet. The problem is, even the most sensitive air-gapped environments need to be accessed for maintenance, updates, and data transfers—and in the case of SecurID, it needed to pull seeds from the air-gapped environment every 15 minutes. This gave the attackers an easy way in—they began using that access point to collect as many seeds as possible, constantly, with thousands of requests for data per second.[12]

Lockheed Martin, L-3 Communications, and others presented evidence that attackers were using SecurID fobs and stolen keys to breach their systems. RSA ultimately offered to replace SecurID tokens for customers, but overall, the monitoring and remediation of this attack (including replacements) cost RSA $66.3 million.[13]

The attack was a devastating moment for the defense community, as it exposed how the very systems built to protect—the security companies' software and hardware itself—could be manipulated to attack.

There was widespread speculation that the attack was perpetrated by a nation-state, especially China, but RSA did not release conclusive attribution or directly state who they suspected perpetrated the attack. Even still, China denied it.[14]

It wasn't confirmed publicly until 2012, when General Keith Alexander, head of the U.S. Cyber Command, said in a congressional hearing that RSA was one example of Chinese cyber espionage.[15]

Flooding Exchange

On March 2, 2021, Microsoft released a blog detailing four new zero-day exploits being used against the on-premises version of Microsoft Exchange Server.[16] Microsoft Exchange enables an enterprise

---

[12]https://archive.nytimes.com/bits.blogs.nytimes.com/2011/04/02/the-rsa-hack-how-they-did-it
[13]www.darkreading.com/cyberattacks-data-breaches/china-hacked-rsa-u-s-official-says
[14]https://www.zdnet.com/home-and-office/networking/us-says-china-behind-rsa-attacks
[15]https://www.armed-services.senate.gov/imo/media/doc/12-19%20-%20 3-27-12.pdf
[16]https://www.microsoft.com/en-us/security/blog/2021/03/02/hafnium-targeting-exchange-servers

to centrally manage email accounts and lets employees share calendars with one another to schedule meetings, provide availability, and so on. The attackers targeted the on-premises version, which is deployed on hardware that the customer manages, often in-person in the customer's own environment.

The vulnerabilities gave attackers access to customer servers, which houses a lot of critical information about a business. Once they had access to the machine, the attackers stole data from email accounts and created a backdoor so that, even if the vulnerability was patched, they could still get access to the servers.[17]

The vulnerability was reported to Microsoft on January 5. Microsoft was preparing to release the patches to fix it in March on Patch Tuesday, the 9th, as Microsoft releases security updates for all its products on the second Tuesday of every month. It's not unusual for patching complex enterprise applications to take two months, given this was an attack with multiple vulnerabilities on an on-premises product. However, as developers were preparing the patch, the attackers ramped up their attacks from hundreds a day to thousands a day. Microsoft rushed to issue the patch on March 2, a week ahead of schedule, but by that point, over 30,000 organizations had been affected, including banks, nonprofits, telecommunications providers, public utilities, and many others.[18]

Other hacker groups in China started targeting the servers at the same time, using the vulnerabilities to deploy ransomware. Microsoft attributed the attack to Silk Typhoon, a state-sponsored cyber espionage group affiliated with China's Ministry of State Security (MSS). All in all, the attack affected 250,000 servers.[19]

The United States, the European Union, the United Kingdom, Australia, Canada, New Zealand, Japan, and NATO condemned the MSS for the attack. China dismissed it as "groundless accusations out of thin air."[20]

---

[17]www.microsoft.com/en-us/security/blog/2021/03/02/hafnium-targeting-exchange-servers

[18]https://unit42.paloaltonetworks.com/microsoft-exchange-server-attack-timeline

[19]www.microsoft.com/en-us/security/blog/2021/03/02/hafnium-targeting-exchange-servers

[20]https://www.npr.org/2021/07/20/1018283149/china-blames-united-states-for-cyberattacks

Chapter 24
The State's Loyal Ears, Eyes, and Tongue

While forms of propaganda had been used by Chinese emperors for thousands of years, the intentional operationalization of propaganda began in earnest in the 1900s. The CCP and the Chinese National Party (KMT) both made liberal use of propaganda, *xuanchuan* (宣传), especially in the form of radio, documentary films, newspapers, patriotic songs, and other media.[1] Propaganda in China is considered legitimate—it is communication that legitimizes the state's rule, educates the public, and mobilizes the masses toward the goals of the state. Ultimately, it is about controlling the people by controlling the narrative.

The late 1930s were when the CCP started to systematize propaganda effectively. The CCP established an international propaganda committee and group to publish the writings of top Party leaders and spread the information internationally.[2]

---

[1] https://hkupress.hku.hk/image/catalog/pdf-preview/9789888390618.pdf
[2] https://www.hoover.org/sites/default/files/research/docs/09_diamond-schell_sec06_2ndprinting_web.pdf

After Mao seized power, he implemented a Leninist approach to the press, establishing that its main goal must be to serve the Party.[3] Private ownership of media was suppressed, and all outlets were brought under state control. Editorial freedom was a thing of the past. Instead, the media served as the "mouth and tongue" of the Party, to spread the propaganda the Party wanted spread.[4] Some of the largest and most popular state media operations include *Xinhua*, the People's Daily, and CCTV.[5] Mao strongly pushed the idea of a "proletarian journalist," one who served as a political operative.[6]

During the Cultural Revolution, many top journalists were purged. The exception was news agencies with ties to the Party, which could be controlled and used to the ends of the Party. The People's Daily, People's Liberation Army, and Red Flag served as the "Two Newspapers and One Journal" propaganda arm for the Party.[7] Mao also called for artists and literary scholars to take up political work as their focus to replace more traditional media.[8]

Language serves as a critical tool in propaganda, in part because the Chinese language can be interpreted in very different ways depending on the context. For example, even a simple syllable like "ma" can have dramatically different connotations: *mā* (妈) means mother, *má* (麻) means hemp, *mǎ* (马) means horse, and *mà* (骂) means to scold. When translated literally, the word for culture in China, *wenhua* (文化) means "transformation through literature."[9] Everything about China's culture is structured around the way things are interpreted, not through an objective reality.

The CCP instituted thought reform as an attempt to fundamentally transform the beliefs of Chinese citizens. Citizens were put into small groups, often based on their danwei, that met to discuss politics, especially communism, and to align on the Party message.[10] Members were required to speak in their own words and be

---

[3] https://rsf.org/en/sixty-years-news-media-and-censorship
[4] Ibid.
[5] Ibid.
[6] https://www.britannica.com/biography/Mao-Zedong
[7] https://chinamediaproject.org/the_ccp_dictionary/two-newspapers-and-one-journal
[8] kennedy.byu.edu/alumni/bridges/features/art-and-politics-in-maos-china
[9] www.baylor.edu/content/services/document.php?id=19565
[10] www.theatlantic.com/magazine/archive/1959/12/thought-reform-ideological-remolding-in-china/642911

criticized for it. "Struggle sessions" publicly humiliated and beat those who did not fall in line.[11]

Creating Realities

In the 1950s, most of the well-trained historians in China were focused on preserving the state-approved version of the history of China at a high level for societal consumption. They created a strong narrative about the greatness of Mao, the CCP, and the Red Army.[12] They downplayed the role of the KMT during World War II, despite its forces taking on a large part of the fight against Japan, instead focusing on the role of the CCP.[13] The rewriting of history served as a key means of controlling the reality of the Chinese people and rendering it malleable to the state.

In growing the cult, one of Mao's most ardent supporters and the head of the PLA, Lin Biao, collated Mao's quotes into *Quotations from Chairman Mao*, more colloquially known as the *Little Red Book*.[14] It became required reading for the PLA and solidified Mao's almost god-like status. Later, Lin was cast out as a traitor; according to the state, Lin attempted to assassinate Mao and was killed while fleeing China. Many speculate this was actually a cover-up and that Mao was threatened by Lin's political popularity and had him assassinated. Records that could have proved either way were destroyed.[15]

The Party's early emphasis on controlling modern thought and historical narratives laid the groundwork for its subsequent information control apparatus. While Mao's China relied on physical

---

[11] https://digitalcommons.ncf.edu/cgi/viewcontent.cgi?article=7394&context=theses_etds
[12] www.cia.gov/resources/csi/static/Edging-in-from-Cold.pdf
[13] https://resolve.cambridge.org/core/services/aop-cambridge-core/content/view/3EC3574E1BCB11AC5C50A6C6266AA5A5/9780511572838c3_p115-176_CBO.pdf/nationalist_china_during_the_sinojapanese_war_1937 1945.pdf
[14] cambridge.org/core/books/mao-cult/little-red-book/8D782F704E841ADE0D BC046F0EB1AB2E
[15] www.odu.edu/ao/instadv/quest/LinBiao.html

coercion and social pressure to enforce ideological purity, later generations of Party leadership adapted these same principles to modern technology. By the turn of the century, censorship and propaganda had shifted from the danwei to the Internet. In spite of the time and technology differences, the core goal of aligning public consciousness with the Party's version of truth remained the same. Only now, the Party could operate at scale through the Internet and the state's control of information networks.

The Illusion of Publicity

Ahead of the 2004 anniversary of the Tiananmen Square massacre, the CCP issued a directive to Chinese media. The document was a top-secret memorandum, illegal to distribute to the public. The directive ordered the media to keep in line with CCP talking points: "adhere to correct theories and sense of responsibility" and influence public opinion in the "right" way.[16]

In the 1990s, the Propaganda Department was renamed the Publicity Department to avoid the negative connotations of the word propaganda in English.[17]

Shi Tao, a journalist for *Contemporary Business News*, was among those who received the directive. Upon receiving it, he sent a summary of the document via his Yahoo! email address to the administrators of the website Democracy Forum, based in New York. While he never explicitly stated why he sent out the summary, it's likely that it was on principle to expose censorship and the lack of freedom of the press. Democracy Forum published his summary in its newsletter

[16]https://cpj.org/awards/shi-tao
[17]scmp.com/article/240408/propaganda-tag-axed-image-facelift#:~:text=Reading%20Time:2%20minutes,in%20an%20internationally%20acceptable%20way

shortly after. Given its top-secret status, Chinese state security officials found out and investigated. They requested the help of Yahoo! to identify who sent the email. Yahoo! turned over Shi Tao's identity, and he was subsequently arrested and convicted of leaking state secrets to a foreign website.[18] Of course, this was a mostly nonsensical ruling – the document did not expose state secrets, just gave orders to the media that the public should be made aware of. Regardless, he was convicted to 10 years in prison, but was released for good behavior just 15 months before the completion of his term.[19] Ten years in prison for disclosing a summary of a document that did not contain what most would consider state secrets, like military plans, intelligence, or sensitive data. All it contained was an internal risk assessment about the upcoming anniversary and the CCP's instructions to journalists. Yahoo! faced significant backlash in Western markets for supporting the investigation, yet it insisted that it was just complying with the local laws of the countries in which it operates.[20]

In March 2015, Yahoo! closed its last physical presence in China, shutting down its research and development center in Beijing.[21] This move was a significant step in the company's gradual withdrawal from the country, which had already seen the termination of its news, community, and email services in 2013.[22]

This was not a tragedy in isolation. As of 2010, China had 34 journalists imprisoned.[23] As of 2021, it was the largest captor of journalists, with at least 127 detained.[24] The reasons: Online expression, covering ethnic unrest in a way the Party did not want to be represented, revealing state secrets, and subversion. All of these are vague charges the state uses to suppress free speech.

---

[18] www.nytimes.com/2005/09/08/business/worldbusiness/yahoo-helped-chinese-to-prosecute-journalist.html
[19] www.hrw.org/reports/2006/china0806/11.htm
[20] www.nytimes.com/2005/09/11/technology/yahoo-had-to-comply-in-china-reporter-case-founder-says.html
[21] www.cnbc.com/2015/03/19/yahoo-closing-last-china-operation-in-beijing.html
[22] https://thechinaproject.com/2021/11/02/yahoo-shuts-down-remaining-china-services
[23] https://cpj.org/2011/02/attacks-on-the-press-2010-china
[24] www.bbc.com/news/world-asia-china-59544226

To make control even easier for the state, China updated its State Secrets law in 2010 to require that Internet and telecommunications companies cooperate with the police, state security officials, and prosecutors in investigating leaks of state secrets.[25] They must also protect the nation's state secrets. In 2024, the law was updated again, this time to make sure that network operators monitor information shared by users for state secrets. The law also broadens the scope of sensitive information, now including "work secrets" like information on the decisions of state agencies.[26] *For journalists, that means ordinary reporting can suddenly look like state security work, with all the legal risk that implies.*

---

[25] www.nytimes.com/2024/02/28/world/asia/china-state-secrets-law.html
[26] https://www.chinalawtranslate.com/en/secrets-law-2024

Chapter 25
The Paper Dragon

In 1949, Soviet propaganda was spreading; the Soviets accused the United States of testing biological weapons against the Inuit people of Alaska. Specifically, Pravda accused the United States of "preparing for new crimes against humanity."[1]

Chinese broadcasts boosted and expanded these stories further, claiming that the United States was coordinating with one of the leaders of the Japanese biological weapons program from World War II to prepare biological weapons against China. This was just the ramp-up of allegations from the Soviets and Chinese, which reached full scale after the breakout of the Korean War.[2]

In 1951, North Korea's Foreign Minister claimed that the United States had used biological weapons to spread smallpox in North Korea. Shortly after, the Chinese made similar claims and argued that the United States used chemical weapons during the war on 10 different occasions.[3]

By 1952, the North Korean Foreign Minister was claiming that the United States had made air raid drops of insects infected with

[1] www.wilsoncenter.org/publication/chinas-false-allegations-the-use-biological-weapons-the-united-states-during-the-korean
[2] www.jstor.org/stable/44074772
[3] Ibid.

microorganisms that caused the plague, cholera, and other diseases. *Renmin Ribao*, China's major newspaper, released stories backing up North Korea's claims with pictures of objects allegedly being dropped by U.S. aircraft. The allegations continued for months. From March to April 1952, a quarter of Soviet media was dedicated to the allegations.[4]

Despite the accusations, North Korea and China both rejected attempts by the World Health Organization and Red Cross to investigate, instead holding their own investigations with Soviet proxy organizations.

It wasn't until years later that reports to the contrary came to the forefront. A Hungarian journalist who spent the Korean War in North Korea relayed stories of North Korean peasants who told doctors they saw paper packets of insects placed in the snow by Chinese soldiers. Eventually, even the Chinese seemed to regret it, with Chinese officials stating in a meeting with Poland and Yugoslavia in 1956,

> They believed the accusations about germ warfare to have been without foundation.[5]

In the present day, it's widely accepted that the claims against the United States were fabricated. However, at the time the allegations sparked a global backlash. Millions of people in the Soviet Union, Eastern European countries, and Western European capitals protested to condemn the alleged use of biological warfare by the United States. It was a successful disinformation campaign—for a time. And that's what's key here: Nation-states do not have to make disinformation campaigns that last decades or centuries, just ones that last long enough to tarnish the reputation of another nation.

Establishing Discourse Power

China treats its external propaganda strategy as a battle for discourse power (话语权), which some say is closer to discourse dominance,

---

[4]www.wilsoncenter.org/sites/default/files/media/documents/publication/cwihp_wp_78_china_false_bw_allegations_korean_war_march_16.pdf
[5]Ibid.

the ability to manipulate the narrative on global governance, values, and norms to legitimize and facilitate a state's approach to power.[6]

China's leaders believe that the United States has been able to establish and maintain global leadership in part due to its massive discourse power. In contrast, China has struggled; the open Internet has enabled free speech and communication to flourish globally, making it incredibly difficult for China to control narratives and avoid responsibility for its human rights abuses. As of 2024, 61 percent of those surveyed in a Pew Research Poll across 25 countries had an unfavorable opinion of China.[7]

China has attempted similar disinformation campaigns to those of Russia over the years, but without the same impact. While it has had significant success at controlling and censoring information within China, controlling narratives in an open media landscape is a different ballgame.

Traditional state media is not appealing to the public like it used to be—people are turning to social media for public discourse. China needs to communicate with the rest of the world if it wants to gain discourse power, but it struggles to do so by design. It closes itself off to the world, prioritizing cyber sovereignty, which makes it difficult to spread its message globally, as websites like Facebook, X (formerly Twitter), and others, which set the public discourse, are being blocked within China. In the case of Facebook, which is banned in China, China even has to outsource its production of disinformation to content farms in Malaysia and convince individuals overseas to spread the messages, since it cannot do so in the country.[8]

China believes that media convergence (融媒体) is the path to enhancing its discourse power. In the eyes of Chinese leadership, media convergence is about blending traditional state media with digital media and leveraging it not only in China but also globally. Through media convergence, China can improve its perception abroad, censor its critics, and promote its ideals.[9]

[6]https://www.atlanticcouncil.org/wp-content/uploads/2023/08/Chinese-Discourse-Power-Capabilities-and-Impact-1.pdf
[7]www.hudson.org/foreign-policy/discourse-power-ccp-strategy-shape-global-information-space-house-select-committee-miles-yu
[8]www.atlanticcouncil.org/in-depth-research-reports/dfrlab-china-reports
[9]https://www.cna.org/reports/2020/08/DRM-2020-U-027331-1Rev.pdf

China presents media convergence as the combination of standards, infrastructure, and message.[10] Standards are straightforward: It wants the world to follow its standards for how the Internet should be, particularly focused on sovereignty and information control. Infrastructure and message are more complicated.

Lie, Cheat, and Steal Up to the Top

China has been expanding its international media presence to establish the infrastructure it needs to spread its message more effectively. Since 2013, it has built a strategy around localizing media and has created many regionalized state media pages. For example, on Facebook, there are many *China Global Television Network (CGTN)* pages for languages local to America, Europe, Africa, and other parts of Asia. In January 2020, over a third of the posts on many of the top Chinese state news pages were dedicated to spreading information on COVID-19.[11]

Beyond media control, China is also pushing to gain market share with apps and other global infrastructure, especially through the Digital Silk Road. For example, in 2019, 44 of India's top 100 apps were Chinese.[12]

China has also tried to improve its reach by paying to gain social media followers; records show that in 2019, China News was offering $177,000 to get more Twitter followers, and the government was offering $108,300 to pay Facebook and Twitter followers to promote the China Association of Southeast Asian Nations (ASEAN).[13]

Since 2019, the Spamouflage network has leveraged these accounts to build up its disinformation operations and harass specific targets. They create a network of hundreds of thousands of accounts across every social media platform. Anyone who has criticized the CCP, or any politician or American company that it deems

[10] https://pmc.ncbi.nlm.nih.gov/articles/PMC10810527
[11] https://misinforeview.hks.harvard.edu/article/pandemics-propaganda-how-chinese-state-media-creates-and-propagates-ccp-coronavirus-narratives
[12] www.thehindubusinessline.com/info-tech/of-indias-top-100-apps-44-are-chinese/article26857166.ece
[13] www.npr.org/2019/08/20/752668835/how-china-uses-twitter-and-facebook-to-share-disinformation-about-hong-kong

anti-China, has been targeted with a flood of disinformation. China posted thousands of comments calling dissidents traitors or dogs, and using racist and homophobic slurs. In 2023, the operation was finally tied to the Chinese police.[14]

In one instance in 2019, Jiayang Fan, a journalist for *The New Yorker,* was targeted by this kind of campaign. She was bombarded with more than 12,000 tweets, all of which used the hashtag #TraitorJiayangFan. They accused her of killing her mother for profit, amid other horrific comments.[15]

All this said, compared to influence operations in Russia, China's information operations are comparatively weak. The Spamouflage crew is not strongly coordinated—activity is constantly happening, but it isn't focused activity. Their biggest differentiator is their scale, with millions of accounts on dozens of platforms. However, while they have been creating substantial content, especially to harass individuals, they haven't been good at creating content for a specific group that will resonate for a viral moment. They also struggle to include cultural context and references, or put them in, but incorrectly, which puts people off. This is a side effect of years behind the Great Firewall: Global cultural context is more foreign to them than most others.[16]

Keyboard Wolf Warriors

China wants to spread a message that gives a positive view of China and its regime while crushing dissent and suppressing counternarratives. But when it can't control the messages being shared on a global stage, the gloves come off, and it fights back.

In 2019, senior Chinese diplomat Zhao Lijian, deputy chief of mission at China's embassy to Pakistan in Islamabad, went on a tweeting rampage about the United States.[17] He brought up what

[14]https://therecord.media/spamouflage-china-accused-largest-covert-influence-operation-meta

[15]www.cnn.com/2023/11/13/us/china-online-disinformation-invs

[16]www.wired.com/story/china-bad-at-disinformation

[17]www.bloomberg.com/news/articles/2019-07-16/chinese-diplomat-deletes-tweet-on-race-that-angered-susan-rice

he considered U.S. hypocrisy on its human rights record, school shootings, and income inequality, among other things. He also said that "You're in Washington, D.C., you know the white never go" in reference to the southeast of DC, where there are historically black neighborhoods. Susan Rice, former U.S. National Security Advisor, responded, calling him a racist disgrace and shockingly ignorant. He responded:

> You are such a disgrace, too. And shockingly ignorant, too. I am based in Islamabad. Truth hurts. I am simply telling the truth . . . To label someone who speak the truth that you don't want to hear a racist, is disgraceful & disgusting.[18]

This type of discourse was typical for Zhao, though he did not previously insult at the level of U.S. national security advisers. This is a dramatically different strategy for China compared to previous decades. Known as wolf warrior diplomacy, it is based on the Chinese action film franchise Wolf Warrior, especially Wolf Warrior 2, which glorifies Chinese special forces protecting Chinese citizens overseas.[19]

Wolf warrior diplomacy was popularized in circles in the CCP in the 2010s, but was put under the global microscope in 2019. The goal: To move away from the low-profile approach of the early 2000s to a more assertive international posture that reflected China's growing status as a global power. Wolf warrior diplomacy vocally defends China, the CCP, and its national interests on social media, in public interviews, and in official Party statements. While wolf warrior diplomacy increased its public profile for a time, especially during the pandemic, for many countries, it has been off-putting, raising mistrust. It is directly at odds with its message of win-win cooperation and a shared future through the BRI.[20]

---

[18]www.bloomberg.com/news/articles/2019-07-16/chinese-diplomat-deletes-tweet-on-race-that-angered-susan-rice
[19]https://www.nbr.org/publication/understanding-chinese-wolf-warrior-diplomacy
[20]www.nature.com/articles/s41599-023-02367-6

Chapter 26
All Under Heaven

The Confucian classic, the *Gongyang Commentary on the Spring and Autumn Annals*, references an important concept in Chinese dynastic history—the idea of *great unity* (大一统). Great unity is a principle that became core to the Chinese state's way of thinking and was embedded in state narratives across many dynasties.[1]

The Chinese have long believed that the authority of the emperor across all regions and officials, *tianxia*, or "All Under Heaven," is paramount to maintaining the stability of China. This is one reason why historical timelines and territorial boundaries in China are so hotly debated—unity is required for stability. Great unity remains pivotal to China's goals and ideology to this day, though the concept has shifted. In modern usage, it is referred to as 不断的大一统 ("continuing great unity" or "unbroken unity"). This is not just about establishing unity, but about preserving it—even in spite of perceived temporary fractures.[2]

---

[1]https://ctext.org/datawiki.pl?if=en&res=394561#wp_en_Content
[2]https://fairbank.fas.harvard.edu/research/blog/the-great-unity-debate

The Center of the Universe

From the Han (东汉) to the start of the Qing dynasty (清朝), China regarded itself as the Middle Kingdom, the center of civilization, with surrounding regions considered less civilized and underdeveloped. In fact, in Chinese, "China" is 中国 (Zhōngguó), which means "Middle Kingdom."[3]

The states surrounding China would come to the Chinese emperor as his vassals and bow down to him with their heads touching the floor in a kowtow, give him offerings, and, in return, he would reward them with even more lavish gifts. Those who agreed to be part of the tributary system acknowledged that he was the ruler of "All Under Heaven." This included polities of what are now the likes of Korea, Vietnam, Thailand, Cambodia, Myanmar, the Philippines, and others. In return for this prostration, China would give the states protection and trade rights.[4]

During the Qing dynasty, Qing emperors perpetuated centuries of geopolitical friction by taking control of several different regions. They conquered Taiwan in 1684, secured control over Outer Mongolia in the same time period, and Xinjiang almost a century later. In the early 1700s, they established a protectorate over Tibet, intervening in Tibetan politics and military affairs in a clear effort to exercise their supposed sovereignty over the country.[5]

However, things began to shift dramatically over the course of the nineteenth century. The tributary system was expensive to maintain; providing protection for that many states was no small endeavor. At the same time, regular diplomatic, trade, and military interactions picked up precipitously between Asia, Europe, and the United States. China shifted from viewing itself as the center of the world to seeing a very different style of diplomacy, trade, and military activity that was competitive, if not superior to, its own.[6]

[3] https://afe.easia.columbia.edu/timelines/china_timeline.htm
[4] https://www.britannica.com/topic/tributary-system
[5] https://theme.npm.edu.tw/exh111/TaiwaneseIndigenous_0/en/page-1.html
[6] https://www.lse.ac.uk/Economic-History/Assets/Documents/Research/GEHN/GEHNWP21-GA.pdf

The Century of Humiliation Begins

China went on to experience defeat after defeat by Japan, the Russian Empire, and Western powers. It was beset by challenges, both domestically and, especially, from foreign interests, which led to its Century of Humiliation and the loss of many territories it considered crucial to its sphere of influence.[7]

During the first Opium War, which started in 1839, it lost control of Hong Kong and was forced to establish British settlements at some of China's most important ports, including Shanghai. "Temporary fractures" had begun.[8]

In the decades leading up to the fall of the Qing dynasty, China lost direct control over Taiwan and saw its traditional influence in places like Korea, Mongolia, and Vietnam erode under Japanese and European imperial expansion. Once the Qing dynasty collapsed in 1913, the Dalai Lama also declared Tibet's independence from China.[9]

Conditions did not improve for China. In World War I, China proclaimed its neutrality, yet Japan attacked anyway and overtook Kiautschou from the Germans. By 1915, Japan's military strength, the distraction of World War I, and political instability rife within China led Japan to issue the Twenty-One Demands to maintain and expand control over Chinese territory. Japan required China not to grant land concessions to any other foreign powers. The agreement was viewed as an abject shame, and May 9 was marked as China's National Humiliation Day.[10]

After World War I ended, negotiations with Japan sparked the May Fourth Movement, a student-led protest in China against the peace talks. This was China's first mass student-led patriotic movement, igniting Chinese nationalism and pushing back against imperialist ideas. China was the only country to refuse to

[7]https://education.cfr.org/learn/reading/china-century-humiliation
[8]https://visualizingcultures.mit.edu/opium_wars_01/ow1_essay01.html
[9]https://apjjf.org/emma-jinhua-teng/2450/article
[10]www.cfr.org/blog/china-japan-and-twenty-one-demands

sign the *Treaty of Versailles* because of the protests and student demands.[11]

World War II brought additional challenges to China. In 1937, Japan launched a full-scale invasion of China, during which the Japanese were horrendously brutal. It was later called the Asian Holocaust due to the war crimes perpetrated by Japan. They carried out the Rape of Nanjing, invading it and murdering over 200,000 Chinese citizens, in addition to rape, torture, looting, and arson.[12] The Japanese had a policy of killing and destroying everything in their path. They carried out live human experimentation, killing contests, and enslaved women en masse to serve as "comfort women" for the soldiers' use.[13]

China fought back, and although defeat seemed all but inevitable, it did not surrender. In a strategically consequential decision for the entirety of World War II, the Chinese resistance forced Japan to commit a large portion of its forces on the Asian front.[14] Despite being on the winning side, World War II and its aftermath were catastrophic for China. Its people and lands were decimated. Its losses and Japan's atrocities were far from equally recognized compared with the European front. Japan renounced all claims to Taiwan, and the Republic of China assumed administration, leaving it in an ambiguous political state. China's people were completely disgusted by the thought of imperialism, Japan, and the West.

Despite suffering so many losses, both of people and land, China continued to hold that certain regions were fundamentally a part of China—All Under Heaven. The losses it faced did not deter it from its mission to keep unity regardless of temporary fractures. Four regions stand out more than any other as China's priorities: Taiwan, Hong Kong, Tibet, and Xinjiang.

---

[11] www.smithsonianmag.com/history/surprisingly-important-role-china-played-world-war-i-180964532
[12] https://books.google.com/books?id=N-vXRgEAPU0C&q=human+beings#v=onepage&q&f=false
[13] https://archive.org/details/nankingatrocity100btwa/page/123/mode/1up?q=animals
[14] www.history.com/articles/china-role-world-war-ii-allies

Chapter 27
Reunification by Other Means

解决台湾问题、实现祖国完全统一,是党矢志不渝的历史任务,是全体中华儿女的共同愿望,是实现中华民族伟大复兴的必然要求。

Resolving the Taiwan question and realizing China's complete reunification is a historic mission and an unshakable commitment of the Communist Party of China.

—*Xi Jinping, 2020*[1]

Taiwan is central to China's goal of unity. In China's eyes, Taiwan is not only a representation of China's territorial integrity, but also the culmination of its own civil war's unfinished legacy. Beijing's diplomatic efforts aim to isolate Taiwan internationally, framing reunification as critical to its national identity.

One of the main places that serves as the testing ground for just how much Taiwan and its allies will accept from China is the Taiwan Strait. The Strait has been home to numerous PLA military

---

[1] https://www.mfa.gov.cn/eng/zy/wjls/3604_665547/202405/t20240531_11367561.html

exercises in the region, heightening tensions as both sides prepare for potential escalation.

One such tense moment was in May 1995, when the United States granted a tourist visa to the Republic of China (Taiwan's) president, Lee Teng-hui.[2] Teng-hui was notably pro-Taiwan and challenged the One China policy. The United States had previously said it would not grant the visa, and between that change and its agreement to sell F-16 fighter jets to Taiwan, this struck a nerve in Beijing. The timing was especially important in light of upcoming legislative elections in Taiwan in December 1995 and presidential elections in March 1996.[3] The CCP recalled its ambassador to the United States and looked for means to intimidate Taiwan, starting with aggressive military exercises.

In July 1995, China closed off an area 80 miles northeast of Taiwan to fire six missiles with little warning and no direct communication to Taiwan or the United States. In August, PLA naval vessels conducted live-fire exercises off the coast of Fujian with at least 59 naval ships and 192 aircraft.[4] After those exercises, China and Washington met to assure China of the United States' commitment to the One China policy, which temporarily appeased the Chinese.[5]

But the appeasement was short-lived. From September to October, the PLA conducted amphibious landing maneuvers north of Taiwan to demonstrate the PLA's naval prowess. It continued with more amphibious exercises south of the Taiwan Strait, including an amphibious landing on Dongshan Island, about 150 miles from Taiwan's Penghu Islands. The PLA announced that it had created a "headquarters for operations targeting Taiwan" in its efforts to intimidate ahead of the election.[6] In the resulting legislative election in December, the Kuomintang, which China wanted to lose, still won, but did fail to win the majority for the first time. While not a blowout, it gave the CCP confidence that the strategy was working.[7]

[2] www.govinfo.gov/content/pkg/GOVPUB-D5-PURL-gpo193511/pdf/GOVPUB-D5-PURL-gpo193511.pdf
[3] https://ndupress.ndu.edu/Portals/68/Documents/stratperspective/china/china-perspectives-17.pdf
[4] www.britannica.com/event/Taiwan-Strait-crises
[5] www.ebsco.com/research-starters/history/third-taiwan-strait-crisis
[6] www.theasiadialogue.com/wp-content/uploads/2017/12/Scobell.pdf
[7] www.jstor.org/stable/2645553

In January 1996, China performed large-scale military exercises to influence the upcoming presidential election.[8] In March, it began missile tests and exercises, again to intimidate. Despite its attempts, Teng-hui won in a landslide.[9]

History Rhymes

China has continued these tactics against Taiwan, but has added a cyberattack and information operations flair. Its goal: Spread disinformation in Taiwan to destabilize the populace and move the country toward a more pro-unification stance. China targets Taiwan at a scale that is not seen in other countries to wear down the Taiwanese people.

Taiwanese elections are the perfect time to strike at faith in government. Ahead of the 2024 Taiwanese presidential elections, Taiwan's intelligence community was more than aware that China was working to influence them.[10] China leveraged Spamouflage, a coordinated influence network, to spread disinformation across social media accounts, impersonating legitimate media outlets and creating and sharing social content promoting a pro-China message.[11] It also funded small news companies to post content that cast doubt on candidates the CCP didn't like. In one case, it spread disinformation that Taiwan's Democratic Progressive Party's (DDP)' vice presidential candidate was secretly a U.S. citizen. While she was a U.S. citizen in the past, she renounced it in 2002.[12]

To protect itself, Taiwan has created a disinformation defense apparatus, prioritizing fact-checking to make sure Taiwanese citizens can trust the information they are getting through tools like the Taiwan FactCheck Center.[13] As a major target of disinformation,

[8] www.ebsco.com/research-starters/history/third-taiwan-strait-crisis
[9] www.jstor.org/stable/44288523
[10] www.cnn.com/2023/12/15/asia/taiwan-election-disinformation-china-technology-intl-hnk
[11] www.aspistrategist.org.au/as-taiwan-voted-beijing-spammed-ai-avatars-faked-paternity-tests-and-leaked-fake-documents
[12] https://factcheck.afp.com/doc.afp.com.34749EQ
[13] https://en.tfc-taiwan.org.tw

these methods have been very impactful in helping Taiwan limit the spread and effects of disinformation.

The Chinese have also taken steps to lock down the media, just like they have already done in China. In 2019, Taiwan's National Security Bureau revealed that the CCP is coordinating with Taiwanese media outlets to spread disinformation and propaganda from China.[14] Tycoons in China have acquired media companies to sway coverage toward unification. For example, Tsai Eng-meng, a pro-unification consumer goods tycoon, acquired three outlets popular in Taiwan: CTV (中視), *Chung T'ien Television* (CTiTV, 中天電視公司), and the newspaper *China Times* (中國時報). In the five years since its acquisition, the *China Times* has reduced its coverage of human rights issues in China by over two-thirds.[15] One hundred percent of *China Times* reports on Xinjiang were based on Chinese state media reports.[16]

Faking Betrayal

In September 2018, a popular online bulletin board in Taiwan, PTT, claimed that Taiwanese citizens were stranded in Japan because of a typhoon and were only being rescued by buses sent by the CCP on the condition that they declare themselves Chinese.[17] Chinese state news agency *Xinhua* and other channels amplified it. Of course, the Taiwanese people felt this was a betrayal by the Taiwanese government. But it turned out these posts on PTT were sent from an IP address in Beijing. Witnesses at the Japanese airport refuted the news, saying that none of it was true. Fake news about this incident spread widely regardless, accusing Taiwanese officials like Su Chii-cherng, director general of the Osaka branch of the Taipei Economic and Cultural Office, of not helping their own people.

[14]https://china-journal.org/2019/05/06/taiwanese-government-says-some-local-media-work-with-china-send-content-to-beijing-for-approval
[15]https://rsf.org/sites/default/files/cn_rapport_chine-web_final_2.pdf
[16]https://globaltaiwan.org/2023/07/assessing-taiwans-media-landscape-and-prc-influence-part-one-the-dangers-of-deregulation
[17]www.nytimes.com/2018/11/22/world/asia/taiwan-elections-meddling.html

Despite this being identified as fake news shortly after, the damage was already done. Su killed himself and stated in his suicide note that the news had troubled him.[18]

Stealth Over Speed

China is also looking for its future military advantage, prepositioning in systems that could be advantageous in a conflict. In June 2023, Microsoft released a joint advisory with the Five Eyes that detailed a massive cyberattack carried out by Volt Typhoon, a Chinese state-sponsored threat actor, targeting critical infrastructure providers in the United States.[19]

The attackers targeted Internet-facing Fortinet FortiGuard devices to gain access. They treated compromised small office devices, like routers from Cisco, ASUS, NETGEAR, and others, as hop points so they could make their network traffic appear more legitimate—or at least like it wasn't coming from China. Once they gained access to target systems, they began working directly hands-on-keyboard instead of deploying malware. They were actively executing actions in the target's network infrastructure to find and steal valuable data, target additional devices, and ensure long-term access.

Volt Typhoon was looking to steal data for espionage, but this marked a turning point: They were also looking to keep long-term access to these systems, especially those of critical infrastructure providers. By maintaining long-term access to these systems, in the event of a military conflict, they could quickly and easily disrupt or destroy critical infrastructure. In doing so, they could effectively cause chaos and delay a military response from the United States at a critical time, such as during an invasion of Taiwan.

---

[18] www.taipeitimes.com/News/taiwan/archives/2018/09/19/2003700718
[19] www.microsoft.com/en-us/security/blog/2023/05/24/volt-typhoon-targets-us-critical-infrastructure-with-living-off-the-land-techniques

The attackers also targeted critical infrastructure in Guam as early as 2021, which is a highly strategic target. The island serves as a critical hub for American military power in the Pacific, especially in light of China's aggressive overtures toward Taiwan. These actions are strongly aligned with China's approach to active defense, gaining a preemptive advantage in a potential future conflict.[20]

When the report was first published by Microsoft, China immediately denied involvement. However, in a secret meeting in December 2024, Chinese officials reportedly acknowledged to U.S. officials that China was behind a series of cyberattacks on U.S. infrastructure as a warning to the United States about Taiwan.[21]

Death by 13 Million Cuts

In some cases, China peppers the Taiwanese people with cyberattacks, looking for any way in so that they can collect information they may either use in the future or release to the public. Most often, this information is best positioned to cause chaos or erode citizens' faith in the government. From November 2023 to April 2024, a state-sponsored group called Flax Typhoon, based in Fuzhou, China, targeted organizations, 60 percent of which were in Taiwan. It targeted academia, government, and electronics companies with cyberattacks to collect information for espionage purposes. The attackers exploited known vulnerabilities to break in and get access to administrative accounts before establishing a backdoor for long-term access. The attackers wanted to steal information on Taiwan's economic policy, trade, diplomatic relations, and any intellectual property they could.[22]

---

[20] www.microsoft.com/en-us/security/blog/2023/05/ 24/volt-typhoon-targetsus-critical-infrastructure-with-living-off-the-land-techniques
[21] www.wsj.com/politics/national-security/in-secret-meeting-china-acknowledged-role-in-u-s-infrastructure-hacks-c5ab37cb
[22] www.recordedfuture.com/research/redjuliett-intensifies-taiwanese-cyber-espionage-via-network-perimeter

In 2024, Chinese-speaking attackers targeted Taiwan's military and satellite industries with a series of attacks that collected information from IT systems for espionage purposes.

Taiwan's public sector was facing 13 million cyberattacks each month in 2024.[23] These attacks also affected critical infrastructure in Taiwan, with a 650 percent increase in cyberattacks from China against telecommunications providers in 2024.[24]

China's attacks on Taiwan are vast, covering different sectors, methodologies, and even countries. But they are all coordinated to tear down the government and its support, and to preposition to ensure they can strike hard when they want to start a conflict.

---

[23] www.politico.com/news/2024/01/11/taiwan-cyberattacks-election-china-00134841
[24] www.nsb.gov.tw/en/assets/documents/%E6%96%B0%E8%81%9E%E7%A8%BF/7d118bec-6a18-4e95-ad85-4055fc48cc31.pdf

Chapter 28
The Revolution Will Be Erased

Late in the Qing dynasty in the 1800s, Great Britain was exporting massive amounts of opium to China against the wishes of the Chinese. This led to the first Opium War, when China destroyed around 1,400 tons of opium in Guangzhou. The war resulted in the Treaty of Nanjing, which gave the British control of Hong Kong, among other measures.[1]

It wasn't until 1997 that China regained sovereignty over Hong Kong from British colonial rule.[2] In the agreement, Hong Kong would be ruled under the principle of "one country, two systems" for 50 years. Hong Kong could maintain its capitalist system and the rights afforded to citizens, while China would control defense and foreign affairs. This was a shaky agreement, as many believed China would not allow Hong Kong to maintain those rights, especially given the disparity between the rights of those in Hong Kong and the rights of those on the mainland.[3]

---

[1] https://www.nationalarchives.gov.uk/education/resources/hong-kong-and-the-opium-wars
[2] www.cfr.org/backgrounder/hong-kong-freedoms-democracy-protests-china-crackdown
[3] https://www.legalhub.gov.hk/details.php?a=10&v=one-country-two-systems-and-the-basic-law

Fast-forward to 2017, when China's preferred candidate for chief executive and major proponent of reunification, Carrie Lam, was appointed as the head of government in Hong Kong.[4]

In 2019, Lam proposed an amendment to *the Fugitive Offenders Ordinance*. This amendment would allow criminal suspects to be extradited, even to countries where there was no formal extradition treaty, like China.[5]

Hong Kong citizens were furious and held a series of protests against the amendment. To try to control the narrative, Chinese state media started pushing messages that the protests were funded by the CIA. The Spamouflage network flooded Twitter and Facebook with pro-CCP posts and targeted ads. To counter the disinformation, Twitter suspended almost 1,000 accounts, and Facebook removed several accounts and pages. Yet still, Twitter bots flooded the site with anti–Hong Kong messages.[6]

Protesters were known to use popular communications apps like Telegram, LIHKG, and FireChat to organize and share information—so, of course, they were targets too.[7] During the June protests, Telegram was hit with a DDoS attack, sending 200–400 Gb/s of junk traffic, like repeated TCP requests, mostly from China. It shut Telegram down for several hours, coinciding with protester activity.[8]

During the September protests, LIHKG was taken down for hours when hit with a DDoS attack which pummeled them with unique visitors and requests, most of which came from China.[9]

Despite these attempts at disruption, the protests succeeded: The government withdrew the bill, and pro-democracy candidates in local District Council elections won in a landslide.[10]

---

[4] https://www.nytimes.com/2017/03/26/world/asia/hong-kong-election-carrie-lam-chief-executive.html
[5] https://www.legco.gov.hk/yr18-19/english/bills/brief/b201903291_brf.pdf
[6] https://www.npr.org/2019/08/20/752668835/how-china-uses-twitter-and-facebook-to-share-disinformation-about-hong-kong
[7] https://westoahu.hawaii.edu/cyber/global-weekly-exec-summary/china-xis-red-cyber-warfare-used-on-hong-kong-protestors
[8] https://www.cnn.com/2019/06/13/tech/telegram-ddos-attack-hong-kong-china
[9] Ibid.
[10] https://www.nytimes.com/2019/09/04/world/asia/hong-kong-carrie-lam-protests.html

Regardless, the Chinese state would not be deterred. In 2020, China started to establish laws in Hong Kong that would censor and bring citizens to heel. The most prominent is *the Law of the People's Republic of China on Safeguarding National Security in the Hong Kong Special Administrative Region*, known colloquially as the national security law. It bans secession, subversion of state power, terrorism, and foreign intervention—specific articles call out those who "incite" or "advocate" for any of these activities, giving the state room to arrest people for speech.[11] It also enabled China's state security agencies to operate in Hong Kong and to set up a national security agency. These security officials use police monitoring to actively watch for online content considered seditious or in violation of the law, even across borders. Hong Kongers have been encouraged to report individuals they suspect of violating the law—many people who are pro-China submit screenshots from social media of potential violations.[12]

The National Security Law was immediately put to the test. In one case, a 30-year-old delivery driver named Ma Chun-man, who was known to join protests in Hong Kong dressed as Captain America, was accused of giving speeches and chanting slogans calling for Hong Kong's independence.[13] He chanted things like, "Be empowered as a people; independence to Hong Kong"—innocuous phrases. He was arrested, denied bail, and held for 10 months before his trial, where he was convicted and sentenced to five years in prison.[14]

In another instance, a university student studying in Japan, Yuen Ching-ting, was arrested on suspicion of inciting secession after she made posts on Facebook and Instagram in Japan. She said things like, "I am a Hongkonger; I advocate for Hong Kong

---

[11] www.chinalawtranslate.com/en/bilingual-hong-kong-national-security-law
[12] https://www.businessinsider.com/china-national-security-law-hong-kong-opens-hotline-report-violations-2020-11
[13] https://hongkongfp.com/2021/09/28/hong-kongs-second-national-security-trial-opens-with-defendant-accused-of-repeatedly-calling-for-independence
[14] https://www.bbc.com/news/world-asia-china-59247659

independence." When she returned to Hong Kong to renew her ID card, she was arrested, detained, and charged with incitement. She was sentenced to two months in prison after she pleaded guilty.[15]

Hong Kong had a 100 percent conviction rate for these crimes over four years. How did they achieve a 100 percent conviction rate? Carrie Lam handpicked the judging panel that handled national security cases.[16]

That record was broken in 2024, when two people from the Hong Kong 47, a group of 47 pro-democracy citizens who were charged with conspiracy to commit subversion, were acquitted.

[15]www.voanews.com/a/hong-kong-sentences-woman-to-2-months-in-prison-for-posts-uploaded-in-tokyo/7349919.html

[16]https://www.law.georgetown.edu/law-asia/wp-content/uploads/sites/31/2021/06/HongKongNSLRightToFairTrial.pdf

Chapter 29
Ghosts in the Himalayas

China invaded Tibet yet again in 1950, as the CCP firmly holds that Tibet is an integral part of China. The Chinese restricted religious rights and imposed forced labor camps, which tried to force assimilation by suppressing Tibetan religious and cultural identities with thought education. In 1959, the Tibetan people revolted, but Chinese authorities crushed the revolt by killing thousands.[1] The Dalai Lama was granted asylum in India and established a government-in-exile.[2] The date the uprising began became known as Tibetan Uprising Day.

China relied heavily on propaganda and disinformation during this time. The official CCP narrative was that the Dalai Lama caused the revolt in Tibet. The Party fabricated a story that the Dalai Lama sent individuals disguised as religious preachers to foment an anti-communist rebellion across Tibet. The story was shared in Party circles before being introduced to the public and historical accounts as a way for the CCP to justify suppressing the revolt.[3]

---

[1] https://media.defense.gov/2023/Dec/04/2003351064/-1/-1/0/TIBETUPRISING_1956-59_20231201.PDF
[2] https://archive.nytimes.com/www.nytimes.com/library/world/asia/040459atibet-special.html?module=inline
[3] https://media.defense.gov/2023/Dec/04/2003351064/-1/-1/0/TIBETUPRISING_1956-59_20231201.PDF

Leading up to the forty-ninth anniversary of Tibetan Uprising Day in 2008, hundreds of protests rocked Tibet over growing frustrations with China's control. Thousands of Tibetans protested and were arrested in March.[4] The Chinese had expelled foreign journalists from the Xiahe region to avoid coverage of the protests and to control the message. By April, in an attempt to demonstrate that tensions were cooling, Chinese authorities gave journalists a tightly controlled tour of Labrang Monastery, one area where protests had taken place. Upon arrival, however, 15 monks rushed out, waved the Tibetan flag, and stated that,

> We are not asking for Tibetan independence; we are just asking for human rights. We have no human rights now.[5]

Enough was enough for the Chinese authorities. Days later, the monastery was raided by the state. Monks were imprisoned. Some claimed to be tortured, and in other cases, disappeared. Protests turned violent, with clashes between protesters, Chinese civilians, and authorities. Rights groups estimate that more than 140 people died during the protests.[6] From then on, China stepped up its policing and surveillance of Tibet, paving the way for it to become one of the most monitored places in the world.[7]

This leads us to 2009, when Information Warfare Monitor, a research group known for cybersecurity training and workshops, went to Dharamsala. They went to meet with the Tibetan Government-in-Exile and brief them on cybersecurity, especially on social engineering and how to use their systems securely. The representative of the Dalai Lama was suspicious that their systems had been bugged for some time and requested a security review. They looked for malware, and malware they found. The Citizen Lab did a sweeping investigation that uncovered GhostNet, a global cyber espionage campaign that stole strategic documents on foreign interests, especially in South and Southeast Asian countries.[8]

---

[4] https://www.cnn.com/2012/01/31/world/asia/tibet-protests-timeline
[5] www.nytimes.com/2008/04/10/world/asia/10tibet.html
[6] www.cnn.com/2012/01/3 et-protests-timeline
[7] www.hrw.org/news/2020/09/07/china-delves-past-police-tibets-future
[8] https://ora.ox.ac.uk/objects/uuid:6d1260fd-b8ee-4a11-8a5f-e7708d543651/files/m0e5334ee23f2b6390f1a69c5d791e618

During the investigation, they identified 1,295 infected computers in more than 100 countries. Of all the targets, 26.7 percent were deemed high-value related to China, Tibet, Taiwan, India, or were devices at foreign embassies, governments, or related international organizations. Some of the targets included ASEAN, TAITRA, the Ministries of Foreign Affairs in Iran, Brunei, Bangladesh, and others. It also targeted embassies in Australia, India, Taiwan, Pakistan, Korea, and many others.[9]

While stopping short of a full accusation against the Chinese government, Citizen Lab did mention them as a potential attacker. Many of the targets of this attack were of high strategic interest to the CCP, particularly from a foreign and defense policy standpoint. Much of the attacker infrastructure, including IP addresses, was traced back to Hainan Island, where the Lingshui Signals Intelligence facility and the Third Technical Department of the PLA reside.[10]

Suspiciously, Chinese authorities also seemed to have access to sensitive information they couldn't have gotten from many other places but the attack. For example, there was one instance where a woman working with Tibetan exiles was detained by Chinese authorities and warned to stop working with them, using her private online conversations as proof.[11]

Following the release of the Citizen Lab report, the domains being used by the attackers went offline, stopping operations. However, for the sake of due diligence, the Information Warfare Monitor and the Shadowserver Foundation, a volunteer watchdog group of security professionals tracking malware, reviewed potentially related incidents. They found a new attack called the Shadow Network, which was mostly targeting the Indian government, some defense-related organizations in India, and some private companies. That attack appeared to be perpetrated by China as well.[12]

---

[9]https://citizenlab.ca/wp-content/uploads/2017/05/shadows-in-the-cloud.pdf
[10]https://www.technologyreview.com/2019/01/10/103560/when-chinese-hackers-declared-war-on-the-rest-of-us
[11]www.nytimes.com/2009/03/29/technology/29spy.html
[12]https://citizenlab.ca/wp-content/uploads/2017/05/shadows-in-the-cloud.pdf

At the time, China and India were in a difficult balancing act. China had become India's largest trading partner, but the Dalai Lama resides in exile in India, and the two countries were in the midst of a border dispute. China was building roads into Indian territory, while India was deploying troops to the border to defend it.[13]

Attackers stole documents and data from the Indian government, including documents about its international relations strategy and security assessments from sensitive regions. They stole documents on Indian missile systems and years of personal emails from the Office of His Holiness the Dalai Lama.[14]

Investigators tied the attack back to individuals in Chengdu, one of whom was affiliated with the University of Electronic Science and Technology. The PLA is known to finance the university's research on computer security and has a technical reconnaissance bureau in Chengdu.[15]

Once again, the Chinese authorities downplayed the attack and cast aspersions on the researchers who discovered it.[16]

[13] https://www.bbc.com/news/world-asia-53171124
[14] https://www.wired.com/2010/04/shadow-network
[15] https://www.nytimes.com/2010/04/06/science/06cyber.html
[16] https://www.nbcnews.com/id/wbna3619658

Chapter 30
Breaking Their Roots

断其血脉,断其根,断其联,断其源 。彻底铲除'两面人'的根子,
挖出来,发誓与'两面人'斗争到底 。

*Break their lineage, break their roots, break their connections, and
break their origins. Completely shovel up the roots of "two-faced
people," dig them out, and vow to fight these two-faced people
until the end.*

*—Maisumujiang Maimuer, Chinese religious-affairs
official, on the Uyghurs*[1]

Over the course of almost 100 years, the Dzunghar Mongol Empire and the Qing dynasty battled for control of parts of Inner Asia, including what would become eastern Mongolia, Tibet, and Xinjiang. After winning the Dzungar–Qing wars in 1758, the Qing dynasty established control over the region. From then on, the region that comprises modern-day Xinjiang was referred to as "new territory," or "Xinjiang."[2]

Xinjiang went on to declare and then lose its independence repeatedly over the centuries. More than half the population in Xinjiang is part of Muslim ethnic minorities such as the Uyghurs.[3] A turning

---

[1] www.hrw.org/sites/default/files/media_2021/04/china0421_web_2.pdf
[2] https://xinjiang.sppga.ubc.ca/timelines/historical-overview
[3] www.nytimes.com/2018/09/08/world/asia/china-uighur-muslim-detention-camp.html

point came in 1990, when the Uyghurs attempted an armed uprising but failed. Since then, China has increased its police presence significantly, implementing Yanda, or "Strike Hard," campaigns to purportedly fight crime. This campaign is similar to the brutal Strike Hard campaign (严厉打击刑事犯罪活动) across China in 1983, which were known as the "bloodiest chapter in post-Mao Chinese politics".[4] In just two months alone in 1996, the authorities killed at least 1,000 people across China in mass executions.[5]

Over more recent decades, a minority of Uyghurs has resorted to violent measures and terrorism, striking out against Chinese authorities.[6] The authorities and Chinese civilians have struck back with revenge attacks that claimed many Uyghur lives, even those who were advocating for their rights through nonviolent means.

In June 2009, a bitter ex-employee of a toy factory in Guangdong Province started a rumor that six Uyghur men had raped two Han women at the factory. The rumor started a brawl, which killed two Uyghurs and left 118 people injured. By July, at least 1,000 Uyghurs in Xinjiang began protesting in the city of Urumqi, demanding a full investigation. The incident ignited the Uyghurs' deep-seated frustration with their persecution. Protests turned into riots, with rioters assaulting police, destroying vehicles, and starting fires.[7] During the riots, at least 156 people were killed, and 800 were injured, though a spokesman for the World Uyghur Congress claimed there were 10,000 protesters and that 600 were killed.[8] Human Rights Watch documented that at least 43 men and teenage boys disappeared.[9]

By the next day, China had taken complete control of the Internet in the Xinjiang region.[10] Locals were told there would be no Internet

---

[4] www.cambridge.org/core/services/aop-cambridge-core/content/view/600987614E4DAD2F81D54B877A84E663/S0305741022001795a.pdf/centralized_law_enforcement_in_contemporary_china_the_campaign_to_sweep_away_black_societies_and_eradicate_evil_forces.pdf

[5] www.amnesty.org/en/documents/asa17/072/1996/en

[6] www.nytimes.com/2009/07/11/world/asia/11china.html

[7] www.nytimes.com/2009/07/06/world/asia/06china.html

[8] http://news.bbc.co.uk/1/hi/world/asia-pacific/8135203.stm

[9] www.hrw.org/report/2009/10/20/we-are-afraid-even-look-them/enforced-disappearances-wake-xinjiangs-protests

[10] www.reuters.com/article/us-china-xinjiang-internet-sb-idUSTRE56513820090706

access for 48 hours; Uyghur forums were blocked; the websites for the regional governments were down; journalists couldn't send texts or make international calls. Phone service was limited, and China Mobile's phone services were cut entirely. Reporters attempting to take photographs were detained. State media pushed a narrative that Uyghur violence was instigated by foreigners. Search engines in the country would no longer give results for terms like Urumqi.[11]

The Internet wasn't restored in 48 hours after all. In fact, the Internet would not be fully restored until 10 months later, in May 2010.[12] In that time, the only websites residents could access were a small number of state-approved local ones. No Internet, no email, nothing. This was the longest period during which the Internet had been blocked in part of China.

This blackout was a strong display of force and control from the CCP. It not only prevented people from organizing, but also enabled the state to completely dominate the narrative about the riots domestically and internationally. It wiped out a large portion of the community of Uyghurs on the Internet, with estimates indicating that over 80 percent of the Uyghur-language websites that existed prior to the shutdown did not return.[13]

The Architecture of Repression

In 2014, Chinese authorities reached a tipping point with the Islamic population in China, especially in Xinjiang. The state began instituting mass detentions using one part of China's Police Cloud, the Integrated Joint Operations Platform (IJOP). IJOP is a surveillance system that collects extensive information on individuals, including names, height, hair color, car registration, religious identity, and other relevant details. It tracks individuals using their phone location data, Internet activity, electricity usage, and personal

---

[11] www.google.com/hostednews/afp/article/ALeqM5jlMPMzVRIgHQFdLL_ShBYw_af3Vw
[12] www.nytimes.com/2010/05/15/world/asia/15china.html
[13] www.wired.com/story/uyghur-internet-erased-china

relationships. The software even tracks when Uyghurs or Tibetans leave their villages or provinces. It deems activities like practicing religion, socializing with neighbors, using the front door, or using WhatsApp to be suspicious.[14]

The surveillance systems track individuals in Xinjiang as high-, medium-, or low-risk, assigning scores up to 100. Simple things like growing a beard or being between the ages of 15 and 55 are enough to make someone considered riskier.[15]

IJOP is used to identify exactly who to put in re-education camps in Xinjiang. As of 2018, more than a million Uyghurs were in detention camps in Xinjiang, while another 2 million were forced into re-education camps for political and religious indoctrination.[16] These camps are known for torture, forced labor, and indoctrination.[17]

Once again, American companies are responsible for supporting the development of these surveillance networks and human rights violations. Thermo Fisher Scientific's websites marketed DNA kits to the Chinese police, describing them as designed for the Chinese population, including for identifying "ethnic minorities like Uyghurs and Tibetans." Dell's official WeChat account promoted a military-grade AI-powered laptop with "all-race recognition."[18]

Meanwhile, China issued blanket denials that the camps existed, with Hu Lianhe, a senior Chinese Communist Party official, stating:

"There is no such thing as re-education centers."[19]

[14]https://www.hrw.org/report/2019/05/01/chinas-algorithms-repression/reverse-engineering-xinjiang-police-mass
[15]https://xjdp.aspi.org.au/explainers/how-mass-surveillance-works-in-xinjiang
[16]www.aljazeera.com/news/2018/8/10/one-million-muslim-uighurs-held-in-secret-china-camps-un-panel
[17]https://news.un.org/en/story/2022/08/1125932
[18]https://www.ap.org/news-highlights/spotlights/2025/silicon-valley-enabled-brutal-mass-detention-and-surveillance-in-china-internal-documents-show
[19]www.nytimes.com/2018/08/13/world/asia/china-xinjiang-un.html

Part III

The Russian Federation

Chapter 31
Red Assembly

The Soviet Union hamstrung itself early on in the development of computers and computing—in the early 1950s, Soviet propagandists took to the term cybernetics like a cat takes to water: Not well. They leveraged Norbert Wiener, widely considered the father of cybernetics, and his ideas on cybernetics, especially his book, *Cybernetics: Or Control and Communication in the Animal and the Machine,*[1] to criticize America, clinging to the idea that cybernetics—and, as such, computers—would destroy the working class.[2]

This idea spread across the Soviet Union, but while the state was an outspoken critic of cybernetics to its own citizens, that didn't mean it stopped experimenting and trying to build computers quietly. In fact, at the same time that the Soviet Union leveled criticisms against cybernetics publicly, it was also developing its first universally programmable electronic computer. This computer could perform complex mathematical calculations that aided the Soviet nuclear weapons program.[3]

---

[1] Wiener, Norbert. Cybernetics: Or Control and Communication in the Animal and the Machine. Cambridge, MA: MIT Press, 1948.
[2] https://ijoc.org/index.php/ijoc/article/view/212
[3] https://scholarworks.uark.edu/cgi/viewcontent.cgi?article=1422&context=etd

It wasn't until de-Stalinization that the perception of cybernetics began to change, thanks to scientists and engineers who had been quietly working on these technologies for years. This brought about a hard pivot for the regime, and by the early 1960s, cybernetics was touted as the future of communism.[4] What a shift!

Unfortunately, politics got in the way of progress. In 1962, Viktor Glushkov proposed a nationwide network to manage the Soviet command economy electronically. It would have been an interstate network for economic planning known as the National Automated System for Computation and Information Processing, or OGAS (Общегосударственная автоматизированная система учёта и обработки информации).[5] He initially had buy-in to this plan; he was appointed head of the new Institute of Cybernetics, a well-funded research institution. However, 8 years later, when he went to the Politburo to seek approval for the project, the finance minister put forward a less ambitious, lower-reward proposal that won out.[6] Instead of creating a network of interconnected computers, computers would be installed at key production facilities but not networked. This missed the true value of what Glushkov originally proposed: A way to coordinate initiatives and share data across vast distances more easily.[7]

The Soviet Union also established the Ministry of the Electronics Industry in 1965 to centralize the development of electronics.[8] Unfortunately, the challenge of Stalin's centrally planned economy plagued every ministry, including (and especially brutal for) the electronics industry: Factories had no incentive to innovate since they were quota-based, and factory managers would intentionally undersell their production numbers to manage expectations in Moscow. The quota-based system meant there was no incentive to provide quality over quantity.[9]

[4] https://terna.to.it/CybCom/2-39%20Cybernetiics%20at%20the%20Service%20 of%20Communism.pdf

[5] https://web.mit.edu/slava/homepage/articles/Gerovitch-InterNyet.pdf

[6] www.jstor.org/stable/26983776

[7] www.bbc.com/future/article/20161026-why-the-forgotten-soviet-internet-was-doomed-from-the-start

[8] https://dbpedia.org/page/Ministry_of_the_Electronics_Industry_(Soviet_Union)

[9] www.elibrary.imf.org/display/book/9789264134683/ch023.xml

Further compounding the problem, the competitiveness between ministries meant that each developed its own set of computer systems incompatible with the others, hamstringing their attempts to eventually connect, modernize, and control the economy. Between that, difficulties with manufacturing, internal bureaucracy, and the massive cost of the project, it failed.[10] Difficulty—or at least the refusal—to coordinate at scale is an inherited trait for Russia's modern hacking groups, thanks to similar challenges; direct competition does not breed effective coordination.[11]

The Copycat Superpower

To catch up with Western innovation, the Soviet Union pivoted from innovating its technologies to stealing and copying Western ones, most notably the IBM Model 360.[12] This was not a trivial endeavor; sanctions were put in place against the Soviet Union at the time to prevent communist states from accessing critical technology. CoCom, short for the Coordinating Committee for Multilateral Export Controls, was established in 1949 as a clandestine effort to prevent the Soviets from getting access to Western technology. CoCom was made up of Cold War allies of the United States and, though it lacked formal status, was an agreement between the countries to coordinate embargoes on strategic goods—specifically preventing the Eastern Bloc from acquiring the advanced computing and telecommunications hardware necessary to close the military gap with NATO.[13]

To circumvent CoCom, much of Soviet-era computing innovation became an exercise in KGB industrial espionage, stealing schematics and then building copies of the technology themselves.[14] Directorate T, the Soviet directorate for scientific and technical

[10] https://ipa.org.au/ipa-review-articles/soviet-cybernetics
[11] Ibid.
[12] https://oldpc.su/lib/docs/ECsft/sovietmainframe.pdf
[13] www.cia.gov/readingroom/docs/DOC_0000309585.pdf
[14] Chan S. (2015) 'Fallen Behind', Intersect, 8(3).

intelligence collection from the West, had a web of front companies and intelligence officers known as Line X that were responsible for stealing or purchasing Western equipment.[15] Line X was tasked with acquiring the equipment in any way possible, by stealing or routing purchases through neutral countries like Switzerland. Directorate T employed engineers to evaluate any hardware or software collected before copying the designs to assess performance.[16]

The Soviets also copied the DEC PDP-11/40 minicomputer, one of the most popular computers of the time, and the one that popularized the operating system that formed the basis for many modern computers, Unix. Some innovation was happening, however, like when, in 1984, a Soviet software engineer, Alexey Pajitnov, created *Tetris*. All that said, he did create it for the Elektronika 60, a Soviet computer that was a clone of the American PDP-11.[17]

Between intentional sabotage efforts by other nations and a focus on copycatting over home-grown innovation, the Soviets were constantly a step behind the West with the most consequential technology of the century.

A few factors made this worse than it had to be. First, the Soviets had an overarching view that computers served as military and research equipment, not as a competitive market product. This limited Soviet investment in the consumer computer market. Second, sophisticated Soviet research institutes were able to design chips and computers effectively, but building them was a completely different story.

And third, the Soviets did not prioritize the use of computers across sectors, as it was seen as reducing labor—the entire system was built on full employment, fixed plans, and the ideology that socialism had eliminated unemployment, so reducing labor was not a palatable option.[18] This was in sharp contrast to other countries, especially the West, which were looking for ways to introduce computers to save time in any way possible.

[15] www.edn.com/farewell-dossier-proves-us-tech-and-research-stolen-july-19-1981
[16] www.cia.gov/readingroom/docs/CIA-RDP86B00338R000300430025-7.pdf
[17] www.vice.com/en/article/the-man-who-made-tetris
[18] www.the-waves.org/2023/01/05/soviet-computer-reasons-for-failing-to-win-the-race

Emailing During a Coup

When Mikhail Gorbachev came to power in 1985, he attempted to reform this system, in part by introducing a nationwide computer literacy program. The program focused on familiarizing students in the 9th grade with computer technology and programming with a course called *Fundamentals of Information Science and Computer Technology*.[19] This course and the ones that followed helped create the Russian cyber attackers who would then pivot Russia into the leading nation-state cyber actor it is today.

In 1990, one of the earliest Russian computer networks was launched: RELCOM. It was launched by Kurchatov Institute employees and DEMOS, a programming cooperative, which included Alexey Soldatov and Vadim Antonov.[20] RELCOM was initially built for email communication for professionals and was linked to machines outside the Soviet Union through a network in Helsinki, Finland, which served as its gateway to the rest of the world. RELCOM became pivotal to Russian citizens' ability to communicate internationally, especially during political conflict.

During the attempted Soviet coup in 1991, which was driven by hardline communists unhappy with the changes under the current regime, the plotters decreed that all television and news be suspended in a media blackout. RELCOM, however, was largely overlooked by the coup plotters and enabled people to get anti-coup messages out to the rest of the world. During the coup attempt, Polina Antonov, a DEMOS programmer, sent a message to Larry Press, a professor of computer information systems at California State University, which said,

> Don't worry, we're OK, though frightened and angry. Moscow is full of tanks and military machines—I hate them. They try to close all mass media, they stopped CNN an hour ago, and Soviet TV transmits opera and old movies. But, thank Heaven, they don't

---

[19] www.jstor.org/stable/1188162
[20] https://demos.ru/upload/soviet_coup_1991.pdf

consider RELCOM mass media or they simply forgot about it. Now we transmit information enough to put us in prison for the rest of our life.[21]

Every RELCOM subscriber was asked to transmit information on exactly what they were seeing under what they called Regime No. 1. All in all, over the course of the three-day coup attempt, REL-COM transmitted 46,000 messages globally, including in the Soviet Union.[22] The messages let the rest of the world know exactly what was happening, and the international pressure on the coup plotters helped lead to the coup's failure. This instance foreshadowed how useful the Internet would become for modern-day uprisings—it served as a system beyond state control where ideas could spread freely . . . if only for a short time.

The Chelnoki Traders

The collapse of the Soviet Union in 1991 took the Soviet computer industry down with it. Nearly all Soviet computer manufacturers ceased operations, and the few that survived into the 1990s did so by assembling small volumes of machines from imported components rather than building full systems domestically.[23] With military and state requisitions gone and Western export controls relaxed, the old Soviet hardware ecosystem was replaced by imports of Western computers. Russia entered the post-Soviet era not as a computer manufacturing power, but as a buyer and integrator of global hardware, setting up the long-term dependence on foreign technology that still shapes its digital landscape today.

When the Soviet Union fell, some of the preeminent Soviet computing experts moved abroad, taking their plans with them.

In one of the more well-known examples, Vladimir Pentkovski, who worked at the Lebedev Institute of Precision Mechanics and Computer Engineering, left the Soviet Union to become the leading microprocessor developer at Intel.[24]

In the 1990s, brand-name computers like Dell were prohibitively expensive for most Russians. This, combined with Russia's reliance on foreign computing equipment, led to a burgeoning gray market.

Small Russian firms and individual technicians would import bulk components like cases, motherboards, and CPUs from Taiwan or China, then assemble them into computers for 30–50 percent lower cost than name brands. The assembly process became known as the Red Assembly.[25] To get the components, Russians who had lost their jobs during the fall of the Soviet Union would go to places like Turkey, China, or the UAE with empty checkered bags and fill them with, among other goods like clothing and shoes, computer parts, before selling them at open-air markets in Moscow. The people were known as chelnoki (челноки), or "weaving shuttles," for the way they shuttled goods to Russia. There is even a monument dedicated to the chelnoki in Yekaterinburg, one of the largest cities in Russia. Millions of ordinary Russians—engineers, teachers, and scientists who lost their jobs—became cross-border traders.[26] By 1996, locally assembled computers accounted for roughly two-thirds of all sales in Russia.[27] The Russians were nothing if not resourceful in spite of hard circumstances.

Russia received its top-level domain, .ru, on April 7, 1994.[28] This largely supplanted the .su domain for most Russian websites, as the Soviet Union had been delegated the .su domain in 1990, before the fall. Russia's .ru domain was a mark of formal recognition of the

[24] www.rbth.com/science_and_tech/2014/09/24/computers_in_the_ussr_a_story_of_missed_opportunities_40073.html
[25] www.hse.ru/data/2021/12/02/1449210308/Computing%20in%20Russia.pdf
[26] https://jamestown.org/how-the-shuttle-traders-save-russia
[27] www.economist.com/unknown/1997/09/04/laptops-from-lapland
[28] https://cctld.ru/en/domains/about

Russian-language segment of the Internet, also known as Runet. New Internet companies were growing in Russia, like Sovam Teleport, which was the first major public Internet site in Russia and was also the first to give Russian banks access to SWIFT, the backbone of international payments and securities transactions.[29] Still, citizens' access to computers was limited to major cities and shared computers through school, work, or community centers. Compounding this was a barrier to entry on the Internet for many nations: Virtually the only language in widespread use online was English. To quote Anatoly Voronov, the director of Glasnet in 1996,

> It is just incredible when I hear people talking about how open the Web is. It is the ultimate act of intellectual colonialism. The product comes from America so we either must adapt to English or stop using it. This just makes the world into new sorts of haves and have nots.[30]

The Blogging Boom

Despite Russia's challenges post–Soviet Union, its adoption of the Internet increased steadily. In 1997, the search engine Yandex launched and would go on to become the largest search engine in Russia. It has become a much broader technology company, now also operating the largest ridesharing company in Russia, among other tech applications.[31]

In 1999, the website LiveJournal was launched. It is a hybrid blogging platform and social network originally created by an American programmer, Brad Fitzpatrick. Despite its creation by an American, it gained a massive early user base of Russians, especially for uncensored political discussion in the early 2000s.[32] By the

---

[29] www.techmonitor.ai/technology/sovam_teleport_launches_russia_on_line_service_targets_anyone_in_russia_with_a_computer
[30] www.nytimes.com/1996/04/14/weekinreview/computer-speak-world-wide-web-3-english-words.html
[31] https://yandex.com/company/history
[32] https://bradfitz.com/misc/bct

mid-2000s, 44 percent of all Russian bloggers were on LiveJournal.[33] The company was sold to a Russian company, SUP Media, in 2007. It moved its servers to Russia by 2016 and became a go-to source for "alternative" news—much of it Russian disinformation.[34] That shift transformed LiveJournal from a personal blogging site into an infrastructure asset for Russia's emerging disinformation apparatus.

The Bulletproof Haven

By the late 1990s and early 2000s, .ru started ranking among the largest country code top-level domains globally by number of registered second-level domains.[35] By contrast, the .su domain continued to operate after the dissolution of the Soviet Union, but became a notorious domain used by cybercriminals. The domain had much looser regulations and terms of service than other country code domain names, which made it easier for cybercriminals to leverage it.

An entire industry was built on .su for bulletproof hosting services—infrastructure services that ignored abuse reports and promised not to take servers down unless they were raided by police or forced by court order.

In 2006, the Russian Business Network (RBN) emerged and came to define the market for bulletproof hosting services.[36] Based in St. Petersburg, it provided a hosting service for illegal content, including child sexual abuse material, spam, and malware distribution. RBN hosted the websites that carried out the majority of cybercrime and profiteering; Rock Group, known for its phishing techniques, used RBN to steal $150 million from bank accounts in 2006.[37]

---

[33] www.bbc.com/news/magazine-17177053
[34] https://jns.scholar.princeton.edu/sites/g/files/toruqf2751/files/jns/files/trends_in_online_influence_efforts_v2.0_aug_5_2020.pdf
[35] www.active-domain.com/dot-ru
[36] www.shadowserver.org/wp-content/uploads/2019/04/RBN-AS40989.pdf
[37] https://newsroom.cisco.com/c/r/newsroom/en/us/a/y2023/m02/security-history-the-evolution-of-phishing.html

This all changed in 2013 after one bulletproof hosting company was blocked by spam watchdog Spamhaus. To strike back, the hosting company hit Spamhaus with a DDoS attack that led to a multiday Internet slowdown.[38] It triggered intense law enforcement scrutiny, especially from German authorities, leading to raids of some of the biggest bulletproof hosting providers.[39]

To this day, .su remains active, especially for patriotic or nostalgic projects. Latin characters had a monopoly on Internet domain names until 2010, when Russia gained a Cyrillic-script ccTLD, .рф. Fourteen years after Anatoly Voronov criticized the Internet as a form of intellectual colonialism, the introduction of Cyrillic domains signaled a long-overdue recognition of other linguistic and cultural communities online.

[38] www.spamhaus.org/resource-hub/ddos/answers-about-recent-ddos-attack-on-spamhaus
[39] www.techtarget.com/searchsecurity/news/252471678/Bulletproof-host-raided-in-former-NATO-bunker

Chapter 32
Jamming Zagranitsa

Information control was essential to the Soviet Union; protecting national sovereignty, including against the spread of information that the state opposed, was fundamental to its approach. Western radio was popular in the Soviet Union from 1948 until the Soviet Union fell, in part because of *zagranitsa* (заграница), a fascination with the world beyond Soviet borders.[1] The music and cultural differences were especially curious, and as time went on—especially into the 1980s—the allure of rock music like The Beatles and songs like Scorpions' *Wind of Change* (which some speculate was a CIA op to bring about the end of the Cold War) was enough for citizens to try to get access to Western radio however they could.[2]

The West used radio stations, like Voice of America and, later, Radio Free Europe, to spread propaganda to Soviet citizens.[3] To stop this, in 1948 the Soviet Union started jamming radio broadcasts. Yet, size and sprawl of the Soviet Union, combined with citizens' interest in Western life, made it difficult to block information completely. The Russians used skywave jamming to block radio stations over large distances, albeit with some difficulty, as its success is

---

[1] www.jstor.org/stable/j.ctt3fgx18
[2] https://crooked.com/podcast-series/wind-of-change
[3] https://firstamendment.mtsu.edu/article/voice-of-america

subject to atmospheric conditions. They also used groundwave jamming, which was effective, but only for smaller areas.[4] Determined listeners still found ways to tune in, keeping Western broadcasts a persistent thorn in the side of Soviet information control.

The Control Doctrine

The state saw the threats posed by cyberattacks early on, particularly the potential for it to lose control over the flow of information. In 2000, Russia released the *Information Security Doctrine of the Russian Federation*, approved by President Putin, which outlined priorities and threats to the Russian populace and Russia's national security in the information domain.[5] This was the first document of its kind in Russia. It outlined information priorities like guaranteeing the freedom of information and prohibiting censorship, bolstering state media, promoting modern technologies, and protecting information technology. It kept to a very Russian ideal about the power of information warfare, and in the document, divided its information security strategy into two core domains: Technical and psychological.[6]

On the technical side, the doctrine prioritized protecting against attacks that accessed or affected data, particularly across telecommunications networks and financial services, both cyber and physical. It highlighted the importance of Russian technological independence, prioritizing homegrown technologies or those developed by allies to avoid adopting sabotaged foreign equipment.

Critically, the doctrine gave the Russian government the basis to legitimize state control over media and the Internet under the guise of protecting against them being used as tools of division. This is the foundation that gave the government wiggle room for the types of censorship and repression it was building behind the scenes. The document was a study in juxtaposition: While it talked of guaranteeing freedom of mass information and prohibition of censorship,

---

[4]https://time.com/archive/6636534/russia-static-defense
[5]https://info.publicintelligence.net/RU-InformationSecurity-2000.pdf
[6]Ibid.

it also left the door open for that same kind of censorship by the government.

It painted a picture of how information warfare was fundamental to national security both inside and outside of the country. It cemented telecommunications providers as information infrastructure, which allowed the state to treat service providers' security as a national security issue. Doctrines like these are critical to coordinating practical defense, but, like this one, they often use fear of potential threats to lay the groundwork for control and surveillance mechanisms.

The doctrine resulted in a material change for the Federal Security Service of the Russian Federation (FSB). It effectively stated that cybercriminals were a national security threat, not just a police issue, which resulted in a semi-militarization of the FSB. In 2003, Putin dissolved the Federal Agency of Government Communications and Information (FAPSI) and moved the majority of its signals intelligence functions under the FSB instead.[7] It recognized that spying, domestic security, and counterintelligence for the state needed to be done under the same roof in the information era.

The doctrine also led to the creation of the Federal Service for Technical Export Control (FSTEC) through a presidential decree in 2004. FSTEC is the civilian counterpart to the FSB, responsible for licensing every piece of encryption, firewall, and antivirus software used in Russia.[8] If you want to sell a router to a Russian bank today, FSTEC has to inspect the source code first—a rule that stems directly from the 2000 doctrine's paranoia about foreign kill switches. They may not be able to crack every type of encryption, but at the very least, companies are required to provide a means for the state to access their data if needed. As a company in Russia, your users' data is not your data, nor your users' data; it is Russia's data.

An incredibly consequential knock-on effect of the doctrine was the establishment of Roskomnadzor (Роскомнадзор) in 2008.[9] Roskomnadzor became the government's Internet and media regulator, responsible for information control. It is charged with supervising mass media and information communications in Russia and has played a pivotal role in limiting access to and controlling free speech online for Russian citizens.

---

[7]http://en.kremlin.ru/events/president/news/28294
[8]Ibid.
[9]https://rkn.gov.ru/en/about/historical-background

Just two years after Roskomnadzor was created, the Russian government began debating separating the Russian Internet from the global Internet. This was a massive undertaking—it would, for all intents and purposes, allow the government to completely bifurcate the Russian Internet from the rest of the world, isolating itself and further controlling its populace. The decision was controversial even within the government: Alexey Soldatov, one of the founders of RELCOM, was Deputy Minister of Communications in Russia at the time, but left the government in protest of the plan.[10] He believed the Internet should be global and not limited in the way Russia planned. In what many see as a politically motivated imprisonment, as of 2024, Alexey is serving a two-year prison sentence for transferring IP addresses to a foreign organization.[11] Dissent will not be tolerated.

The Failed 2013 Strategy

In 2013, the Russian government considered rethinking its approach to more holistically prioritize public-private partnerships and align with international cybersecurity standards. The Federation Council, the upper chamber of the Russian Federal Assembly, held a parliamentary hearing on *Legislative Support for National Cybersecurity in the Russian Federation* to debate the potential changes.[12] Attendees included representatives from government and top industry leaders, and their goal was to establish the basis for legislation to ensure Russia's cybersecurity strength in collaboration with the private sector.[13]

The session was unique in its emphasis on collaboration between government and industry, a rare approach in Russia. It also made use of terms accepted by international groups, like "cybersecurity"—terminology rarely put to paper and defined for public consumption in Russia, especially compared to terms

---

[10] www.themoscowtimes.com/2024/07/29/how-does-russia-treat-its-modernizers-by-locking-them-up-a85859
[11] www.eff.org/deeplinks/2024/09/eff-calls-release-alexey-soldatov-father-russian-internet#:~:text=EFF%20was%20deeply%20disturbed%20to,connection%20to%20the%20global%20internet
[12] http://council.gov.ru/media/files/41d4c80aee277857ad9c.pdf
[13] Ibid.

like "information space." In all other situations, Russia has used the term "information security" rather than "cybersecurity" to reframe the argument around the sovereignty of its national information, thereby giving it greater opportunity to establish control over both domestic infrastructure and the information citizens can access. This session differed greatly from that idea. For example, Senator Ruslan Gattarov, the champion of the session, stated,

It is impossible to regulate cyberspace exclusively at the national level—it has no borders.[14]

That statement alone was a dramatic reframing of how the government approached the domain, which had relied on terms like "information sovereignty" to articulate its ultimate belief that it should have control over the information its citizens create or consume.

The session resulted in the drafting of a strategic framework, the *Concept for the Cybersecurity Strategy of the Russian Federation*, for public consideration and review; however, it was never adopted.[15] It came under scrutiny by the FSB and academics for its acceptance of international terminology and recommendations for international collaboration and support.[16]

This was far, far from the status quo that the FSB had set . . . or wanted to keep. Since the turn of the century, the Russian government has agreed not to extradite its citizens, in part so that it could use them for its own cybercrimes; this new strategy would threaten the operations it had built. Much of its cyber operations rely on a safe harbor for cybercriminals in Russia, and this proposal was directly opposed to it.

Not only did the strategic framework fail, but Russia took the exact opposite approach a few years later, pushing further into information sovereignty and isolationism. In 2016, a new update expanded beyond the 2000 doctrine. It codified the direction the government had already begun moving in and expounded on three key beliefs: (1) information security is a domain of national sovereignty; (2) the

---

[14]http://council.gov.ru/media/files/41d4c9afd3145b3a6264.pdf
[15]http://council.gov.ru/services/discussions/themes/38324
[16]https://sites.middlebury.edu/cyber/2014/01/20/russias-crowdsourcing-experiment-getting-the-peoples-opinion-on-the-new-cyber-security-strategy

Russian state, citizens, and media face blatant discrimination globally; and (3) Russia is facing threats from other geopolitical forces
and must establish an international security system to protect itself.[17]

On the first point, the updated doctrine put a heavy emphasis
on information security as critical to the national sovereignty of
Russia. It highlighted that state control over information infrastructure, data, and communications is fundamental to its ability to act
as an independent state and protect its interests.

On the second point, the doctrine breaks down how Russia per-
ceives that its media system faces discrimination, which raised the
stakes on why these major changes and increases in government
control were so important; the state, you as citizens, our youth . . .
we are all under attack! From everyone!

On the third point, the doctrine reiterated its intention to address
threats from other groups by developing an international information
security system that is vertically and centrally organized at the federal
and regional levels. It stayed in line with the top-down approach to
securing the country, with the private sector at the mercy of government
decisions instead of helping shape them. It also laid the groundwork to
push for further developments in data sovereignty requirements.

As part of its efforts to pull away from foreign imports, both technology and software, in December 2019, Russia's consumer protection law was amended to require manufacturers to preinstall certain
government-approved apps on devices like computers and smartphones sold in Russia.[18] The amendment requires certain browsers,
search engines, navigation, instant messaging apps, social networks,
and payment system apps to be installed—many of which are
made by Russian companies.[19] The amendment boosted domestic
technology and reduce reliance on Western devices and software.

All of these pieces come together to push Russia further away
from an open Internet and closer to the isolation the state craves.

---

[17] http://www.scrf.gov.ru/security/information/DIB_engl
[18] www.themoscowtimes.com/2019/12/02/russia-bans-iphone-sale-without-russian-apps-a68313
[19] https://schneider-group.com/en/news/countries/russia-mandatory-pre-installation-of-russian-software-on-electronic-devices-from-01-01-2021

Chapter 33
Killing Samizdat

The Soviets became extremely concerned about samizdat (самиздат), or self-publishing, in the late 1950s.[1] At the time, self-publishing was considered a form of dissent: Individuals reproduced and spread content that was otherwise censored by the state. For example, a major political document that the Soviets wanted censored was Khrushchev's secret speech of 1956, *On the Cult of Personality and Its Consequences*, which was given to the 20th Communist Party of Congress.[2] It denounced Stalin and marked the beginning of a political and cultural thaw, so the state tried to prevent it from being released publicly. It was leaked, and bootlegged versions spread like wildfire.[3]

When it came to preventing samizdat, photocopy equipment was an invention that served as a thorn in the Soviets' side.[4] Photocopiers were incredibly useful for self-publishing, as individuals didn't have to manually copy each word into a new document. The KGB considered photocopiers to be such a big problem that they strictly inventoried them. They even went so far as to sequester them in a

---

[1] https://samizdat.library.utoronto.ca
[2] www.bbc.com/culture/article/20170724-the-writers-who-defied-soviet-censors
[3] www.nytimes.com/1989/04/06/world/soviets-after-33-years-publish-khrushchev-s-anti-stalin-speech.html
[4] www.latimes.com/archives/la-xpm-1989-10-05-mn-913-story.html

spetsotdel (Спецотдел), a special department with barred windows and a dedicated person to guard the key. To use a machine, you had to log every individual page in a ledger, and the KGB maintained files documenting the exact typeface and unique output characteristics of each copier. This meant that if a piece of samizdat was found by security officers, they could compare it to their records and find the person responsible.[5]

It wasn't until 1989 that the ministry began to loosen its grip on photocopiers.[6] However, that didn't stop the KGB from controlling samizdat—it just recognized that samizdat now came in a new form. Now, they needed control over the new communications infrastructure services that were emerging, especially telecommunications and the Internet. The state approached control over this infrastructure in a similar way: They implemented controls to surveil the equipment and, when information they didn't approve of was found, censored it.

Surveillance-as-a-Service

Russia started to monitor citizens' telephone and electronic traffic through the System of Operative-Search Measures (SORM).[7] SORM was a nationwide telecommunications surveillance system initiated in the 1990s. It required telecommunications providers to buy and install probes for the FSB that enable them to monitor user communications and content.[8]

SORM expanded quickly from telecommunications to Internet monitoring. By 1998, SORM-2 was embedding devices in Internet service providers (ISPs) that gave the FSB access to Internet data and could be used without the ISPs' knowledge or intervention.[9] The kicker? The ISPs were still forced to pay for and install the equipment. With this equipment in place, the only thing stopping

---

[5] Ibid.
[6] Ibid.
[7] https://www.csis.org/analysis/reference-note-russian-communications-surveillance
[8] www.cogitatiopress.com/mediaandcommunication/article/view/808/498
[9] www.csis.org/analysis/reference-note-russian-communications-surveillance

the FSB from accessing the data was the need for a court-issued warrant. Even that requirement was short-lived. Over the next two years, the state defanged the warrant requirements, removing the need for a warrant in the case of collecting metadata like phone call times, origins, destinations, and SMS. They also removed the requirement for the FSB to present documentation to telecom providers on which wiretaps were being done or which users were being tapped, effectively hollowing out oversight at the operator level.[10]

SORM-3 was introduced in 2014. Its introduction was not just a minor update, but the most far-reaching of any version, allowing authorities to intercept and track data from all devices, social media, and Wi-Fi.[11] SORM-3 requires telecommunications providers and ISPs to install deep packet inspection equipment to enable the FSB to read all messages passing through these providers. It also allows the FSB to route and store all this data for 3 years, so that it can return to it later (say, for a criminal investigation) or retrospectively analyze past data. The FSB can take all of this action without any intervention from ISPs.

Legally, SORM is still framed as lawful interception, so in theory, its use should be tied to warrants and investigations. In practice, Russian law and its implementation grant the FSB broad, minimally supervised powers; providers must pay for and host the equipment, but do not control what the FSB captures or how it routes the data. Any attempt at privacy was shredded once SORM-3 went into effect.

That said, SORM is not a perfect system. Russia lacks the same degree of centralization as China's system of ISPs, which makes it much more difficult to enforce compliance. Some ISPs struggle with aging infrastructure incompatible with the surveillance technology,

---

[10]http://www.libertarium.ru/libertarium/37988
[11]www.recordedfuture.com/research/tracking-deployment-russian-surveillance-technologies-central-asia-latin-america

or they simply cannot afford it. From 2016 to 2017 alone, Russia Business Consulting found that Roskomnadzor issued over 450 SORM violations at over 200 providers.[12]

Even with SORM-3, there have been gaps that made it more difficult for the Russian government to surveil as they wished. The VPN has helped users access websites otherwise restricted by Roskomnadzor. To stop it, in 2017, Russia passed the *VPN Law*, explicitly requiring VPN services and anonymizers to prevent access to restricted websites.[13]

Tor, the onion router, has also enabled users to access restricted information and to communicate anonymously online. In December 2021, Russia tried to block Tor, but due to its open-source nature and widespread community, many have found workarounds to continue using it. Some users have run bridges separate from the broader Tor infrastructure, which makes it more difficult to track and censor.[14]

Volodin's Prism

Vyacheslav Volodin, First Deputy Head of the Presidential Staff and a known Putin loyalist, once said,

"There is no Russia today if there is no Putin."[15]

In 2012, Volodin was known for his role in, among other things, managing internal dissent in Russia. After the Euromaidan protests, he began to develop a broader function to monitor social media, particularly bloggers. One critical piece of this puzzle was created by the company Medialogiya, which developed software called Prizma.[16] Known to some as Volodin's Prism, the software allowed Volodin to track the activity of Russian citizens on social media and blogs. Volodin used it to help gauge when unrest was rising in the

[12]https://css.ethz.ch/content/dam/ethz/special-interest/gess/cis/center-for-securities-studies/pdfs/RAD298.pdf
[13]http://publication.pravo.gov.ru/Document/View/0001201707300002
[14]https://www.themoscowtimes.com/2021/12/08/russia-blocks-tor-anonymity-service-a75760
[15]https://www.themoscowtimes.com/2014/10/23/no-putin-no-russia-says-kremlin-deputy-chief-of-staff-a40702
[16]www.mlg.ru/about

nation.[17] The government tracked and analyzed 60 million sources for real-time notifications of activity. More of these systems were installed in state offices over time, and they continue to be used to this day.[18] This cemented the Russian government's view that the information space must include blogs and social media. It also showed them that these sources had begun to have greater potential than traditional media manipulation.

In 2014, the state took that visibility to the next level when a consequential law on bloggers was passed, which defined any independent blogger with more than 3,000 daily visitors as a media outlet.[19] Once that happened, site owners were required to register with Roskomnadzor, which enabled the government to maintain an up-to-date record of emerging sites to monitor in Prizma to identify potential dissent or protests. It also made the site owners responsible for the accuracy of any information published on their sites, prompting them to self-censor and censor their followers to avoid government scrutiny. By hard-coding bloggers into the state's media ecosystem, the Kremlin was able to weaponize it as core censorship infrastructure.

Moscow Never Sleeps

In parallel to online government surveillance, total in-person government surveillance began in earnest in 2014 under the guise of digital transformation. In December 2014, the government released an order to construct the Safe City, a nationwide surveillance and emergency management initiative.[20] Safe City was meant to create more interconnected, digitally advanced infrastructure for Russia. It connects monitoring equipment across cities, improves emergency response by processing emergency calls more quickly, and helps manage safety for large events. While the implementation has been promoted under the guise of public safety and law and order,

---

[17] www.forbes.ru/sobytiya/vlast/92590-kak-vlasti-chitayut-vashi-blogi-rassledovanie-forbes
[18] https://www.rbc.ru/society/27/08/2012/5703fbef9a7947ac81a6b1cd
[19] https://merlin.obs.coe.int/article/6935
[20] http://government.ru/docs/16082

some of which it has delivered, the technical reality of the order meant heavier surveillance measures, data collection, and analytics that could be applied to dissidents.

Once the COVID-19 pandemic hit, the Russian government leaned into its surveillance infrastructure. In addition to the Safe City deployments, in 2019, it deployed facial recognition systems throughout Moscow. In early 2020, in the peak of the pandemic, the surveillance systems exposed more than 200 individuals who violated the mandated isolation requirements.[21]

That said, not every region has the technical advancements and surveillance capabilities of Moscow. Regions outside of urban areas, especially those with less surveillance equipment, like Murmansk, had to adopt alternative methods. Some used tracking bracelets akin to those used for house arrest to track sick patients.[22] Others required the use of mandatory tracking apps. Digital tracking became a mainstay of Russian compliance with COVID-19 restrictions. What began in the name of public safety morphed into infrastructure for monitoring behavior at scale, laying the groundwork for how Russia now manages not just crises, but dissent itself.

Reactionary Censorship

Once the vehicle for surveillance is in place, next comes the action: Censorship. However, censorship is not an easy thing to retrofit onto an Internet distributed across thousands of ISPs. Russia has invested in a slew of government regulations over the years, attempting to plug all holes in the free flow of information, but it's been difficult, especially given its aging equipment and the growing global standard of encrypting network traffic.

In 2011, the Arab Spring was a not-so-distant memory; it served as one reason why the Russian government's response to massive protests from 2011 to 2013 was so heavily focused on

---

[21] www.hrw.org/news/2020/03/25/moscow-silently-expands-surveillance-citizens
[22] www.ponarseurasia.org/russia-and-digital-surveillance-in-the-wake-of-covid-19

information control.[23] The demonstrations were some of the largest since the fall of the Soviet Union, caused by Putin's run for reelection in 2012 and reports of potential election fraud. Tens of thousands of people attended the protests.[24] The turmoil was palpable. Mikhail Gorbachev called for Putin not to seek a third term as president and for the results of the parliamentary election to be reevaluated.[25]

The state saw Internet circles and social media coverage as uncontrollable, independent tools of mobilization and dissent. Just one protest meetup on Facebook had over 35,000 people signed up.[26] Protesters made sure anti-Putin hashtags went viral as often as possible. Videos that seemed to show voter fraud, including ballot stuffing, took off on social media websites. At one of the rallies, Alexei Navalny said to the crowd,

They can laugh with their 'zombie boxes' [televisions], they can call us microbloggers and little social-network hamsters . . . I am a little social-networking hamster! And I'll gnaw through the throats of these cats![27]

Meanwhile, DDoS attacks intermittently took down LiveJournal, radio stations, and other media sources.[28] Russian state media ignored the protests or portrayed them as chaotic and full of radicals.[29] Their attempt to shift the narrative did not put a dent in the overwhelming social media coverage. The traditional means of information control over the population was failing the Russian government, now that users had fully embraced social media.

As predicted by many in Russia, this led the government to introduce laws to monitor and crack down on Internet usage. In

---

[23] www.ponarseurasia.org/wp-content/uploads/attachments/pepm_159.pdf
[24] www.politico.com/story/2011/12/moscow-rallies-protest-putin-alleged-voter-fraud-070234
[25] www.bbc.com/news/world-europe-16066061
[26] www.hrw.org/news/2011/12/13/era-apathy-russia-post-election-protests
[27] www.rferl.org/a/russian_protesters_mobilize_online_as_leaders_jailed/24414881.html
[28] www.reuters.com/article/2011/12/07/russia-protests-socialmedia-idUSL5E7N62NM20111207
[29] https://academic.oup.com/book/33649/chapter-abstract/288179909

2012, Roskomnadzor implemented Federal Law No. 139-FZ, which empowers the government to maintain a registry of IP addresses that telecommunications and ISPs are required to block; Roskomnadzor can update the list at any time without a court hearing. They claimed the list was to protect minors from websites featuring child sexual abuse material (CSAM). Think of the children![30]

The blocklist is not publicly available, which helps the state hide what's actually being blocked from broader scrutiny. That said, there are known examples of the blocking infrastructure being abused (repeatedly), as the government blocks websites because of their dissenting opinions, such as when it blocked Grani.ru, a popular opposition news site.[31] It was supposedly blocked because it called for unlawful activity, a vague charge that ultimately boils down to one thing: They were posting scathing critiques of the Kremlin.

In 2017, Russia banned instant messaging providers from allowing anonymous accounts.[32] Mobile operators are required to associate instant messaging user accounts with their actual mobile phone numbers to ensure they can be identified. The ban also required instant messaging providers to comply when Russian authorities request that they block messages that distribute prohibited content, which effectively ended anonymous messaging. It also laid the groundwork for tracking what citizens were saying and when. From here on, any messaging platform that wanted access to Russian users also had to accept visibility and control by the Kremlin.

The Navalny Effect

Alexei Navalny had been a persistent challenge for Putin for years, consistently growing in popularity among the Russian population.

[30] http://kremlin.ru/events/president/news/16095
[31] www.rferl.org/a/russia-blocks-websites-critical-of-kremlin/25297188.html
[32] www.hrw.org/news/2017/08/01/russia-new-legislation-attacks-internet-anonymity

In 2018, he was disqualified from running for president due to prior politically motivated convictions.[33] He launched a voting strategy known as Smart Voting to help organize the opposition party, with a website, Telegram channel, and app. Beyond his pressure on the oligarchy, his wit, and his charisma, many attributed the results in the 2019 Moscow City Duma elections to his digital strategy.[34]

Because of the success of the strategy, days before the 2021 parliamentary elections, Russian authorities ordered Google and Apple to remove the Smart Voting app.[35] While Google and Apple initially spurned these requests, both companies had offices in Russia, which were points of leverage. The Kremlin sent authorities to Google's Moscow office and summoned representatives from Google and Apple to the Russian parliament, where they were threatened.[36] The authorities made a list of specific Google employees whom the government threatened to prosecute if the app was not removed. Shortly after, Google and Apple both removed the app from their app stores. If regulatory requirements fail, physical threats are more likely to prevail.

Roskomnadzor labeled the Smart Voting websites extremist and blocked them websites too. According to Russian state justice database records obtained by the BBC, in 2021, the majority of content Russia wanted removed was in support of Navalny—about 67 percent across Twitter, Facebook, Instagram, YouTube, and TikTok.[37]

In yet another censorship test for Russia, in August 2020, Navalny was poisoned with a Novichok nerve agent, which the EU said was only possible with the consent of the Presidential Executive Office [of Russia].[38] After the poisoning and his recovery, Navalny

---

[33] www.cnn.com/2017/12/25/asia/russia-alexey-navalny-barred-election

[34] https://electoralpolitics.org/en/articles/otsenka-effektivnosti-umnogo-golosovaniia-spor-analiticheskikh-podkhodov

[35] www.reuters.com/world/europe/google-apple-remove-navalny-app-stores-russian-elections-begin-2021-09-17

[36] https://meduza.io/en/news/2021/09/14/court-marshals-visit-google-s-moscow-office-in-connection-with-injunction-against-smart-vote-search-results

[37] www.bbc.com/news/blogs-trending-59687496

[38] https://www.npr.org/2020/10/15/923982672/eu-sanctions-russian-officials-over-navalny-poisoning-citing-chemical-weapons-us

returned to Russia and was immediately arrested. This led to a nationwide wave of protests from January to April that took social media by storm. To address it, in March, Roskomnadzor began throttling Twitter under the guise of it being used to spread information on supposed "unauthorized rallies" in support of Navalny, claiming some were illegally calling for minors to participate.[39] Roskomnadzor throttled websites with t.co to control Twitter's mobile website, but as an unintended consequence, this ended up with collateral damage. It affected any website with t.co, which included the Kremlin's own website, the website of the Duma, and other services like Google and Yandex.[40] Not a great look for Roskomnadzor's powers of censorship and control.

The Cost of a Like

In 2014, Putin signed into law an addition to the *Russian Criminal Code, Article 280.1, Public Calls for Action Aimed at Violating the Territorial Integrity of the Russian Federation.*[41] The law is very broad and criminalizes public calls for actions that could affect the territories of Russia. The law does not require physical violence: Even a simple post online can lead to a criminal charge, which is exactly what happened to Darya Polyudova. She was found guilty in a Russian court of "public calls to extremist activities" after posting three messages on VKontakte: One about how supposed ethnic Ukrainians were calling for the Krasnodar region to become part of Ukraine; one of a poster that said, "No war in Ukraine but a revolution in Russia!"; and one stating that Russians needed to take to the streets to protest. She had merely 38 followers at the time of her posts . . . not exactly inciting a mob. She served two years in a penal colony for the crime of posting on social media.[42]

---

[39] https://censoredplanet.org/#/throttling
[40] www.accessnow.org/russia-throttled-twitter
[41] http://en.kremlin.ru/events/president/news/46297
[42] www.hrw.org/news/2015/12/22/dispatches-crime-speaking-russia

Beyond *Article 280.1*, one of the most consequential pairs of statutes Russia instituted in the modern era is the *Yarovaya Laws*, which were signed by Putin in July 2016.[43] The laws serve as the legal data retention framework for SORM, mandating data storage and access for telecommunications, Internet service providers, messaging apps, and email providers. Providers must store the content of communications for 6 months in Russia, and metadata for up to three years for telecommunications providers and one year for ISPs and online services.

One of the most important parts of the laws also expanded what qualifies as a terrorist act to include "justification of terrorism." It also made it a crime to fail to report information on terrorist attacks. Many Crimean Tatar activists and Ukrainian supporters were charged, prosecuted, and jailed under these laws.[44] The laws are, once again, vague—what is considered a public call to a terrorist act doesn't rely on terrorist activity taking place, terrorists being mentioned, or even a call for violence. Instead, the laws ultimately just instill fear of pushing back against the government and force individuals to self-censor or report on others. This is yet another instance where the FSB gained incrementally more control, more context, and more access.

One of the more public and embarrassing (for Russia) tests of the *Yarovaya Laws* in action happened against Telegram. In April 2017, Saint Petersburg was shaken by a terrorist attack in the metro system that killed 15 people and injured 45.[45] According to the FSB, the perpetrator used Telegram to communicate with his accomplices in the attack. There has been no corroborating third-party evidence that proves the terrorists were using Telegram in this attack, though Telegram has been used by terrorist organizations in the past, including during the attacks in Paris in 2015 and Brussels in 2016.[46] As part of its investigation into the

---

[43] www.eff.org/deeplinks/2016/07/russia-asks-impossible-its-new-surveillance-laws
[44] https://zmina.info/en/news-en/moscow-weaponizes-terror-laws-against-civilians-in-occupied-crimea-crimeasos
[45] https://carnegieendowment.org/posts/2017/04/st-petersburg-bombing-exposes-chinks-in-russias-counterterrorism-strategy
[46] www.cnn.com/2016/03/30/europe/inside-paris-brussels-terror-attacks

metro attack, the FSB requested access to Telegram's encryption keys to break into the application.[47] This was a major, public, and emotionally heated test of the *Yarovaya Laws*.

At the time, Telegram stated that it could not provide access to the FSB because of its end-to-end encryption capabilities; keys are stored locally on the device, per industry standards, and therefore are inaccessible by Telegram. In October 2017, a Russian magistrate ruled that Telegram had committed an administrative offense by failing to provide decryption keys to the FSB.[48] While Telegram appealed the ruling, by 2018, its appeal had failed, and the district court ruled to restrict access to Telegram across Russia immediately.

The state ordered ISPs to block the IP addresses it associated with Telegram, but Telegram used domain fronting to dodge the block. Domain fronting is a technique to hide the true domain destination behind a seemingly legitimate domain. In response, the Russian government proceeded to block almost 20 million IP addresses, many of which were owned by legitimate Internet services like Google, Amazon, and Microsoft; this disrupted online banking, shopping, and other services in Russia. Seeing that this was less effective than they wanted, Roskomnadzor found a new path forward: It requested that Google and Apple remove Telegram from their app stores, but neither company complied. Russia's attempts to block Telegram were largely a failure and highlighted the gaps in the Internet control Russia has set up.[49]

Russia continued trying to restrict access to Telegram until 2020, when it effectively gave up on the ban, in part because state agencies were actively using the app during the pandemic. You can't ban an app that the government relies on. However, Telegram also acquiesced and agreed to aid the Russian government in extremism investigations by blocking extremist channels.[50]

---

[47] https://carnegie.ru/commentary/68579
[48] https://rsf.org/en/russia-telegram-block-leads-widespread-assault-freedom-expression-online
[49] www.wired.com/story/telegram-in-russia-blocked-web-app-ban-facebook-twitter-google
[50] https://interfax.com/newsroom/top-stories/69068

The Splinternet

A series of laws slowly gave Russia more control of the data its citizens create, particularly by keeping that data within the physical borders of Russia.

In 2014, Russia passed a law that requires any company, Russian or otherwise, that collects or processes personal data of Russian citizens to process that data within Russian borders. In 2016, a Russian court found LinkedIn guilty of violating the law, and because of the violation, LinkedIn has been blocked in Russia ever since.[51]

In 2021, Putin signed a related law that required social media companies with over 500,000 daily Russian users to open offices in Russia.[52] It claimed this was to ensure compliance with Russian national security requirements, but it ended up serving a deeper purpose. It gave authorities a potential point of leverage: If a company was taking an action the Russian government felt was incongruous with its goals (for example, refusing to censor its users), it could simply raid the local office and threaten the staff to force change, as it did with Google.

In 2019, Russia enacted the *Sovereign Internet Law*, fulfilling some of the promises laid out in the *National Security Strategy*. The government claimed this law supported Russia through deterrence by denial: Stopping attacks or making hostile actions less effective by ensuring Russia could disconnect from the external Internet at any time. Russia calls this *tsifrovoi suverenitet* (мировой суверенитет), or digital sovereignty, which, in Russia, is the government's right and capability to control its information environment. It is divided into two main aspects: Electronic sovereignty and information sovereignty. Electronic sovereignty encompasses robust Internet and electronic infrastructure (for example, the electric grid) to protect against attacks, including cyberattacks, while information sovereignty is about ensuring self-sufficient control of information and resilience against external attacks. It gives Russia more power in an emergency, but it also gives the government

---

[51] www.bbc.com/news/technology-38014501
[52] www.reuters.com/technology/putin-signs-law-forcing-foreign-it-firms-open-offices-russia-2021-07-01

more control overall, especially over information entering and leaving the country, and thus the information consumed by its citizens.

Russia's difficulty blocking websites like Telegram fueled the need for the *Sovereign Internet Law*. Prior to 2019, Roskomnadzor had to maintain the single register to block sites, which required it to coordinate with ISPs. This left Roskomnadzor relying on ISPs instead of having direct control over what was blocked and when. The *Sovereign Internet Law* changed that—it required ISPs to install deep packet inspection and other technologies that the government could remotely access to ensure it could track, filter, and route Internet traffic. It also required ISPs to give diagrams of their networks to Roskomnadzor so it could ensure the controls were installed appropriately and that no data was missed. The law mandated that the government create a national domain name system responsible for routing and monitoring Internet traffic within Russia, and that it run annual tests to isolate the Russian Internet from the rest of the world. With this equipment, Roskomnadzor could independently control the Internet, from blocking certain content to providing the equivalent of a wiretap, without the knowledge of the ISPs or citizens. The system isolates Russia as much as possible from the rest of the world to maintain control.[53]

A few ISPs had installed and tested the equipment by mid-November 2019, but the maintenance requirements of the equipment and the investments required to align with these new laws are taxing. Overall, the law set an aspiration to have 90 percent of Russian Internet traffic routed through Russian servers by 2024. This was a massively ambitious goal, since as of 2017, foreign servers transmitted around 60 percent of Runet traffic.[54] Much of Russia's Internet traffic relies on foreign infrastructure that was developed as a decentralized mesh of thousands of ISPs. Forcing all that traffic through Russian government chokepoints means reengineering the entire system.

---

[53] www.brookings.edu/articles/putins-internet-plan-dependency-with-a-veneer-of-sovereignty

[54] https://meduza.io/en/news/2018/07/11/russian-officials-draft-an-initiative-to-reduce-domestic-internet-traffic-routed-through-foreign-servers

As one step in that process, ISPs were mandated to use the Russian national DNS by 2021. With the Russian national DNS instantiated, the government has complete control over what websites citizens can or cannot access. A national DNS gives Russia power over the Russian Internet's phonebook—if you want to go to a particular website, the government gets to decide which IP address your request resolves to (which site you actually reach), or whether it resolves at all (whether the site is blocked entirely).

However, different parts of Russia experience this system very differently. ISPs with legacy infrastructure suffer from slow Internet speeds caused by these controls. There are significant doubts that all ISPs have started using the Russian national DNS.[55]

The first Internet isolation test took place in December 2019, which attempted to demonstrate that Russia could successfully disconnect from the Internet and remain operational.[56] The test took several days and included four different Russian operators, targeting specific segments of their infrastructure, especially signaling planes used for mobile services. The results did not demonstrate success. The *attackers* succeeded in 62.5 percent of attacks on the SS7 protocol (legacy interconnect/roaming) and 50 percent through the Diameter protocol (LTE/5G).[57] Though Russia called it a success, the reality was that even one segment of the Russian Internet, under specific conditions, wasn't able to disconnect and prevent the attacks. Rather than showcasing a hardened, independent Runet, the exercise revealed that even under controlled conditions, Russia could not reliably shield its core mobile signaling from attack.

[55] https://dgap.org/en/research/publications/russias-quest-digital-sovereignty
[56] www.themoscowtimes.com/2019/12/24/russias-interent-ready-isolation-officials-say-after-partial-shutdown-a68728
[57] https://www.vedomosti.ru/technology/news/2019/12/23/819484-suverennom-runete

Chapter 34
Centralized Defense, Centralized Control

I n 2013, the Russian government recognized the Internet's potential, both to advance its interests and to undermine them. It had wielded the power of offensive cyberattacks on countries like Ukraine and Georgia with success, and it became evident that it needed to defend its own country from the very actions it was perpetrating against others.

To this end, in 2013, Putin issued a decree establishing a state system for preventing, detecting, and eliminating computer attacks on Russia's information resources.[1] This system would serve as Russia's cybersecurity defense for any "critical information infrastructure," though the term was not defined until 2017, which caused challenges for its implementation. "Critical information infrastructure" was assumed to be any sector crucial to the stability of the nation, such as the defense sector, financial sector, transportation, and so on; however, since it was not explicitly defined, many companies had to make judgment calls as to whether the government would consider them part of it, leading to self-imposed compliance. There were also others who wanted to avoid

---

[1] https://rg.ru/documents/2013/01/18/komp-ataki-site-dok.html

being classified as critical information infrastructure so they could avoid giving the government access. Similar to Soviet times, companies do not want to report on incidents and be put under a microscope by the government, especially since it can result in penalties.[2]

The Shield That Watches

Russia's system to defend critical information infrastructure is called the State System for Detection, Prevention, and Elimination of the Consequences of Computer Attacks (GosSOPKA), which the FSB, Roskomnadzor, and FSTEC created collaboratively at Putin's direction.[3,4]

GosSOPKA (ГосСОПКА) is a combination of capabilities, in part built by contractors like Kaspersky Lab and Astra Group, among others.[5] Every critical information infrastructure provider is required to install sensors within its networks that continuously monitor network traffic for cyberattacks. Industry-specific bodies and regional FSB offices aggregate data from these sensors, enabling them to identify attacks that span multiple sectors more effectively—if ten banks are seeing the same attack, there's a pattern.

The implementation was a massive undertaking that took years, with the first pilot of the system kicking off in 2015.[6] Managing the implementation of a system like this is not trivial, given competing data formats, hardware and software requirements, and difficulty retaining talent in Russia. It's a complicated system that needs people with a very specific set of skills to manage it.[7]

2017 was the year of control for GosSOPKA. Putin signed *Federal Law No. 187-FZ, On the Security of the Critical Information*

---

[2] https://ftp.treadstone71.com/files/Unit29155-APT28-GosSPOKA/Unit%2029155%20with%20GosSOPKA.pdf

[3] https://cis-legislation.com/document.fwx?rgn=98928

[4] https://jamestown.org/russia-ramps-up-cybersecurity-systems

[5] Ibid.

[6] www.internetgovernance.org/wp-content/uploads/IGPWhitePaper_STADNIK_RUNET-1.pdf

[7] https://support.kaspersky.ru/KATA/7.1/en-US/301735.htm

Infrastructure of the Russian Federation, which defined computer incidents and computer attacks and finally defined critical information infrastructure, though still quite broadly.[8]

Also passed in 2017, *Presidential Decree No. 620* made the FSB directly responsible for detecting and preventing cyberattacks on Russian internal networks, which formalized its control over Gos-SOPKA. This further fueled mistrust of the system, as the FSB is Russia's primary internal intelligence agency. The data collection for which it is responsible doesn't just help it protect against cyberattacks; it also gives it direct, government-mandated access into the most important companies in Russia. There are no legal protections that prevent the FSB from surveilling companies with this data, even if it wasn't its original purpose.[9]

In 2018, *the Law on the Security of the CII of the Russian Federation* required critical information infrastructure to report computer incidents to federal executive bodies. It also specified a tight timeframe by which incidents have to be reported, within 24 hours, and mitigation results within 48 hours. These requirements are challenging, as some incidents take days to weeks to investigate and respond to fully.[10]

The National Coordination Center for Computer Incidents NKTsKI (НКТсКИ) is where the FSB tracks and coordinates responses to cyberattacks as part of GosSOPKA. Regional offices are expected to provide the NKTsKI with curated data so that it can correlate attacks across the entire country. As of 2024, the FSB claimed that 70 percent of the calls the NKTsKI received were related to ransomware attacks.[11]

---

[8]https://rkn.gov.ru/docs/18.06.2015_-_ZHarov-PJEF-intellekt._sobst vennost6_ang.pdf
[9]http://www.kremlin.ru/acts/bank/42623
[10]https://tadviser.com/index.php/Article:State_System_for_Detection,_ Prevention_and_Elimination_of_Consequences_of_Computer_Attacks_(State_ system_of_detection,_prevention_and_elimination_of_consequences_of_computer_ attacks)#The_Law_on_the_Security_of_the_CII_of_the_Russian_Federation_ obliged_the_subjects_of_the_CII_to_inform_government_agencies_about_ cyber_incidents
[11]www.tadviser.ru/index.php/%D0%9A%D0%BE%D0%BC%D0%BF%D0%B0%D0%BD%D0%B8%D1%8F :%D0%9D%D0%B0%D1%86%D0%B8%D0%BE%D0%BD%D0%B0%D0%BB%D1%8C%D0%BD%D1%8B%D0%B9_% D0%BA%D0%BE%D0%BE%D1%80%D0%B4%D0%B8%D0%BD%D0%B0%D1%86%D0%B8%D0%BE%D0%BD%D0% BD%D1%8B%D0%B9_%D1%86%D0%B5%D0%BD%D1%82%D1%80_%D0%BF%D0%BE_%D0%BA%D0%BE%D0% BC%D0%BF%D1%8C%D1%8E%D1%82%D0%B5%D1%80%D0%BD%D1%8B%D0%BC_%D0%B8%D0%BD%D1%86 %D0%B8%D0%B4%D0%B5%D0%BD%D1%82%D0%B0%D0%BC_(%D0%9D%D0%9A%D0%A6%D0%9A%D0%98)

The Shield That Censors

A parallel operation took place to ensure that telecommunications providers were appropriately monitored as well. In 2013, the government authorized the creation of the Center for Monitoring and Control of the Public Communications Network (TsMU SSOP).[12] Much of its funding and authority were expanded by the *Sovereign Internet Law*. This group operates under Roskomnadzor and centralizes the monitoring of the Internet and telecommunications in Russia to ensure its stability and security. It protects against some cyberattacks as part of its duties, particularly DDoS attacks.[13]

This is critical—a DDoS attack against telecommunications infrastructure could feasibly knock out large portions of the Internet or communications systems, which would be especially valuable for an enemy in a wartime scenario. TsMU SSOP supports the network resilience needed to prevent this from happening. However, much like GosSOPKA, TsMU SSOP has a dual use: Roskomnadzor can use it to throttle Internet traffic, block domains, or even drop specific packets, effectively enabling large-scale censorship.[14]

---

[12] https://tadviser.com/index.php/Company:Public_Communication_Network _Monitoring_and_Management_Center
[13] https://tadviser.com/index.php/Project:National_System_for_Countering_ DDoS_Attacks
[14] https://tadviser.com/index.php/Company:Public_Communication_Network _Monitoring_and_Management_Center

Chapter 35
The Kremlin's Information Monopoly

Ничего наши танки не будут стоить, если души у них будут гнилыми, Вот почему я говорю: производство душ важнее вашего производства танков. И вот почему выпьем за вас, писателей, инженеров человеческих душ!

The production of souls is more important than the production of tanks . . . and therefore I raise my glass to you, writers, the engineers of the human soul!

—*Joseph Stalin, 1932*[1]

O ne of the early ways Vladimir Lenin, Joseph Stalin, and others in the party saw the power of the written word was via *Pravda*, which became the official paper of the Communist Party of the Soviet Union. It was an early lesson in the power of propaganda, as it helped shape public opinion during the Russian Revolution and helped the Communist Party spread its

---

[1] Stalin, I. V. Sochineniya (Collected Works), Vol. 15, Moscow: Gosudarstvennoe izdatel'stvo politicheskoi literatury (Gospolitizdat), 1951, pp. 356–357.

ideals. However, what was originally a way to spread ideas became a disinformation weapon. In 1935, Stalin commissioned a book, *The History of the All-Union Communist Party: Short Course,* which served as the definitive history and ideals of the party, considered "a book of our own, in place of the Bible."[2] Stalin took great pains to edit the book to his specifications—including reframing his role in the Communist Party to be more significant than it truly was and downplaying, deriding, or completely removing Bolshevik leaders with whom he conflicted.[3]

Propaganda was rampant in Russia during World War II as well, when the Soviet Union joined the Allied Powers for revenge and survival against an invading Germany. This alliance was critical for the war's outcome, but it did not mean a new alignment of values between the nations. The war demonstrated the Soviet Union's total brutality, especially to its own troops as part of Order No. 227 ("Not a Step Back"). Any attempts at unauthorized retreat were punished severely by forcing troops to serve in penal battalions, which faced suicide missions like walking across minefields.[4] The order also increased the number of blocking detachments, which sat behind the front lines and were charged with shooting anyone who retreated or attempted to desert. This brutality was juxtaposed against one of the most pivotal moments of propaganda for Russia, when they defined the war as "the Great Patriotic War," depicting Stalin as a father figure and great leader, and positioning participation in the war as patriotic, despite the death toll.

Over time, communism became the message, but control was held by a select few at the top only. This transition was aided by Russia's early forays into propaganda and information warfare, executed against its citizens. The goal: To convince the working class that they held the power. The method: To contort reality by changing it.

The Soviet Union maintained a tight grip on the populace through censorship, propaganda, and suppression of dissent. The

[2]https://books.google.com/books/about/Writing_History_in_the_Soviet_Union.html?id=NqJS-H-odnYC
[3]www.tandfonline.com/doi/full/10.1080/09546545.2022.2065740
[4]https://notevenpast.org/order-no-227-stalinist-methods-and-victory-eastern-front

idea of "reflexive control" was pioneered by Soviet strategists and scholars; reflexive control is about manipulating the flow of information to an adversary, including inundating them with truth, half-truths, and outright falsehoods, to manipulate a target into making decisions that benefit Russia.[5] The KGB used it against domestic targets, including Soviet citizens, by surveilling the populace, relying on informants, and controlling all major sources of information in the country across state media, radio, television, and literature.

While reflexive control was used initially to shape Russian minds, disinformation requires constant reinforcement, action, and destruction of opposing viewpoints at scale. It isn't easy to maintain. Ultimately, it did not entirely hold, in part because of exhaustion over the Cold War and the opportunity for knowledge brought about by *Glasnost* (гласность), Mikhail Gorbachev's policy in the mid-1980s of increasing transparency, loosening censorship, and allowing a more open discussion of political and social issues.[6]

Russian scholars defined the term "information space" (инфо рмационное пространство) when they began preserving the circulation of print media in the country during the fall of the Soviet Union.[7] By 1996, the government put out a formal definition that reflected a foundational mindset: The information space in Russia is a strategic asset, essential both for governance and for the broad function of society. The information space is not one system, but a collection of systems used to manage citizens' information needs.[8]

For a brief moment, Russian media was guaranteed freedom of speech thanks to *Glasnost*. In 1985, Gorbachev introduced reforms in an effort to promote freedom of expression, which weakened the Soviet communist mindset and control over the public. Censorship declined significantly, the Soviets were given access to previously banned history, travel restrictions were eased, and opposing political parties had more room to grow. In 1993, Gorbachev even helped the newspaper *Novaya Gazeta* with funds from his Nobel Peace Prize.

---

[5] https://calhoun.nps.edu/server/api/core/bitstreams/f770a2ad-2f1b-48c8-9d8b-a34a5be2df1d/content
[6] https://www.ebsco.com/research-starters/law/gorbachev-initiates-policy-glasnost
[7] https://stratcomcoe.org/cuploads/pfiles/5-kovaleva.pdf
[8] http://library.zntu.edu.ua/zakon/98ru-gip.html

The newspaper became well known for being critical of the Russian government up until 2022, when it ceased operations in Russia.[9]

The freedom journalists enjoyed was slowly eroded once Boris Yeltsin was elected, as journalists backslid into a similar mindset to Soviet times. By the 1996 election, the media had changed its tune, and Yeltsin was openly and overwhelmingly backed by the media, thanks to bribery and oligarchic pressures.[10]

The Architecture of Control

Putin officially came to power after being elected in March 2000, in part because of a massive support campaign by the media and Boris Berezovsky through *Russian Public Television, ORT*.[11] It once again demonstrated the power of controlling the media narrative in Russia, which Putin continued to hone through the next several decades via the consolidation of media power. After Putin's win, he immediately began the pendulum swing away from Gorbachev-era policies of openness, positioning himself as a strongman and establishing control over Russia's federal structure. He began slowly and systematically exiling oligarchs and destroying news outlets that disagreed with him.

One of Putin's biggest media targets early on was *NTV*. *NTV* is a media channel known for its independence from the state and for being critical of the Second Chechen War and Vladimir Putin in the late 1990s. In one of the more ridiculous yet darkly consequential moments, *NTV* had aired a puppet show, called *Kukly*, since 1994. In previous episodes through the years, the show had made fun of Yeltsin as a bumbling drunk. Where things took a turn was in 2000, when *NTV* aired episodes that made fun of Putin, portraying him as, among other things, an ugly little gnome from a fairy tale called *Little Zaches Called Cinnabar*, who appears beautiful to people but only by magic.[12] They continued to mock Putin until, two years later, masked

---

[9] www.reuters.com/world/europe/russia-revokes-independent-novaya-gazetas-last-media-licence-2022-09-15
[10] https://cpj.org/reports/2000/03/russia-analysis-march00
[11] www.themoscowtimes.com/2013/03/03/putin-saw-tv-parody-before-it-airedspokesman-says-a22055
[12] Ibid.

federal agents raided the offices of its parent company, Media-MOST. This kicked off a barrage of different measures by the government to pressure Media-MOST to sell a controlling interest in the company.[13] The state went so far as to jail Vladimir Gusinsky, founder of Media-MOST, on fraud charges, which would only be lifted after he agreed to sell his stake in *NTV* to *Gazprom Media*. At least 42 staff members, including journalists and anchors, quit shortly after in protest, and those who remained took to self-censoring over the next decade. *NTV* became a shell of its former self, and Gusinsky fled to exile.[14]

> From 2000 to 2024, 44 journalists have died in Russia, and over half of them were murdered.[15]

This is but one example of how Putin and his supporters consolidated media control under the state and slowly destroyed alternatives. Even Berezovsky fell under pressure. Berezovsky controlled *ORT*, which carried coverage after the Kursk submarine disaster in August 2000. It streamed videos of the sailors' wives and exposed lies about the rescue operation.[16] An *ORT* journalist, Sergey Dorenko, accused the prime minister and president and pulled no punches, saying,

> The main conclusion is that the authorities don't respect any of us, and that's why they lie. And the main thing here is that the authorities treat us like this only because we let them.[17]

Berezovsky alleges that Putin's Chief of Staff, Alexander Voloshin, told him that if he did not surrender his shares in *ORT*

[13] www.themoscowtimes.com/2013/03/03/putin-saw-tv-parody-before-it-aired spokesman-says-a22055
[14] www.pbs.org/newshour/nation/media-jan-june01-russia_04-03
[15] https://cpj.org
[16] www.rferl.org/a/kursk-disaster-putin-turning-point-russia/27184505.html
[17] https://meduza.io/en/feature/2019/05/10/sergey-dorenko-the-journalist-who-trashed-putin-s-rivals-before-sacrificing-his-career-to-criticize-him-has-died

to the Russian state, he would be imprisoned just like Gusinsky.[18] Berezovsky sold his stake to Roman Abramovich, an oil tycoon who was regarded as fairly neutral. However, once Abramovich acquired a stake in the media company, he installed Kremlin loyalists to control the organization. *ORT* was rebranded as *Channel One* and has promoted state talking points ever since. Berezovsky fled to London in late 2000.[19]

The Kremlin has also supported the creation of new, state-owned news agencies. As a knock-on effect of the 2004–2005 Orange Revolution, during which Kyiv overturned a rigged election favored by Moscow, the Kremlin supported the creation of *Russia Today*. *Russia Today* was established by *RIA Novosti*, a state-owned news agency, with the mission of improving Russia's image abroad. It was meant to serve as the country's soft power, spreading information to convince the world of Russia's perspective. Instead, it has morphed into a core part of Russian information operations. It influences other outlets around the world, including those that are not explicitly branded as Russian, to spread disinformation.

RIA Novosti was liquidated by Putin and replaced by the new state media conglomerate, Rossiya Segodnya, in 2013. The conglomerate kept the trusted *RIA Novosti* brand name for domestic news, but in 2014, launched Sputnik, a state-owned news agency and radio broadcast service. It is widely recognized as a tool of Russian propaganda.[20]

The Five Pillars of the Lie

In modern-day Russia, there is a multifaceted approach to information operations and propaganda campaigns. You can think of the

---

[18] www.judiciary.uk/wp-content/uploads/JCO/Documents/Judgments/berezovsky-abramovich-summary.pdf
[19] Ibid.
[20] www.nytimes.com/2016/08/29/world/europe/russia-sweden-disinformation.html

Russian propaganda ecosystem as being made up of five pillars, adapted from the U.S. State Department categorization:

- *Official government messaging*, which comes directly from the Kremlin.
- *State-funded global messaging*, which comes from state-run media tightly controlled by the Kremlin.
- *Proxy sources*, which disseminate news from state-funded media channels. These are often characterized as unrelated to Russia; they may mimic American news, like *The Washington Post* or *The New York Times*, or just appear as independent media.
- *Social media campaigns,* where the Kremlin amplifies disinformation.
- *Cyberattacks,* in which the Kremlin attacks governments or businesses, steals their data, and then either releases it to the public or uses it to inform its campaigns.

These pillars are often used together to best propagate a certain message or series of messages, or to dodge a particular narrative and cause confusion.[21] One example of this system at work took place during the tragic crash of Malaysia Airlines Flight 17.

The Five Stages of Denial

On July 17, 2014, a plane carrying 283 passengers and 15 crew members was traveling from Amsterdam to Kuala Lumpur, the capital of Malaysia. The plane never made it there. Debris from the plane was scattered over different areas in Ukraine near its border with Russia. There was much speculation early on that the crash was caused by a missile striking the plane.[22]

Twenty minutes after the downing, Russian militants were caught on several tapped calls talking about the incident and admitting that they were the ones who shot down the plane.[23]

[21] https://2017-2021.state.gov/wp-content/uploads/2020/08/Pillars-of-Russia%E2%80%99s-%20Disinformation-and-Propaganda-Ecosystem_08-04-20.pdf
[22] www.government.nl/topics/mh17-incident/achieving-justice/russia-responsible-for-downing-of-flight-mh17
[23] www.cnn.com/2014/07/18/world/europe/ukraine-mh17-intercepted-audio

Shortly after the crash, the VK page *Reports from Igor Ivanovich Strelkov*, which was managed by his supporters who reposted local militia chats or Girkin's private forum posts, posted about shooting down the plane, confirming that it was them. The post showed two videos of black smoke rising from a crash site, which were videos of the MH17 wreckage. Within minutes of realizing it was not a Ukrainian plane but a civilian airliner, the post was deleted.[24]

Once the Russians realized what had actually happened, they began to craft a new narrative in earnest. They recognized that, if the incident was traced back to them, it would have far-reaching consequences beyond the human toll. This was for one reason: Russia wasn't supposed to be fighting a war with Ukraine at that time. They had fervently denied being involved in the conflict, framing it as a civil war and an internal conflict between Kyiv and "freedom fighters." Weeks before the downing, Putin had made a spectacle of asking the Russian Federation Council to revoke parliamentary authorization to use military force in Ukraine, just so it could appear as though they had nothing to do with the battles happening there. Even though parliament did revoke this permission, it was all for show—the Russians were still providing heavy weaponry like Buk TELAR in the region, and many of the troops in the region were affiliated with the Russian military.[25]

If the Russians didn't find a fall guy for the downing of the plane, there would be definitive evidence that Russia was involved in the conflict, cracking the careful narrative they had created on the global stage.

Thus began Russia's disinformation and propaganda campaign. Most agreed that the MH17 plane had been hit by a missile, with many stating that it was likely a Buk missile, which both Ukraine and Russia were using during the war.

On July 23, 2014, the Dutch Safety Board (DSB) took the lead on the technical investigation of the incident. Meanwhile, the Joint

---

[24] www.bbc.com/news/blogs-trending-28371461
[25] https://time.com/3019915/russian-media-narrative-on-mh17-tragedy-highlights-kremlins-grip-on-public-opinion

Investigation Team (JIT) began the criminal investigation into war crimes on August 7. The JIT comprised law enforcement officers from the Netherlands, Australia, Belgium, Ukraine, and Malaysia.[26]

Pillar 1: The Russian Ministry of Defense Sets the Message

On July 21, the Russian Ministry of Defense blamed Ukraine, specifically a Ukrainian Su-25 jet, for the incident.[27] Lieutenant-General A. V. Kartapolov, Chief of the Main Operations Directorate and Deputy Chief of the General Staff of the Armed Forces of the Russian Federation, held a press conference in Moscow and stated that Russian air traffic control had detected a Ukrainian Air Force aircraft, presumably an Su-25, gaining height toward the Malaysia Airlines Boeing 777.

The Ukrainian Ministry of the Interior released a video on July 18 that showed a Buk carrying three missiles, with one missile missing, on the morning after the plane went down in Luhansk. It was heading toward Russia. The Russian Ministry of Defense stated that a video of the Buk system was fabricated and not actually filmed in Luhansk, but rather in Ukrainian-controlled territory.[28]

The Russian Ministry of Defense also argued that the Malaysia Airlines plane had diverted from its expected flight path into a war zone. Separately, they showed satellite images that indicated Ukrainian Buk TELAR surface-to-air missile launchers were active and within firing range of the plane.[29]

Journalists at Bellingcat proved that the video the Ukrainian Ministry of the Interior released had actually been filmed in Luhansk, and that the Russian ministry was lying. They also found that the satellite images the Russian ministry showed in the July 21 briefing had been falsified; the images had actually been from June, a month earlier than the downing of the plane, and were composite images. The Ukrainians did not have any Buk systems in the area when the plane was downed.

---

[26] https://www.government.nl/topics/mh17-incident/achieving-justice/the-criminal-investigation
[27] https://docs.un.org/en/A/68/954
[28] www.bellingcat.com/news/uk-and-europe/2018/01/05/kremlins-shifting-self-contradicting-narratives-mh17
[29] Ibid.

In the days following the downing, Russian ambassadors and leadership vehemently denied any involvement in the incident. In an interview on the same day it was shot down, the Russian Ambassador to Malaysia, Lyudmila Vorobyeva, presented several other potential theories.[30] She speculated that the Ukrainians could have been targeting President Putin's plane but hit the Malaysia Airlines plane instead. She also posited that Ukrainian armed forces fired on the plane with an air defense system.

By July 30, an independent Russian research firm, Levada Centre, found that 82 percent of Russians blamed Ukrainian forces for the downing of the flight. And if you're thinking, wow, a whole 18 percent saw past the disinformation—you'd be wrong. Sixteen percent said they didn't know what happened.[31]

Pillar 2: State Media Pollutes the Information Space

When reporting on this, RT and Sputnik followed a spaghetti strategy—throw it all at the wall and see what sticks. In many instances, they would posit the articles as "asking questions that need answers," without providing any answers to those questions. Their goal was to pollute the information space to the largest extent possible, such that the average viewer would eventually conclude that the truth was unknowable.

One segment would claim a Ukrainian Su-25 fighter jet shot down the plane, citing the evidence provided by the Russian Ministry of Defense. In the next, RT would publish an article on how the incident was a false flag operation perpetrated by the CIA. Others would promote articles from Western authors, highlighting their location and Western accolades to give them legitimacy. For example, a false flag accusation was written by William Engdahl, who was positioned as an award-winning geopolitical

---

[30]www.thestar.com.my/news/nation/2014/07/21/mh17-russian-ambassador-to-malaysia-speaks
[31]www.theguardian.com/world/2014/jul/30/mh17-vast-majority-russians-believe-ukraine-downed-plane-poll

analyst based in Germany.[32] In reality, he is better known as a vocal conspiracy theorist whose views align with those of the Kremlin.[33]

In the next hour, *Channel One* and *Interfax* would be pushing the theory that the Ukrainians were trying to assassinate Putin.[34] Russia 24 posited that the Ukrainian flight dispatcher gave the pilot instructions to intentionally steer the plane into a war zone to get shot down.

These stories were all mutually exclusive, yet were still promoted with the same zeal to appeal to various demographics. Flood the zone such that at least one theory would appeal to everyone, while also making Western journalists spend precious time debunking theories instead of focusing on the evidence. It speaks to RT's slogan, unveiled in 2010: "Question More"—better known as "Believe Nothing."

Pillar 3: Proxy Sources Cast Dispersions on Investigators

In 2019, former RT journalist Yana Yerlashova and Dutch blogger Max van der Werff founded Bonanza Media. Bonanza Media positioned itself as a platform for "alternative journalism" dedicated to dismantling the credibility of the JIT.

Yerlashova and van der Werff had histories of pro-Kremlin journalistic ties. In her time at RT, Yerlashova created two different documentaries critical of the Dutch investigation into the downing of the plane, one in 2014 and one in 2015. Van der Werff had also been involved in the conversation around the downing of the plane from the beginning. After the crash, he went to eastern Ukraine twice to "verify" the facts on the ground. In one instance, he claimed to go to the place where photos were taken of the smoke from the wreckage, claiming they had been doctored, as he couldn't find equivalent indicators at the site, like electrical cables present in the pictures. It turned out the reason he couldn't find them was because he filmed

---

[32] www.rt.com/op-ed/177388-mh17-cia-false-ukraine
[33] www.hurriyetdailynews.com/opinion/mustafa-akyol/did-zbigniew-brzezinski-blame-cia-for-turkeys-coup-103647
[34] www.washingtonpost.com/world/russians-have-many-theories-about-the-mh17-crash-one-involves-fake-dead-people/2014/07/22/9a1c5ec9-11b6-4384-b585-53fff62e5779_story.html

in a different location than where the pictures were taken. Even though these lies were proven false, the time between the messages spreading and being contradicted gave room to fuel some of the conspiracies coming out of Russia.

But what truly takes this to another level is the coordination Bonanza Media had with Russian intelligence. According to a Bellingcat investigation, Yerlashova was regularly emailing, calling, and coordinating with Col. Sergey Chebanov, a graduate of Russia's Military Intelligence Academy associated with the GRU. In most of their phone calls, the cell phone data they collected showed him at GRU headquarters at Khoroshevskoe Shosse 76B, Moscow. Yerlashova and Chebanov talked at least twice a day from September 2019 to mid-2020. Via email, Yerlashova would send Chebanov drafts of articles she intended to publish and promotional documents for review.[35]

Yerlashova and van der Werff also coordinated with the GRU to secure passage into the Donbas region, subsequently releasing "leaked" documents upon their return. In 2020, the documents they leaked were internal JIT documents suggesting that no Buk missile systems were in the area where MH17 was shot down. While the documents were real, they were out of context. The documents were from an early intelligence assessment that stated investigators had not seen a Buk at a particular time, not that none were present at all.

They got access to these documents through the GRU, which had illegally obtained them, but did not necessarily want to release them through Russian state media, as it would not preserve the documents' legitimacy. By instead passing them to Bonanza Media, the GRU could create a veneer of European legitimacy. This allowed the disinformation to spread to fringe media in the West while also being amplified back to the Russian state media as supposedly independent findings.

For all intents and purposes, Bonanza Media was functionally an external asset of the GRU to spread propaganda.

Pillar 4: Social Media Campaigns Flood the Zone

The Russian government and its associates, especially the IRA, went into overdrive once the MH17 downing came out. Forty

---

[35]https://www.bellingcat.com/news/europe/2020/11/12/the-grus-mh17-disinformation-operations-part-1-the-bonanza-media-project

minutes after the plane was downed, the IRA began spreading disinformation about it. In just the first 72 hours after the crash, Russian trolls posted almost 111,486 tweets. Their goal was to flood the zone with theories until people did not know what to believe and give up.[36]

In the first few hours, the message the trolls were pushing was not yet aligned with Kremlin talking points. They started out posting that a Ukrainian plane had been shot down by the rebels, and it wasn't until the next morning that the trolls realigned their message to claim that Ukraine had shot down MH17.

Just that day, they posted 40,931 tweets with hashtags like # Kiev-shot-down-Boeing.[37] IRA trolls were required to tweet and write blog posts for LiveJournal and other platforms about MH17; the day after the incident, the most popular topics on LiveJournal were "MH17," "border conflict," and "US sanctions." Quantity was the message: 192 different blogs were created by trolls on LiveJournal that day alone.

In one particularly sticky instance, hours after the downing of the plane, a man named Carlos on Twitter claimed to be a Spanish air traffic controller working at the airport in Kyiv. He said there were two Ukrainian military jets in the air near the site of the downed plane before it crashed. That same day, RT cited Carlos' statements and his status as a Spanish air traffic controller without any validation of his credentials.[38] *NTV, LifeNews, Vesti, RIA Novosti, Interfax*, and many other outlets cited Carlos' Twitter posts, treating them as legitimate.[39]

Trolls retweeted posts describing Carlos' experience with reckless abandon. In one instance, a blog about Carlos from a known troll, Katya Timofeeva, was retweeted nearly one hundred times in six minutes.[40]

Carlos, the air traffic controller, was a lie—there were no records of him existing or working in air traffic control at the Kyiv airport.[41] The whole premise was a farce from the start; only Ukrainian

---

[36] https://ui.adsabs.harvard.edu/abs/arXiv:2005.06558
[37] www.groene.nl/artikel/het-mh17-complot
[38] https://ria.ru/20140719/1016660745.html
[39] www.bbc.com/russian/international/2014/07/140718_tr_mh17_fake_controller
[40] https://archive.khpg.org/en/1557928691
[41] Ibid.

citizens can work as air traffic controllers in Ukraine. The account that "Carlos" was publishing from had a history of posting pro-Russian content and was later revealed to be a man living in Romania with no relation to air traffic control in Ukraine.[42]

The story persisted, however. The Russians were like a dog with a bone when it came to Carlos, the air traffic controller. Even as late as 2017, Putin continued to spout these ideas, even referencing Carlos in interviews with Oliver Stone in 2015 for the book *The Putin Interviews*.[43]

When Bellingcat began systematically debunking Russian talking points regarding its role (or lack thereof) in the downing of the flight, the IRA responded with a swarm of cyber activity. Bellingcat founder Eliot Higgins and other members of his team received a flood of phishing emails.[44] The IRA broke into the accounts of Bellingcat contributors, posting messages to their LiveJournal accounts. CyberBerkut, one of Russia's hacktivist groups linked to the GRU, defaced the Bellingcat homepage in February 2016.[45] It also doxed a Bellingcat researcher. Nearly every day for a week after Bellingcat published its findings, a new article came out from RT or Sputnik attacking them.[46] Russia was trying to harass and humiliate anyone effectively communicating the truth into submission.

Doxing, derived from "dropping docs," is the act of aggregating a person's private or semi-private information—home address, phone number, Social Security number, family details—and publishing it publicly without their consent.

[42]https://www.rferl.org/a/catch-carlos-if-you-can-mh17-russia-ukraine/29065244.html
[43]https://www.rferl.org/a/putin-debunked-spanish-air-traffic-controller-claims-oliver-stone-interview/28709936.html.
[44]www.itpro.com/hacking/27324/bellingcat-vs-fancy-bear-how-hackers-tried-to-halt-the-mh17-investigation
[45]www.washingtonpost.com/world/national-security/russian-hackers-harass-researchers-who-documented-russian-involvement-in-shootdown-of-malaysian-jetliner-over-ukraine-in-2014/2016/09/28/d086c8bc-84f7-11e6-ac72-a29979381495_story.html
[46]Ibid.

Pillar 5: Cyberattacks to Gather "Proof" to Manipulate

On April 10, 2018, four Russian men landed at Amsterdam Schiphol Airport on diplomatic passports. They were met by a member of the Russian embassy in The Hague. With a surplus of technical equipment, including an antenna meant to intercept traffic, they spent days scouting out the Organization for the Prohibition of Chemical Weapons (OPCW) headquarters, taking pictures for reconnaissance purposes. The equipment they brought was used to target the OPCW Wi-Fi network, looking for vulnerabilities that would allow them to intercept the signal, gather login details, and compromise the computers in the building. Their scouting was spotted by the Dutch General Intelligence and Security Service, and they were sent packing back to Russia without their equipment.[47]

One of the men, Yevgeny Serebriakov, had his laptop seized by authorities. His search history showed that the laptop had been used in Brazil, Switzerland, and Malaysia.[48]

Months later, in October, the Dutch defense ministry gave a briefing on disrupting the attempted attack. During it, they concluded that this was not a solo engagement—the GRU's Fancy Bear had been sending officers to locations around the world to perpetrate similar activity.[49]

Fancy Bear also targeted the Malaysian government, including the attorney general's office and police force. At the time, it was unclear what, if anything, they stole. However, in the two months leading up to the MH17 court case at The Hague, Bonanza Media published documents from the JIT—specifically, documents that seemed to be obtained from offices in Malaysia.[50] These were internal documents not meant to be disclosed to the public, detailing evidence, including images from the operation, witness statements, etc. Bonanza Media took quotes out of context to make their point, and the Russian media immediately started spreading the quotes.

---

[47] https://www.the-independent.com/news/world/europe/russia-hack-spies-chemical-weapons-doping-us-evidence-opcw-hague-gru-a8569326.html
[48] www.bbc.com/news/world-europe-45747472
[49] www.flightglobal.com/safety/russian-military-accused-of-hacking-mh17-investigation/129753.article
[50] https://maxfromthewharf.com/5510-2

One headline from *Kommersant* read: "Peskov: New publication on the MH17 crash proves Russia is right."[51] (Spoiler alert: The document did not prove that.)

Dmitry Peskov, Press Secretary of the President of the Russian Federation, used a leaked document that included a map from Dutch intelligence supposedly showing no Buk missile systems in the area of the crash. Peskov and state media presented this as "proof" that there was no Buk missile there at all. However, what the document actually showed was that Dutch intelligence had not independently spotted a Buk in that specific timeframe with their own limited assets. It did not contradict the overwhelming evidence the JIT used to prove the Buk was there.[52]

The Reality: Attribution and Attempted Accountability

There was a very different story being told outside of Russia. Ukraine stated definitively that the attack was perpetrated by Russia and went so far as to characterize it as a terrorist attack. Just a few days later, on July 21, 2014, U.S. Secretary of State John Kerry stated publicly that there was overwhelming evidence of Russian complicity, particularly because it was believed that Russia provided the rebels with the Buk system used in the attack.

On the same day the incident happened, Bellingcat began to post publicly available breakdowns debunking claims about the incident. They were actively posting about the Buk missile launcher the same month as the incident, and continued to post about the downing for years as more disinformation cropped up to be debunked.[53]

It wasn't until 2018, when the JIT explicitly concluded that the 53rd Anti-Aircraft Missile Brigade of the Russian Army was the perpetrator, that the broader public could definitively accept the reality.[54]

The JIT concluded that the downing of MH17 was not the result of a rogue militia act, but of a direct military operation facilitated by Russia. After years of forensic reconstruction

---

[51] www.kommersant.ru/doc/4259834
[52] https://www.bellingcat.com/app/uploads/2015/10/MH17-The-Open-Source-Evidence-EN.pdf
[53] Ibid.
[54] www.rferl.org/a/mh17-criminal-probe-to-appeal-to-the-public-for-help/29246988.html

efforts, the JIT proved that the weapon used was a Buk TELAR belonging to the 53rd Anti-Aircraft Missile Brigade of the Russian Army, based in Kursk. The system was convoyed across the border into eastern Ukraine, and the missile was launched from an agricultural field near Pervomaiskyi before being hurriedly trafficked back into Russian territory the following morning to hide the evidence.[55]

On November 17, 2022, the District Court of The Hague delivered a verdict on the case. It found three men guilty in absentia of mass murder and bringing down the plane. None of them have been apprehended or served their sentences for these crimes; since they are all based in Russia, the Russian government has protected them and not extradited them to face their sentences.[56]

War on the Free Press

To this day, Russia still uses tactics against the independent media, particularly in wartime scenarios where the media it does not yet control is at work, to intimidate journalists. During the war in Ukraine, Russian forces have maintained lists of individuals who could resist the occupation, such as Ukrainian journalists, activists, or war veterans, whom they are meant to kidnap on sight.[57] In one instance, Ukrainian journalist Viktoriia Roshchyna, who was reporting in Russian-occupied territories, disappeared in August 2023. She was detained and held in Russian detention facilities for over a year, despite Russia never accusing her of a crime or bringing official public charges against her. During her captivity, she was tortured.[58] In October 2024, her father was

---

[55] www.prosecutionservice.nl/topics/mh17-plane-crash/prosecution-and-trial/court-sessions-june-2020/investigation-on-the-main-scenario
[56] www.prosecutionservice.nl/topics/mh17-plane-crash/criminal-investigation-jit-mh17
[57] https://kyivindependent.com/ukraine-shocked-by-torture-of-captive-journalist-as-over-30-remain-in-russian-hands
[58] https://kyivindependent.com/ukrainian-journalist-roshchyna-dies-in-russian-custody-in-september-2024-investigation-says

officially notified by Russia of her death while she was being held in a pretrial detention center. Her body was returned to Ukraine in February 2025, labeled as an unidentified man. She was missing organs, which many speculate was intended to hide her true cause of death, likely strangulation. Journalist torture is, unfortunately, not an isolated event in Russia. At least 26 Ukrainian journalists are currently held in Russian captivity.[59] They are often charged or framed with espionage or terrorism and subjected to medical neglect or physical abuse.

Ultimately, Russia's approach to media is consolidation and control through whatever means necessary. The message must be consistent, and it must align with the Kremlin's wishes, or else.

---

[59] https://imi.org.ua/en/monitorings/ukrainian-journalists-in-russian-captivity-the-up-to-date-list-i64252

Chapter 36
Information Confrontation

In 1987, German hackers Markus Hess and Karl Koch started targeting American defense contractors. The hackers were loosely affiliated with the Chaos Computer Club, a German group that was widely regarded as the center of German hacker culture. Unrelated to the club, Hess and Koch realized the value of the data they had found in the systems of defense contractors and the access they had gained to critical American defense operations. They worked with two other hackers with connections to the KGB to sell the data to the KGB, in part to fund Koch's cocaine habit. The criminals were eventually caught by a system administrator, Clifford Stoll, who noticed a slight accounting discrepancy—merely 75 cents—that led him to the attackers.[1]

After a long back-and-forth, including Stoll setting up a honeypot to catch the attackers, they were arrested by West German authorities. All served between one and two years in prison, except for Koch, who was unfortunately found burned to death in the woods in Germany in a suspected suicide. The attack was one of

---

[1] Clifford Stoll, The Cuckoo's Egg: Tracking a Spy Through the Maze of Computer Espionage (New York: Doubleday, 1989).

the KGB's first internationally reported, criminally prosecuted forays into offensive cyberattacks, and it set the stage for future collaboration between the government and cybercriminals. The attack was recognized by the *Guinness Book of World Records* as the first incident of cyber espionage.[2]

A *honeypot* is a trap or decoy designed to mimic a legitimate asset—like a server or network—to attract and engage attackers. It lures adversaries away from real production systems and lets defenders gather threat intelligence without risking sensitive operational assets.

Hacking for Bush Legs

For many in Russia in the late nineties and early aughts, it was a time of extreme hardship. There was widespread unemployment and unpaid work; in the late 1990s, as many as 60 percent of Russian workers were paid late.[3] Food insecurity was common; the United States made a deal to send over surplus chicken to Russia, which was known as *nozhky boosha,* or "Bush legs."[4]

People needed a way to make money. Hacking was relatively easy to break into, and it could be done remotely. It could be extremely financially lucrative, as few organizations had significant defenses at the time.

Between Internet service providers cropping up, the economic hardship post–Soviet Union that led to the 1998 Russian financial crisis, and the importance placed on computing courses in Russian

[2] www.guinnessworldrecords.com/world-records/612868-first-incident-of-cyber-espionage

[3] https://jamestown.org/russian-firms-rapidly-falling-behind-in-paying-workers

[4] www.npr.org/sections/thesalt/2018/12/06/673806672/chicken-diplomacy-how-president-bush-went-for-the-gut-in-the-former-ussr

schools, the mid- to late-1990s led to a boom in early cybercriminal activity in major cities in Russia.

In one of the more well-known examples, Vladimir Levin and accomplices stole more than $10 million from Citibank customers in the first globally known online bank heist in 1994.[5] They targeted Sprintnet, one of the competing Internets at the time, and narrowed down a list of all Sprintnet numbers to those associated with Citibank. Once they had the list, they continuously connected to the node listings for over a year, looking for an open node. Eventually, one of the nodes, which had been password-protected, wasn't—someone had forgotten to log out of the computer. They used this access to find the username and password, stored in a text file on the machine, and to then gain access to other Citibank machines. This was how two cybercriminals eventually found and broke into the Citibank cash management system in New York. They didn't want to use the information for fear of getting caught, so instead they sold it to Levin for $100. Levin stole more than $10 million with it, all while he was safely tucked away in St. Petersburg, Russia. Or so he thought. In what would now seem impossible, the FBI worked closely with Russian authorities to gather evidence against Levin.[6] He was later lured to London before being arrested, indicted, and prosecuted. He was sentenced to three years in jail.

Everything changed for the Russian cybercriminal community in 1996. Russia adopted a new post-Soviet Constitution and criminal code, which included *Article 61*, which states,

A citizen of the Russian Federation may not be deported from Russia or extradited to another State.[7]

This serves as the legal bedrock for Russian cybercriminals. No matter how many crimes they commit, the Russian state will not extradite them.

---

[5] www.isc2.org/Insights/2024/03/CISSP30-The-CitiBank-Cyber-Heist-30-Years-On
[6] www.fbi.gov/news/stories/a-byte-out-of-history-10-million-hack
[7] https://hrlibrary.umn.edu/research/constitution-russia.html

For example, in late 2014, two FSB officers recruited two cyber-criminals for a major operation. One was a Latvian-born Russian national who had already made the FBI's Cyber Most Wanted List and had been indicted twice by the U.S. government. He was arrested in Greece at the request of the U.S. government, but managed to escape and flee back to Russia. In July 2013, Interpol issued a Red Notice (a request to law enforcement agencies world-wide to locate and arrest a specific person) for him, which Russia promptly ignored. Instead, the FSB began using him as a tool for their operations.[8]

On this mission, their target was Yahoo! one of the world's most popular email providers. The FSB provided insider intelli-gence to the cybercriminal so that he could evade detection during his attacks. In the Yahoo! cyberattack, they successfully stole over 500 million user accounts with account names, email addresses, tel-ephone numbers, dates of birth, passwords, and security questions and answers—all the information Yahoo! uses to verify the owner of an email account. The attackers also gained unauthorized access to Yahoo!'s Account Management tool, which helped them access 6,500 Yahoo! user accounts that were of particular interest to the FSB—accounts of Russian journalists, employees in the commer-cial sector, and Russian and U.S. government officials, including diplomatic and military personnel.

Beyond access to Yahoo! accounts, the FSB assumed that some of the breached individuals would reuse their usernames and passwords across accounts on different websites, like Gmail. The assumption was correct: They hired a second cybercriminal, a Canadian national and resident who purported to be a hacker for hire, to reuse the breached usernames and passwords to break into 50 Gmail accounts and 30 accounts at other companies, many of which were targets of Russia.[9]

---

[8]https://www.justice.gov/archives/opa/pr/us-charges-russian-fsb-officers-and-their-criminal-conspirators-hacking-yahoo-and-millions
[9]https://abcnews.go.com/US/russian-agents-facing-charges-yahoo-hacking-attacks/story?id=46142396

This attack was a huge win for the FSB and, initially, for both cybercriminals. It rocked the security industry, as it was the largest data breach ever reported at the time, and brought cybersecurity into the forefront of business minds because of its impact on Yahoo!'s financials. It cost Yahoo! $117.5 million in a class action settlement, $35 million in a fine to the SEC, and $80 million in a settlement to shareholders over the drop in stock price.[10,11]

The Russia-based cybercriminal continues to evade capture and prosecution by the U.S. government, thanks to the protection provided by Russia. The Canada-based hacker was not nearly as lucky, despite being involved in a much smaller part of the operation and claiming he didn't know he was being hired by the FSB. He was arrested in Canada in March 2017, transferred to the United States, and then pleaded guilty to nine felony hacking charges, earning him five years in prison.[12]

The Proxy Pivot

In 2000, Putin signed *the Information Security Doctrine*, which took this to the next level: It identified the information threat to Russia as a national security issue, formalizing information confrontation and prioritizing state control over the domain.[13] The FSB took this as an opportunity to start actively recruiting and working with criminal proxies, which gave them plausible deniability. This is a win-win for the cybercriminals and the government; cybercriminals get to continue illegal activities, while the government has a tool that offers plausible deniability on the global stage ("the criminals did it, not us").

---

[10] www.sec.gov/newsroom/press-releases/2018-71
[11] www.reuters.com/article/technology/yahoo-strikes-1175-million-data-breach-settlement-after-earlier-accord-rejecte-idUSKC
[12] https://www.justice.gov/archives/opa/pr/us-charges-russian-fsb-officers-and-their-criminal-conspirators-hacking-yahoo-and-millions
[13] https://www.itu.int/en/ITU-D/Cybersecurity/Documents/National_Strategies_Repository/Russia_2000.pdf

That said, Russian cybercriminals are aware that they can still be prosecuted *within* Russia and that they may be, with dire consequences. There are a few unwritten rules between cybercriminals and the government that allow cybercriminal activity, as long as you follow them. First, if the state requests support on a cyber operation, you provide it. Cybercriminals operate as proxies for the government. Second, you are not to target within the .ru zone. That means no targeting Russian, Belarusian, Kazakh, or individuals from other former Soviet states with cyberattacks. To avoid targeting former Soviet states, cybercriminals bake controls into their malware—the malware looks for the keyboard settings and system language, and if it is located within former Soviet states, it will not execute. Any other country is fine, but you cannot target Russians.

The Rise of the Digital Mafia

The cybercriminal community in Russia thrived thanks to cybercriminal forums like Antichat, Mazafaka, and DaMaGeLab. Russia was known for its collaborative cybercriminal networks, where people could ask questions, get answers, sell and buy stolen data, and potentially even get malware samples, which enabled new cybercriminals to build their skills quickly.[14]

Russian-speaking cybercriminals congregated on underground forums and chats in the early 2000s.[15] Their collaboration enabled decades of cybercriminals to flourish in Russia and Russian-speaking countries.

One of the most prolific was the community and forum CarderPlanet, predominantly in Russia and Eastern Europe. Founded in

---

[14] https://flashpoint.io/blog/breelite-cybercrime-forum-maza-breached-by-unknown-attacker
[15] www.own.security/ressources/blog/russian-language-cybercriminal-forums--chapter-i-an-excursion-into-the-core-of-the-underground-ecosystem

2001 by Dmitry Golubov and Roman Vega, it specialized in criminals monetizing credit card numbers and it arguably created the
framework by which cybercriminal forums now operate. At its
peak, it had over 6,000 members and resembled a mafia hierarchy:
The head was the Godfather, who had a number of dons, who had
consiglieri, all to manage the operation.[16] They connected sellers
with buyers and facilitated other services like money laundering. It
became quite audacious; at one point, they organized a real-world
meetup for the members of the forum at a resort outside of Odessa.[17]
It was eventually shut down in 2004 by the creators, as they saw the
signs that other forums were being taken down by the police.[18]

Once cybercriminals in Russia gained enough mainstream
acclaim—often in the form of indictments by the U.S. Justice
Department or other countries—they were given two options:
Get extradited or support the interests of the Russian government
and military.

Competing for the Crown

In the early- to mid-1990s, there was early work by scholars to explore
Russia's approach to information in warfare, known as *informat-
sionnoe protivoborstvo* (информационное противоборство). Often
mistranslated as "information warfare," which oversimplifies a very
complex topic, a more accurate interpretation of the term is "information confrontation." This more closely captures the essence of a
persistent, multidimensional struggle that is ongoing, and not limited to a single battlefield or conflict.[19]

[16]https://flashpoint.io/blog/usa-vs-roman-vega
[17]www.recordedfuture.com/blog/russian-chinese-hacking-communities
[18]www.bbc.com/news/technology-40671091
[19]https://cgsr.llnl.gov/sites/cgsr/files/2024-08/Information-Confrontation-
in-Great-Power-Competition.pdf

Information confrontation weakens adversaries from within by creating instability and confusion. Offensive cyber operations are one part of the broader, continuous struggle for information superiority, a struggle that encompasses technological and psychological dimensions, aiming not just to disable or disrupt infrastructure but to influence perceptions and decisions over the long term.

Three main agencies comprise the Russian intelligence services structure, which contributes to information confrontation efforts: The Federal Security Service (FSB), the Main Directorate of the General Staff of the Armed Forces of the Russian Federation (GRU), and the Foreign Intelligence Service of the Russian Federation (SVR). The Director of the FSB is appointed by and accountable to the President of Russia, and the SVR director reports directly to the President. The GRU's chain of command runs through the military hierarchy. The groups often have overlapping responsibilities that unwittingly encourage competition.[20] The competition matters: One of the most important parts of effective nation-state cyber operations is coordination, so attackers do not accidentally expose an ally in an operation. With this model, cooperation is out the window—like Ptolemy XIII's presenting Pompey's severed head to Caesar, bringing forth the most impressive wins to curry favor is far more critical.

The FSB is the successor to the KGB and Russia's most influential security agency. The FSB plays a crucial role in maintaining Russia's internal information security; it oversees much of the internal surveillance throughout Russia, including wiretapping and monitoring Russian Internet traffic. This extensive monitoring allows the FSB to keep a tight rein on information flow in Russia. The FSB includes Center 16, a group responsible for signals intelligence in domestic and foreign operations. Center 16 is home to threat groups like Ghost Blizzard and Turla, which have primarily targeted U.S. and European critical infrastructure and conduct cyber espionage operations on government agencies and military

[20]https://ecfr.eu/wp-content/uploads/ECFR_169_-_PUTINS_HYDRA_INSIDE_THE_RUSSIAN_INTELLIGENCE_SERVICES_1513.pdf

targets. Center 18 is also part of the FSB and includes the Gamaredon Group, which has primarily targeted the Ukrainian government and military with cyber espionage operations.[21]

The GRU is Russia's military intelligence agency. It was initially perceived as a secondary player to the FSB in cyber operations, yet it has grown increasingly prominent in offensive cyber activities and has several specialized units with specific geopolitical targets. One of its most well-known units is Fancy Bear, a group responsible for many widely publicized attacks, including on the 2016 U.S. presidential election and the Olympics.[22] Sandworm is known for its attacks on the Ukrainian power grid, including NotPetya, and attacks on the Olympics.[23] Ember Bear targets Ukraine and Georgia, especially with wiper attacks.[24]

The SVR is Russia's primary external intelligence agency that specializes in strategic intelligence. Unlike the GRU, which engages in espionage and sabotage, the SVR's activities are primarily focused on intelligence gathering. One of its most well-known groups is Cozy Bear, whose hallmark is subtlety and which has been responsible for prolific attacks like the ones on the U.S. Democratic National Committee and SolarWinds.[25]

Navigating Moonlight Maze

The turning point for the increase in Russian state cyber operations came in 1996, with an attack known as Moonlight Maze. Attackers stole thousands of documents from organizations in the United Kingdom, Canada, Brazil, Germany, and the United States. The attackers

---

[21] www.gov.uk/government/publications/russias-fsb-malign-cyber-activity-factsheet/russias-fsb-malign-activity-factsheet
[22] www.nsa.gov/Press-Room/Press-Releases-Statements/Press-Release-View/Article/4193749/nsa-and-others-publish-advisory-warning-of-russian-state-sponsored-cyber-campai
[23] www.isaca.org/resources/news-and-trends/industry-news/2024/understanding-sandworm-a-state-sponsored-threat-group
[24] www.crowdstrike.com/adversaries/ember-bear
[25] www.ic3.gov/CSA/2021/210426.pdf

established a backdoor, then stole unclassified but sensitive documents, including bidding documents, contracts, and other defense-related data. U.S. investigators initially suspected Russia perpetrated the attack, as parts of it originated from Russian IP addresses. Russian officials were initially cooperative as the United States investigated the case, but shortly after, a Russian intelligence service spokesman denied culpability, and Russia refused any further support in the investigation. This was a turning point for the Russians; from here on out, their response to most accusations of cyberattacks was to deny, deny, deny. The attacks were publicly exposed in 1999.[26]

Hacktivists for Hire

The Russian government will sometimes leverage hacktivists to execute some mundane operations, like DDoS attacks, because, much like with cybercriminals, it avoids revealing its infrastructure, which could be used to track it later.

The line between hacktivists and nation-state actors can be a blurry one. A well-known example of this is the Internet Research Agency, or IRA (also known as the Trolls of Olgino or the Kremlin-bots). The IRA was a privately held organization that, while masquerading as legitimate, was engaged in widespread information warfare leading up to the 2016 U.S. presidential election. It operated as a massive troll farm to mass-produce and spread disinformation to worsen societal divides. It also spread a lot of pro-Kremlin content through comments, posts, infographics, and videos, all meant to divide other countries and highlight Russia.[27]

[26] www.pbs.org/wgbh/pages/frontline/shows/cyberwar/warnings
[27] https://www.justice.gov/archives/opa/pr/grand-jury-indicts-thirteen-russian-individuals-and-three-russian-companies-scheme-inter

While this may seem like a hacktivist group and nothing more, it's more complicated than that, as the group was founded and funded by Yevgeny Prigozhin in 2013. A year later, Prigozhin founded and led the Wagner Group, a state-funded private military company that played a crucial role in many conflicts Russia entered. Yevgeny was an oligarch close to Putin for many years, known to be "Putin's Chef," who secured many catering contracts with the Russian government and military before pivoting to mercenary work. While the IRA was technically independent, it had significant ties to the Russian government that undoubtedly influenced and potentially directed its operations as a proxy.[28]

---

[28] https://www.abc.net.au/news/2022-10-23/yevgeny-prigozhin-the-rise-of-vladimir-putins-so-called-chef/101555386

Chapter 37
The Red
Orchestra Rewired

In the mid-1930s, a Polish Jew and communist named Leopold Trepper joined the Soviet Red Army Intelligence Service. He also joined the Soviet secret police and espionage agency, the People's Commissariat for Internal Affairs (NKVD). While there, he created a network of communist sympathizers throughout Europe, which, once the Second World War started in 1939, he turned into a spy ring to gather information, both on the Europeans and the Nazis.

The network was so vast that there were multiple regional spy rings run by different people, including units in France, Belgium, the Netherlands, Berlin, and Switzerland. They transmitted so much data that the sheer volume of traffic became a hazard in itself; their agents had more high-level German sources than any other spy network of the time.[1]

The Swiss ring, known as the Lucy Ring, had spies high up in the German military, including a senior officer in the Wehrmacht's communications branch and an intelligence officer for the Army Group Center on the Eastern Front.[2] It was there that they collected details on

---

[1] www.cia.gov/readingroom/docs/CIA-RDP88-01350R000200340017-9.pdf
[2] www.archives.gov/iwg/research-papers/red-orchestra-irr-file.html

the Nazis' plan to invade the Soviet Union, back when they were still allies. The intelligence they collected was so detailed that it included dates for the launch of the offensive, which they promptly turned over to the Soviet Army. Soviet leadership ignored the intelligence, as Soviet intelligence had received many previous warnings about a potential invasion that did not prove fruitful. However, their intelligence was correct, and because of this, the Lucy Ring was considered one of the most important sources of intelligence during the war.[3]

Unfortunately, by the early 1940s, many of the spies were found out and arrested by the Gestapo; more than 600 people were arrested from 1942 to 1944.[4] Some were tortured for information, others were murdered, and others still were sentenced to imprisonment. The Abwehr named the group "Rote Kapelle," which means "Red Orchestra;" this was because the agents transmitted reports by radio (radio transmitters were referred to as "music boxes" in Soviet intelligence jargon) to a "musician" in the field (radio operators were called "musicians") at one of the regional deployments, then back to their "conductor" in Moscow.[5]

After their arrests, the network largely fell apart and could not be rebuilt to its former glory. Even so, in its heyday, it was widely considered the most successful intelligence operation of the war. The Russians continued the legacy of the Red Orchestra with many of the cyber operations and strategies perpetrated by its most infamous threat actors.

The Digital Uroburos

Once the early- to mid-2000s hit, the Russian government began leaning into its nation-state offensive cyber capabilities. As early as 2003, a unit within FSB Center 16, codenamed Turla by Western researchers, started developing malware known as Uroburos, or Snake. The initial version of this malware was finalized in 2004 and spread by creating a peer-to-peer network of infected machines,

---

[3] https://www.jstor.org/stable/260932
[4] www.encyclopedia.com/politics/encyclopedias-almanacs-transcripts-and-maps/red-orchestra
[5] www.archives.gov/iwg/research-papers/red-orchestra-irr-file.html

enabling attackers to hide and route activity through them. Over the course of the next 20 years, the malware would be reverse-engineered by security researchers, and then the FSB would develop a new version to improve capabilities, much like a cat-and-mouse game. The Snake malware became notorious for cyberespionage, stealing data from governments, researchers, and journalists in over 50 countries, including the United States. It is widely considered one of the most powerful offensive cyber tools in FSB Center 16.[6]

In February 2014, BAE Systems published a report on reverse-engineering the latest iteration of the Snake malware, shortly after G Data published its own analysis.[7] Up until this point, the Snake malware had not been attributed to Russia or Turla, but had been running rampant since 2004. Though BAE's analysis did not explicitly state that the malware was attributable to Russia, many indicators, such as who was targeted (NATO governments, journalists, and research facilities), how the working hours of the attackers aligned with Russian time zones, and portions of Russian text written into the code, implicated it. At the time, Snake was especially prevalent in Ukraine and NATO countries.[8] Understanding such a prolific piece of malware was a big step toward understanding the motivation and potential threat actor behind it.

Espionage in the Bundestag

2013 was also a time of change. Though not a formal, public reordering, researchers started to notice a change in which Russian threat actors became the dominant, public-facing offensive cyber operations group. The FSB started to take a back seat to the ostentatious, more prominent GRU.[9] Russia's largest foreign intelligence agency, the GRU, sits within the Russian military command and strictly targets external actors. Their transition to the louder frontrunner may

---

[6] https://www.rferl.org/a/russia-fsb-malware-snake-takedown/32407612.html
[7] www.baesystems.com/en/digital/feature/the-snake-campaign
[8] www.nytimes.com/2014/03/09/world/europe/suspicion-falls-on-russia-as-snake-cyberattacks-target-ukraines-government.html
[9] https://nsarchive.gwu.edu/media/31755/ocr

not have been directed from the top down; given the structure of each organization and the competitiveness between the divisions, the GRU may have become more inclined to curry favor with Putin by executing conspicuous and more direct confrontations with its cyberattacks. At the same time, the FSB had enough on its plate with its broad remit of internal surveillance and intelligence, as it would soon be given formal executive control over GosSOPKA at the end of 2017. Its internal role would only grow further as Russia continued to tighten monitoring, censorship, and control.[10]

One example of this change in strategy came in early 2015, when German MPs received emails from what purported to be United Nations news bulletins. Though they seemed legitimate, these messages were actually phishing emails from the Russian threat actor Fancy Bear, attempting to break into the systems of the Bundestag—which they ultimately succeeded in doing. Though the attack was found and stopped just a few weeks later in May, attackers were still able to collect 16 GB of information, including confidential emails, some of which came from then-Chancellor Angela Merkel. In 2016, Germany's domestic intelligence agency officially attributed the attacks to Russia.[11] By October 2020, the EU sanctioned the GRU and two Russian intelligence officers over the attack.[12]

This attack was all in the name of espionage, but it had bigger consequences. It was seen as a turning point in how cyberattacks could begin to escalate geopolitical confrontations, and it served as a landmark case for state-sponsored cyber espionage in Europe.

Cozy Bear's Vaccine Hunt

In 2020, countries around the world were in a fierce arms race to find a COVID-19 vaccine. Russia named its vaccine Sputnik V, framing vaccine creation as a competition and demonstration of Russia's soft power. Given how big a priority the vaccine was to Putin, and

---

[10] https://www.atlanticcouncil.org/content-series/russia-tomorrow/unpacking-russias-cyber-nesting-doll
[11] https://www.bbc.com/news/technology-36284447
[12] https://eur-lex.europa.eu/legal-content/EN/TXT/?uri=uriserv%3AOJ.LI.2020.351.01.0001.01.ENG&toc=OJ%3AL%3A2020%3A351I%3ATOC

how fierce the geopolitical competition was, Cozy Bear had its next objective. Through 2020, Cozy Bear targeted vaccine development groups in Canada, the United States, and the United Kingdom, looking to steal intellectual property about the COVID-19 vaccine as it was being developed.[13] By July, the United States and the United Kingdom publicly accused Russia of trying to steal information from researchers developing the vaccine. Security agencies, such as the CISA (United States), CSE (Canada), and the NCSC (United Kingdom), issued a joint advisory accusing Cozy Bear, detailing the specific tactics and techniques they used, and recommending how companies defend themselves against future activity. The vaccine race was all hands on deck to prove which nation was the most developed, not just in healthcare but in espionage efforts.[14]

The Perfect Backdoor

One of Cozy Bear's largest operations happened in September 2019, when it would strike again, this time targeting a company known for its network management software: SolarWinds. SolarWinds started in 1999 in Tulsa, Oklahoma, and by 2019 had grown to around 2,000 employees and over 300,000 customers, including more than 425 of the Fortune 500. On its website, it listed the U.S. military, Pentagon, State Department, NSA, and many other U.S. government agencies as customers, making it an ideal target.[15] Break into one small, potentially less secure organization and gain access to hundreds through its software. And that's exactly what Cozy Bear did.

In October 2019, the attackers tested whether they could successfully inject code into SolarWinds' flagship software, Orion. It would take several more months, into February 2020, before they would inject the malware used to establish a backdoor into the build process of Orion. A month after that, SolarWinds unwittingly

[13] https://media.defense.gov/2020/Jul/16/2002457639/-1/-1/0/NCSC_APT29_ADVISORY-QUAD-OFFICIAL-20200709-1810.PDF
[14] https://www.ncsc.gov.uk/news/advisory-apt29-targets-covid-19-vaccine-development
[15] www.cybersecuritydive.com/news/Solarwinds-orion-cisa-government-cyberattacks/592101

sent out a software update with that backdoor to thousands of customers. It would not be found until months later.[16]

In late November 2020, a security analyst at the security firm Mandiant reviewed sign-on logs from its customers from the previous day (often a source of insight into what attacks may have been attempted) and found a discrepancy: A user had an additional registered device on their account, one more than usual. When the analyst called the user to ask if they had registered the new device, they said they hadn't—even more suspicious. This simple moment of due diligence led to the discovery of one of the largest hacking operations in history. Over the course of the next few weeks, the teams at Mandiant and Microsoft uncovered the full extent of the attack and how it started: With the initial compromise of SolarWinds in 2019. The breach was disclosed to the public in December 2020 and started a firestorm as 18,000 SolarWinds customers rushed to disconnect and remediate any affected systems.[17]

U.S. government agencies like the Treasury, Commerce, State, Homeland Security, and intelligence services—as well as the U.S. military, Fortune 500 companies, leading tech and telecommunications firms, and international governments—were all affected. CISA issued emergency directives to collect forensic evidence, disconnect systems running Orion (the affected SolarWinds software), and report the incident.[18]

Attackers stole sensitive emails from government agencies and enterprises, reports, corporate files, and other data.[19] It highlighted the current reality of interconnected software systems: Even if your organization has a strong security posture, if your partners and vendors do not, it can lead to a breach that affects your company, not just theirs. It was not until 2021 that the U.S. government attributed this attack to Cozy Bear.

---

[16] www.wired.com/story/the-untold-story-of-solarwinds-the-boldest-supply-chain-hack-ever

[17] https://cloud.google.com/blog/topics/threat-intelligence/evasive-attacker-leverages-solarwinds-supply-chain-compromises-with-sunburst-backdoor

[18] www.cisa.gov/news-events/directives/ed-21-01-mitigate-solarwinds-orion-code-compromise-closed

[19] www.microsoft.com/en-us/security/blog/2020/12/18/analyzing-solorigate-the-compromised-dll-file-that-started-a-sophisticated-cyberattack-and-how-microsoft-defender-helps-protect

Chapter 38
Disinformation, Inc.

Many KGB operations correspond to modern-day Russian offensive cybersecurity and information security strategy, particularly those executed under *aktivnye meropriyatiya* (активные мероприятия), or active measures. *Active measures* are covert influence and subversion campaigns used heavily after World War II by the KGB.[1]

Active measures were used as covert operations, leveraging disinformation, blackmail, and bribery to destabilize and create divisions within the enemy. These practices were rampant during the Soviet Union and were foundational to Russia's future thinking regarding offensive cyber operations. One (very successful) example of this was Operation Denver in the 1980s.[2]

Operation Denver

Operation Denver was a multi-year disinformation operation perpetrated by the KGB to spread the falsehood that the United States created HIV/AIDS in a series of biological weapons experiments

---

[1] cia.gov/readingroom/document/cia-rdp89g00720r000500060008-2
[2] www.marshallcenter.org/en/publications/security-insights/active-measures-russias-covert-geopolitical-operations-0

gone wrong. The operation started with a letter to the editor in *The Patriot*, a newspaper in India, in 1983. The letter was written by someone claiming to be a "well-known American scientist and anthropologist" who remained anonymous. In actuality, the letter was written by the KGB. The article said AIDS was a bioengineered weapon created at Fort Detrick, spread by the U.S. government through blood donations.[3]

By 1986, Jakob Segal, a biophysicist born in Soviet-controlled territory, published a report that alleged AIDS had been engineered in an American lab. The KGB took this report and spread it in the media, especially through its allies in the Eastern bloc, like *Pravda*. Over the years, the KGB continued to push this lie in fringe media until it spread to reputable sources in the Western world. The campaign was one of the major successes of the KGB's disinformation efforts, in part because of the substantial resources that the KGB put into it. The Internet enabled Russia to take what it had done so successfully for years and spread it faster, further, and more effectively than ever.[4]

Trolls Without Borders

Russia's initiatives in the information domain expanded after a series of early wins. Central to this effort was Project Lakhta, a disinformation and influence campaign active since at least 2014.[5] Project Lakhta leveraged many Russian organizations, including the *International News Agency*, *the National News*, and *the Federal News Agency*.[6] The largest of the supporting organizations was the IRA.

---

[3] https://archive.org/details/1983-07-16-patriot/page/n1/mode/2up?view=theater

[4] https://www.wilsoncenter.org/blog-post/operation-denver-kgb-and-stasi-disinformation-regarding-aids

[5] www.unsw.edu.au/content/dam/pdfs/unsw-canberra/dri/2023-02-research/2023-02-Understanding-Mass-Influence---A-case-study-of-the-Internet-Research-Agency.pdf

[6] www.npr.org/2018/10/23/659545242/heres-how-russia-runs-its-disinformation-effort-against-the-2018-midterms

Project Lakhta targeted countries worldwide with disinforma-tion. The IRA hired thousands of workers to post online, many of whom were young, struggling to get work, and had no experience. They had quotas to meet, much like a call center agent. They had to post five political posts, ten nonpolitical posts, and 150 comments per shift.[7] It operated as a business, with a graphics department and social media analytics.

One of the IRA's specialized units was the "Translator Project," which focused specifically on targeting and manipulating public opinion in the United States. Their strategic goal was to sow divi-sion and discord. This group ramped up its efforts ahead of the 2016 U.S. presidential election. It spread disinformation through fake accounts and by having people pose as U.S. citizens online. As early as 2014, the IRA began targeting the 2016 U.S. presidential elec-tion as part of the Translator Project. IRA staff used fake personas—supposedly of U.S. activists—to create social media accounts and group pages on Facebook and other platforms. Over two years, they built up legitimacy and a large following. Two IRA employees even came to the United States for three weeks to take photographs they could later use in social media posts and to gather intelligence in battleground states like Colorado and Michigan. Others traveled to Atlanta. They used stolen U.S. Social Security numbers to help cre-ate and validate bank accounts and made email and social media accounts on sites like Facebook, YouTube, and Twitter; later, some even started to post on Tumblr and Instagram.[8]

The IRA created so many fake social media accounts that they established networks of fake personas commenting on other fake per-sonas to build up their credibility with actual Americans. The groups the IRA created had hundreds of thousands of followers. On Face-book alone, they purchased over 3,500 advertisements. While they initially posted negative comments about all U.S. presidential candi-dates, by 2016, they honed their efforts to posts that supported Trump

[7] www.nytimes.com/2015/06/07/magazine/the-agency.html?_r=0
[8] www.justice.gov/d9/fieldable-panel-panes/basic-panes/attachments/2018/02/16/internet_research_agency_indictment.pdf

and third-party candidates and maligned Clinton, creating a snowball of support and virality. The IRA had at least 470 Facebook accounts that made 80,000 comments over two years; Twitter shut down 3,814 related accounts that had directly interacted with 1.4 million people.[9,10]

Meanwhile, in 2014, the agency responsible for domestic security and counterintelligence in the Netherlands, the Dutch General Intelligence and Security Service (AIVD), broke into the computer infrastructure of Cozy Bear. The Dutch monitored Cozy Bear for over a year, tracking its targets and attacks and learning its methodology. They noticed suspicious activity against targets based in the United States, and in 2015, they alerted the FBI. What the AIVD didn't know was that they had seen initial access activity that would lead to an attack on the U.S. Democratic National Convention and result in the release of thousands of stolen emails and documents, damaging the reputation of the DNC and causing significant controversy during the election.[11]

The FBI alerted the DNC to the breach in September 2015 via a phone call and voicemail, but the contractor responsible for security thought it was a prank call and did not take action. The contractor eventually investigated but found no evidence of the attack. The FBI reached out another three times in October, November, and December, asking the DNC staff to check again. Yet their calls were not returned, even after the FBI attempted to notify higher-level officials.[12] In the meantime, Cozy Bear was having a field day exfiltrating thousands of documents and operating with impunity in the DNC network. It was not until April 2016, over six months later, that the contractor found unusual activity on the network that tipped him off—but that activity wasn't even from Cozy Bear. It was from a different Russian threat actor, Fancy Bear. Fancy Bear, more of the bull in the china shop of the two, was accessing password

[9] www.nytimes.com/2018/02/16/us/politics/russia-mueller-election.html
[10] www.pbs.org/newshour/politics/at-facebook-im-responsible-for-what-happens-read-mark-zuckerbergs-prepared-house-testimony
[11] www.dutchnews.nl/2018/01/dutch-security-service-hackers-monitored-russian-interference-in-us-media
[12] www.nytimes.com/2016/12/13/us/politics/russia-hack-election-dnc.html

vaults from multiple different users and performing other noisy activities that the contractor was able to spot. Cozy Bear continued undetected.[13]

But that wasn't all that Fancy Bear was up to; it had gained access to the DNC infrastructure through a previous attack on the DCCC. It had targeted a DCCC official, gained access to her account, and spent April through June 2016 stealing information like employee passwords, files, and communications. Fancy Bear used this access to break into the DNC; they stole the credentials of a DCCC employee who had access to the DNC network around April 18, and from there, they could access DNC infrastructure unimpeded.[14]

It was around this same time that Fancy Bear set up a site called DCLeaks. A short while earlier, in March 2016, Fancy Bear had broken into the personal email of John Podesta, the chair of Hillary Clinton's 2016 U.S. presidential campaign. To get into the system, Fancy Bear used a phishing email: It sent a legitimate-looking but actually malicious email to Podesta's inbox claiming to be from Gmail that said he needed to change his password. Podesta's staff were well-trained and reported the email to the IT team. However, in a bizarre moment of human error, when one of his aides found the email suspicious and forwarded it to IT, the technician responded that it was a *legitimate* email and that Podesta's password needed to be changed ASAP. Unfortunately, the technician later claimed this was a mistake and that he meant to write "illegitimate," not "legitimate." The aide diligently followed the IT team's instructions and made sure Podesta's password got changed by clicking on the link in the email chain, which directed them to an attacker-owned webpage where, once Podesta's username and password were entered, the attacker gained access to the account. Because of this error, Fancy Bear was able to access and exfiltrate thousands of Podesta's emails, which WikiLeaks later published.[15]

---

[13] www.crowdstrike.com/en-us/blog/bears-midst-intrusion-democratic-national-committee
[14] www.justice.gov/storage/report_volume1.pdf
[15] Ibid.

While the bears were fighting for access to the DNC, the IRA was pumping disinformation into the social media ecosystem to further sway public opinion and to amplify WikiLeaks and DCLeaks posts. IRA operators were told to use any opportunity to criticize Clinton.[16]

The influence of the IRA was so significant that news outlets in the United States often cited posts from fake accounts created by the IRA as legitimate. Thirty-two out of thirty-three major news outlets referenced tweets from IRA-controlled accounts between 2015 and 2017, skewing perspective in favor of the IRA's point of view, not the American one.[17] High-profile Americans like Roger Stone, Sean Hannity, and Kellyanne Conway retweeted and responded to posts from IRA accounts.[18]

Coming back to the bears and the DNC attack, in June, Fancy Bear started publishing some of the stolen DCCC emails on DCLeaks and used a pseudonym, Guccifer 2.0, to try to throw investigators off the trail and ensure they did not tie the attack and release back to Russia. Guccifer 2.0 was an homage to Guccifer, a well-known Romanian hacker jailed in 2014. In a cringeworthy choice for a name, Guccifer is a combination of Gucci (for style) and Lucifer.[19]

DCCC and some DNC-related documents continued to be published to DCLeaks through July and August. In August, DCLeaks posted personal information on more than 200 Democratic lawmakers, including details like their phone numbers. On July 22, just three days before the 2016 Democratic National Convention, WikiLeaks published thousands of DNC emails and documents. The documents ran the news cycle for weeks, increasing political infighting among Democrats, implicating news outlets in less-than-ideal political conversations, and prompting lawsuits. But things were far from over. On October 7, WikiLeaks began publishing the 50,000 emails of John Podesta, vowing to publish new emails every day leading up to Election Day. In response, Guccifer 2.0 (a.k.a. Fancy Bear) was quoted

---

[16]https://www.justice.gov/d9/fieldable-panel-panes/basic-panes/attachments/2018/02/16/internet_research_agency_indictment.pdf
[17]www.cjr.org/analysis/tweets-russia-news.php
[18]www.intelligence.senate.gov/wp-content/uploads/2024/08/sites-default-files-documents-report-volume2.pdf
[19]www.bbc.com/news/technology-36913000

as saying, "Together with Assange we'll make America great again." WikiLeaks published the last batch of DNC emails—over 8,000—on November 6, just two days before the election.[20]

Knowing how to respond to such a multifaceted attack was difficult. In many ways, this was a watershed moment: Two of the largest countries in the world were facing off, but through new, nonmilitary means. Knowing when to escalate versus when to hold was new territory. At the G20 summit held in China in September of that year, then-President Barack Obama told Vladimir Putin to "cut it out"—in reference to the cyberattacks against the DNC.[21] He said he was concerned about potential tampering with the election process. When the hacked documents continued to be released, Obama took a major step to use the Red Phone in the Oval Office, the Cold War–era hotline between the US and Russia. While the Red Phone isn't an actual physical phone, it is a way to communicate in times of emergency and to convey the gravity of a situation when it comes to cyberattacks.[22] The administration used the channel for the first time to warn Putin off from further offensive cyber operations around the election. Part of the message from Washington to Moscow said, "International law, including the law of armed conflict, applies to actions in cyberspace. We will hold Russia to these standards."[23] While Obama claimed success given that the vote on Election Day remained legitimate, other Democrats thought it did not go far enough. They wanted a red line, though what that red line was, no one knew.

In July 2018, the FBI indicted 12 individuals believed to be associated with the GRU and specifically with the election interference in 2016.[24] The Russian government did not cooperate in the extradition of these individuals, and they remain in Russia to this day.

---

[20] www.bloomberg.com/politics/articles/2017-11-03/inside-story-how-russians-hacked-the-democrats-emails
[21] www.politico.com/story/2016/12/obama-putin-232754
[22] www.theverge.com/2013/6/18/4443076/us-russia-putin-obama-hacking-hotline-cyberwar-nrrc
[23] https://www.nbcnews.com/news/us-news/what-obama-said-putin-red-phone-about-election-hack-n697116
[24] www.fbi.gov/wanted/cyber/russian-interference-in-2016-u-s-elections

Election Season Continues

After finding success targeting the 2016 U.S. presidential election, Fancy Bear decided to target a slew of other elections in 2017. In the Netherlands, before the 2017 elections, it attempted to breach the Dutch Ministry of General Affairs and was reportedly unsuccessful.[25]

In 2016, the United Kingdom held a referendum entitled the *2016 United Kingdom European Union membership referendum,* also known as Brexit. Shortly after the referendum, which resulted in the United Kingdom moving forward with Brexit, it held snap elections in 2017. Leading up to and following the referendum and elections, there was widespread speculation that Russia would attempt to influence the results. Of the cyberattacks Russia was perpetrating at the time, Theresa May was quoted in a speech addressing Russia directly, saying,

> We know what you are doing . . . And you will not succeed.

Whether or not she was correct, in some ways, we will never know. While the United Kingdom confirmed that the paper-based voting and counting system would make digital interference difficult, disinformation campaigns were a different story. According to a report presented to Parliament by the Intelligence and Security Committee on Russia and its potential interference, no post-referendum assessment of Russia's attempts to interfere was ever done as of 2020.[26]

On many fronts, the operation to understand and identify potential interference before, during, and after Brexit and the snap 2017 elections was sorely lacking. They likely chose to avoid a large investigation because of the divisiveness of Brexit and to avoid chipping away at the legitimacy of the vote by further inquiry into Russian meddling.

---

[25] https://english.aivd.nl/publications/annual-report/2018/03/09/annual-report-2017-aivd
[26] https://isc.independent.gov.uk/wp-content/uploads/2021/03/CCS207_CCS0221966010-001_Russia-Report-v02-Web_Accessible.pdf

On May 7, 2017, the second round of the French presidential election was due to be held in a runoff. The top candidates were Emmanuel Macron, a defender and supporter of the European Union, and Marine Le Pen, a vocal supporter of some of Russia's activities, including its annexation of Crimea.[27] In January 2017, she said to the French news channel *wBFM TV*:

> I absolutely do not believe that it was an illegal annexation . . .
> There was a referendum and residents of Crimea wanted to join Russia.

Disinformation was spread online through Twitter, Russian media, and other channels leading up to the election. For example, on February 2, *Sputnik International* released an article titled "Ex-French Economy Minister Macron Could Be 'US Agent' Lobbying Banks' Interests."[28] One of the key quotes from the article came from Nicolas Dhuicq, a vocal opponent of Macron known to spread baseless accusations about him in the media. Dhuicq is also known to have visited Moscow, Crimea, and the Russian State Duma, and serves on the board of the Association Dialogue Franco-Russe, a group known for its pro-Kremlin lobbying in France. The man is not without a clear bias and conflicts of interest.

The Macron campaign had been raising warnings that it had been a target of email credential-stealing attempts since January. In a surprise tactic to fight back against the attackers, the Macron campaign identified phishing emails and intentionally input the wrong credentials into the hackers' website to try to waste the attackers' time.[29] Just two days before the election on May 5, 2017, 9 GB of emails from the Macron campaign, amounting to around 20,000 documents, were published on Pastebin. The Macron campaign claimed that fake documents had been included in the leak

---

[27] www.vocaleurope.eu/emmanuel-macron-stand-russia
[28] https://sputnikglobe.com/20170204/macron-us-agent-dhuicq-1050340451.html
[29] www.weforum.org/stories/2017/05/how-macrons-team-thwarted-the-hackers-with-one-simple-trick

and that attackers were trying to spread disinformation. Far-right activists in the U.S. and Russian state media helped amplify the emails alongside automated bots and messages on 4chan, Twitter, and Facebook.[30]

The entire campaign harkened back to the attack on the Clinton campaign emails, and later, it was proven to have been executed by one and the same: Fancy Bear. However, in this instance, Macron still won the election. France named the Russian GRU responsible in 2025, taking years to publicly attribute the attack.[31] Unfortunately, that much time between attack and attribution gives the disinformation enough space to breathe, as it leaves enough ambiguity about the motive of the attackers for them to appear legitimate.

While Russia had much success early on with disinformation, over the next several years, its efforts stopped being as explosively effective as they had been previously.[32] Social media companies boosted their detection capabilities and takedown efforts to suppress attacks. The public is far more knowledgeable and skeptical of disinformation than they were before, especially when it is spread through traditional social media applications. Many governments have also taken up the responsibility to help identify and alert the public to fake news, fighting back in their own way.

---

[30] https://www.atlanticcouncil.org/in-depth-research-reports/report/the-macron-leaks-operation-a-post-mortem
[31] https://www.diplomatie.gouv.fr/en/country-files/russia/news/2025/article/russia-attribution-of-cyber-attacks-on-france-to-the-russian-military-intelligence-service-apt28-29-04-25
[32] www.hybridcoe.fi/wp-content/uploads/2024/03/20240306-Hybrid-CoE-Working-Paper-29-The-impact-of-Kremlin-disinformation-WEB.pdf

Chapter 39
Olympic Mind Games

No country has weaponized its cyber capabilities as maliciously or
irresponsibly as Russia.
                        —*U.S. Assistant Attorney General John Demers*[1]

In July 2016, the World Anti-Doping Agency (WADA) recommended to the International Olympic Committee and the International Paralympic Committee that they decline all entries
of athletes submitted by the Russian Olympic Committee and the
Russian Paralympic Committee for the Rio 2016 Olympic Games,
based on WADA's findings that the Russian government had a
secret, state-sponsored doping program for Russian athletes during
the 2014 Sochi Winter Olympics.[2] Less than a week later, the IOC
released a statement that it would not accept the entry of any Russian athlete into the Olympic Games in Rio unless they met specific
criteria and could provide specific evidence. After the report was
published, Putin stated that calls to ban Russia represent a "danger-
ous slide toward political interference in sport."[3]

---

[1]https://www.justice.gov/archives/opa/pr/six-russian-gru-officers-charged-
connection-worldwide-deployment-destructive-malware-and
[2]www.wada-ama.org/en/news/wada-statement-independent-investigation-
confirms-russian-state-manipulation-doping-control
[3]www.themoscowtimes.com/2016/07/19/russia-reacts-to-doping-report-
findings-a54632

Just a few months later, WADA reported that Fancy Bear had targeted the Anti-Doping Administration and Management System with a phishing attack. They broke into the system, took information about athletes, and released data on 26 of those athletes.[4] This was retaliation by the Russian government for banning its athletes from participating in the Olympic Games.

Over the next decade, Russia continued to attack the Olympics as it looked for ways to punish the Olympic Committee while dodging outright attribution and the consequences that would come with it.

In December 2017, the Russian Olympic Committee was officially suspended, banning Russia from formally participating in the 2018 Pyeongchang Winter Olympics. Russian athletes were allowed to compete, but not under the Russian flag, nor were they allowed to accept medals on behalf of Russia. They could compete under the name Olympic Athletes from Russia (OAR), but the Russian anthem was replaced during ceremonies by the Olympic anthem. This frustrated many in Russia who spoke out against it, including Putin.

Leading up to the start of the Olympics in South Korea, security researchers at McAfee discovered a campaign of attacks targeting South Koreans, especially those in the departments working on the Olympics in Pyeongchang. The researchers named the campaign Operation GoldDragon.[5] The attackers timed the sending of Korean-language phishing emails to coordinate with legitimate terrorism drills in Pyeongchang, counting on users' desire for information about the imminent event to make them more likely to click. Once the users did, the malware scoured the device for information to send back home.

The researchers loosely tied the attack to North Korea under the assumption that, given how vociferously it is known to target South Korea overall, it would be the most likely aggressor leading up to an event as big as the Olympics. As true as that typically was,

[4] www.wada-ama.org/en/news/wada-confirms-attack-russian-cyber-espionage-group
[5] www.mcafee.com/blogs/other-blogs/mcafee-labs/gold-dragon-widens-olympics-malware-attacks-gains-permanent-presence-on-victims-systems

it was at odds with the political environment of the time, as the North Korean government was extending diplomatic overtures in the lead-up to the Olympic Games. It was running a charm offensive, even sending Kim Yo-jong, Kim Jong-un's sister, to the Games.[6] Espionage operations do not stop because of a simple charm offensive or a round of the Olympic Games, so suspicions remained.

The attacks continued. At the very start of the Winter Olympics, the official Olympic website was taken offline for 12 hours, preventing attendees from downloading tickets or getting information on the event. The Wi-Fi in the stadium stopped working, and the network connections in the press center failed, making reporting on the opening of the Games challenging. This cyberattack used a new kind of malware that became known as Olympic Destroyer. It got access to devices from Olympic officials, sponsors, ski resorts, service providers, and broadcasters, then immediately deleted their data.

Many speculated that the attack was perpetrated by North Korea, especially given McAfee researchers' early findings. A series of technical indicators suggested that the attribution was legitimate. Within the malware, there was logic that mimicked the techniques used by some North Korean attackers (specifically the Lazarus Group) to write their own malware. However, there were potential links that could attribute the attack to other groups as well. The malware used a function to generate AES keys for encryption, which had only ever been used by the Chinese threat actor APT 10 until that point. The attribution process for the attack was a veritable mess; everyone wanted answers, and every researcher wanted to be first to provide them. Microsoft, Intezer, Cisco Talos, SecureList, Kaspersky, and many others published articles examining the attack and raising suspicions that it was not, in fact, perpetrated by North Korea at all.[7]

---

[6]www.cnn.com/2018/02/07/asia/kim-jong-un-sister-olympics-korea-intl
[7]www.wired.com/story/untold-story-2018-olympics-destroyer-cyberattack

It turned out that the attack was actually the Russian GRU all along. Researchers found that the attackers had reused command-and-control infrastructure they had also leveraged when attacking election systems during the 2016 U.S. presidential election. This led investigators right to the GRU. By February 2018, two unnamed U.S. intelligence officials spoke to the *Washington Post* and verified that the attack had been meant to frame North Korea and had actually been perpetrated by Russia.[8] In 2020, the United States charged six Russian GRU officers with the attack, and the United Kingdom condemned it and formally blamed Russia.[9,10]

This cyberattack embarrassed the Olympic Committee and South Korea, a country known for its advanced digital infrastructure. It is considered one of, if not the best, examples of a cyberattack as a false-flag operation for deception and to avoid attribution. At the same time, it showed that even the best threat actors can slip up when recycling resources for different operations, and just a single IP address or reused piece of infrastructure can be traced back to the source.

The attacks didn't stop there. UK and U.S. officials accused Russia of reconnaissance ahead of the Tokyo Olympics, which they believe was meant to lead to disruption. The Tokyo Olympics were postponed due to COVID, so these potential plans were not confirmed. Ahead of the Paris Summer Olympics in 2024, Russia perpetrated attacks against entities in France, with the French National Cybersecurity Agency, ANSSI, seeing a 15 percent increase in attacks.[11] Even still, none of these attacks had the same level of disruption that the Pyeongchang Olympics demonstrated.

---

[8] www.washingtonpost.com/world/national-security/russian-spies-hacked-the-olympics-and-tried-to-make-it-look-like-north-korea-did-it-us-officials-say/2018/02/24/44b5468e-18f2-11e8-92c9-376b4fe57ff7_story.html
[9] www.justice.gov/archives/opa/pr/six-russian-gru-officers-charged-connection-worldwide-deployment-destructive-malware-and
[10] www.gov.uk/government/news/uk-exposes-series-of-russian-cyber-attacks-against-olympic-and-paralympic-games
[11] https://www.cert.ssi.gouv.fr/uploads/CERTFR-2025-CTI-004.pdf

Chapter 40
A Bear for a Brother

The mindset of the Russian state is mired in its history, driven by its attempt to return to and expand beyond its former perceived glory as the Russian Empire. The drive to expand, particularly across Eurasia, goes far beyond the Soviet Union and spans back to the fifteenth century. Russia peaked in its territorial expansion in the nineteenth century and was locked in a fierce competition with the British Empire, known as the Great Game, a rivalry between the two that led to significant expansion in Central and South Asia.

The Russian Revolution of 1917 caused the fall of the Russian Empire. Its collapse led to declarations of independence by Ukraine, Finland, Poland, Estonia, Latvia, Lithuania, and several Caucasus entities, which Russia recognized in various treaties and armistices but often only under duress. Over the years, the Soviet Union regained some of this territory, but Russia never recovered many of the independent states it had lost.

Disillusionment with the communist system, or in this case, the communist curtain hiding the autocracy within, was one of many factors that led to the Soviet Union's collapse. Once the Soviet Union fell, Russia once again lost control of many of its former territories, including Armenia, Azerbaijan, Belarus, Estonia, Georgia, Kazakhstan, Kyrgyzstan, Latvia, Lithuania, Moldova, Tajikistan, Turkmenistan, Ukraine, and Uzbekistan.

Some losses hurt more than others. Georgia controls key Black Sea ports and sits at a unique crossroads between Europe, Asia, and the Middle East that is particularly important to Russia. Over the centuries, Ukraine was the traditional invasion route into Russian territory, and many Russian elites see it as the cradle of early Russian civilization.

To bridge some of this gap, Russia has established strategic partnerships. It is a leader of the Eurasian Economic Union (EAEU) to help promote better economic integration, and it works with the Collective Security Treaty Organization (CSTO) to help ensure mutual defense and military cooperation between members.[1] Russia participates in non-Western blocs like BRICS to offer a direct counter to the G7; it has also begun setting up joint digital sovereignty and financial systems for members.

However, for some of its larger integration priorities, it relies on military incursions and warfare, including cyberattacks, to assert control. Russia has prioritized its attacks on Georgia, Estonia, and Ukraine to further its geopolitical advantage, though in very different ways.

Escalating Control

In 1783, the king of the Eastern Georgian kingdom signed a treaty with Russia's Catherine the Great to turn Georgia into a Russian protectorate in exchange for military protection.[2] The tsars annexed Georgia between 1801 and 1804, abolishing the Georgian monarchy and exiling the royal family.[3] Georgians resisted, and once the Russian Revolution happened, Georgia declared its independence in 1918, but the Soviet Union quickly invaded and annexed it in 1921. It took another 70 years before Georgia would again declare its independence after the Soviet Union collapsed. Russia has not forgotten. It exerts control over Georgia through military occupation and diplomatic and economic influence.

---

[1] www.eaeunion.org/?lang=en
[2] www.britannica.com/event/Treaty-of-Georgievsk
[3] https://georgia.to/en/annexation-by-the-russian-empire

In July 2008, a short month before it invaded Georgia, Russia-backed hackers, most likely hacktivists, took down the website of the President of Georgia through a DDoS attack. It took the website offline for 24 hours and was a precursor to what was to come post-invasion.[4] On August 1, South Ossetian forces, with the backing of Russia, began shelling Georgian villages. The Georgian's did not respond until the forces picked up the intensity of the attacks. Once they did, Russian forces twisted the narrative to use the Georgians' advance as justification to launch a full-scale invasion.[5] *Russia Today* called Georgian actions a genocide.[6] Russian troops closed in on South Ossetia, while its naval forces blockaded the coastline and air forces targeted land. During the invasion, the Russian media was portraying it as a justified peace enforcement mission, and the Russian people were primed to accept the disinformation about Georgia thrown their way.

The Ministry of Defense of the Russian Federation stated that more than 2,000 people were victims of the supposed Georgian attack on South Ossetia, and that most of the victims were Russian citizens—a number far inflated from the 365 South Ossetians total, civilians and combatants, that were later verified.[7] The disinformation prompted an outraged, unified response from the underground hacker community in Russia, which even created a website, www.StopGeorgia.ru, to coordinate Russian hacktivist activities and enable more individuals to participate in the attacks. It even had a scoreboard to track and gamify what websites they took down. Given the timing and coordination, it's unlikely the hacktivists acted alone. The Russian government likely coordinated with the hacktivists on the attacks.[8]

---

[4] www.army.mil/article/19351/georgias_cyber_left_hook
[5] https://warroom.armywarcollege.edu/articles/enduring-impact
[6] www.rt.com/news/we-have-evidence-of-genocide-russian-investigators
[7] http://casebook.icrc.org/case-study/georgiarussia-independent-international-fact-finding-mission-conflict-south-ossetia
[8] https://jamestown.org/the-cyber-dimension-of-russias-attack-on-georgia

The hacktivists targeted websites of the president of Georgia, the government of Georgia, the Ministry of Foreign Affairs, and parliament. They also attacked Georgia-friendly media and online news outlets like *Civil.ge* and *The Messenger* to limit the information civilians could get. Instead, Georgians were forced to rely on Russian media. Over the next several days, 54 websites, including government sites and those of Georgian banks, were taken down or defaced. Some were defaced with fascist symbols and photos comparing the Georgian president to Hitler. The National Bank of Georgia had to suspend electronic operations from August 8–19.[9]

Russian bloggers also called on their followers to contribute to a CNN poll questioning the validity of the Russian invasion. They wanted to skew the results more favorably toward Russia.[10]

The invasion of Georgia was the first time in history that Russia leveraged hybrid warfare during a war. The cyberattacks isolated Georgia from the outside world during the invasion and confused its citizens and the international community.

---

[9] https://jamestown.org/the-cyber-dimension-of-russias-attack-on-georgia
[10] Ibid.

Chapter 41
The Bronze Night

In June 1940, an independent Estonia was invaded by the Soviet Union before being annexed into the USSR. During the Soviet Union's occupation, thousands of Estonians were killed, and tens of thousands were mobilized into the Soviet military. In 1941, a different oppressor came: German troops invaded, executing thousands of Estonian civilians and imprisoning thousands more. Just three years later, Soviet troops retook Estonia from the Germans through even more bloodshed. The Soviets retook Tallinn, the capital, on September 22, 1944. During this four-year period, in a country of just over 1 million people, a devastating 39,000 Estonians were killed, and 250,000 were displaced.[1]

But it wasn't over. Estonians waged an insurgency to regain independence from the Soviets that started in October 1944. The Estonian people wanted independence and were willing to fight for it.

Three years after the Soviets retook Tallinn and in the middle of the Estonian insurgency, the Soviets erected a six-foot-tall statue of a soldier in a Red Army uniform in the center of the city. The

---

[1]https://tuna.ra.ee/en/registration-of-the-population-in-estonia-on-1-december-1941-background-organisation-sources/#:~:text=The%20population%20figure%20was%201,population%20had%20decreased%20by%209.5%25

statue was called the Monument to the Liberators of Tallinn, which stood over a burial site for Soviet soldiers. That statue stood through to the end of the rebellion in 1956, during which another 19,000 Estonians were killed and 80,000 were displaced. It lasted through the next several decades, when Estonia gained independence, and the Soviet Union fell. It was a historical fixture of the relationship between Estonia and the Soviet Union.

The statue—later known as the Bronze Soldier of Tallinn—has always been a polarizing symbol. For Estonians, it served as a reminder of Soviet repression. For Russians in Estonia, who were about a quarter of the population in the early 2000s, it served as a proud reminder of the Soviet victory over Germany. The statue was so controversial that it was protested and vandalized to the point of requiring guards,and it was petitioned to be destroyed.[2,3]

Of all things, this statue was the impetus for one of the earliest large-scale, politically motivated cyberattacks considered to be perpetrated by a government.

The Bronze Soldier had stood at the center of the capital for 60 years before things finally came to a head in January 2007. The Estonian government decided to relocate the Bronze Soldier and the remains of the Soviet soldiers buried beneath to a nearby military cemetery in April. The Russian government was outraged. The Minister of Foreign Affairs, Sergei Lavrov, said:

> This is blasphemous, and will have serious consequences for our relations with Estonia.[4]

In the months leading up to the relocation, Russia began to spread disinformation about the Bronze Soldier. Russian state media claimed the statue had been cut into pieces and was completely gone, which was not true.[5] This disinformation riled up many of the

---

[2]https://news.err.ee/592070/monument-of-contention-how-the-bronze-soldier-was-removed
[3]http://news.bbc.co.uk/2/hi/europe/6255051.stm
[4]www.nytimes.com/2007/04/27/world/europe/27cnd-estonia.html
[5]www.pbs.org/newshour/show/inside-estonias-approach-in-combating-russian-disinformation

Russian-speaking protesters, and by the evening of April 26, 2007, a thousand of them had gathered near the site and turned violent.

Property was vandalized and looted, protesters threw stones and bottles at police, and police used water cannons and tear gas on protesters. It became known as the Bronze Night and resulted in over $3 million in damages, over 100 people injured, and one person dead.

The Russian government continued to target Estonia in the days following. It blocked transit trade, especially that of coal, which fell by 60 percent. More covertly, Russia wanted to cripple Estonia's Internet infrastructure and leave it isolated. It started weeks of cyberattacks, leveraging DDoS attacks to disable the websites of the Estonian president and parliament, government ministries, political parties, media, banks, and communications companies. Government email accounts were spammed with messages to the point that they could not communicate. Journalists could not post news stories, leaving a vacuum that Russian state media was eager and willing to fill. ATMs were shut down for hours at a time. The common emergency number, 112, was blocked. The Estonian Reform Party website was targeted, and a forged apology from the Estonian prime minister was posted on the site.[6]

In response, Estonia blocked much foreign traffic into the country. It stopped the attacks, which was a win for the Estonian people. However, it was a double-edged sword: It isolated Estonia from the rest of the world, preventing foreign individuals from using Estonian services.

While we now have the benefit of hindsight, it was difficult to definitively attribute these cyberattacks to Russia when they happened—certainly not with enough certainty to respond in kind or escalate. Difficulties with attribution enabled Russia to have plausible deniability, even as it strongly implied it was involved and coordinated other types of attacks against the Estonians.

---

[6] https://ccdcoe.org/uploads/2018/10/legalconsiderations_0.pdf

Aside from challenges with attribution, it was difficult to know what the appropriate response to this type of attack should be; if Russia spreads disinformation, should Estonia respond in kind? Should it launch a DDoS attack against Russian assets, or worse, escalate to military conflict? Who is held responsible for the response, especially given defense partnerships like NATO? These are the kinds of questions that were being considered at the time, given that this was one of the earliest politically motivated, large-scale cyberattacks against a state.

There is no clear point at which nations consider escalation from a cyberattack to a kinetic one. Much like economic sanctions, cyberattacks do not necessitate a military response—they are one part of a larger operation that drives a nation to war. It's a slow erosion, where the constant frustration of cyberattacks can wear down an opponent until they acquiesce or escalate.

Chapter 42
The Hybrid Crucible

At this point the question of Ukraine is the most important. The situation in Ukraine is very bad. If we don't take steps now to improve the situation, we may lose Ukraine. The objective should be to transform Ukraine, in the shortest period of time, into a fortress of the USSR.

—A letter from Joseph Stalin on Ukraine in 1932[1]

Ukraine has a long and tumultuous history with Russia that has only become more tense over time, in part driven by its size as the largest country entirely in Europe, its farmland and industrial base, and its time under Soviet occupation.[2] This has made it a petri dish for Russian cyber aggression over the years, especially in hybrid warfare.

In late 2013 and early 2014, there was a series of protests in Ukraine known as Euromaidan, or the Revolution of Dignity.[3] Ukrainian citizens were pushing back on President Viktor Yanukovych's choice not to sign an association agreement with the European Union, which instead pushed its ties closer to Russia.

---

[1] Joseph Stalin to Lazar Kaganovich, 11 August 1932, in The Stalin–Kaganovich Correspondence, 1931–36, ed. Oleg V. Khlevniuk et al. (New Haven, CT: Yale University Press, 2003), page.
[2] https://www.bbc.com/news/world-europe-18018002
[3] https://war.ukraine.ua/faq/revolution-of-dignity-ukraine

During this time, telecommunications providers in Ukraine were targeted with DDoS attacks that blocked communications between protesters, which many suspect were perpetrated by Russian hacktivists.[4] Websites such as Radio Free Europe and Television News Service was hit with DDoS attacks to prevent communication between demonstrators and the outside world.[5,6]

During Euromaidan, a special Ukrainian police force known as Berkut was notorious for its police brutality and for beating protesters, including peaceful demonstrators. Berkut was disbanded immediately following the protests, but not soon enough. The majority of the Heavenly Hundred, the protesters who died during the demonstrations, were killed by Berkut.[7,8] Some of the worst cyberattacks happened when these protesters were shot: Mobile phones were flooded with messages and phone calls to prevent protesters from coordinating at a critical moment.[9]

The protests eventually succeeded; on February 21, 2014, opposition leaders and President Yanukovych signed an agreement to resolve the situation by restoring Ukraine's 2004 constitution, implementing constitutional reform, and holding presidential elections in December. On February 22, Yanukovych fled to Russia, and the Ukrainian Parliament voted to remove him.[10]

Just five days later, on February 27, 2014, Russia took the next step in plans that had been laid out for quite some time: An invasion and occupation of Crimea. Though it initially denied that unmarked Russian forces, the "little green men," were overtaking parts of Crimea, a few weeks later, Putin confirmed it to the Russian Parliament.[11] Unmarked forces invaded Crimea, removed the government, and replaced it with one that was pro-Russia. They issued a referendum to vote on whether Crimea

[4] https://nsarchive.gwu.edu/sites/default/files/documents/semon9-ryglx/2024-02-02-Cyber-Diia-A-Decade-in-the-Trenches-of-Cyberwarfare.pdf
[5] www.rferl.org/a/rferl-ddos-attacks/25196217.html
[6] https://imi.org.ua/en/news/tsnua-survived-powerful-ddos-attack-i24994
[7] https://euromaidanpress.com/2017/12/04/the-maidan-beatings-november-30-2013-what-we-know-and-dont-know
[8] www.kyivpost.com/post/22913
[9] https://ccdcoe.org/uploads/2018/10/Ch07_CyberWarinPerspective_Pakharenko.pdf
[10] www.bbc.com/news/world-europe-26304842
[11] www.reuters.com/article/markets/us/putin-admits-russian-forces-were-deployed-to-crimea-idUSL6N0N921H

wanted to rejoin Russia or restore the Crimean constitution as part of Ukraine.

Meanwhile, Russian state media flooded the zone with claims to justify the invasion of Crimea, such as how annexation was necessary to protect Russia's access to the Black Sea.[12] Fake personas claiming to be Ukrainians popped up on Facebook, Twitter, and VKontakte, all too eager to comment on articles and make posts about their frustrations with the Euromaidan protests.[13]

This flood of attacks, combined with the sham of an election process—Russian soldiers manned many public buildings, including polling stations and military sites during the election to intimidate voters—led to a vote in overwhelming favor of joining Russia. Crimea's occupation and annexation gave Russia a foothold in Ukraine, giving it free rein to continue to target Ukraine with cyberattacks, which it has to this day. All this said, Russia was hit back with cyberattacks as well; in March 2014, *Russia Today* had its website defaced, with all references to "Russia," "Russian," or "military" replaced with the word "Nazi."[14]

Because of its invasion, Russia faced deteriorating relations from the West and sanctions from the United States, the EU, Canada, and Australia.[15,16,17,18] It was suspended from the G8, which then became the G7 again.[19] In response, Russia sped up its "turn to the East"—a pivot that had been attempted many times in its history, especially during imperial and Soviet periods—reorienting its economic, political, and diplomatic focus toward Asia.[20] This shift led to strategic partnerships with China, India, Bangladesh, and

---

[12] www.files.ethz.ch/isn/181102/PW42_the_anatomy_of_russian_information_warfare.pdf
[13] https://stratcomcoe.org/cuploads/pfiles/russian_information_campaign_public_12012016fin.pdf
[14] https://css.ethz.ch/content/dam/ethz/special-interest/gess/cis/center-for-securities-studies/pdfs/20181003_MB_HS_RUS-UKR%20V2_rev.pdf
[15] www.consilium.europa.eu/en/infographics/eu-sanctions-against-russia-over-ukraine
[16] www.international.gc.ca/world-monde/international_relations-relations_internationales/sanctions/russia-russie.aspx?lang=eng
[17] www.aph.gov.au/About_Parliament/Parliamentary_departments/Parliamentary_Library/FlagPost/2022/February/Sanctions_on_Russia
[18] www.nytimes.com/2014/03/25/world/europe/obama-russia-crimea.html
[19] https://2021-2025.state.gov/division-for-counter-threat-finance-and-sanctions/ukraine-and-russia-sanctions
[20] https://static.rusi.org/297_EI_RFE.pdf

other countries in the Asia-Pacific, and to further the development of Russia's Far East through expanded trade opportunities.

After Yanukovych's ouster, Ukrainian elections were set to take place to replace him on May 25, 2014. The Russian government was far from pleased with Yanukovych's removal, and it attempted to tip the scales back in its favor during the elections. The way Ukrainian election infrastructure was set up helped Russia—Ukraine had inherited a similar structure to that of Soviet times, and was highly centralized, with one body managing presidential elections. Centralized infrastructure is ideal for cyberattackers; it means there's only one target they have to break into. To try to increase transparency in the election process, Ukrainians had put new software in place to allow citizens to track the election in real time—a valuable addition for the electorate, but also a new piece of software to attack.[21]

Before the election, attackers gained access to the Central Election Commission systems, including the electoral network. They stole passwords and deleted files critical to the counting system, which ultimately took down parts of the central system for elections, including the new real-time election tracking, for roughly 20 hours.[22] The Ukrainians recovered, but forty minutes before the election results were announced, they discovered malware that would have changed the election results to show the far-right candidate as the overwhelming winner, with 37 percent of the vote instead of his actual, measly 1 percent.[23] Ukrainian cybersecurity experts removed the malware and ensured the integrity of the results. Even so, the attackers cast doubt on the results by defacing the Central Election Commission's homepage, claiming that the far-right candidate had won the election just twelve minutes before the polls closed.

The Russian hacktivist group CyberBerkut took responsibility for the attacks.[24] CyberBerkut first came on the scene in 2014, and,

[21] https://securingdemocracy.gmfus.org/incident/russian-government-connected-hacktivist-group-cyberberkut-breaches-ukraines-election-commission
[22] https://nsarchive.gwu.edu/sites/default/files/documents/semon9-ryglx/2024-02-02-Cyber-Diia-A-Decade-in-the-Trenches-of-Cyberwarfare.pdf
[23] www.csmonitor.com/World/Passcode/2014/0617/Ukraine-election-narrowly-avoided-wanton-destruction-from-hackers
[24] www.crowdstrike.com/en-us/blog/lessons-from-past-cyber-operations-against-ukraine

in a grotesque display of its commitment to Russia, it takes its name from the brutal special Ukrainian police force, Berkut.

Despite CyberBerkut taking credit for the attacks, Ukrainian cybersecurity experts were convinced that the attack was actually perpetrated by Russian state actors, given the uniqueness of the malware and its target.[25] Some of the malware also matched that used previously by Fancy Bear.[26] Their suspicions were all but officially confirmed when, immediately after the polls closed, Russian state media published the exact election results that the malware was intended to change the results to.[27] The Russians had built a one-two punch to the attack, trying to change results and then propel awareness of the fake results through legitimate websites and state media.

The vote tally system was also subjected to a DDoS attack in the early morning after the polls closed, delaying the vote count.[28]

These attacks led the Central Election Commission (CEC) to institute a series of reforms to secure election infrastructure for the future. It segmented the election network to limit how far the attackers could spread, made sure there was a complete log of events happening in the network, and made major infrastructure updates. Over the next few years, Ukraine also adopted its first cybersecurity strategy and passed its first comprehensive cybersecurity law. These changes helped make sure future elections were far more secure despite continued attacks.[29]

The Long, Cold War

On a cloudy, foggy, 60-degree day on November 21, 2015, the electricity went out in most of Crimea for 1.2 million consumers for 6 hours. Four transmission lines had been blown up. Some of the power was

---

[25] https://time.com/magazine/us/4512760/october-10th-2016-vol-188-no-14-u-s
[26] www.atlanticcouncil.org/in-depth-research-reports/issue-brief/defining-russian-election-interference-an-analysis-of-select-2014-to-2018-cyber-enabled-incidents-2
[27] https://ccdcoe.org/uploads/2018/10/Ch06_CyberWarinPerspective_Koval.pdf
[28] https://nsarchive.gwu.edu/sites/default/files/documents/semon9-ryglx/2024-02-02-Cyber-Diia-A-Decade-in-the-Trenches-of-Cyberwarfare.pdf
[29] https://cepa.org/article/bolstering-electoral-cyber-resilience-in-ukraine

restored via generators, but for others, it took over a week to get power back. At the time, it was unclear exactly who caused the outage, though Russia suspected and implied that it was the fault of Ukraine. No group claimed responsibility, but most suspect it was Ukrainian supporters like the Crimean Tatar groups and anti-Russian activists, as they had been blockading supplies into Crimea as part of the protest.[30]

In a parallel operation, just a month later, on a cloudy, foggy, 40-degree day on December 23, 2015, in Ukraine, 230,000 consumers lost power for anywhere from 1 to 6 hours, depending on the region. Three different energy distributors (with over a dozen substations) were knocked offline unexpectedly, yet in a coordinated fashion, within half an hour of each other. The GRU unit Sandworm had hit all three companies with a coordinated cyberattack.

Sandworm had been preparing to hit the distributors since springtime and had spent months gaining access. They infiltrated with a phishing attack, then installed a backdoor so they could access the infrastructure as they pleased. They conducted reconnaissance for months to make sure the timing and the operation went off without a hitch. To make sure stations could not get backup power once the cyberattack hit, Sandworm reconfigured the uninterruptible power supply.[31] The attackers went so far as to generate malicious firmware updates for each serial-to-Ethernet converter to prevent the electrical system from reinitiating the breakers and restarting. This made it simpler to execute the attack in a coordinated way at a specific time across distributors. Once they initiated the attack, they also launched a DDoS of the phone lines, blocking up support lines so customers could not report the outage.

The attack was the first of its kind—a geopolitically motivated cyberattack aimed at disrupting critical infrastructure on a large scale. But as sophisticated as the attack was, it required months of expert preparation and execution. The juxtaposition of the electricity going down due to a simple blown-up power line versus an

---

[30] www.osw.waw.pl/en/publikacje/analyses/2015-11-25/crimea-left-without-power
[31] www.wired.com/2016/03/inside-cunning-unprecedented-hack-ukraines-power-grid

intricate, detailed cyberattack is especially stark. Though the attacks were similar in some ways, in others, they differ entirely. The physical attack lasted longer and affected more people, while the cyberattack was smaller and shorter-lived. The physical attack took just a few explosives; the cyberattack took months of careful planning and execution. It's a lesson in resource utilization: Why attack with a cyberattack when physical destruction is more effective and more permanent?

Russia continued its attacks on Ukraine's power grid. In December 2016, Sandworm unleashed an attack using the Industroyer malware to cause a blackout in Ukraine. The blackout started just before midnight, taking out one-fifth of the power consumption in Kyiv for a little over an hour. The attack differed from the previous attack on the Ukrainian power grid in 2015. This one targeted the transmission facility instead of the distribution facility, which could cause more damage: Transmission facilities act as the backbone of the electric grid and are much more likely to trigger cascading failures. By contrast, distribution centers—when they fail—tend to be more localized, minimizing the impact. Sandworm also made the attack more automated than it had been previously. Once the devices were infected, the malware automatically mapped out control systems and located targets for the attack, reducing the amount of manual activity the attackers would have to execute. The more automation, the more targets Sandworm could attack at once. Even still, the impact was much smaller than that of a kinetic attack, though it was also less escalatory.[32]

Years later, on April 8, 2022, Sandworm again tried to take out the electricity in Ukraine, this time in the midst of war. They compromised a Ukrainian energy provider in February, just before the start of the Russo-Ukrainian war, and waited for the opportune moment to strike. The attack was methodical . . . yet it failed miserably. It went wrong when the attackers configured the malware to execute at 5:58 p.m. on a Friday, thinking most employees would be on their way out of the office or preparing to leave for the weekend.[33] What the

---

[32] www.wired.com/story/crash-override-malware
[33] www.welivesecurity.com/2022/04/12/industroyer2-industroyer-reloaded

attackers failed to recognize was that most employees *would* be out of the office, which meant their computers would be shut off for the weekend. Malware can't execute if the computer isn't on. Even highly capable state actors can be tripped up by mundane things like work schedules.

The Eye of Hurricane NotPetya

Ukrainian Constitution Day is on June 28. It serves as the anniversary of the ratification of the Constitution of Ukraine, a symbol of its independence since 1996. The day before its anniversary, on June 27, 2017, became the day of a disastrous, wide-scale, politically motivated cyberattack. The attack hit Ukraine's state power company and Kyiv's airport with malware known as NotPetya (it was a variant of Petya, a notorious ransomware, hence "Not" Petya). To break in, it first compromised a widely used Ukrainian tax software application, M.E.Doc, to infect as many Ukrainian businesses as possible. Once in, it leveraged exploits, including a modified version of EternalBlue, a leaked NSA tool, to spread to Microsoft Windows machines. The malware initially presented as ransomware and requested a ransom of $300 in Bitcoin from its targets. The thing was, it wasn't actually ransomware. It was a wiper masquerading as ransomware, *destroying* files instead of offering a way to decrypt them. It spread to machines outside of Ukraine quickly, and it spread far. It hit companies in over 65 countries, including Maersk, one of the world's largest shipping and logistics companies. Maersk operates in over 130 countries and had around 75,000 employees at the time of the attack.[34]

The attack left Maersk with 49,000 computers rendered unusable. It also lost access to 1,200 critical business applications. Any machine online at the time of the attack was affected, which was the vast majority. It took down almost all 150 of their domain controllers, the servers responsible for managing user access to a Windows

---

[34] www.macrotrends.net/stocks/charts/AMKBY/ap-moller-maersk/number-of-employees

network; if domain controllers go down, the organization loses the ability to operate. If they have backups, operations can be restored, but if they do not, the damage may be irreversible, meaning there would be no way to access user accounts. Every employee account would be inaccessible, including everything they had worked on. Imagine losing access to everything you have worked on for your company, permanently. Each account would need to be re-created from scratch, which would be the type of catastrophic event that could destroy a company.

Maersk was facing a nightmare. However, in a stroke of sheer luck, just one Maersk domain controller survived: One in Ghana. At the time of the attack, the domain controller had been knocked offline thanks to a common occurrence in Sub-Saharan Africa—a blackout. The blackout prevented the domain controller from connecting to the network and getting infected with NotPetya. If the blackout had not occurred, that machine would have been inaccessible too, and Maersk would have had no machines to recover from.

Maersk's challenges were not over though. Bandwidth issues in Africa prevented Maersk employees from uploading a backup of the domain controller, so instead, employees had to physically carry and fly with the server from Ghana to Nigeria, then from Nigeria to London. It took 10 days to get back core business technology and weeks to get the rest.[35,36] In that time, Maersk lost $300 million from the attack.[37]

The damage inside Ukraine was also undeniable. Ukrainian hospitals (four just in Kyiv), six power companies, two airports, dozens of banks and ATMs, and government agencies were all affected; a senior government official estimated that 10 percent of the computers in Ukraine were completely wiped of data. At the end of the day, estimates indicate the attack cost up to $10 billion in total damages worldwide.[38]

---

[35] www.bleepingcomputer.com/news/security/maersk-reinstalled-45-000-pcs-and-4-000-servers-to-recover-from-notpetya-attack

[36] www.sipa.columbia.edu/sites/default/files/2022-11/NotPetya%20Final.pdf

[37] www.zdnet.com/article/maersk-forced-to-reinstall-4000-servers-45000-pcs-due-to-notpetya-attack

[38] www.wired.com/story/notpetya-cyberattack-ukraine-russia-code-crashed-the-world

By July, the Ukrainian authorities had confiscated equipment used in the attack and attributed it to Russian security services.[39] By January 2018, the CIA attributed the attack to the GRU; by February, the United Kingdom Ministry of Defence had attributed it to Russia.[40] In a first for the European Union, in 2020, it announced sanctions on four Russian attackers and the GRU for NotPetya, the attacks directed at the Ukrainian power grid in 2015 and 2016, and the attack on The Hague.[41]

Hybrid War Put to the Test

In January 2022, over 100,000 Russian troops were amassed on Ukraine's northern and eastern borders.[42] Talks between Russia and NATO members were misaligned; while NATO looked to avoid a Russo-Ukrainian war, Russia's foreign minister railed against NATO in the press. Soon after these talks, a barrage of cyberattacks targeted Ukraine.

This was the moment when the Russia-Ukraine conflict spilled over into all-out war, and when true hybrid warfare, the kind that melded kinetic and cyberattacks together, was tested at an unprecedented scale.

It started out experimental. Prior to this, there were limited expectations of how cyberattacks could be used in warfare—for espionage, perhaps to take out parts of the electric grid, but even much of that was untested. The cyberattacks during the early days of the war were all over the place, and attackers used a bit of a spray-and-pray approach, with threat actors trying different attacks, evaluating their success, then pivoting to a new method and new target.

The attacks were rampant: DDoS, wipers, physical hardware attacks, and many others. Some of the malware used in the attacks had been compiled years in advance, showing just how long they had been planning. Once the war started, waves of DDoS attacks

---

[39] www.reuters.com/article/technology/police-seize-servers-of-ukrainian-software-firm-after-cyber-attack-idUSKBN19P1Y0
[40] www.wired.com/story/white-house-russia-notpetya-attribution
[41] https://eur-lex.europa.eu/legal-content/EN/TXT/HTML/?uri=CELEX:32020D112 7&from=EN
[42] https://www.congress.gov/crs_external_products/IN/PDF/IN11806/IN11806 .5.pdf

were perpetrated year after year to knock out banks, government sites, and critical infrastructure providers, and were often paired with additional attacks, like wipers. In the first year of the war alone, DDoS attacks made up the vast majority of attacks targeting critical infrastructure.[43]

The Computer Emergency Response Team of Ukraine (CERT-UA) responded to over 2,000 cyber incidents in 2022.[44] Some allies of Russia also executed attacks, including Belarus and North Korea, in active coordination and support for Russia. During the first month and a half of the war alone, Ukraine reported 362 cyberattacks, three times more than the same period the year before.[45] The majority targeted government, local authorities, and security and defense firms.

The Russo-Ukrainian war is the first true hybrid war that leverages multidomain operations, from kinetic warfare to electronic to cyberwarfare, together in a cohesive way. Amid this experimentation, a clearer pattern began to emerge: Most Russian cyber operations clustered into a few repeatable playbooks. In particular, four categories defined the cyber side of the campaign—denial of service attacks, espionage operations, psyops, and wipers—and each evolved alongside Russia's kinetic strategy.

Knocking Ukraine Offline

From the start of the war to early 2023, 276 distinct outages hit Ukrainian Internet and telecommunications providers.[46] During the first months of the war, Russia had seized some key cities but was being stalled by Ukrainian defenders. To help turn the tide, Russia used cyberattacks to complicate and disable Ukrainian command and control and create operational uncertainty.

---

[43] https://cyberpeaceinstitute.org/news/ukraine-conflict-one-year-anniversary
[44] www.computerweekly.com/news/252529292/Ukraine-cyber-teams-responded-to-more-than-2000-attacks-in-2022
[45] https://cip.gov.ua/en/news/za-pivtora-misyacya-viini-kilkist-khakerskikh-atak-zrosla-vtrichi
[46] www.networkworld.com/article/971980/war-tests-ukrainian-telecom-internet-resilience.html

Cyberattacks targeted and took down VinAsterisk, an Internet provider in the region, on March 13, 2022.[47] Ukrtelecom, one of the largest Internet providers in Ukraine, experienced numerous outages at the beginning of the war, some caused by cyberattacks and others by damage to critical cables. In one instance, on March 28, attackers used stolen employee credentials to break in and disrupt services for 15 hours. The outage dropped network traffic across Ukraine to 13 percent of pre-war levels.[48] Similarly, Triolan, a major broadband provider and a collective of independent network operators in Ukraine, had services disrupted on the day of the Russian invasion and again in early March for more than 12 hours.

Contrast these cyberattacks with an example of one of many kinetic attacks: On March 6, 2022, the last functioning cell tower in Mariupol was hit by a shell and destroyed, making emergency coordination incredibly difficult. Services were only partially restored by the second half of 2022, and only on Russian-controlled networks, not on Ukrainian ones.

There's a stark difference between the effects of cyberattacks versus physical attacks on infrastructure like this: Restoration times. While providers were able to get services back up and running in less than half a day after a cyberattack, critical services affected by physical attacks were expected to be back up and running within three days (though they often would take much longer)—a much longer time offline.[49]

In another instance in early December 2023, nearly 24 million Ukrainians lost mobile and Internet service across Ukraine.[50] Kyivstar, the largest telecom operator in Ukraine, had been hit with a cyberattack. The war was heading into its second winter, and Russia was putting intense pressure on Ukraine with front-line fighting and missile attacks. Taking out the Internet was another way to exhaust the Ukrainian military as well as civilians. Telecom

---

[47] https://cyberdefensereview.army.mil/Portals/6/Documents/2022_fall/02_Lin.pdf

[48] www.infosecurity-magazine.com/news/attack-ukraine-telecoms-employee

[49] www.kmu.gov.ua/en/news/hotovnist-ukrainy-do-novykh-vyklykiv-kiberbezpeka-i-zviazok

[50] https://reliaquest.com/blog/russia-linked-threats-to-operational-technology

services are also how most Ukrainians received advanced warning of Russian air attacks, and because of this cyberattack, some residents missed air-attack warnings.[51]

As early as March 2023, attackers had attempted to infiltrate Kyivstar. They eventually succeeded and compromised an employee account, and by November, had leveraged it to gain access to the full infrastructure. Once they got in, attackers took out both virtual and physical servers. The attack disabled and damaged 40% of Kyivstar's infrastructure, especially its virtual servers.[52] According to its CEO, "(The attack) significantly damaged (our) infrastructure, limited access, we could not counter it at the virtual level, so we shut down Kyivstar physically to limit the enemy's access."[53]

It took Kyivstar multiple days to recover and weeks to fully restore systems. They ultimately reported a revenue impact of $95 million USD because of the attack.[54]

The group Solntsepek took credit for the attack in a message directed at President Volodymyr Zelenskyy on Telegram.[55] Ukraine's State Service of Special Communications and Information Protectorate (SSSCIP) has stated that Solntsepek is a front for the GRU, specifically for Sandworm.

The Glass Battlefield

Attacks to gather espionage have been constant during the war. Espionage is one of the most valuable uses of cyberattacks on the battlefield for visibility, planning, and situational awareness. What makes this even easier is just how digitally enabled society has become. The more digital, the more opportunities for attackers to break in and use the equipment to their advantage—in war, to track

[51] https://therecord.media/kyivstar-ceo-on-russian-cyberattack-telecom
[52] https://babel.ua/en/news/102106-the-president-of-kyivstar-stated-that-hackers-destroyed-40-of-the-operator-s-infrastructure
[53] www.reuters.com/technology/cybersecurity/ukraines-biggest-mobile-operator-suffers-massive-hacker-attack-statement-2023-12-12
[54] www.kyivpost.com/post/26948
[55] www.wired.com/story/ukraine-kyivstar-solntsepek-sandworm-gru

troop movements, aid routes, and other important battlefield intelligence. That's exactly what Fancy Bear started doing at the time of the invasion. Fancy Bear used password-guessing, spearphishing, vulnerability exploits, and brute-force attacks to break into cameras and systems owned by logistics and technology companies. The information gave the Russian military intel on targets in key positions and the supply chain, like critical access points, aid routes, and schedules.

Sandworm also struck for espionage purposes, this time in 2023, with a new approach: Infamous Chisel. On the battlefield, the GRU stole devices from Ukrainians, especially tablets and phones used by the Ukrainian military, then broke into them and used them to distribute malware to other devices.[56] They effectively physically took trusted Android devices from Ukrainian soldiers, then used them as a foothold to deploy Infamous Chisel and gain access to other trusted devices. Once the malware infected other devices, it used a connection over the Tor network to hide its traffic, then exfiltrated system device information and information from any apps on the device, especially apps specific to the Ukrainian military. It continuously scanned the devices for new information or files, especially those on troop deployments, movements, or provisioning details, before exfiltrating them. The Security Service of Ukraine stated that it managed to prevent the Russians from gaining access to the sensitive information they were looking for.[57]

Hacking the Narrative

The espionage operations took place in tandem with ongoing psychological campaigns conducted by both sides. According to the State Service of Special Communications and Information Protection of Ukraine, over 200 successful cyberattacks on Ukrainian media occurred from 2023 to 2025.[58] Russian attackers used these attacks to spread propaganda and to erase existing news content they did not agree with. They also targeted journalists' social media

---

[56] www.computerweekly.com/news/366550454/Sandworm-attacks-Ukraine-with-Infamous-Chisel-malware

[57] www.ncsc.gov.uk/static-assets/documents/malware-analysis-reports/infamous-chisel/NCSC-MAR-Infamous-Chisel.pdf

[58] https://therecord.media/ukraine-media-cyberattacks-russia-ssscip-report

accounts so they could spread more disinformation on supposedly reliable, trustworthy accounts, adding to their believability. Telegram became a popular destination for attackers to publish stolen documents, propaganda, and disinformation.[59]

Before the invasion on January 14, close to 70 official Ukrainian government websites were targeted with a DDoS attack and defaced with the message:

"Prepare for the worst."[60]

Russian media posted about the attack before Ukrainian outlets. Ukraine and Poland blamed Russia for the cyberattack, though the forensic evidence was tenuous. It was likely carried out by Russia or by Russian hacktivists to try to scare Ukrainians into submission.[61]

Competing Deepfake Presidents

In March 2022, a deepfake video of President Volodymyr Zelenskyy circulated on Telegram, Twitter, and other platforms.[62] The video called for Ukrainian troops to stand down and go back to their families. While this deepfake was not realistic and was easy to spot as a fake, particularly because of the ratio of his head to his body, it still convinced some individuals and forced a response from Zelenskyy. This is in part because the attackers targeted a Ukrainian media channel, *Ukraine 24 TV*, with a cyberattack, broke into its systems, and posted the video on its website. Since the video was being broadcast by a trusted news source, people were more inclined to believe it.

Meanwhile, Putin faced down his own deepfake: A video spread on Twitter in March 2022 that showed Putin suggesting the war should end, that Russian soldiers should lay down their weapons and go home, and even saying that Russia had reached peace with

---

[59] https://therecord.media/ukraine-media-cyberattacks-russia-ssscip-report
[60] www.europarl.europa.eu/RegData/etudes/BRIE/2022/733549/EPRS_BRI(2022)733549_EN.pdf
[61] www.bbc.com/news/world-europe-59992531
[62] www.bitdefender.com/en-us/blog/hotforsecurity/deepfake-president-zelensky-calls-on-ukraine-to-surrender-as-tv-station-hacked

Ukraine. At least in this deepfake, they got the ratio of his head to his body right.[63]

The Wiper Epidemic

Wiper attacks have taken center stage as some of the most prominent malware used during the war, with many variations being used against critical infrastructure. Just some of the wipers used during the war include WhisperGate, HermeticWiper, IsaacWiper, Acid-Rain, CaddyWiper, DoubleZero, AwfulShred, Soloshred, ZeroWipe, SDelete, and BidSwipeSince. It's a lot. The wipers overwrite data and, in some cases, firmware, rendering devices inoperable and forcing rebuild or replacement. In some ways, it's as close as a cyberattack can get to a kinetic attack in its ability to disrupt and destroy critical operations.

In mid-January 2022, WhisperGate masqueraded as ransomware, while, in actuality, it was built to destroy its targets and any related data with little chance for recovery. It targeted government agencies providing emergency response functions, non-profits, and information technology organizations. Some of those affected were the same organizations that had been targeted by the DDoS attack and defacement messages from January 14, 2022. Much like those attacks, WhisperGate was intended to force political concessions from Ukraine prior to invasion, effectively as a demonstration of Russia's military might.[64]

The NSA later attributed this attack to Unit 29155 of the GRU. While this unit is better known for and has historically been focused on covert operations, sabotage, and assassinations, since 2020, it has expanded its cyber capabilities.[65] It's also likely that the war created an all-hands-on-deck mentality among cyber warfare units in Russia.

In another instance, just a day before the invasion on February 23, 2022, several more Ukrainian banks and government websites

---

[63] www.reuters.com/article/fact-check/doctored-video-appears-to-show-putin-announcing-peace-idUSL2N2VK1CC

[64] https://blogs.microsoft.com/on-the-issues/2022/01/15/mstic-malware-cyberattacks-ukraine-government

[65] www.nsa.gov/Press-Room/Press-Releases-Statements/Press-Release-View/article/3895808/nsa-fbi-cisa-and-allies-issue-advisory-about-russian-military-cyber-actors

were knocked out by a DDoS attack.[66] The attack was followed by a new wiper malware known as HermeticWiper, which targeted a small number of Ukrainian organizations, including government and financial institutions, and affected hundreds of devices. ESET first identified the malware, and Symantec subsequently confirmed it. These attacks were meant to destabilize and soften Ukraine in the hours prior to the invasion. Given that the code used in HermeticWiper was compiled as early as 2021, researchers suspect that the attackers had pre-positioned in victim networks well before the invasion and were waiting for the right moment to pull the trigger.[67]

In parallel, similar operations were happening in defense of Ukraine. Leading up to the initial invasion in January 2022, many Russian troops and military supplies were traveling through the Belarusian rail system to get to the Ukrainian border.[68] To prevent troops from reaching the border, a Belarusian hacktivist group, the Cyber Partisans, targeted the Belarusian railway network. The hacktivists encrypted many of the state railway computer systems to shut down the railway and stop troop movements.[69] The hacktivists treated it as a kind of ransomware attack, just instead of ransoming for money, they were ransoming for strategic military changes. The hacktivists promised to provide encryption keys to the railway company, but only if 50 political prisoners were released and the presence of Russian troops in Belarus was prevented. A spokesperson for the Cyber Partisans said the attack successfully affected rail freight. The railway company confirmed that electronic tickets were unavailable at the time, but didn't confirm why. The railway was able to restore systems in the weeks after the attack. While the cyberattack didn't stop the invasion, it did create friction for the Russians and Belarusians, forcing manual dispatch and disrupting train schedules.

[66] www.sentinelone.com/labs/hermetic-wiper-ukraine-under-attack
[67] www.elastic.co/security-labs/elastic-protects-against-data-wiper-malware-targeting-ukraine-hermeticwiper
[68] www.washingtonpost.com/world/2022/04/23/ukraine-belarus-railway-saboteurs-russia
[69] www.reuters.com/legal/litigation/belarusian-group-claims-hack-railway-system-after-russian-troop-moves-2022-01-24

Forecast: Acid Rain

The day before Russia's invasion, Russian attackers executed a coordinated, two-part cyberattack against Viasat, an American telecommunications company that owns the KA-SAT, a geostationary telecommunications satellite that gives Internet access across Europe, including Ukraine.

Viasat was hit with a DDoS that overwhelmed its servers with requests and prevented customer modems from accessing the network, effectively knocking out the Internet for those customers.

In parallel, attackers repeatedly attempted to access a VPN appliance at Viasat—they failed for an hour before gaining access and using it to send over-the-air commands via KA-SAT to thousands of modems across Ukraine. These commands pushed AcidRain, a wiper malware, to the modems. Once AcidRain was executed on the modems, it wiped those devices entirely.[70]

AcidRain rendered between 40,000 and 45,000 modems inoperable—not permanently destroyed, but unable to connect back to the network without support.[71] Combined with the DDoS attack, this meant that thousands of customers got knocked off the Internet, then could not get back online because of the wiper. Even if they could recover from the wiper, the DDoS attack prevented them from getting back online and made it more difficult for Viasat to support customers in restoring service.

Viasat struggled to address the attack in the initial hours due to on-the-ground logistics: It works primarily with distributors in Europe and maintains most operations in the United States, and thus does not have direct access to the hardware to fix the problem. For many of these customers, they needed on-the-ground support to get back online.

Viasat was used by both the Ukrainian military and government, and it affected Ukrainian command and control at a time when communications were desperately needed—just as the invasion

---

[70] www.sentinelone.com/labs/acidrain-a-modem-wiper-rains-down-on-europe
[71] https://cyberconflicts.cyberpeaceinstitute.org/law-and-policy/cases/viasat#:~:text=The%20attack%20on%20Viasat%20also,fixed%20broadband%20customers%20across%20Europe

began. Customers lost Internet access for up to two weeks. It's one of the reasons the Ukrainians brought in Starlink, to ensure a more resilient communications infrastructure.[72]

The attack also spread farther than just Ukraine, with organizations in Europe also losing Internet access. The attack knocked out access to over 5,000 wind turbines in Germany. The operational impact was not a single, brief outage; disruptions continued intermittently for months after February. Many countries condemned the attack on Viasat and blamed the Russian Federation for it.[73]

Piercing the Veil

Ukraine has taken a more direct tack since 2023: Going on the offensive and targeting inside Russia. There have been instances where Ukraine has sent missiles into targets inside Russia, and in parallel, instances where they have launched cyberattacks against companies inside Russia.

Take, for example, on July 5, 2023, when the IT Army of Ukraine launched a DDoS attack to take down Russian Railways (RZhD) public-facing services.[74] The attack targeted its main website and mobile application, taking them down for several hours and making it so that passengers across Russia could not access or buy tickets on the site. By hitting access to the railway in the middle of the summer travel season, the attackers brought the war home to Russian citizens who were trying to go on vacation, piercing the veil of normalcy the Kremlin tries to maintain.[75]

In another instance, on July 23, 2024, the Main Intelligence Directorate of the Ministry of Defense of Ukraine orchestrated a multi-day cyberattack against the Russian banking sector to knock out access to ATM and banking services. Customers in Russia

---

[72] www.cnbc.com/2022/02/28/ukraine-updates-viasat-says-cyber-event-disrupting-satellite-internet-service.html
[73] www.consilium.europa.eu/en/press/press-releases/2022/05/10/russian-cyber-operations-against-ukraine-declaration-by-the-high-representative-on-behalf-of-the-european-union
[74] https://therecord.media/russian-railway-site-taken-down-by-ukrainian-hackers
[75] https://mazebolt.com/wp-content/uploads/2024/04/Summer-of-2023-DDoS-Attacks.pdf

could not withdraw cash from ATMs across multiple banks. The attack also affected Russian telecommunications service providers, national payment systems, social networks, and government resources.[76] Russia was forced to acknowledge the attack, despite initially calling it a series of technical failures. However, rather than acknowledging it as a Ukrainian cyberattack, Russian officials referred to it as the work of "politically motivated hackers."[77]

Multidomain War, Realized

The Gulf War was the first to demonstrate the power of joint military operations across domains and what that could look like; Ukraine is the first war where those domains are treated as a single, continuous battlespace. Russian units and their proxies have iterated through denial-of-service attacks, wipers, telecommunications and satellite disruption, espionage, and psyops in lockstep with missiles and troop deployments, turning Ukraine into the working prototype of true hybrid war.

---

[76] www.bitdefender.com/en-us/blog/hotforsecurity/ukraines-military-intelligence-service-takes-down-banking-services-in-russia
[77] https://securityaffairs.com/166214/cyber-warfare-2/atm-services-russian-banks-hacked.html

Part IV

The Future

Chapter 43
Three Broken Promises

Though the United States remains the world's leading power, it now operates in a competitive environment where influence is increasingly contested. The unipolar era has ended, and the coming decades will define the balance of power in a world no longer centered on a single place.

Here's the wrench that is being thrown in the works of all three of these nations—the United States, China, and Russia: Leadership across the board is failing to live up to the social contracts it has established with its people.

The Divide of the United States

For the United States, its economic prowess is creating a divide between the ultra-rich and the middle class, such that the promise that you can make a living and have opportunities for upward mobility and security through hard work has completely failed. America's top 0.1 percent have more wealth in stocks alone than the bottom 50 percent have combined across all their assets.[1] As of 2024,

---

[1] www.visualcapitalist.com/wealth-asset-breakdown-americas-top-0-1-vs-bottom-50

only 47 percent of millennials owned a home in the United States compared to 74 percent of baby boomers.[2] In 2025, the U.S. Federal Reserve found that more than a third of Americans could not pay for an unexpected $400 expense due to their economic situation.[3]

From a cybersecurity standpoint, the United States is taking a deregulation-first approach, where industry partnerships replace mandates. In his first six months in office in 2025, President Trump issued a slew of executive orders that have changed the landscape. Just a few include:

- *The Executive Order on Initial Rescissions of Harmful Executive Orders and Actions* rescinded President Biden's executive order on artificial intelligence (*Safe, Secure, and Trustworthy Development and Use of Artificial Intelligence, EO 14110*), which required AI providers to report safety testing results for large-scale AI models. It leaves much of the AI model market untested.[4]
- *The Executive Order on Achieving Efficiency Through State and Local Preparedness* effectively shifted the burden of disaster and cyber preparedness from federal agencies to state and local governments. This creates a patchwork defense where resilience varies wildly by ZIP Code.[5]
- *The Executive Order on Sustaining Select Efforts to Strengthen the Nation's Cybersecurity and Amending Executive Order 13694 and Executive Order 14144* removed the requirement that CISA validate self-attestations for software supply chain requirements. Now, you just have to trust that companies use secure development practices that meet federal requirements.[6]

[2]https://www.apartmentlist.com/research/millennial-homeownership-2025
[3]www.investopedia.com/here-s-how-many-americans-can-t-afford-a-usd400-emergency-the-numbers-may-shock-you-11814788
[4]www.fisherphillips.com/en/news-insights/trump-rolls-back-bidens-ai-executive-order.html
[5]www.whitehouse.gov/presidential-actions/2025/03/achieving-efficiency-through-state-and-local-preparedness
[6]www.whitehouse.gov/presidential-actions/2025/06/sustaining-select-efforts-to-strengthen-the-nations-cybersecurity-and-amending-executive-order-13694-and-executive-order-14144

What's more, the administration cut CISA's budget by 15 percent. Roughly 1,000 people at CISA were either laid off or went into early retirement, about a third of CISA's staff. This leaves the premier federal critical infrastructure security and election security agency underfunded and understaffed ahead of the 2026 midterm elections, the co-hosting of the FIFA World Cup, and the United States Semiquincentennial.[7]

Meanwhile, ICE signed a one-year, roughly $2 million contract in late September 2024 with Paragon Solutions, a spyware company. Paragon makes tools to exploit mobile devices so that authorities can get access to messages, calls, and device data once a phone is compromised, without the user's knowledge. Immigration enforcement often operates in constitutional gray zones, where courts have historically granted the government more leeway at borders and in immigration contexts than in standard criminal cases, making powerful spyware especially attractive and dangerous.

In line with actions taken in China and Russia to control media companies within their information spaces and to pressure them to self-censor, the United States has also begun down that path. Within the right-wing blueprint Project 2025, major social media platforms are recast as common carriers, which would bar them from discriminating against political viewpoints. It also recommends using federal agencies to investigate and punish those who would censor core political content, either by downranking, demonetization, or account restrictions. It pushes the platforms away from active moderation of their own technologies, placing control in the hands of the state.

At the same time, the 2025 FCC chair has warned that certain broadcasters could face investigations, fines, or license revocations if they allow people on their programs to say things the FCC doesn't agree with. This happened with Jimmy Kimmel and ABC, though he has also floated using his powers to investigate *The View* as well.[8]

---

[7] www.cybersecuritydive.com/news/cisa-departures-trump-workforce-purge/749796
[8] www.politico.com/news/2025/09/18/fcc-brendan-carr-the-view-00572178

The United States' alliance with the Five Eyes is on rocky ground over changing policy decisions and strained alliances.[9] It is in a period of high volatility and change.

The Crumbling Prosperity of China

For China, its latest economic statistics are directly at odds with the core tenet of its social contract: Prosperity. In August 2025, youth unemployment reached 18.9 percent, and more than 84 million people were employed in the gig economy.[10] The state is punishing the people who speak out: Weibo suspended more than 1,200 accounts that were allegedly spreading rumors about the economy.[11]

China is in a race against its own economic clock. From a cybersecurity standpoint, espionage has increased in concert with its desperation to improve the country's economic conditions. In 2024, Chinese cyber espionage jumped by 150 percent. In critical industries like finance, media, and manufacturing, it jumped 300 percent.[12] China will likely become more aggressive with its cyberattacks as it seeks to address its economic state.

The CCP has begun to recognize that the Great Firewall imposes friction that foreign businesses are not willing to incur. Because of this, China is exploring options that would allow foreign businesses to bypass the Great Firewall for some websites, not all, as it works to attract foreign investment.[13] However, its economic interests are unlikely to reduce censorship long term.

As of September 2022, China requires state-owned companies in critical sectors to replace foreign IT software and hardware by

---

[9] www.cbsnews.com/news/gabbard-barred-sharing-intelligence-russia-ukraine-negotiations-five-eyes-partners
[10] www.atlanticcouncil.org/blogs/econographics/chinas-economy-remains-trapped-in-the-doldrums
[11] www.nytimes.com/2025/10/08/world/asia/china-censorship-pessimism-despair.html
[12] www.infosecurity-magazine.com/news/chinese-cyber-espionage-jumps-150
[13] yahoo.com/news/shanghai-mulls-plan-bypass-great-093000332.html

2027.[14] This removes a key foreign dependency that makes it vulnerable to sanctions. This self-sufficiency, combined with Made In China 2025 to replace Western tech with Chinese alternatives, makes China more prepared to endure sanctions in the event of war, such as if it chose to invade Taiwan.[15]

Contrast that with just how dependent other countries are on China's goods and services—for example, the United States' defense industrial base is moderately to highly dependent on China for materials.[16] It controls the majority of global processing capacity for some of the world's most important minerals, such as rare-earth elements.[17] China is also the United States' largest supplier of critical pharmaceutical inputs by volume.[18] The Belt and Road Initiative and the Digital Silk Road position China to control a large part of the information economy and to potentially use it to surveil its global customers.

China is well-positioned for a future conflict; if war were to come, it controls infrastructure in many places and can strangle them if it needs to. In a wartime scenario, China has positioned itself to win the information war.

The Dangerous Landscape of Russia

For Russia, the invasion of Ukraine violated the core tenet of its social contract: Safety. The regime will no longer guarantee that if you turn a blind eye, you will be left alone. The state is now reaching into private lives: Taking sons for the front, demanding public displays of loyalty, and militarizing schools. The blind eye is no longer enough; the state demands active participation.

---

[14] https://ginterfaces.com/the-silent-tech-purge-chinas-plan-to-replace-all-western-software-by-2027
[15] www.csis.org/analysis/made-china-2025
[16] https://files.gao.gov/reports/GAO-25-107283/index.html?_gl=1*1vawoov*_ga*MTc3ODkzNzQ0OS4xNzY0NTYwNjAz*_ga_V393SNS3SR*czE3NjQ1NjA2MDMkbzEkZzAkdDE3NjQ1NjA2MDMkajYwJGwwJGgw
[17] https://carnegieendowment.org/research/2025/10/securing-americas-critical-minerals-supply?lang=en
[18] www.atlanticcouncil.org/blogs/econographics/sinographs/pharmaceuticals-are-chinas-next-trade-weapon

The sanctions against Russia because of the war in Ukraine hurt, but they didn't kill. That said, Russia is teetering on the edge of stagnation in 2026, and households are cutting back amid persistent inflation and the strain of sanctions.[19]

From a cyberattack standpoint, Russia will continue to act as the global aggressor. It has become emboldened to attack more countries and to even stretch its cyberattacks to target NATO allies, so long as it can get away with it.[20] That will continue, and most of the focus will remain on leveraging cyberattacks to support the war effort.

Russia is on the cusp of enabling true Internet isolation from the rest of the world. New amendments are enabling the FSB to take control, as seen in China, allowing it to disconnect individuals or entire regions without a court order on national security grounds.

Instead of the bombastic cyberattacks and immediate destruction we have come to expect from Russia, it is prioritizing long-term, stealthy access to energy, water, and logistics grids in North America and Europe.[21] There is growing concern over Russian hybrid operations targeting undersea cables, a fragile bottleneck for global connectivity that remains a high-priority target.

China, Russia, Iran, and North Korea are cooperating and aligning more with one another every day.[22] Russia is cementing its alliances with them to secure an alternative to foreign equipment and to address ongoing sanctions. It is leveraging this partnership to address gaps in its domestic hardware supply chains resulting from Western sanctions.

There's one more stakeholder that is orthogonal to all of this, but that hasn't been called out explicitly and should: The veritable fourth power, the largest tech companies in the world.

---

[19] www.imf.org/external/datamapper/profile/RUS
[20] www.theguardian.com/world/2025/oct/16/russian-cyber-attacks-against-nato-states-up-by-25-in-a-year-analysis-finds
[21] www.microsoft.com/en-us/corporate-responsibility/dmc/en-us/corporate-responsibility/cybersecurity/microsoft-digital-defense-report-2025
[22] www.csis.org/analysis/crink-10-charts

Chapter 44
The Fourth Power

In July 2025, NVIDIA's market cap—the company's total value based on its current stock price and outstanding shares—was $3.972 trillion. That's larger than the GDP of all but the top five countries in the world. It's larger than the GDP of the United Kingdom, at $3.8 trillion.[1]

The Magnificent Seven—the largest and most influential technology companies (Apple, Amazon, Alphabet, Meta, Microsoft, NVIDIA, and Tesla)—make up 37 percent of the S&P 500's total market capitalization.[2]

Instagram has three billion monthly active users.[3] That's more than double the population of any country in the world.[4] Apple's Siri has more active users than there are people in the United States.[5]

[1] www.imf.org/external/datamapper/profile/GBR#:~:text=Datasets,General%20 government%20gross%20debt
[2] https://finance.yahoo.com/news/magnificent-seven-makes-one-third-140006761.html
[3] www.cnbc.com/2025/09/24/instagram-now-has-3-billion-monthly-active-users .html#:~:text=Instagram%20has%20installed%20a%20new,to%20an%20automatic% 20private%20mode.&text=Bell%20%7C%20Getty%20Images-,Instagram%20now%20 has%203%20billion%20monthly%20active%20users%2C%20Meta%20CEO,than%203% 20billion%20monthly%20actives.%22
[4] www.worldometers.info/world-population/population-by-country
[5] www.businessofapps.com/data/apple-statistics

Privately owned undersea telecommunications cables carry 99 percent of transoceanic digital communications.[6] Pretty much all the traffic on the Internet goes through these cables. That includes every Netflix stream, Zoom call, WhatsApp message, and every transfer of cloud computing data. These cables are the roads that enable communication for networks like the SWIFT global banking system to process trillions of dollars in daily transactions. Google, Microsoft, Facebook, and Amazon own or lease nearly half of the undersea bandwidth.[7]

Many governments, including the United States, Israel, and the United Kingdom, store some of their top-secret data in Amazon, Google, or Microsoft cloud services.[8]

A handful of private companies are capturing people's attention more effectively and producing more economic value than most countries. They have more economic power and are beholden to subscriber bases that are more vast than most countries have citizens.

The Border Is the User

But here's the obvious catch: These companies are not countries. They are subject to the laws of each country in which they operate. What they lack in physical sovereignty, they almost make up for in digital sovereignty. These devices, applications, and websites, owned and operated by private companies, have the data that countries compete to collect and surveil.

These companies are, for all intents and purposes, proto-states: Political entities that look, act, and function like a country but lack the full international recognition or total legal authority to be one.

For these companies, users are digital peasants living in a world of corporate feudalism. Users till the soil (create data), pay

---

[6] www.congress.gov/crs-product/R47237
[7] https://techcrunch.com/2020/05/14/2africa-africa-middle-east-facebook-subsea-cable
[8] https://privacyinternational.org/long-read/5683/big-techs-bind-military-and-intelligence-agencies

taxes (through attention, ads, or fees), and live in the castles (platforms) for community, but they have no say in how the kingdom is governed.

A great example of this is the changes that took place on Twitter, now X. When Elon Musk took over the platform, he made big changes that many would have scoffed at before. The company shifted from a constitutional monarchy governed by rules to an absolute monarchy, in which the sovereign sets the rules.

For example, before Musk, the blue checkmark was an iconic verification of identity. Musk changed that, distorting it and turning it into a sign of subscriber status. Instantly, the visual language of credibility flipped. Random users looked official, and actual officials looked untrustworthy.[9]

Musk ordered engineers to artificially boost his own tweets by a factor of 1,000 so they would dominate. Hundreds of millions of people were forced to see his thoughts, not because they followed him, but because he, as the ruler, wanted to prioritize his voice above all others.[10]

Musk reinstated Donald Trump, Alex Jones, and others who had been, for all intents and purposes, exiled. He dissolved the Trust and Safety Council and dismantled the structure of accountability.[11] This proved that "Community Standards" are nothing more than the whims of the current monarch.

All of this said, the metaphor is not perfect. There are key differences between Internet companies and proto-states.

As a citizen of a state, you have a one-to-one relationship. Perhaps you have a one-to-two relationship if you are a dual citizen, but for the majority, it is a one-to-one relationship. With online companies, you have a one-to-many relationship. They are competing for your attention and your interest. The greater the diversification across websites and apps, the less power these companies individually hold.

---

[9] https://www.cnn.com/2023/04/24/tech/musk-twitter-blue-check-mark
[10] www.platformer.news/yes-elon-musk-created-a-special-system
[11] https://www.npr.org/2022/12/12/1142399312/twitter-trust-and-safety-council-elon-musk

Governments still control and regulate companies, so they have the power to help manage the direction of the future of tech companies. At the end of the day, a government can nationalize or dissolve a company with the stroke of a pen. A monopoly on violence is far more consequential than a monopoly on your online reality. Nature cannot be fooled.

Governments have the power to shape how strong individual users are in the tug-of-war: Whether they control or own their data, whether they have rights to it, and whether they have rights over how it is used. This is exemplified by regulations like the EU's *General Data Protection Regulation (GDPR)*, which gives users the right to control their personal data.

Take, for example, in January 2025, when Chinese AI company DeepSeek announced a new large language model, DeepSeek-R1. The announcement rocked the AI industry, as it showed that it required only a fraction of the computer chips other companies needed to train their models. It claimed to require only $6 million in raw computing power (a figure that remains contested), compared with others like Meta, which cost ten times that.[12]

It caused a frenzy. NVIDIA's market cap dropped by $589 billion in a single day.[13] Every developer wanted to get the model and test it. Just days after the announcement, DeepSeek hit number one on the Apple App Store's Top Free Apps chart.[14]

But there was one glaring problem: DeepSeek's privacy policy states that it can collect "your text or audio input, prompt, uploaded files, feedback, chat history, or other content" and use it for training purposes. Not only that, but it can share information with law enforcement agencies at its discretion.

This is directly at odds with the GDPR. One reason the GDPR has had such an outsized impact on data processing globally, not just in the EU, is that it applies to any company, even those that don't operate there. Since the EU regards personal data protection

---

[12] www.businessinsider.com/deepseek-number-one-app-apple-store-openai-chatgpt-2025-1

[13] www.bloomberg.com/news/articles/2025-01-27/asml-sinks-as-china-ai-startup-triggers-panic-in-tech-stocks

[14] www.businessinsider.com/deepseek-number-one-app-apple-store-openai-chatgpt-2025-1

as a fundamental right, it must protect its citizens' personal data regardless of where it resides. This means that businesses that operate entirely outside the EU can still be subject to EU data privacy regulations if they have users that are citizens of the EU.

Italy's data protection authority, Garante, launched an investigation into whether DeepSeek was complying with the GDPR's requirements: What Italian data is being collected by the app, how it is used, and whether it is stored in China. The responses it received from DeepSeek were not sufficient for Garante. DeepSeek pushed back. According to Garante,

> "Contrary to what the authority found, the companies declared that they do not operate in Italy and that European legislation does not apply to them."[15]

Garante ordered DeepSeek to cease processing data on Italians, and the app was also removed from the Google Play and iOS app stores in Italy.[16] The Italians aren't the only ones: Belgium, Ireland, and France are all investigating how DeepSeek uses their citizens' data. Certain U.S. government agencies banned the app on government-issued devices. Taiwan also banned government agencies from using DeepSeek's AI model for national security reasons.[17]

Complicit

Governments can take action for better or for worse. Take, for example, Apple and Google's initial refusal to remove the Smart Voting app in Russia at the government's request. Regardless of how big they get, how many users they have, or how big their economic value is, the government is always bigger. The government can come to a company's office with armed soldiers and intimidate and threaten it until the company does what it says.

---

[15] www.silicon.co.uk/cloud/ai/italy-blocks-deepseek-over-data-concernsdeepseek-italy-block-597854

[16] www.politico.eu/article/italy-blocks-chinas-deepseek-over-privacy-concerns

[17] www.aljazeera.com/news/2025/2/6/which-countries-have-banned-deepseek-and-why

Beyond government intervention, we should expect companies to recognize their ethical responsibility to something more than the almighty dollar. We've seen time and time again that companies fail at this and try to find justifications for a lack of moral clarity.

Companies that believe they are large enough to affect national change while still complying with government abuse are simply justifying their complicity. This is the lesson history teaches us time and time again.

Tech companies have much power, but they do not have infinite might. They would have none at all were it not for the individual users who truly power their platforms. But users are also changing the boundaries of nations. National boundaries are not just geographic; they are determined by what citizens do and where they do it. If a company wants access to a market, it must comply. If a government wants to maintain strong geopolitical ties with another government, it has to make sure its companies comply.

Chapter 45
Reality Does Not Exist

W̶e are in a new arms race that kicked off on November 30, 2022: The one to make generative AI and AI technologies ubiquitous and useful. Artificial intelligence is one of the biggest innovations of our time and is fundamentally changing the ways we interact with technology. It is also changing how cyberattacks are perpetrated and how society understands the world we live in: It makes it easier to build more effective malware, and it can be used to manipulate our reality.

Protean Attacks

AI has both offensive and defensive applications. In late 2025, Anthropic announced that it had observed and stopped an espionage campaign that leveraged Claude and AI agents to break into organizations and steal data.[1] It attributed this campaign with high confidence to a Chinese state-sponsored actor. The attack was not entirely automated—there was still a human involved in orchestrating parts of it. However, it was far more automated than ever before

---

[1] www.anthropic.com/news/disrupting-AI-espionage

and is a sign that there is a future where attackers can automate attacks so that they can automatically adapt to changing scenarios—like changing operating systems, domains, and vulnerabilities.

In a typical attack, an attacker must conduct reconnaissance to identify the target infrastructure in the environment: Whether there are Macs or PCs, Android or iPhone devices. An attacker must identify vulnerabilities in those devices that can be exploited. An attacker must understand network infrastructure, the underlying operating system of a computer, and cloud operations. Now, they don't have to do any of that—they can rely on AI to do the reconnaissance for them, and to do it far faster than a human being can. Soon, cyberattacks will be faster, more dynamic, and harder to attribute.

A False Reality

Artificial intelligence can also be used to create more believable disinformation. It is being used to do that very thing today. But there's a greater risk here than simply using AI as a tool for spreading disinformation online.

Toward the end of 2025, CrowdStrike Counter Adversary Operations released research detailing how, when certain terms and phrases are used in prompts to DeepSeek-R1, it is more likely to introduce severe vulnerabilities into the code it generates. These trigger words include topics like the Falun Gong, Tiananmen Square, Uyghurs, Taiwan, and Tibet.

The CrowdStrike team posits that DeepSeek may generate vulnerable code due to inherent biases introduced by CCP requirements. This is an important distinction—the DeepSeek team is not necessarily directing the large language model (LLM) to make vulnerable code; it's just that the model is inherently biased because of the requirements the state puts on the provider.

The Cyberspace Administration of China has already begun mandating a process for testing LLMs and censoring certain results. The link between ideological training and poor code quality is plausible, given the known side effects of fine-tuning

LLMs: Fine-tuning a model in one area can degrade performance in another, or introduce unexpected issues. The fine-tuning required to navigate China's censorship rules could compromise the logical consistency and precision needed to generate secure, high-quality code. If the AI system holds negative biases toward certain topics, it may be less inclined to prioritize security or high performance.

AI providers are capable of adjusting their models to craft the reality they or the government wants us to have. Visibility into its the decisions that models make, opaque, which makes it even more difficult to understand why they produced the outputs they did.

We have come even further than the disinformation-ridden world of the past. We are firmly in a world where reality no longer exists. It is what we decide. Nations, enterprises, and individuals face a battle for believability.

Chapter 46
Conclusion

There is one single thing that has remained throughout this entire book. One single focus that is ever-present and never leaves the page.

It isn't China, or Russia, or the United States. It isn't a weapon, a doctrine, or a war. It isn't a specific exploit, tactic, or campaign.

The one through line in this book is you.

What do nation-states want? Your data. What do they want to influence? Your worldview. What are you to them? Someone to protect or to persecute.

What do tech companies want? Your data. What do they want to keep? Your attention. What are you to them? A user to serve and a resource to exploit.

You may not think your data is important, but I guarantee you, a nation-state does. Your data trains their models, reveals your habits, and makes it cheaper to manipulate, intimidate, and pressure you at scale.

None of this exists without you. If there is no real-world outcome to a cyberattack, attackers do not do it. You are that impact. You are the real-world outcome.

The Internet would not exist if people did not participate. The largest and most powerful companies in the world would cease to exist tomorrow if users threw away their cell phones and laptops.

But it isn't going to happen. The Internet will continue. Nation-states will continue to steal data, sabotage enemies, and surveil their citizens.

We did not choose our role here; it was imposed on us by how the Internet and modern states evolved. We don't get to decide that now. But what we do get to decide is where we click, what we share, and what we choose to believe. That can look small: using strong and unique passwords, scrutinizing the facts of a rage-bait post, or backing laws that treat your data as your property instead of their gold mine. We get to choose what we demand from governments and companies—and what we are no longer willing to accept.

Index